TECHNOLOGY AND SOCIETY

TECHNOLOGY AND SOCIETY

Advisory Editor
DANIEL J. BOORSTIN, author of
The Americans and Director of
The National Museum of History
and Technology, Smithsonian Institution

THE STORY OF THE

BALTIMORE & OHIO RAILROAD

1827～1927

BY

EDWARD HUNGERFORD

v. 2

ARNO PRESS

A NEW YORK TIMES COMPANY

New York • 1972

Reprint Edition 1972 by Arno Press Inc.

Reprinted from a copy in The State Historical
Society of Wisconsin Library

Technology and Society
ISBN for complete set: 0-405-04680-4
See last pages of this volume for titles.

Manufactured in the United States of America

———————————

Library of Congress Cataloging in Publication Data

Hungerford, Edward, 1875-1948.
　　The story of the Baltimore & Ohio Railroad, 1827-1927.

　　(Technology and society)
　　1. Baltimore and Ohio Railroad. I. Title.
II. Series.
HE2791.B3H8　1972b　　　　385'.0974　　　72-5054
ISBN 0-405-04706-1

WHERE THE PAST MEETS THE PRESENT.

A scene in the Valley of the Potomac between Point of Rocks and Harpers Ferry, showing an ancient canal barge on the Chesapeake and Ohio Canal and the highly modern *Capitol Limited* on her way from Washington to Chicago.

From a photograph.

THE STORY OF THE
BALTIMORE & OHIO RAILROAD
1827~1927

BY

EDWARD HUNGERFORD

PROFUSELY ILLUSTRATED WITH MAPS,
PRINTS, PHOTOGRAPHS, ETC., ETC.

G. P. PUTNAM'S SONS
NEW YORK - LONDON
The Knickerbocker Press
1928

Made in the United States of America

CONTENTS

iii

CONTENTS

CONTENTS

CONTENTS

CHAPTER XVIII

APPENDIX

ILLUSTRATIONS

vii

ILLUSTRATIONS

ix

THE STORY OF
THE BALTIMORE AND OHIO RAILROAD

THE STORY OF
THE BALTIMORE AND OHIO RAILROAD

CHAPTER I

BALTIMORE AND OHIO BENDS TO WAR-TIME TASKS

Stonewall Jackson Prays to God and Helps Himself to Its Loco-
motives—A Brilliant Raid and What Came of It—Guerilla
Warfare—And the Unending Struggle to Keep the Bridge at
Harpers Ferry—The Destruction of the Monocacy Bridge.

THE beginning year of the Civil War—1861—was for the
Baltimore and Ohio probably the most difficult. At no other
time during that conflict was its Main Stem severed, con-
tinuously, for so long a while. From the fourteenth of June of
that year until the twenty-ninth of the following March, no
through trains moved between Baltimore and Wheeling.
Even then, there was but a short period of through operation;
from March 29 to May 25. At this later date, General N. P.
Banks, commanding the Union forces, fell back from Winchester, through Martinsburg toward the Potomac and Maryland; and the Main Stem was again captured by the Confederates. It was soon recovered, however, and on the fifteenth of
June was again reopened for its entire length; and remained so
open until the fifth of the following September (1862).

But the summer and fall of '61 marked a period of great
travail for the road. Not only was it deprived of the revenues
that should have come, had its Main Stem been open for the
vast volume of business that was offering itself, but the property destruction—track and bridges and buildings, engines and

3

cars—in the fighting zone was terrific. Yet, despite all of this, the passenger receipts increased, perceptibly. In the fiscal year which ended September 30, 1861, these totaled $887,159.05 on the Main Stem alone; as compared with but $697,735.44 for the preceding twelvemonth. But, at the same time, the revenue from freight on that backbone of the property dropped from $3,224,467.50 (for 1860) to $2,324,467.50. Here was where the long blockade of the Main Stem showed itself most clearly; as well as the restrictions placed upon ordinary traffic by the government authorities and their occasional commandeering of the road's cars; many of them for months at a time. . . . When all was taken into consideration, the net earnings for the system, for the fiscal year of 1861, $2,182,664.73, reflected no small credit upon its efficiency of operation.

.   .   .   .   .   .

We left Mr. Garrett and his associates, at the end of April of that same year, viewing with no small consternation the work of the Baltimore mob on the nineteenth; reports of the threats and suspicions and actual outbreaks up the line coming through to them every hour. . . . Baltimore was blockaded from the rest of the world. . . . The federal authorities, despite the terrible confusion that reigned at Washington, began to move, however; and to move effectively. One of the first things that they did was to complete the blockade of Baltimore. At the Relay House, an armed camp was established, with two small brass six-pounders (evidently relics of the Mexican War) set up so as to sweep and to guard the main tracks of the railroad and to prevent any trains coming out of the city. General Benjamin F. Butler, of Boston—a name which was not to be unknown in the South during the other years of the war—was placed in charge at Relay, which presently became known as Camp Essex. Acting under instructions from Washington, Butler, at the very first, placed a complete interdiction on all traffic out of Baltimore.[1] On the eighth day of May, however,

---

[1] Among the young Union soldiers who helped guard the viaduct at the Relay House at that time, was Sergeant John M. Schoonmaker, of Pittsburgh, who had

both Mr. Garrett and William Prescott Smith, his master of transportation, went out to Relay and pleaded with General Butler to permit the resumption of traffic. They asked him to regard the real contrition of Baltimore and the absolute stagnation of trade that was resulting there. They also called attention to the great need for food and other supplies in overcrowded Washington, into which the troops were now pouring (by the Annapolis route) by the thousands each day.

The last argument probably was the most potent with Butler. At any rate, he permitted the embargo to be lifted; to a slight extent. Now it was that groceries, sugar, teas and coffees might go through to the capital and to the West; dry goods, however—save that cloth from which uniforms might be made—were especially interdicted. . . . The following day, a freight train of thirty-six carloads of provisions was loaded and sent out of Camden Station at four o'clock in the afternoon for Washington. Thereafter, its operation became daily. . . . Other trains were added, until the full capacity of the single-track branch was reached and passed. Afterward, a wagon train was placed upon the highway and operated intermittently.

. . . .

In the meantime, the situation up the Main Stem was becoming more and more precarious. Even though from Wheeling a United States expeditionary force, under command of Colonel (afterwards Brigadier-General) B. F. Kelley, of the Virginia Volunteers, was starting forth by train for the relief of Grafton and Cumberland and intermediate towns known to

joined the army at the age of eighteen. Young Schoonmaker rose rapidly. At the age of twenty years and four months, he was commissioned as Colonel of the Fourteenth Pennsylvania Cavalry. He was then the youngest man ever commissioned as a colonel in the United States Army. Much of Colonel Schoonmaker's experience with the Union forces in the Civil War was in guarding the line of the Baltimore and Ohio through the area of hardest fighting; although it was in the fight at Winchester, September 19, 1864, that his great heroism won for him the Congressional Medal of Honor. . . . In the years after the war, he became identified with railroading and, at the time of his death (October, 1927), he was the chairman of the board of the Pittsburgh and Lake Erie Railroad.

be in sympathy with the Union. This troop moved on May 29. It captured Grafton—then but a tiny railroad junction—after a brief pitched battle with the Confederates, and moved at once on its way toward Cumberland. All of this developed into the movement which was headed, first by Brigadier-General T. A. Morris, and afterwards by Major-General George B. McClellan, and which did so very much toward keeping the sections of the Baltimore and Ohio west of Cumberland so generally protected and open to the transport of Union troops and their munitions. . . . The sympathies of the folk of those parts did much to help. A straw vote, taken in Grafton at the beginning of the war, showed some five hundred Northern sympathizers there; as contrasted with but a single Southern adherent.

It was in the territory twenty or thirty miles to the east and to the west of Harpers Ferry where the struggle early took on its most dramatic phases. The Virginia militia—augmented by those Marylanders who were most outspoken in their sympathies for the Confederacy—who had marched in and taken possession of the Ferry on April 18, hung steadily on. For a time, despite many threats to do otherwise, they permitted the trains of the Baltimore and Ohio, moving east and west, to pass through it without serious hindrance.

Gradually their control tightened. Command of the forces there was assumed by that great and tragic and much beloved figure of the Valley of Virginia—Stonewall Jackson. Jackson felt that the continued operation of the Baltimore and Ohio was, in many ways, a menace to the success of the Confederate army. The war was so very new that real measures of reprisal had not as yet been seriously entertained. The Norfolk steamboats still ran down the Bay from Baltimore, and those to the railroad connection for Richmond down the Potomac from Washington, and one could still go quite freely between all of the warring states of the North and the South. Slowly the control of this traffic also tightened.

In these tightening days of May, 1861, Jackson did a

characteristically shrewd thing: At all times during the war,
the South stood in desperate need both of locomotives and cars
—particularly of locomotives. The Southern railroads, never
rich, had not been generously supplied with motive power.
Now, in the stress of war, with vastly increased burdens thrust
instantly upon them, they needed engines—at once. Jackson
sought to obtain them. And at the outset resorted to a bit
of strategy.

The Baltimore and Ohio, at that time, was double-tracked
from Point of Rocks through to Martinsburg, thirty-one miles.
Its coal traffic bound east, already large, was, in that month
of May, tremendous. The federal authorities were accumulating fuel upon the seaboard. . . . Night and day, the heavily
loaded coal trains pounded their way down toward both
Baltimore and Washington; night and day, the long lines of
empties rattled their course back up the Main Stem once again.

"The noise of your trains is intolerable," Jackson notified
Garrett. "My men find their repose disturbed by them each
night. You will have to work out some other method of
operating them."

Garrett was helpless. On so slender a thread his entire
Main Stem hung; he was in no position to defy the wily Confederate general at Harpers Ferry. Finally, Smith and he
worked out a plan with General Jackson, by which all trains
were to be operated through the Ferry only in the middle
of the day. When this was done, Jackson made his next move.
Upon an appointed day in that month of May, he held up all
trains moving through Harpers Ferry and helped himself to
four small locomotives; which were not too heavy to go safely
over the poorly built branch line to Winchester, thirty miles
away. These engines, once obtained, were hauled by horses
over the famous Valley Turnpike to Strasburg, but twenty
miles from Winchester, where they again were placed on rails—
on the track of the Manassas Gap Railway, which connected
with the Virginia Central and the entire railroad system of the
Confederacy.

This was real strategy and Jackson undoubtedly would have repeated it, had it not been that Harpers Ferry was beginning to be untenable for him. The North, slowly but surely, was organizing its army and preparing to take and hold every strategic point along its frontier; among which, few ranked higher than Harpers Ferry. And so it was that, when —on June 14—Stonewall Jackson received his orders to evacuate the Ferry, he took good pains to complete the work of destruction that had been well started there.

This day, the long-hanging threat of the destruction of the combined railroad and highroad bridge was carried out. At four o'clock in the morning, a gigantic explosion marked for the countryside the moment of destruction of the historic structure. Torches aided the gunpowder in setting fire to it; and within an hour the flames had done their work; the entire structure was a mass of charred ruins lying in the bed of the Potomac. A few days later, the long span which carried the Winchester Railroad from the main structure was destroyed; and a fine, large locomotive—too heavy to be attempted on the rail route through to Winchester—thrown into the river. Swiftly the work was done. The bridge gone, its companion over the Shenandoah, then what remained of the arsenal, as well as the Hall's Rifle Works not far away were burned and battered. . . . Harpers Ferry was destroyed—for all time. Never again was it to be the brisk and thriving industrial town that it had been prior to the outbreak of the war.

Six days later, Jackson's command was obliged to fall back upon and occupy Martinsburg. In the meantime, it continued its destruction. The many-spanned highway bridge over the Potomac at Shepherdstown was destroyed . . . and, finally, the great Baltimore and Ohio property at Martinsburg. . . . The commands of Johnson—Jackson's superior officer—were absolute. "Destroy all the railroad property at Martinsburg," they read. Jackson was a good soldier. He obeyed orders. Some forty-two locomotives and their tenders at that important railroad center, in addition to 305 cars, chiefly coal gondolas, were given the torch. And, all the while, the tall figure, sadly surveying the work of destruction, realized how desperately the cause for which he fought needed both locomotives and cars. The waste alone was appalling to him. Of that day's work, he wrote to his wife:

> . . . It was a sad work; but I had my orders and my duty was to obey. If the cost of the property could have been disseminating the gospel of the Prince of Peace, how much good might have been expended!

A letter from Martinsburg, written a month later, gives an idea of the thoroughness with which Stonewall Jackson obeyed orders. It reads, in part:

> . . . Yesterday we rode three miles along the Baltimore and Ohio Railroad and then went across the country three miles. All along the railroad were scattered coal-cars . . . in long lines . . . with the coal still burning. . . . Heavy fires had been built around them, burning all the wood and warping the iron. . . . All were fine iron cars, holding about twenty tons each. Their insides still were a mass of red-hot coals.

In some cases, small bridges, or culverts, had been burned, with the cars that had stood upon them. And the burned engines now were all red, and blistered with heat.

To Stonewall Jackson, however, this wreckage gradually began to mean something far more than an absolute and hopeless destruction. There still came to him word from his beloved Southland of the desperate need of locomotives. Some of these Baltimore and Ohio engines had not been so very badly burned; after all, there is comparatively little about a locomotive that can ever be destroyed by fire. . . . Slowly a great idea formulated itself within his mind. If only some of the best of those locomotives could be moved down upon those Southern railways. . . . Over the turnpike; as he had done with the little Harpers Ferry engines, from Winchester to

Strasburg. True it was that the distance from Martinsburg through Winchester to Strasburg (thirty-eight miles) was considerably longer, but the highroad was good and the thing was not impossible. It must have appealed to Jackson tremendously.

At any rate, one bright morning in July, he arranged to take the first of the engines out over the turnpike. The thing had been carefully rehearsed in advance. A picked group of about thirty-five men, including six machinists, ten teamsters and about a dozen laborers, had been told off to the task. They were placed under the immediate charge of one Hugh Longust, an experienced and veteran railroader from Richmond. Longust reported in turn to Colonel Thomas R. Sharp, at that time ranked as captain and also as acting quartermaster-general in the Confederate army.[1]

The farmers in the valley brought forty of their strongest and best horses to Longust to haul the engines, one by one, on their thirty-eight-mile trek to Strasburg. These were marshaled in double teams—four abreast, a quartet ten horses deep. To pull a fifty-ton locomotive over thirty-eight miles of even passably good dirt highway was no child's play.

Longust singled out a big and grimy wood burner standing on a side track, close beside the ruins of the Martinsburg roundhouse.

"That's the fellow we've got to begin on," he shouted. "Go in, boys."

They went in. The machinists and the skilled laborers began stripping the bulky mechanism. First, they uncoupled and drew away the tender; then by means of jacks, they raised the engine itself, and stripped it of all the parts that were removable—side rods, piston rods, valves, levers, pumps, lamps, bell, whistle and sand box. Then they removed all the wheels, save the flanged drivers at the very rear. . . . In this

---

[1] In after years Colonel Sharp was to succeed William Prescott Smith as master of transportation of the Baltimore and Ohio, and was so to become Mr. Garrett's right-hand man.

THE ARSENAL AT HARPERS FERRY.

Not long after it had been evacuated and destroyed by the Union army. The temporary pontoon bridge can be seen.

From a military photograph of the time.

THE FIRST ROUNDHOUSE AT MARTINSBURG, VIRGINIA.

With locomotives and three-pot coal gondolas in the foreground —destroyed by the Confederate army in 1861.

From a very old photograph.

way, the weight of the locomotive was reduced, materially.
Moreover, it was not so easily apt to be damaged. . . .

Next, they swung their bulky, helpless prize around, at
right angles with the track upon which it had been standing,
and substituted for its forward wheels a crudely constructed
emergency truck, fitted with thick wooden wheels, iron-shod
and fastened to the engine's bumper by an iron bolt serving as
a linchpin. When the jacks had been taken away, the engine
rested solely on its flanged drivers and its emergency forward
truck. A massive chain connected this with the forty horses;
or rather with the single, double and "fou'ble" whiffletrees to
which they were all hitched. . . . This crude arrangement
was ingenuity itself and insured steady and united effort.

.   .   .   .

The start from Martinsburg was made easily enough.
At each double team, a teamster was mounted. When Longust gave the starting signal, the cracks of their ten whips rang
out like rifle shots, the traces and the great chain creaked
and straightened, and the iron horse, groaning its indignation
at the humility to which it was being subjected, began its
long trip inland. . . .

For long hours—until the coming of dark—the effort continued. Then there was rest—until the coming of another
dawn. Gradually, as other locomotives were brought down
the pike, something like a schedule began to show itself. The
eighteen miles from Martinsburg to Winchester generally could
be done in a day; but all the way through to Strasburg and the
rails of the Manassas Gap generally was accounted a three-
day task. . . .

The forty horses filled the turnpike, side to side, and
stretched a full hundred feet ahead of the creaking, groaning,
careening locomotive. A mighty dust filled the air. . . .
Sometimes, when there was a sharp grade ahead, they fastened
long ropes to the protesting bulk and then a hundred—two
hundred—men added their muscles, their shouts, their curses

and their wild singing to the racket. But the engine went ahead, all the while—almost all the while. Occasionally, under the unwonted weight, the macadam shell of the road would break and let the huge iron horse sink into the soft dirt underneath. And then the expert men, with the jacks and the timbers, would have to come along, work long hours and hard, and put it on its feet again, and again on its march forward. The Trojan horse could not have been half the trouble.

And, sometimes, night would fall while they still sang and cursed and struggled under their burden, and up into the Southern summer sky would come the soft moon and all the stars. Then the men would light their torches and the flames would fall unevenly upon the rusted black sides of the captive locomotive. . . . More men at the ropes. . . . Fresh horses. And the steady cry, all the while, "On to Strasburg."

And, sometimes, there would come the crackle of musketry out from the misty bushes—Yankee snipers were making trouble over there—and then perhaps the entire outfit, horses and men, would be off, leaving their burden in the middle of the road until they could find time and opportunity to come back for it once again. . . . Then the horses would strain again in their traces, every muscle taut and holding, and the lines of men would pull at the ropes again. And "On to Strasburg" remained all the while their steady refrain.

.   .   .   .

In this way, fourteen Baltimore and Ohio engines, of every sort and variety, "made the Gap" that summer of '61. In fact, it was not until the following spring that the last engine that Jackson succeeded in helping himself to was carried successfully off and into the Confederacy. This was the *199*, a Ross Winans camel-back—one of those curiously ugly but not entirely inefficient freight pullers, with its long cab perched atop of and well to the front of its high boiler. The *199* reached Strasburg, with no more difficulty than had attended its fellows; but it never crossed Manassas Gap. . . . Second Bull Run had come and gone, and the army of the South had

fallen back from Manassas. That road was closed—to the South, at any rate. And still the *199* must be delivered at Richmond—which had been set aside as the point where all the seized locomotives were to be reconditioned and made fit for hard service.

The railroad through Manassas Gap closed . . . and the engine to be taken through to Richmond. The thing must be done. . . . Somehow. . . . Some way. Those were days that tried the courage and ingenuity of every man, and "no" was not the word to be spoken.

If the *199* could not go to Richmond by way of Manassas, it could take the main line of the Virginia Central (main line of the present Chesapeake and Ohio Railroad) through from Staunton. But Staunton was nearly a hundred miles distant from Strasburg. Of course, the Manassas Gap Railway (now a part of the Southern) went on as far as Mount Jackson; but there still remained a gap of seventy miles where there was nothing to be done but to take to the highroad. And this, it was determined to do.

The thing was done—one might almost add "of course." In four days after leaving Mount Jackson—by far the most hurried and exciting of the series of engine movements—the *199* came drunkenly careening into the main street of Staunton. It had been found necessary to strengthen many of the bridges on the way; and, on some of the lightest of these, block and tackle finally was substituted for the horses. . . . Early in the morning of the fourth day, Staunton and the rails of the Virginia Central were reached; but not so early but that the greater part of the population of the valley town was up, and staring at the strange spectacle. . . . It was easy enough to replace the engine on the rails, to put back in their proper positions all the parts that had been stripped from it. Fortunately for the Confederates, the gauge of most of their main line railroads was precisely the same as that of the Baltimore and Ohio.

.   .   .   .

About a dozen of the Baltimore and Ohio engines— together with their tenders, which had been hauled separately —finally reached Richmond and were assembled there for their overhauling. Two or three never even reached Strasburg. The Union forces had a way of coming up and interrupting the scheme of engine movement. Until, finally, it was necessary to ditch the mechanisms at the side of the pike, where they remained—a melancholy sight, indeed—until the war was ended. After that, they were hauled back to Martinsburg and there made ready for service on the road for which they had been builded.

The engines that finally reached Richmond were, a little later, taken further south; to the well equipped shops of the Raleigh and Gaston Railroad, at Raleigh, North Carolina, where they were speedily made ready for war service. One of the finest of them—*No. 188*, a passenger locomotive of the William Mason type—was made quite ornate, fitted with a walnut cab and was named the *Lady Davis*, in honor of the wife of the President of the Confederacy. All of these engines did yeoman service in the war. The Winans camel-backs came so close to the Northern lines at times that they were with difficulty saved from recapture. Their peculiar shrieking whistle carried its note a long way off. When, years afterwards, Blind Tom used to render his pianistic description of the Battle of Manassas, he had a certain point at which, with his voice, he imitated the whistle of a Ross Winans camel with a blood-curdling accuracy.

.   .   .   .

Jackson moved much more than locomotives and tenders south from Martinsburg during that summer and fall of '61. A goodly number of freight cars as well. But, what was far more necessary to the Confederacy,—a large quantity of valuable machinery . . . and the turntable from the round-house. A clean job it was. To be followed by one or two others. It is in the records how the "Railroad Corps" of the

Confederate army, on one occasion, actually tore up and took away about five miles of the Baltimore and Ohio track—ties, chairs, rails, spikes, everything—reaching from Duffields to Kearneysville, and relaid it between Manassas Gap and Centerville. The next day, the Northern army swooped down and recaptured the track.

The usual method, however, when the advancing wave of the Confederacy in its great periodic tide movements swept north up over the Baltimore and Ohio Main Stem, was to completely destroy the track. This was done, most effectively, by ripping up the comparatively light iron rails of that time and gathering up the ties and making of these huge pyres, which, when lighted and fully ablaze, were used for heating the rails red hot in the middle. After which, these were taken to the nearest tree and twisted around and around it; and there allowed to cool. A more complete destruction hardly could be found. Bridges, where of wood, were burned; and so, whenever possible, were the railroad's cars and buildings. . . . The loss amounted to a tremendous figure. Baltimore and Ohio eventually was repaid more than three millions of dollars reparation for the actual destruction of its property during the four years of the war.

. . . .

Not all of the loss was in pitched battles or in skilfully organized depredations, such as that of the locomotives.[1]

[1] "The Baltimore and Ohio Railroad was much more of a factor in winning the war for the preservation of the Union than is generally known, it being the nearest railroad on the north to the imaginary Mason and Dixon Line . . . while the Virginia and Tennessee Railroad, which practically paralleled the former, was south. So far as the movement of troops between the Eastern and Western Confederate Armies was concerned, the latter railroad, which went over to the Confederacy when the State of Virginia seceded, had a decided advantage in the movements of large bodies of troops, either east or west. and oftentimes before any such movement was known to the North, as in the case of what is known as the Hunter Raid, by the Federal troops in an endeavor to get behind the defenses of Richmond and Petersburg, occupied by the Confederate Army, and which movement General Lee easily defeated by diverting Early's entire corps one night

Desultory fighting, sniping, guerilla warfare of every sort was continuous. . . . Mr. David Lee, who, until a comparatively few years ago, was master of way of the line west of the Ohio, at the time of the war was in charge of the track in the Harpers Ferry sector. His was a real task at all times. For no sooner would he, acting under the orders of his superior—John L. Wilson, master of way—replace a bit of track badly wrecked, than some marauding band of Confederates would descend again upon the defenseless railroad, and again pull it to pieces.

Mr. Lee used to tell of a summer morning in '62, when he came around the turn of the line at Point of Rocks to find a group of greycoats indulging themselves in rolling huge boulders down upon the track. Back of them stood their leader, Colonel John V. S. Mosby.

Now it so happened that Lee and Mosby were long-time friends. The fact that, for the moment, they were allied with opposing forces, was not to be permitted to interfere with such a friendship. Lee went straight up to the Confederate commander and protested at the work of his men.

"They are beginning to draft our men now," he said sorrowfully. "And I can't get men enough to maintain our track

---

from the defenses of Richmond, defeating Hunter the following morning at Lynchburg, forcing his army into the Kanawha Valley, which had to be ultimately moved east via the Baltimore and Ohio Railroad to join Sheridan's Army in the Shenandoah Valley in the Fall of 1864, while Early came unmolested within sight of Washington before Hunter's Army could be returned to the Shenandoah Valley. Both Northern and Southern troops were actively engaged in their endeavor to interrupt traffic movements on both railroads; the Union forces, knowing that the Confederate Army was assembling large supplies of material at Salem (an interior point on the Virginia and Tennessee Railroad, available for movement either east or west) forced their way to that point, destroying immense supplies of material for both their Eastern and Western Armies. . . . I was fortunate in having the splendid support of the operating department of the Baltimore and Ohio . . . as otherwise it would have been impossible for me to have kept the road open and the movement of troops, supplies, etc. uninterrupted, which service ended after Sheridan had defeated General Early's Army for the third time at Winchester, Fishers Hill and Cedar Creek respectively. . . ."—From a letter to the author from Colonel Schoonmaker, written in April, 1927.

properly without you fellows coming along and doing a trick of this sort."

Mosby thought for a moment.

"Very well . . . this time, David," said he. . . . And promptly ordered his men to roll the boulders off the track again.

Not always was it so laughable as this.

W. W. Shock, who was an operator on the line during those early days of the war and who afterwards helped rebuild and replace its shattered telegraph lines, used to recall an episode at Point of Rocks that had rather more of tragedy than comedy in it.[1] From the diary of the late John Edward Spurrier, a veteran Baltimore and Ohio officer of a long-time Baltimore and Ohio family, and the grandson of a Spurrier who had a distinguished Civil War record, the following excerpt is taken:

. . . Shock says Frank Mantz, Christ. Smith, John R. Smith, Bob French and a half a dozen others came from Sandy Hook to Point of Rocks on the yard engine hurrying away from the rebels who had crossed the Potomac at Harpers Ferry. . . . The engine stopped in front of the office and Mantz said, "Climb on, Billy. This is your last chance." Billy [Shock] replied, "I can do nothing East and will be of valuable service here and cannot leave my post on account of military duties." Just then a rifle ball whizzed and the next second a scream was heard. Miss Fisher, standing on Dixon's upper porch, fell dead with a bullet through her heart. Mr. Mantz cried to the engineman, "Pull away quickly," remarking, "if Billy is fool enough to remain here, we are not." And away they went and did not return for at least two weeks. . . .

[1] A letter from Mr. Shock to the author in October, 1927, showed that he was alive, healthy and prosperous in Pasadena, California. His record is a remarkable one. In 1857, at the age of fourteen, he entered the service of the Northern Central Railway as a telegraph operator at York, Pennsylvania. Soon after, he moved to Baltimore and, a little later, joined the forces of the Baltimore and Ohio, with which he remained many years. For his loyalty and his heroism in the days of the war, he was commended both by President Lincoln and by Mr. Garrett.

In the meantime, Shock, with the assistance of a track foreman and his gang, repaired not only the telegraph line, but the track and culverts as well. . . . He kept moving eastward all the while, and finally came to Sykesville. There he learned that there was a break in the telegraph line a mile further east. He found the break and, having repaired it, tried to get the chief operator at Camden Station. Without success. Then he called the Relay House. The operator there answered but replied, very craftily:

"Oh, you, Johnny Reb, you can't fool us. S [Shock] at 7 [Point of Rocks] was killed a week ago."

Shock kept his head and merely asked Relay if there were any extra troops there. The operator brought General Lew Wallace, at that time in command of the sector, to the wire. . . . Wallace satisfied himself that a loyal Union operator of the Baltimore and Ohio was on the line. Shock convinced the general that he himself had repaired and reopened the line through to Point of Rocks. General Wallace then said that he would send troops through. Shock went ahead, much of the distance afoot. He made sure that the long Monocacy bridge was safe, then cut the telegraph wire west of Point of Rocks, so that the Confederates up at Harpers Ferry could get no news of the advancing Union movement. At about three o'clock in the morning, he stumbled up to the door of the little log house of Fred Stunkle, not far from the Point of Rocks, and demanded rest and shelter.

Stunkle refused to admit him to the house.

"Shock was killed last week," he kept repeating.

Shock finally dropped into the German vernacular of the neighborhood. Then it was that Fred Stunkle slipped back the bolt of the door.

"Mein Gott! I never expected to see you again," he gasped.

Shock lost no time in explanations. Where were the grey-coats? They had crossed back over the river into Virginia early the preceding afternoon. Stunkle was sure of this.

Upon this information, Shock went to the place where he had cut the telegraph line and hidden its ends, and reconnected them. Then he signaled General Wallace that he might come in safety all the way through to Harpers Ferry.

.   .   .   .

Incidents such as this—repeated, not once or twice, but dozens of times—proved the war-time loyalty of the Baltimore and Ohio and its rank and file. As has been said already, many, if not all, of the men on the eastern end of the system were, at heart, sympathizers with the cause of the Confederacy. But they had learned the lesson, not only that a good railroader, like a good soldier, always obeys orders, but that there must never be for a moment a question of his loyalty.

.   .   .   .

The chronology of those beginning months and years of the Civil War, as set down in the annual reports of the Baltimore and Ohio company, gives but little more than an index to the intensity of the struggle that was going on all the while. . . . Thus, when one reads that on May 28, 1861, the Confederates took possession of more than one hundred miles of the Main Stem, not relinquishing all of it until March 29 of the following year, that they seized or destroyed 42 locomotives with their tenders, 386 cars, 23 bridges—embracing, all told, 127 spans and a total length of 4713 feet—one may gain an idea of the vast property damage, but little else. The bridges destroyed were, many of them, covered wooden structures of a type that continued in use upon the highways in many parts of the United States for long years afterwards. The first to go (on May 28, 1861) were the nearby ones at Pattersons Creek and at the North Branch, about 171 miles from Baltimore. Opequan Bridge went on the second day of the following June; Harpers Ferry, as we have seen, on the fourteenth of the same month. On the day before, the famous Pillar Bridge—nine spans of forty feet each—and the 263-foot structure at the Great Capacon at Martinsburg had been destroyed. . . . The two iron bridges a few miles away were thrown off their abutments a little later, and the fine stone arch of 180-foot span at Back Creek blown up and utterly destroyed.

So runs the record.

The track gangs and the bridge gangs endeavored, as fast as the Confederates were beaten and forced to retire, to repair the severed sections of the railroad. Temporary timber trestling was their constant expedient. They became expert in this form of emergency bridge construction; not only on the Baltimore and Ohio, but elsewhere in the war territory.[1]

. . . .

For the men of the Baltimore and Ohio, the bridge job was an unending one. Harpers Ferry Bridge alone was repeatedly built, destroyed, and rebuilt. More than once, by men working against terrific odds of weather, as well as the constant danger of surprise by the enemy. The Potomac often went on a rampage at just the wrong moment. When, in March, 1862, it seemed at last as if the Main Stem could be safely restored to traffic once again, and W. E. Porter, the assistant master of road, and William Allee, its supervisor of bridges, were ready to proceed with the building of an emergency bridge, they found the river suddenly flooded into a raging and impassable torrent. . . . They finally communicated their troubles to Mr. Garrett. He reflected upon a bridge-building method that had been used for beginning the first suspension structure at Niagara, and at once telegraphed that the expedient of flying a kite over the river, or shooting a rocket, be used for the beginning

[1] The four-storied trestle close to the Potomac below Washington, 414 feet long and 82 feet high, which the United States Army engineers built in nine working days, became one of the record bridge construction feats of the world. Into it went more than two million feet of lumber. . . . Abraham Lincoln rode out to it and dubbed it "the bridge of cornstalks and bean poles." Yet the record was broken later, when the Army engineers by the same methods built the emergency bridge over the Chattahoochee River, in Georgia—780 feet long and 90 feet high—in just four and a half working days!

cable. Whether either of these methods was used, the records do not show; but the fact remains that, despite the flood, great iron cables were put across the river, and on these were swung the heavy timbers for the trestles. So swiftly and so surely that, between the fourth and the eighteenth, the long trestle bridge was finished; and for the first time in nine months a locomotive and its train crossed the river in safety to Harpers Ferry. Not a remarkable record perhaps; but accomplished in days of torrential rain and flood and temperature so cold that the ropes were constantly becoming frozen and unusable.

A real record of achievement.

Within three weeks, the Potomac was aflood again. High water and seven inches of snow imperiled the bridge. . . . Only locomotives and heavily laden cars placed out upon each of its spans saved it. But not for long. That was the ninth of April. On the sixteenth, the river rose, dangerously high, again . . . and there was resort again to the loaded cars.

Spring came but slowly in '62.

On the twenty-second of April, it was bitterly cold once again—and the river running at flood height. Close to the Maryland side of the river, the old Chesapeake and Ohio Canal bent its way under the cliff and around its nose; and, then as now, was crossed by a single span of the railroad bridge.

At eleven thirty o'clock that morning, the temporary structure, strong as it was and held in place by fourteen car-loads of coal, no longer could stand the strain and the pull of the roaring waters underneath. With a tremendous crash, the two spans nearest the Maryland side went out, and the householders down the river all the way to Washington would not lack for firewood for many a day to come. Four hours later, a canal boat, having become unmanageable, swept out of its accustomed pathway and into the main river channel. It carried away another span . . . ten more loaded coal cars. At seven forty-five that evening, most of the rest of the bridge went out . . . with twelve more cars. . . . It was a day not soon to be forgotten.

For six more days the river was absolutely impassable. Then the bridge gangs went back to the beginning and began their huge task once again. This trestle lasted just one month and three days. On the seventh of June, the river again rose in flood and the 800-foot structure went crumbling down, like a tiny thing builded of matches.

Yet, Garrett and his fellows never gave up. As Harpers Ferry Bridge was being destroyed again and again and again—now by the hand of man and now by the hand of God—they were fashioning a new one at Mount Clare, a new one of more permanent sort. This one—of the now celebrated Bollman truss type—was to be of iron and at least fire-resisting. The third wooden trestle began to go into place at Harpers Ferry on June 9, and was completed on the sixteenth. This structure was, however, replaced gradually by the iron spans, as the members were completed at Mount Clare, sent out to the Ferry and carefully fabricated and set up. Construction work began July 25, and, with the exception of the fifth span, was completed by August 21. . . .

About that time, however, troubles of another sort were beginning. The grey flood tide of the Confederacy was advancing northward once again. By September, it overwhelmed the entire country between Harpers Ferry and Martinsburg, and the bridge gangs could not work without removing the accumulation of bodies of dead men and horses.

On the twenty-fourth day of September, the fifth bridge of the Baltimore and Ohio at Harpers Ferry was fired, blown up and completely destroyed.

It was not until the middle of the following February that Mount Clare had new iron spans ready for fabrication. By April of '63, it was again completed. Two weeks later, there was another flood and again loaded cars had to be rushed out upon the structure. Free of the complicated underpinning of the trestles, it stood—successfully. Until the fifth of July, when it was again burned; this time by the United States Army, as a military precaution. Yet the structure itself held

Harpers Ferry After the War.

Showing the wrought-iron highway and railroad bridge built by Bollman and still (1927) in partial use for highway traffic.

From a photograph.

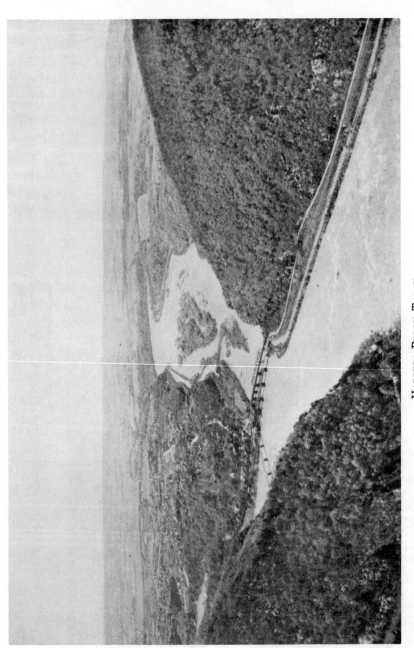

HARPERS FERRY TODAY.

The Potomac at the right, the Shenandoah at the left. The parallel bridges of railroad and highway can be seen.

From an aerial photograph.

so well that it was refloored and again opened to trains and vehicular traffic before the first of August. . . . It then stood intact again until the early part of April, when floods of greater violence than ever before were known in the history of the valley of the Potomac beat against and wiped out two of its principal spans. Hurried orders were sent to Baltimore for steel cables of the heaviest known strength; and these, rushed by special trains, were so interwoven with the other spans as to save them. . . . Until the sixteenth of May, when the temporary pontoon bridge, which had been used at the Ferry in the seasons when the main bridge was down, broke under high waters; and throwing itself and piling high against the main structure broke it, absolutely and effectually. Several spans were completely lost and the bridge was almost an absolute wreck.[1] And so

---

[1] In the dispassionate language of the report of John L. Wilson, master of road of the Baltimore and Ohio at that time, one reads as follows of that sixteenth of May, 1864:

"The Potomac River at Harpers Ferry was much higher than in April. The pontoon bridge at Falling Water (just above) was carried off; also the pontoon at Harpers Ferry. Several boats from these bridges lodged against the trestles at Harpers Ferry, upon which loaded cars had been previously placed. In consequence of the heavy weight upon the top, and the immense accumulation of drift, combined with the wreck of the pontoon bridges, the sixth trestle in the wide span broke and fell at 2 P.M. The second trestle in the same span broke shortly after, followed by four trestles going out from the curved and four from the Winchester span, carrying also two cars into the river. The loss of these supports so weakened the structure, that at 3:30 P.M. the wide span entire, the Winchester span, and all of the curved span, except six trestles near the Virginia shore, were swept out, and fourteen cars (in addition to the two previously mentioned) went into the river. On the 18th an attempt was made, by use of a life boat, to get a cable across the river to establish a ferry. The men in charge of the boat were compelled, from the condition of the current, to throw the cable into the river to save themselves. Another cable was sent from Baltimore by special train, which reached the bridge at 7 A.M. This was successfully placed, and the ferry thus established. All passengers, baggage and mails from delayed trains were transferred by 9:40 A.M. Several regiments of Ohio one-hundred-day troops were also brought safely over the river in a large boat, which had been built upon the previous day for the purpose. The trestling was commenced on the 19th and finished at one o'clock on the 21st inst., when Mail train east passed, also all delayed Troop and Tonnage trains."

.   .   .   .

remained until the twenty-first of May, when an emergency trestling was completed which continued in constant service until replaced by a permanent iron bridge, designed and built by Wendel Bollman.

After such a strenuous record of four years, it is a pleasure to add that thereafter the Harpers Ferry Bridge, finally rebuilded, stood (as has already been shown, eventually relieved of the railroad portion of its burden) until the spring of 1924; when, it will be recalled, the Potomac again rose to record flood height and swept out the two spans nearest the Maryland shore. These have been replaced, temporarily, awaiting the advent of a permanent stone and concrete arched structure; but the rest of the highway bridge across the Potomac at Harpers Ferry today consists of the same stout Bollman spans that were wrought in the Mount Clare shops in those trying days of the Civil War.

.   .   .   .

As went Harpers Ferry, so went—although in slightly lesser measure—the war-time record of many other bridges of the Baltimore and Ohio. . . . Damaging and pillaging, all the while . . . and rebuilding. Damaging and pillaging and rebuilding. Faith never lost. Nor heart.

Take the Monocacy, for a single other instance. The railroad had erected, in a period prior to the outbreak of the war, a fine bridge over that river, near Frederick Junction. Yet it had been by no means immune from Confederate attack. And, early in September, '62, it had been completely destroyed. Yet one finds in the *American Railway Journal* of the twenty-seventh of that same month the following:

After an interruption of about two weeks, the Baltimore and Ohio Railroad is once more open as far as Harpers Ferry. The new bridge which crosses the Monocacy is a very substantial structure of wood and was put up in the wonderfully short period of five days. The previous bridge was of iron,

resting on two stone piers, about thirty feet above the water.
It was blown up by the insurgents who poured powder into the
cores of the iron castings on which the beams rested, but so
hurriedly was the work of destruction done that the destroyers
were blown up with the bridge itself.   There is no saying when
the road will be opened throughout, as the Harpers Ferry
Bridge will have to be rebuilt.   Fortunately the piers are still
sound, however, in spite of attempts made to destroy them.
. . .   The enemy still holds the southern shore of the upper
Potomac. . . .

Pillaging and damaging . . . and rebuilding. But faith
never lost. Nor heart. The railroad forever is an undy-
ing thing. Its great main line is like the backbone of the
human body; save for one thing; the railroad main line may be
severed and then again reunited—indefinitely . . . just as
long as there is faith . . . and hope . . . and courage. These
things—in large measure—were the possessions of Baltimore
and Ohio men in those days of the Civil War.

CHAPTER II

A RAILROAD IN WAR TIMES

Mr. Garrett Runs His System—Asks Questions and Keeps His Eyes
Open and Misses no Opportunities—Lively Times on the Line
—Major Harry Gilmor Halts a Train—And Mr. Lincoln Goes
to Gettysburg.

THROUGH all these throbbing years, there stalked erect the
dominating figure of John W. Garrett. President of the
Baltimore and Ohio, he made himself far more than a mere lay
figure to fit that title. President of the railroad he was—in
every full sense of the word. Captain of the ship, as well.
Smooth, suave; upon most occasions, imperturbable; on others,
he could—if he felt the immediate moment called for it—
domineer, bombast, storm . . . like any other high-strung
and high-tempered man. But always he was resourceful; rarely
ever was he to be found napping. . . . In every way an
executive. Yet, even in minute details, Mr. Garrett was not
to be found lacking interest. True it is that great executives
are not supposed to be men given to detail. John W. Garrett
then must have been the exception that proves the rule. For the
smallest detail in the operation of the Baltimore and Ohio in
those strenuous years was not beneath the attention of its
president.

Why were the gas bills higher this month at Camden
Station than they had been for a full year previous? And why
was the quality of sperm oil furnished the company inferior
to that with which it had been supplied heretofore? Why were
ladies suspected of riding daily between Camden Station and

Washington—free of all expense whatsoever? Mr. Garrett
had understood that these were "females employed in the war
business at the capital"; yet that was no reason why they
should go back and forth the forty miles each way daily without paying one cent of fare for the privilege. He was, as will be
seen, preparing a commutation scheme for this new and growing traffic. But why, Mr. Smith, was this free riding being
allowed? An answer, Mr. Smith, and quickly.

Truly this William Prescott Smith was, during Civil War
days, called the "man Friday" of the Garrett administration.
Upon his head was heaped everything; questions, recriminations, occasionally—not often—even abuse. That he kept
that head and kept it cool and resourceful was one of the
wonders of all who came into contact with him. Questions
. . . demands . . . orders . . . came to him . . . in constant bulletins from his superior officer. The office boy in the
auditor's office had taken the horse and buggy used by that
important financial officer of the road in the performance of his
duties in Baltimore City, had gone joy riding with it and there
had been a runaway and the horse scared and the buggy badly
smashed. Why, in heaven's name, Mr. Smith, such sky-
larking as this in serious days of war?

And why was engine *25* left standing on the main track outside of Camden Station that October day and train No. 6,
bound south, detained five valuable minutes in consequence?

. . . detention being caused by Engine *25*, standing on the
main track, *with no one on it* [writes Mr. Garrett] which prevented train from passing until it had been removed. Through
whose neglect did this occur? The engineman and all parties
responsible should be severely reprimanded for a neglect leading
to such consequences. Is it not wrong, at any rate to leave
an Engine in such a position, even with proper parties in
charge?

A president with observant eyes in his head, Mr. Smith.
A president who goes poking his way and investigating into this

corner and into that, Mr. Smith. A president who even observes, Mr. Smith, that, upon a single occasion, two trains which were due to depart from Camden Station were delayed all of sixty seconds each, because of the failure of some one to pull the starting bell, right on the dot. Of this lapse, Mr. Garrett writes:

> . . . This is unpardonable. See that it does not occur again. The party whose duty it is to pull the bell, failing without proper cause, must pay the fine.

There is trouble up on the Northwestern Virginia Branch— a sort of chronic thing up there. Mr. Van Winkle, the president of that line, still a separate railroad, has complained of the dilapidated state of the passenger coaches that Mount Clare is furnishing it. This time it is not Smith, but Thatcher Perkins—the master of machinery of the Baltimore and Ohio —who catches the hot shot. Mr. Garrett sends him a personal note; in it, he says:

> It is said that in hard rains, passengers inside [the cars] are obliged to use their umbrellas. I have not personally had this experience, but can testify that the cars are greatly out of repair in their internal arrangements.

At the same time, another officer of the company—Mr. King, the auditor—hears from the president. A large "customer" of the road desires it to find a gentleman going to St. Louis the following week who will escort a lady—a relative of his—to that city. Can the auditor's office locate a "respectable gentleman" who is willing to take this task to himself?

.   .   .   .

More often, however, the matters are of far more serious import.

The War Department over at Washington has called for ironclad cars (box cars, covered with rails—an unsuccessful scheme for a sort of predecessor of the modern tank) and there is not a moment to be lost. Lee already is on his way toward Gettysburg and the entire North is aroused and in fear of invasion. Baltimore itself is in the shivers. Garrett turns to Thatcher Perkins; his highly competent master of machinery, to be known in after years as a locomotive designer of exceptional abilities. Perkins lets no stone go unturned in the prompt preparation of the cars and (on July 3, 1863) reports to his chief:

> I telegraphed you on the 30th ulto., about 4.30 P.M., that I would have one of the ironclad cars completed on the morning of the following day, Wednesday, another on yesterday, Thursday A.M., and the remaining three if it were possible, by the last of this week. The first two were completed according to promise and the last three at 3 o'clock, this morning.
>
> You will remember that I did not receive the order from the Government to construct these cars until between 3 and 4 o'clock on last Sunday. Immediately I went after our employes, many of whom were at Church and Sunday School, and they all promptly responded and prepared for operation. From that time to the completion of the cars, three hundred men have worked steadily, day and night, only stopping for meals. It becomes me to speak of my high appreciation of the zeal and energy of the workmen who, without a single exception, displayed marked earnestness in facilitating the completion of the cars as if upon them depended the safety of Baltimore. . . .

In more ways than one, Mount Clare worked those years; for the safety of Baltimore. The Confederates might—and repeatedly did—come rolling up out of the South and destroy the Baltimore and Ohio Railroad and its equipment, but Mount Clare was always at work to replace the damage; in some instances, almost even before it had been done. Seemingly, it was tireless. Its endeavors were well-nigh unending. And the editor of the *American Railway Journal*, who visited the place in the autumn of 1863, gives a rather graphic description of its activities. In his paper he writes:

. . . Some idea of the extent of the work done at Mount Clare may be formed when it is learned that since the commencement of the present war, there have been built there 525 cars and now arrangements are making for the construction of 200 additional coal-cars, and all of these are to have iron trucks, instead of wood.

They also are building new passenger cars at Mount Clare, the interiors of which, the editor avers, present "the taste and the elegance of the parlor and the dining room." He goes into detail:

. . . The inside panellings are filled with a species of gold cloth and those of wood on the outside have been polished and rubbed down, until they present the gloss and brilliancy of the finest coach bodies. The corner panels are elaborately ornamented with gilded scrollwork of rich design which gives an artistic finish to the whole. . . .

"And yet," adds the commentator, "there is no unmeaning ornamentation about this work." It is with difficulty that he tears himself away from such fascinating magnificence and faces the more sordid evidences of war. He continues:

. . . Among the curiosities of the Mount Clare Depot are the debris of the rails, locomotives, etc., which were destroyed by the rebels. There are successive piles of twisted rails, sections and rods of bridges, bolts, screens, carwheels and boilers of excellent locomotives, fragments of coal-cars, axles and demolished tenders.

These articles having fallen into the hands of the rebels, they seem to have adopted the most effective mode of destroying them. The rails, some of which are of the finest quality of English iron, after having been torn from the road-bed, were laid upon piles of crossties and fire applied to the latter. Whilst in heated state they were dragged off by tongs and twisted and turned in almost every conceivable manner. . . . There are millions of pounds of damaged iron, but it is

not lost to the company, for no matter how small the piece it
is collected, placed into the melting furnaces and again wrought
into such parts of engines and cars as are required. The
process, instead of deteriorating the quality of the metal, is
said to improve it.

.   .   .   .

Well did Mount Clare need to put forth its best efforts
all the while; for the destruction of the railroad's property went
on apace, all the time. Take, for instance, such a fight as went
on at the Great Capacon in the very beginning days of January,
1862.

Great Capacon had hitherto been known merely as a point
where one of the wild and picturesque streams from out the
Virginia mountains poured itself into the Potomac; at Bath,
about ten miles above Hancock and near the confluence of the
two rivers, was the home of Porte Crayon, an early American
illustrator, whose work in the pages of *Harper's Magazine*
already had attracted national attention.

In the summer of '61, the Great Capacon bridge of the Main
Stem of the Baltimore and Ohio had been destroyed by Confederates; and later had been rebuilded as a trestle, by the
working forces of the road. It was an effective bridge, however, and, under guard of two companies of Union soldiers,
trains were passing and repassing upon it. In the darkening
shadows of the late afternoon of January 4, a picket of twenty-
three men, under command of Lieutenant Rudd, was on duty.
At about four o'clock, they noticed sharpshooters, evidently
from Stonewall Jackson's forces, making their way through
back of the trees and bushes. . . . At a signal, these men, who
had placed themselves in safe position, began firing. The
Union pickets fell back slowly. When over the mountain
came General Swing (one of General Jackson's aides) with
many more men. The purpose of their maneuvering was clear.
Great Capacon bridge again was to be destroyed.

The two companies on guard fortunately had as reinforce-
ment a good part of the Thirteenth Regiment of Indiana,

which was in retreat by train from Hancock. This regiment continued in retreat, taking with it most of the two companies which had remained on guard near the Porte Crayon home. But eighty men were left to guard the bridge. That they actually succeeded in holding it for two whole days, remained one of the stirring chronicles of the Potomac Valley. Finally, however, they were compelled to fall back. The Confederates under General Swing, in superior numbers, came down upon the railroad bridge, fired it and utterly destroyed it. But, all the while, under the steady fire of Union outposts. Four men, at least, of the Southern army were killed in this last phase of the fight. An old negro buried them beside the Great Capacon— and was paid for all his trouble, one dollar, in Confederate scrip. He reported later to the Union officers that a number of Confederate wounded had been hastily carted away in wagons.

Multiply these instances for four years up and down the Main Stem of the Baltimore and Ohio and you will begin to gain some faint idea of the unending battle that it was to keep one single and much needed railroad line in successful operation. As has been said, it was the very theater of the conflict. The little town of Winchester, Virginia, in the four years of the war, changed hands between the armies more than sixty times.

. . . .

Swing ahead two years in the conflict. This time it is February 11, 1864, and the place is not far east of Martinsburg —between Duffields and Kearneysville. Conductor Horatio C. Perry is in charge of the westbound night express, moving slowly and cautiously from Baltimore out toward Wheeling. Well it is, to go cautiously. For, just west of Duffields, timbers have been placed across the track and the engineer is not quick enough to avoid gently derailing his bulky craft. There is a bump, a sudden stop . . . silence. . . . And Conductor Perry finding his way to the front of the train and a group of men in the uniform of the Confederacy. They level guns at him.

GUARDING THE BRIDGE AT THE RELAY HOUSE.
The Boston Battery of the Union Army keeps the bridge.

From a contemporary drawing in *Leslie's Weekly.*

ANOTHER VIEW OF THE BOSTON BATTERY.

Also taken from a contemporary print from *Leslie's Weekly*.

They ask him if he is armed. Coolly he replies that he is not. Then, with a pistol against his forehead, they relieve him of his pocketbook. . . . Practical warfare, this! . . . They find that Perry is carrying money, the railroad company's money—some $4350 of it, all told. They take that also—of course. Then they stand up the passengers, in true Western hold-up style, and take from them another thousand dollars and four watches—two of gold and two of silver. A hard night on the Baltimore and Ohio. But worse to come—more confusion still. Let Mr. Perry tell it in his own words, as he reported it to William Prescott Smith three days later:

> . . . The man in charge of the Rebels represented himself as Harry Gilmor; inquiry was made particularly about yourself, they did not seem disposed to shed blood. With great persuasion, I got the Major, Gilmor, to let me go forward to stop the express. I proceeded to Kearneysville; met no pickets between the disaster and Kearneysville. . . . I waited at Kearneysville until I found by the book that the express east could not come. I then returned to my train. Mr. Porter was on the train, but learning the trouble got out of the hind end of the sleeping-car. Went on to Harpers Ferry on a coal-train, laying at the east end of Quimbys Siding. Whilst there he arranged with Mr. Darby to let nothing leave Martinsburg. He left the Ferry with Engine 56 to come to the wreck; he there informed me that he and C. Smith, also General Sullivan had arranged with Martinsburg to let nothing leave there; I took Engine 56 and proceeded to Martinsburg; when about one mile east of Martinsburg, I came in collision with Engine 72. Damage, I suppose, about $100.

To all of which, may fitly be added the testimony of Mr. Darby, the railroad agent at Martinsburg. Mr. Darby says:

> Your despatch received. Would say in reply that the first intimation I had of the train being stopped last night was a despatch from Mr. Porter that the express train had been captured by the rebels and to send nothing east of Martins-

burg. From what I can learn, about thirty men, commanded
by Major Harry Gilmor, stopped the train at Browns Crossing
by placing obstructions on the track and throwing the engine
off; as soon as the train stopped they entered the cars and
robbed the passengers of their money, watches, clothing, etc.
In regard to the collision would say that Mr. Smith ordered
the express eastbound and the stock-train to run on stock-train
time and had ordered the conductor of Engine 56 that had
been sent up to get the train to Harpers Ferry. Mr. Porter
not knowing that these trains had been ordered on, started
express train on to Martinsburg. We had started an engine
and . . . car which met express west, about one mile east
of this, near the rattling bridge, causing a collision. The
amount of damage done was the breaking of the pilots of both
engines and breaking in the end of the baggage-car and head
lamps on both engines.

Very respectfully yours,

B. DARBY, Agent.

There was no lack of excitement, operating the Baltimore
and Ohio in those war days!

. . . .

Sometimes the excitement took another turn. Consider
that memorable day when Mr. Lincoln again passed through
Baltimore—not stealthily nor in secret this time, but acclaimed
by all the folk of the town as its protector. The occasion was
the consecration of the battlefield cemetery at Gettysburg, just
five and a half months after one of the decisive battles of the
world had been fought in that old Pennsylvania-Dutch town.
In those five and a half months, great progress had been made
in cleaning up the battlefield; the bodies of the slain had been
assembled, identified whenever it was possible, and decently
interred in what was to become in after years one of the sacred
shrines of America. . . . It was thought fit that the new
cemetery be dedicated, and this at once. And no less a
personage than Mr. Lincoln to perform the rite, even though

the chief oration of the day was to be delivered by Senator Everett, of nation-wide fame as a public speaker.

November 19 was the day set for the consecration and, two weeks before, the railroad authorities were busying themselves arranging for the safe and comfortable conduct of Lincoln and his party to the battlefield. On November 8, William Prescott Smith wrote to J. N. DuBarry, superintendent of the Northern Central Railroad, at Harrisburg, saying:

> Mr. Lincoln and a portion of the Cabinet expect to go to the Gettysburg Consecration, and have sent to me making inquiries as to the route and facilities.
>
> Will you take them up in our private-cars, through from Washington, if we will deliver them to you at Bolton [the outer terminal of the Northern Central at Baltimore]? How near to Gettysburg can you take them by rail? Which is the best route—by Hanover or Westminster?
>
> Please answer promptly. I will confer with you further about details, after the route is determined.
>
> W. P. SMITH.

Mr. DuBarry replied at once, by telegraph, saying:

> Message received. Will be most happy to take your cars with party mentioned. Route, Baltimore to Hanover Junction, by N. C. Ry.; thence to the town of Gettysburg by Hanover Branch Road. Westminster is not on the route. Advise me fully of time etc., as early as possible to make all necessary arrangements.
>
> J. N. DuBARRY.

To all of these, and many other, detailed arrangements, Mr. Garrett added his own note of warning. On the very morning of the day that the Lincoln party was due to pass through Baltimore, he wrote an urgent letter to Mr. Smith, saying:

> Superintendent DuBarry's telegram of 17th inst. indicates a design to attend thoroughly to the President and suite. You

will of course see fully to having Howard Street clear, and that all arrangements upon our line are as perfect as possible for the comfort, safety and rapidity of movement of the party.

Be very vigilant regarding an understanding for their return. Have this point understood as early as practicable, and be specially careful to have the street track clear for them, and your arrangements so made that there will be no cause of complaint.

Respectfully yours,

J. W. GARRETT, President.

That very noon Lincoln was leaving Washington; accompanied by Seward, his Secretary of State; and Usher, the Secretary of the Interior; the French Minister, M. Mercier; and the Italian, M. Bertinatti; together with members of their legations and several Italian naval officers. Various members of Congress were in the party; and also Captain Henry A. Wise and his wife. Mrs. Wise was a daughter of Senator Everett. There were also in attendance the two Lincoln secretaries, John G. Nicolay and John Hay; and the chief marshal of the occasion, the redoubtable Colonel Ward Lamon, who always made it his business to protect the life of the President—with his own, if necessary.

The train moved swiftly over the Baltimore and Ohio. At one twenty—after just one hour and ten minutes of actual running time from Washington—it pulled into Camden Station, where it was greeted enthusiastically by a large group, including Mr. Garrett, Mr. Smith and Mr. J. D. Cameron, the president of the Northern Central. The Marine Band, which was also on the Lincoln Special, piled out of the cars and played a selection, while the locomotive was being taken from the cars and horses were hitched to them, to haul them individually up the long Howard Street hill to the Bolton Station.

All the way up Howard Street, the sidewalks were thronged —the passing of the President had been well heralded—and the crowds were not only orderly but enthusiastic. This time,

Baltimore was doing herself proud. . . . Repeatedly Mr. Lincoln came to the platform of the car and acknowledged the cheering. The pleasure of that hour showed upon his face. . . . At the Bolton depot there was more cheering and, as the train, brought together once more and fastened once again behind a locomotive, moved off, Lincoln came to the door for a final time and lifted his great hat to the populace. That was to be his last—almost his only—public appearance in Baltimore.

The Lincoln party, to which had been added General Schenck, in command of the Federal forces at Baltimore, and others, reached Gettysburg promptly at six thirty that evening. Mr. Lincoln spoke modestly and informally to the crowd for a few moments, but finally withdrew in favor of Mr. Everett, whose speech upon the morrow had been much heralded. . . . All that afternoon and evening, Gettysburg filled itself with humanity. There were many excursion trains and folk drove in from many miles around. Hotels and private houses were full to overflowing, and finally the churches were opened so that men and women could sleep in their pews.

Of the following day, history has told in detail; of Mr. Everett making his flowery oration and of Mr. Lincoln making a few remarks thereafter—scarcely noticed in the daily papers of that day, but which were to become recognized as one of the finest single contributions ever made to our national literature. Then the crowd turning about and toward home. But no trains were permitted to move ahead of the presidential one. It left Gettysburg at seven o'clock that evening and reached Bolton at eleven. The trip through Baltimore was quiet and unheralded. Mr. Lincoln, tired from the events of the stirring day, remained in his car. . . . At eleven thirty the train left Camden Station and, at a little after one, it was safely in the station at Washington. And every man who had been concerned in its safe progress breathed easily once again.

.   .   .   .

From the consideration of such momentous events in the history of the Baltimore and Ohio, all other things seem mundane, indeed.[1]   Yet the business of Mr. Garrett and his associates was the business of running a railroad.   Mr. Garrett, who could not have failed to be thrilled by the responsibilities that had been thrust upon him as president of the Baltimore and Ohio, not only running through the theater of the war, but also, in its Washington Branch, serving as the most important connecting link between the chief cities of the Union and its seat of government, never lost track of the details of conducting his business.   Many of these details were perplexing.

Take, as a single instance, the matter of competition:

The Vanderbilt system was being formulated.   True it was that the doughty Commodore, already in full ownership of both the New York and Harlem and the Hudson River railroads, had not yet acquired full control of the New York Central (then extending from Albany to Buffalo), but his hands

[1] " Night and day the young and vigorous railway president worked—at one time in conference with President Lincoln, the general of the army, the Secretary of War, or other officials, and later on, out on the road, encouraging and commending his men.   The next day he would be in Baltimore, looking after and inspecting terminals, conferring with his assistants, or holding conferences with the state and city authorities, to prevent hostile attacks by the secret Southern sympathizers, on his bases of supplies, his connections with the states to the north, and with the shipping to and from over the seas, for a great part of the importations from abroad, especially those for the use of the Union forces, were landed in Baltimore, as the nearest open port to the capital and the seat of the war.   The writer has a distinct recollection of Mr. Garrett as he appeared at that time (1863).   He was in the Treasury Department as Mr. Garrett came along the corridor with Secretary Chase—arm in arm, these two eminent men walked slowly along, Mr. Garrett talking in a low tone and the great financier of the war, the man who has been known ever since as the 'father of the greenbacks,' and later as the great Chief Justice of the Supreme Court, listening intently to what was said.   Those were nerve-racking days in Washington, and although Mr. Garrett was still a young man, his face had a tired, worried look, showing that he felt the awful strain caused by the great task imposed upon him.   These two great figures of the history of the war, walked slowly down the steps of the Treasury, and crossed over to the White House."—From *Graphic Sketches from the History of the Baltimore and Ohio Railroad*, by Paul Winchester.

were close upon it. His influence was being felt. And the group of roads of which the New York Central was, and is, the great main stem, were forming themselves into a strong and well united system; which reached from the city of New York to Buffalo, to Cleveland, to Cincinnati, to Chicago and St. Louis. Its lines were low grade and it was in a position to quote extremely low rates; to cut them—ruthlessly—whenever it was needed.

Tom Scott, despite his splendid war activities, was bringing the Pennsylvania—in those days often called the Pennsylvania Central—into a similarly strong strategic position. With Pittsburgh always as the key city of that growing system, he was acquiring lines—later to be known as the Panhandle and the Fort Wayne systems—which were to give him a fighting opportunity against the Vanderbilts and Garrett in all the important traffic centers of the mid-West.

A third system, in those days not to be ignored, was the Erie. The influence of Daniel Drew and James Fisk and Jay Gould—baneful as it was to be, in many, many ways—had not yet begun to exert itself harmfully. The Erie still was in a constructive phase of its existence. If it scorned Chicago— no one then dreamed that "the Garden City of the West," as it then was popularly known, was yet to become its dominant metropolis—it aspired to Cincinnati. And, from the obscure little town of Salamanca, in western New York, it was building its own railroad straight down to the "Queen City" upon the Ohio. This line, at the outset broad-gauged, like its parent, was known originally as the Atlantic and Great Western. English capital went heavily into its construction, and it was heralded as about to become one of the important railroads of all the world. Its first station at Meadville, Pennsylvania, was solemnly averred to be the "finest in the United States," with its vast dining hall, windowed and roofed "like the nave of an English cathedral." The Atlantic and Great Western afterwards came to hard times and most of the Britishers who had invested in it lost all of their money.

But in the closing years of the Civil War—'63 and
'64 and '65—it was just being completed and opened and
was taking on the appearance of a formidable competitor for
the vast business between the Atlantic seaboard and the
hinterland.

.   .   .   .

Against these three competitors, Garrett and the Baltimore
and Ohio were in a hard position.   Their line had many grades
and steep—more so even than the Pennsylvania Central, which
also passed through highly mountainous country.   Moreover,
at its two crossings over the Ohio—at Benwood, just below
Wheeling, and at Parkersburg—there were as yet no bridges.
Freight and passengers must be transferred on ferry boats,
always a tedious and, not infrequently, a disagreeable experience.   The three other systems, with direct rails all the way
from the seaboard to the important cities of the middle portion
of the country, were physically in a far stronger position.
Financially, they were, for the moment at least, in as strong
a place as the Baltimore and Ohio, if not stronger.   And that
road, it must never be forgotten, was engaged all the while in
playing a most important rôle in the saving of the Union.

The representatives of the competing lines met frequently
in rather vain efforts to adjust the delicate and destructive rate
situation.   Rarely they came to any real basis of agreement.
They would make agreements, and then promptly break them.
They were, thus, a court without authority to enforce its
decisions.   They were seemingly impotent.   And they were
two decades ahead of any attempt at governmental effort to
regulate and control and enforce a rate structure.

Mr. Garrett did not attend these conferences.   His job was
at Baltimore, and he knew it; and to Baltimore he stuck very
faithfully during those four years of the war.   At all times, he
was the general in immediate charge, the captain who refused
to leave the bridge while his ship was endangered.   His very
soul waxed wroth at the inroads of his shrewd competitors upon

A WAR-TIME LOCOMOTIVE AND ITS TRAIN.
And some of the passengers who rode upon it.

From an early photograph.

MOUNT CLARE TODAY.

The historic works at Baltimore—probably the oldest railroad shops in the world—as seen from the roof of the nearby elevator.

the traffic that rightfully he thought to be his.   He had, in his
resourceful mind, many plans for harassing and for fighting
them.   But during the years of the larger war, these must
remain in abeyance.   To be put into effect, however, as soon
as a much delayed peace was to be accomplished between
North and South.

  .   .   .   .

One of these plans for the physical improvement of the
Baltimore and Ohio could not, however, wait for the termination of the war.   It was, in no small degree, a war measure.
 This was the completion of the double-tracking of the long-
overburdened through rail route between New York, Philadelphia, Baltimore and Washington.   This, in the days of the
Civil War, was still composed of not less than three different
railroads, not always sympathetic nor entirely harmonious in
their relations with one another.   They were what soon was to
be known as the United Railroads of New Jersey, connecting
Jersey City and Philadelphia; the Philadelphia, Wilmington
and Baltimore, joining the cities that its name indicates; and
the Washington Branch of the Baltimore and Ohio, comprising
the final forty miles of the joint route—from Baltimore to
Washington.   The Camden and Amboy, reaching from the
lower harbor of New York to a point on the Delaware directly
opposite Philadelphia, also fought for its proportion of this
traffic, although with decreasing success after the route across
the Delaware, at Trenton, and thence down the west bank of
that stream to Philadelphia had been perfected.   The first large
step in the bettering of this through rail route between Jersey
City and Washington had come in 1860, when the Philadelphia,
Wilmington and Baltimore had joined with the Philadelphia
and Reading and the Pennsylvania in the immediate construction of the Junction Railroad, connecting all three lines
along the west bank of the Schuylkill in West Philadelphia.
An important final step was to be accomplished, and this was
not even begun until 1864, when the Connecting Railroad was

started between the Philadelphia and Trenton near Frankford and Mantua Junction on the Pennsylvania, the beginning point of the Junction Railroad.[1]   But this Connecting Railroad was not finished and ready for traffic until well after the close of the war, and so rendered no military service to it, even though it then became a great convenience to through travelers between New York and Washington.[2]

The Connecting Railroad was not finished until 1867—there had been so many delays; the most of them arising from the inability to get hold of both men and materials in the days of the war.   But another thing was done so that, in the fall of 1863, it became possible for passengers to go through in ten hours from Jersey City to Washington, and this was then considered a very great achievement.   The completion of double track for the entire distance had made this possible. While work had been begun on a much needed improvement—the bridging of the Susquehanna at Havre de Grace.   This last also was much delayed in its completion.   Grave difficulties were encountered in construction—on one occasion, when practically all of the spans were in place, they were blown down by a tornado and completely demolished—and it was not

---

[1] Prior to the completion of the Connecting Railroad, the main line of the Pennsylvania had been almost entirely dependent for New York traffic upon the so-called Allentown Route, a combination of the Central Railroad of New Jersey and the Philadelphia and Reading between New York and Harrisburg.   A few years after the Connecting Railroad had been finished (1867), the Pennsylvania abandoned this Allentown Route as a through link.

[2] The importance of this new line could only be realized by one who had ever tried to pass through Philadelphia on the rail route between New York and Washington in the days before it was done.   If one came on the original Camden and Amboy, after a tedious boat trip down the full length of the harbor of New York and around back of Staten Island, there was another ferry trip across the Delaware from Camden to Philadelphia; and then an additional journey through the streets of the Quaker City to the uptown station of the P. W. & B.   On the road from Jersey City through Trenton, conditions were only a little better.   For a number of years after it had been completed, it led to the edge of the Delaware at Tacony, seven miles above the heart of Philadelphia, where the traveler took another steamer to the center portion of the city. . . .   All of these changes meant great delays.

until November 28, 1866, that the bridge was formally open for traffic and the historic ferryboat, *Maryland*, which had achieved a real war record, sent around into New York harbor to carry for many years thereafter trains from Jersey City to the Bronx.

.   .   .   .

But the fact that through passengers could at last go from Jersey City to Washington in ten hours was deemed sufficient occasion for a celebration—even in war times. The more important fact, of course, was that the line was now double-tracked the entire distance—at a cost roughly estimated at $2,000,000. No longer would so many aggravating delays to traffic come to pass. By more closely linking the nation's chief seaboard cities and its capital, a real contribution had been made toward the prompt ending of the war.

On Thursday, December 3, 1863, a large party of prominent citizens and newspaper men had journeyed by special trains from Jersey City to Washington—in the appointed ten hours. At the national capital that evening, there was the inevitable banquet . . . at Willard's Hotel, where the proprietors, Messrs. Sykes and Chadwick, had laid themselves out to prepare a meal of more than ordinary magnificence. There were many speeches. Among them, one by William Prescott Smith, who mentioned the fact that the Baltimore and Ohio portion of the double-tracking would have been completed long before, had not Stonewall Jackson three times helped himself to the track material that had been set aside for the job. Mr. Smith also paid a fervent tribute to Mr. Garrett. He said, according to the *National Intelligencer* of the following day:

. . . Some were strongly prejudiced against him [Mr. Garrett] but he was the body and brain of that railroad [the Baltimore and Ohio] and to his immense force of character and his patriotism were to be ascribed the success of the herculean labors he had performed during the war. Mr. Garrett was nothing to him; he was too poor to own railroad stocks; his present railroad connection might cease at any time; he did not always agree with Mr. Garrett in his plans. . . .   "But," said he, "*such is the man!*"

.   .   .   .

With its double-tracked line in full operation between Washington and Baltimore, the Baltimore and Ohio greatly improved the quality of its passenger service between the two cities.   Now there were seven trains a day, in each direction. Trains left the handsome Washington station at 8 o'clock and 11:50 o'clock in the morning, and at 5 o'clock and 8:30 o'clock in the evening for Baltimore, Philadelphia and New York.   The night trains had sleeping cars.   Additional trains left for Baltimore at 6:35 in the morning and at 3:10 o'clock in the afternoon.   And there was, at 4:30 o'clock each afternoon, the commutation train.

This last was to be adjudged a real novelty.   It came as a war-time necessity.   The outbreak of the conflict found Washington a rather haphazard overcrowded town, of say fifty thousand folk.   To take care of the great influx that the war brought was no easy problem.   At no time in the four years of the war, did the building operations quite catch up with the housing demands.   And so folk employed in the capital began living in Baltimore and going back and forth each working day; a practice which has continued to this day. . . .   At first, a flat charge of $200 a year was made for an annual ticket good on any train back and forth each day between the two cities.   This seemed high, and finally Mr. Garrett was induced to make a yearly rate of $125 good on the commutation train which left Baltimore at 7:10 each morning and reached Washington at 8:45; returning, as we have just seen, at 4:30 o'clock each afternoon.   Later he was induced to sell a six-months' ticket for $75—the second six months, if wanted, to be paid for by an additional $50.   He said that he would have made the figure even lower than this, had it not been for that absurd Maryland tax which took a flat one-fifth of all gross revenues of the Washington Branch for the state treasury at Annapolis.

Here, then, was a beginning, if not the earliest one, of a form of traffic that was to grow greatly in its volume at most of the large cities of America and was to form, not only a considerable source of steady revenue to the railroads, but also no small problem in the design of their stations and other terminal facilities.   The short-distance daily rider on the railroad was a new creature in the 'sixties; by the 'eighties, however, he was to become a recognized fixture upon it; a citizen forever to be patronized and never, never to be scorned.

CHAPTER III

THE ARMY TAKES TO THE RAIL

Troop Movements on the Baltimore and Ohio—The Eleventh and
the Twelfth Army Corps Move West—And the Twenty-Third
Comes East—Lincoln's Final Journey—The Dispersal of a
Mighty Army.

IN September, 1863, General Rosecrans and the Union
forces suffered smashing defeat at Chickamauga, Georgia.
The people of the North, still exultant over Gettysburg and
Vicksburg, paid but little attention as a whole to the disaster.
Washington, however, had full significance of its import. Its
carefully planned strategy for the strangling and the downfall
of the Confederacy had suffered a severe setback.

Here was genuine disaster. Of the extent of the catastrophe,
the War Department had full realization. It knew that
an entire army had almost been lost. A little later, it was
to remove General Rosecrans from his post and to replace him with that highly energetic man from out of the
West, Ulysses S. Grant. In the meantime, the immediate
need was that the Army of the Cumberland, much depleted
by the casualties of Chickamauga, should at once be supported
and reinforced. More troops were needed, and at once. The
problem was, where to obtain these reinforcements.

It so happened that, at that very time, the Army of the
Potomac was, for the moment, resting on its laurels. It had
more men than it needed. It could spare troops for the Army
of the Cumberland, if only there were some way that they

46

could be transported for a thousand miles or more into the western theater of the war.

If only there were some way they could be transported!

One easily can see the bearded Edwin M. Stanton, Secretary of War, sitting at his desk with a vast map of the eastern portion of the United States spread before him; his fingers tracing it in detail. . . . Across that map, although well to the north of the fighting area, ran certain black lines. These denoted the railroads of the North; already these had become the swiftest, admittedly the most dependable, agents of its transport.

If only these railroads could be brought to bear in this rather critical situation.

Why not?

That must have been the question that E. M. Stanton asked, not only of himself, but of his chief generals in those September days of '63. Some of them must have replied that it never had been done. Which certainly would not be the sort of answer for the energetic and resourceful Stanton. And presently we shall see him sending for his friend, Garrett, of the Baltimore and Ohio.

The close and intimate relationship existing between Mr. Garrett and Mr. Stanton already has been mentioned in these pages. Just before the beginning of the war, we have seen Mr. Garrett beginning to absorb the lines of the Central Ohio Railroad, as a continuation of the Baltimore and Ohio west from Wheeling. Stanton, whose home was at Steubenville, had been at one time the general counsel of the Central Ohio. As such, he must have seen that much of his future progress rested in Garrett's hands. Be that as it may, the men became close friends. Garrett did many things for Stanton. Did Stanton . . . did Mrs. Stanton . . . wish to go to New York? At the appointed hour, the Garrett private car was ready in the Washington station. . . . On the other hand, it quickly became noised about Washington that John W. Garrett was almost the only man who could "handle" Stanton;

particularly, when he went into one of his obstreperous
moods.   And in Baltimore it still was being said that, when a
local citizen became too outspoken in his sympathies for the
South and in consequence found himself incarcerated in a
Federal prison, it was Garrett who could—and who generally
did—get him out again.   After promises of no repetitions of
the indiscretion.

.   .   .   .

Yet, on that afternoon of September 23, 1863, when
Rosecrans began appealing for help from distant Chattanooga,
Stanton had brought Meade, then commanding the Army of the
Potomac, into his office and asked him what could be done.
Meade apparently did not know.   Neither did Halleck, at that
moment general-in-chief of the entire situation.   When Stanton had asked General Halleck how quickly fifteen or sixteen
thousand men (eventually twenty thousand went) could be
transported from Virginia to Tennessee, Halleck guessed
"three months."   He really did not know.

One man came nearer knowing.   His name was T. T.
Eckert, and at that time he was known as the chief of telegraph
of the United States Army.[1]   Eckert, upon being asked how
long it would take to accomplish such a stupendous move,
said that *he* was sure it would not take so long as three months.
He asked for a few hours to study out maps and time-tables.
When he returned to the War Department at eight o'clock, he
expressed his definite opinion that the entire movement could
be accomplished within sixty days—perhaps within forty.
Later, Eckert reduced this estimate to fifteen days.[2]   It was

[1] In later years, Mr. Eckert was to become head of the Baltimore and Ohio
telegraph service; then he was for years president of the Western Union Telegraph
Company.

[2] "By 8 A.M. (September 24) Eckert had his report ready and after discussing it
with Assistant Secretary Watson, took it to Stanton's room.   When the latter
read it and learned that Eckert allowed only fifteen days, instead of his previous
hastily expressed opinion of 'sixty and perhaps forty,' he jumped for joy and began
eagerly to ask for details.   His first inquiry was, 'How do you propose to get so
large a number of men, with batteries and horses, across the river at Louisville

A POWDER CAR OF CIVIL WAR DAYS.

Built of sheet iron, with a little copper intermixed, it still retains its strength.

From a recent photograph.

A TROOP TRAIN ON THE TRAY RUN VIADUCT.

Colonel Irvine's Sixteenth Regiment of Ohio Volunteer Militia on its way to Rowlesburg, Virginia.

From a contemporary drawing in *Leslie's Weekly*.

discovered that fast freight had been known to go from Washington to Nashville in seven or eight days; passenger traffic, of course, was quicker.

With this opinion in hand to confirm him, Stanton decided to hesitate no longer. He prepared to go to Lincoln and recommend the movement—the first great troop movement upon a railroad in the history of the world. Two full corps—fifteen or sixteen thousand men, at the least—could be spared from the Army of the Potomac. It was decided that the Eleventh and Twelfth corps would be chosen.

.   .   .   .

All this took time.

In the meantime, Rosecrans was growing desperate. Another dispatch came through from him at 10:35 that evening demanding help—just as soon as it could be forwarded. The men who sat in Mr. Stanton's office decided that Mr. Lincoln must be consulted; that very night. The President, following his usual custom of the hot months of those war years, had vacated the White House and taken up his summer residence at the Soldiers Home, on an eminence just north of the capital. He was summoned by messenger and came into the city on horseback, arriving at the White House at about one o'clock in the morning. Stanton and his aides were awaiting him there. Secretaries Seward and Chase and some others joined the group.

---

safely and quickly?' Eckert replied that at that season the Ohio River was full of coal barges, loaded and empty, and that a pontoon bridge could be got ready in twenty-four hours. The next question was, 'How will you feed the hosts without losing time?' Answer was made that the Quartermaster's Department could establish a force of cooks and waiters every fifty miles or so along the route and at each eating station a supply of hot coffee, bread, etc., with waiters, could be put on the train and be carried to the next eating-place, and the waiters could then come back to their starting-point on regular trains. The plan was so well laid and withal so sensible, that Lincoln and Stanton both indorsed it, subject to the approval of the railroad authorities and military officials."—From *Lincoln in the Telegraph Office*, by David Homer Bates. The Century Company, New York, 1907.

In those quiet hours of a sultry September night, President Lincoln and his little Cabinet again faced, as so many times before they had faced, a real crisis in the history of the nation. . . . The President slowly read the dispatches from Rosecrans, listened attentively to each detail of the situation as they were given him. Then he began asking for opinions. . . . He turned to Hooker.

"Fighting Joe" had little faith in the proposed movement. And said so. For one thing, he felt that the protection of two army corps should not be withdrawn from the national capital; for another, he very much doubted the possibilities of the movement itself. . . . Men would desert, the railroads would probably prove in a final analysis entirely unable to handle so great a number of men.[1]

Lincoln turned next to Stanton.

The Secretary of War reaffirmed his belief that the thing could be done and would be done—handsomely. For an hour . . . two hours . . . the Cabinet and the general debated on the momentous undertaking. Then the President spoke.

"We will do it," he said.

And instantly word went into action. Waiting messengers outside the door sped off . . . in this direction . . . and in that.

It was half past two o'clock in the morning when this decision was reached. A dispatch was sent at once to Meade, then commanding the Army of the Potomac and resting soundly on his Gettysburg laurels, to ask him to send the Eleventh and the Twelfth corps at once to Washington . . . to reach the capital not later than the morning of the twenty-fifth. There was little time to be lost.

Within a half hour, General Meade responded with a tele-

---

[1] It must be remembered that, up to that time, the American railroads never had handled great numbers of human beings for any considerable distance, at any time or under any excuse. Today, the movement to any one of the large football games—fifty or sixty thousand folk—is hardly regarded as more than an incident in the everyday operation of any well organized and equipped railroad.

gram, saying that the Twelfth Corps was on guard along the front—which, at that moment, meant along the Rappahannock River, sixty miles below Washington—and that some little time would be required to find replacement troops for it. He was told to find them and to send the Twelfth on, without delay.

It was at about this time that it was decided to bring practical railroaders into the conference. Accordingly, dispatches were hurried off; to Baltimore for Mr. Garrett and for William Prescott Smith of the Baltimore and Ohio; and to Philadelphia for S. M. Felton, of the Philadelphia, Wilmington and Baltimore, and Colonel Thomas A. Scott, of the Pennsylvania. Garrett and Smith were the first to arrive; soon after them, Felton and Scott.

.   .   .   .

Throughout that night and clear into the dawn of the twenty-fourth, the council continued. Still others came in. Then it was again that Eckert confirmed his very definite opinion that the movement to the Tennessee could be accomplished within fifteen days. With his maps and his timetables he had figured it all out; by this time to a nicety.

For the movement itself, the best qualified men that it was humanly possible to secure were placed in command. The embarkation of the troops at the easterly end of their long trek was placed in charge of Colonel D. C. McCullon, the superintendent of the United States Military Railroad, which comprised practically all the railroads in the active theater of the war—save the Baltimore and Ohio.[1] At the west end of the movement, Quartermaster-General M. C. Meigs, who already was at Nashville—on his way to Chattanooga—was asked to look after matters. Dispatches were sent to the various railroads over which the troops would move, asking them to state their resources in cars and in engines and to be

---

[1] Garrett had always succeeded in keeping his own line quite free from governmental domination. He had shown himself to be quite as capable of its war-time operation as any one who might possibly be brought in from the outside.

fully prepared for the prompt handling of the great column.
And Colonel Scott went forward, to assist in preparing the
way.

.   .   .   .

The route laid down for the movement led from the Orange
and Alexandria Railroad, along which the Eleventh Corps
already was stretched, in protection of the line up into Washington; thence over the Baltimore and Ohio, by way of the Relay
House, Martinsburg, Cumberland and Grafton to Benwood,
just below Wheeling.   At Benwood, the troops would leave the
cars, cross the Ohio and reëmbark in other trains, through
Columbus to Indianapolis.   At Indianapolis, there would be
another movement between trains—involving marching the
men about a mile and a half across the town, to the train for
Louisville; a difficult business it all was, but seemingly there
was no way out of it.   A more logical route would have been
by way of Cincinnati and the old Kentucky Central (now a part
of the Louisville and Nashville) directly south through Paris,
Kentucky, to Chattanooga.   But, in the crudely organized
national railroad system of that day, there still remained many
variations of track gauges.   The Kentucky Central was six
feet between rails.   For through troop movement, it was
practically useless. [1]

Mr. Garrett was most concerned and anxious about the
success of this important movement.   He felt that, having so
largely sponsored it, he was personally responsible for its success.   He bombarded Smith and all the other members of his
organization with letters of instruction.   Kept them all on
"tenter hooks" until the whole thing had been accomplished—
successfully.

.   .   .   .

[1] It is worth noting, however, that, within a week afterward, the track of the
Kentucky Central was changed to the standard four feet, eight and a half inches
gauge.   They were beginning by that time to learn the real strategic value of a
railroad in the conduct of a war.

One can look back through the long years and see the morning of the twenty-fifth of September, 1863. The troops moving along the hot and dusty Virginia roads to the trains waiting for them—at Manassas Junction and again at Bristow. Marching up to the cars and entering them, in a more or less military fashion all the while.

They were crude trains, indeed. For the first leg of the journey, few passenger coaches could be secured. Flat cars and box cars, without even the semblance of seats, would have to do. The American army, which fifty-odd years later would be bumping its way over France in similar cars, labeled "Hommes 40, Chevaux 8," was getting its first dose of rail transport—under the hardest possible conditions.

Only a few miles of this first leg of the journey. There must have been many to mutter a "Thank God" to that. . . . Then the Long Bridge, and the trip across Washington City. Here there was no detraining and forced marching. For, but a few months before, under military necessity and the stress of actual war, a track had been laid in the broad streets of Washington connecting the Long Bridge and the Baltimore and Ohio passenger station and yards in New Jersey Avenue . . . At the passenger station there were other trains waiting—these composed of passenger cars of many sorts and styles, and box cars, into which rude seats had hastily been fitted. If the men traveled henceforth in seatless flat cars, it would be because they so elected.

Off and away again. . . . Up over the Washington Branch to the Main Stem at the Relay House.[1] Off and away. . . . Up through Point of Rocks and Harpers Ferry and Martinsburg; the scenes already of many heroic conflicts; but, for the moment, held tightly by Union forces. . . . Cumberland passed. . . . And then up over the Seventeen Mile Grade and through Kingwood Tunnel

[1] There had been installed at that place a direct or "Y" track (long since removed) which enabled through trains moving west from Washington to pass on to the Main Stem, without turning or switching, as formerly had been necessary.

and past Grafton, through the Board Tree Tunnel and down to Wheeling. . . . What a new experience to most of these Northern boys. What sights, what experiences, to be written to the folks back home and to be retold for forty years thereafter around the pleasant glow of a hearthstone!

At Wheeling, they were ready for the oncoming host. The tricky Ohio at low water was not to be trusted for ferriage, but it was compelled to bear upon its yellow bosom a stout pontoon bridge over which the column moved . . . men, horses, wagons . . . hour after hour . . . and boarded the waiting trains at Bellaire, upon the west bank of the river.

After which, long hours across the rich, flat fields of Ohio. Cambridge passed . . . and Zanesville . . . and Newark . . . and finally Columbus, the smart capital town of an enterprising state. More hours of darkness and of light and, finally, Indianapolis. . . . But still good order and good discipline upon the long trains moving steadily upon their way.[1]

From Indianapolis south, the rail arrangements were worse. The railroad companies were younger and weaker, and ill provided with rolling stock of every sort. But Tom Scott and Meigs, between them, had accomplished wonders; and the column moved unhesitatingly down to Jeffersonville, where again it crossed the Ohio; this time to Louisville. A rough bridge, builded of coal barges anchored in the stream just as had been planned, helped the passage. . . . Louisville represented a final transfer into the cars; a thing accomplished with becoming quickness.

On the evening of October 3, General Hooker reported to Washington that the Eleventh Corps already was going into camp at Bridgeport, but twenty-six miles from

[1] The correspondent of the *Chicago Evening Journal*, in a dispatch from Indianapolis, dated September 29, tells of the seemingly endless succession of trains coming into the depot there; the cars jammed, men riding upon their platforms and even upon their roofs. Those who were not fortunate enough to get seats in passenger cars had taken the butts of their muskets and knocked enough boards off the sides of the box cars to give them both ventilation and a sight of the passing country.

Chattanooga.   The Twelfth Corps already was arriving.
This was but a fraction over seven days from the departure at
Manassas, Virginia.   The final company of the final regiment
swung into camp on the seventh. . . .   The entire great
movement was accomplished in eleven days.   And, once again,
a vast crisis to the Union had been passed.

It seems easy enough to sit back, in this day and age, and
contemplate the movement of twenty thousand troops, in
addition to their horses, their mules and their supplies, 1100
miles in eleven days; but, when one recalls the still primitive
railroads of the 'sixties, the unending miles of poorly laid single
track, the small and ofttimes inefficient cars and engines, the
absence of bridges over important rivers, the poor telegraphic
service, the feat accomplished in that first military rail-trans-
port movement of all history looms as something vast and truly
monumental.

The archives of the Baltimore and Ohio are singularly
reticent as to the really important part played by the road
in the movement—the sole link for more than a third of its
entire distance.   Yet, here and there, one does find a passing
reference to the size of the task that had been accomplished.
As, for instance, in the long message sent by William Prescott
Smith to Secretary Stanton and dated 11:35 P.M., October 1,
1863.   It reads:

> Your despatch of inquiry received.
> As the movement is now entirely completed on our line,
> except a small remnant of horses about starting from the
> Manassas road, and as all the reports continue of a uniformly
> successful character, I thought it would be tedious to send
> you more bulletins, unless some change occurred which, I am
> happy to say, is not the case.   The only place where any real
> impediment has been threatened is Indianapolis; and I am
> more than ever satisfied of the correctness of my judgment
> when I advised you and General Hooker this day a week ago
> that the troops should have gone to Cincinnati direct by rail,
> and taken steamers for Louisville.

The change of cars at Indianapolis, with the march of over a mile across the town has been very tedious and difficult, because there was no track room or other facilities for such an occasion; nor were they familiar in that quarter with the details of such things, on such a scale. Under the circumstances, however, wonders have been achieved even there—the average delay at that point being only about six hours.

Up to 12 o'clock noon yesterday (Wednesday) fourteen out of the twenty thousand men had passed Indianapolis and by dark last evening that number had reached Jeffersonville. The last trains of troops proper crossed the Ohio River at Bellaire yesterday afternoon and are now nearly due at Jeffersonville. Some of the batteries are following closely, but even they have all crossed the Ohio River, and are on the way to Indianapolis. I hope to send you the final report tomorrow morning.

In summing up results, I find over twenty thousand men, ten batteries and their horses—besides other horses—and more than one hundred cars of baggage, etc., have gone, being, in the whole movement, an average of thirty-five per cent beyond the requisition and our expectations; and we can only wonder, that under such circumstances, such results have been secured.

I am glad to say, however, that even without previous notice, we feel ready to undertake it again, with all the anxiety and constant effort involved.

W. P. Smith.

Eventually, William Prescott Smith was to have his opportunity to "undertake it again," and in a much more difficult time than in the pleasant days of the end of September and the beginning of October, 1863. Fifteen months later, the entire movement was to be reversed; and the Twenty-Third Army Corps, 17,000 men strong, was to be moved east; from the Tennessee River, where things were comparatively quiet and the Union forces at last had the situation well in hand, to Washington, for the final move to Richmond. January is always a treacherous month for a heavy rail movement. And even though that January of 1865 started in pleasantly enough, before the troops were half done with their journey, they were to encounter bitter, freezing weather, not only greatly hampering their prompt movement, but adding much to their personal discomfort. Yet, again, the entire movement—about 1400 miles, by both river and railroad—was accomplished in eleven days or less; and a great triumph recorded for American railroad enterprise; particularly for that American railroad enterprise which bore the name, Baltimore and Ohio.

The men rode both in passenger cars and freight; from twenty to forty cars—depending upon their size and weight—to each locomotive and train. Yet, before they came to the cars, they had a long and tedious passage by water, in badly overcrowded steamboats.

Originally, it had been planned to use the Tennessee and Ohio rivers, all the way from Clifton, Tennessee, where the column embarked, through to Pittsburgh; thence east over the Pennsylvania, by way of Harrisburg, the Northern Central and the Baltimore and Ohio, through Baltimore to Washington. Tom Scott evidently was most anxious to show what *his* road could do in the mass movement of an army.

But the opportunity was not to be given him. The upper Ohio is far too treacherous for dependable or even swift river transport. Moreover, with the good record of the Baltimore and Ohio in the first movement, the War Department felt assured of its ability; and so it ordered the Twenty-Third Corps to go through as far as Parkersburg, where they would board the cars for the East. Parkersburg never was reached, however. The men, who with their horses, mules and munitions had been loaded upon sizable steamboats at Clifton (being transferred to smaller craft at the canal locks at Louisville), started in January days so pleasant and so mild that the warm promise of oncoming spring seemed fairly to hover in the air. That was up to the seventeenth of January. That night the weather marched about-face, and the mild and genial temperature of the preceding evening changed into bitter cold and freezing. Floating ice, and fixed, began to fill the Ohio, and the men in charge of the expedition began to wonder if their armada could even reach Cincinnati.

Cincinnati *was* reached. On the twenty-first, some three thousand men, the advance guard of the army, disembarked on the broad levee there, and were without delay marched to the station of the Little Miami Railroad, where the first of the troop trains stood awaiting them. . . . This was but the beginning. The story is not half told as yet. . . . The weather changed again. The wind swung around into the south, the air became warm and fetid . . . tremendous fog settled down upon town and river and levee and all the processes of unloading the corps.

Yet the work went steadily ahead. Despite all the difficult conditions, three thousand more men and their paraphernalia were unloaded on the twenty-second; four thousand, on the twenty-third. After which, the wind swung around into the north again, became biting; with astounding swiftness the glass fell. Parkersburg as a point of disembarking for any portion of the expedition was abandoned; the railroaders were told that they must handle the entire column from Cincinnati, and this with the least possible delay. They took their added burden . . . and made the best of it.

The Ohio Central received the trains from the Little Miami at Columbus and carried them east to the pontoon bridge crossing over the Ohio just below Wheeling, where Garrett and Smith and the rest of the Baltimore and Ohio had a long succession of cars and engines awaiting the soldiery. . . . The Ohio Central was still a very new railroad. It had encountered large financial difficulties in building itself and, at the best, it was not a well constructed railroad. Under the stress of mid-winter, it became a very poor railroad. Its rails were constantly cracking and breaking under the extreme cold; the small locomotives were going to pieces . . . the troop trains were sadly delayed in their passage across the state of Ohio. Colonel L. B. Parsons, who, as chief of river and rail transportation, supervised the movement and afterwards reported it to the

Executive Mansion
Washington, Jan. 10. 1865

Mr. J. W. Garrett
My dear Sir:

It is said we shall soon all be in the dark here, unless you _can_ bring coal to make gas— I suppose you would do this, without my interference, if you could; and I only write now to say, _it is very important to us_, and not to say that you must stop sup-plying the army to make room to carry coal— Do all you can for me in _both matters_.

Yours truly
A. Lincoln

MR. LINCOLN WRITES MR. GARRETT.

And asks him to make sure that Washington does not lack for its coal supply.

Reproduced from the original on file in the Library of Congress.

Baltimore & Ohio Railroad

RE-OPENED.

THIS GREAT NATIONAL THOROUGHFARE

IS AGAIN OPEN FOR

FREIGHTS & TRAVEL.

The Cars and Machinery destroyed are being replaced by

NEW RUNNING STOCK,

With all recent improvements; and as the

Bridges and Track are again in Substantial Condition,

The well-earned reputation of this Road for

SPEED, SECURITY and COMFORT

Will be more than sustained under the re-organization of its business.

In addition to the *Unequalled Attractions of Natural Scenery* heretofore conceded to this route, *the recent Troubles upon the Border* have associated numerous points on the Road, between the Ohio River and Harper's Ferry, with painful but instructive interest.

CONNECTIONS

At the Ohio River, with Cleveland and Pittsburg, Central Ohio, and Marietta and Cincinnati Railroads; and through them with the whole Railway System of the Northwest, Central West and Southwest.

At Baltimore with Five Daily Trains for Philadelphia and New York.

TWO DOLLARS ADDITIONAL ON THROUGH TICKETS

To Baltimore or the Northern Cities, give the

Privilege of Visiting WASHINGTON CITY en route

This is the ONLY ROUTE by which Passengers can procure *Through Tickets and Through Checks* to or from WASHINGTON CITY.

W. P. SMITH, Master of Transportation, Balt.

A WAR-TIME ADVERTISEMENT.

Published in a Baltimore city directory in the early 'sixties,
it notes "recent troubles upon the border."

From the company's archives.

War Department at Washington, said that there were several narrow escapes from serious disaster.   He added:

> . . . I remained on the line from Columbus to Bellaire [opposite Benwood, just below Wheeling] until the 31st, taking personal supervision of the transfer of the troops until the last car was loaded on the Baltimore and Ohio Railroad and on its way over the mountains, when I took the train and reached the city [Washington] on the 1st, where, upon the following day, I found upon the bank of the Potomac, the 23rd Army Corps safely encamped.

.   .   .   .

It all seems easy enough when one looks back at it over sixty years of dimming perspective, but when that one realizes the small engines and cars and the light track and bridges upon all American railroads of that day, the thing begins to take herculean proportions.   Then it is that one realizes that the railroaders of that day would have to concede nothing to those who have followed on and who are in the harness today.   Men who, with limited resources of every sort, did not hesitate to attempt the impossible . . . and who generally accomplished it.[1]

.   .   .   .

[1] Colonel Parsons, in that selfsame report to the Quartermaster-General at Washington, pays honest tribute to the Baltimore and Ohio men who did so much to make the difficult second movement also a tremendous success.   He says:

"The circumstances, I think, render it not invidious that I should especially refer to the management of the Baltimore and Ohio Railroad, where indomitable will, energy and superior ability have been so often and conspicuously manifested and where such valuable services have been rendered to the government—a road nearly 400 miles in length, so often broken and apparently destroyed, or constantly subjected to rebel incursions that, *had it been under my management* [the italics are those of Colonel Parsons] it would have long since ceased operation. Yet, notwithstanding all the difficulties of the severe winter season, the great disorganization of employés to a road thus situated, its most extraordinary curves, grades, bridges, tunnels and the mountain heights it scales, it has moved this large

Plainly enough, the Baltimore and Ohio was now equipped, both mentally and physically, to undertake the movement of almost any body of troops.   Yet the opportunity was not again to be given to it; not, at least, in any organized single movement, as a strategy of war.   For the war was approaching its end; swiftly, as Grant clamped his iron ring around Richmond and brought it closer and still closer all the while on the beleaguered city and the gallant Lee and his men.   Until there came that April day in the unforgettable spring of 1865, when Grant and Lee met in the little house at Appomattox and the Stars and Stripes went shimmering out in the sunlight of all the Northern towns, big and little. . . .   And then, five short days after Lee's surrender, rejoicing changed to deepest sorrow; in Ford's Theater in Washington, Lincoln was assassinated and a season of mourning inaugurated which did not halt at the Potomac's unseen line.

On the morning that Lincoln died and all eastern Maryland was in man hunt for his murderers, all trains of the Baltimore and Ohio were halted until noon at the Relay House. Washington was in panic; for a few brief hours, seemingly, there was no man that might be trusted.

Gradually, out of this panic, there came order; the preparations at the national capital for the most impressive funeral it had ever known.   Never before in all the history of the land had a man dared to raise a hand against its chief executive.   Never before had the United States been subjected to such an indignity.   Public rage rose to white heat.   And white heat gave way to the inevitable; to the blackness of a national sorrow.

Once again, and for the final time, Mr. Lincoln rode the Baltimore and Ohio.   At eight o'clock on the morning of Friday, April 21, the funeral train—eight cars in all and carry-ing, in addition to the murdered President, about three hun-

---

force in the shortest possible time, with almost the exactness and regularity of ordinary passenger trains and with a freedom from accident that I think has seldom, if ever, been paralleled."

dred men and women—left the Washington station and, running decorously slow as well befitted the solemnity of its mission, reached Camden at ten, where Mayor Chapman of Baltimore and other local dignitaries awaited it.

Despite a disagreeable rainy spring day, a great crowd of folk had been assembling since dawn at the Camden Station, which had been heavily draped for the occasion in an intertwining of flags and funeral black. . . . The train itself was preceded by several minutes by a pilot engine. The coffin was slowly unloaded and taken through the waiting room of the station to the hearse waiting outside, which carried it to the City Hall, where for four hours a vast number of people slowly passed by it and gazed upon the features of the martyred President. . . . At three o'clock, the body was carried to the Calvert Station and sent on its way to Philadelphia and New York, by way of Harrisburg. In the five hours that it rested in Baltimore, business—even the street cars—was entirely suspended and church bells tolled all the while.

. . . .

A final paragraph completes the remarkable Civil War record of the Baltimore and Ohio: In that same quartermaster-general's report in which Colonel Parsons tells the story of the second great troop movement over its Main Stem, there is recorded the fact that, in the swift dispersal of the Union army, there moved out of the Washington passenger station in two brief months (June and July, 1865) 233,300 soldiers and more than 2000 tons of baggage. From the adjoining freight tracks, more than 27,000 mules and horses were shipped in the same period of time. The greatest portion of this enormous hegira went north and east from Baltimore. Yet, of the returning and disbanded army, not less than 96,796 soldiers and 9896 animals returned home over the full length of the Baltimore and Ohio, either to Wheeling or to Parkersburg. From this last town, in a mere twenty-eight days, 92 steamboats, laden with returning soldiers and their impedimenta, were dispatched . . .

to Cincinnati, to Louisville, to St. Louis and a host of smaller river ports.   And it is put down that the average cost to the government for the movement of all these soldiers was a mere $3.40 a man.   No one might accuse the railroads of profiteering at any corner of the situation.

CHAPTER IV

BALTIMORE AND OHIO AGAIN EXPANDS

Post-War Years—Mr. Garrett Extends His Railroad Into Ohio —Many Improvements to the Line—The Metropolitan Branch is Opened—And the Baltimore and Ohio Goes to Sea.

THE Civil War over, the Baltimore and Ohio was, once again, to face the hard realities of ordinary life. No longer were the exaltations and the super-endeavors, the tremendous splurge and inflation of a vast war machine, hard at work . . . of men individually straining each nerve and being carried forward in fervors of enthusiasm. Henceforth, there was to be for the whole land the grubbing of humdrum days and weeks and months and years; the hard sharpness of business competitions, all the grueling things that put the temper of men—and railroads—upon mettle; that test full well their every resource of diplomacy.

Four years of hard internecine conflict in the land must have proven certain things very definitely to John W. Garrett and his fellows. The first of these was that their railroad finally had attained organization . . . real administration. It had ceased to be a weakling; the cat's-paw of politicians, large and small. It had showed its ability, under capable direction, to stand at last for itself, to be a going agent of transport—in every full sense of the word. The Civil War had shown, or should have shown, Baltimore that it now possessed—after nearly forty years of effort—an agency which should be truly effective in maintaining its parity, if not its supremacy, as an entrepôt in the still rapidly growing traffic into and out of the hinterland.

The war, of course, had acted very largely as a stimulant to the business of the road. It had been a tremendous help, financially, to all the Northern railroads—even though a deadly blow to most of the Southern ones. The Baltimore and Ohio, in the thirty-third year of its existence as a railroad, had handled a traffic—both freight and passenger—far in excess of the rosiest dreams of its original promoters. Its profits rose to a huge figure. In the twelve months ending September 30, 1864 (in those days the closing of the fiscal year of the company), the gross earnings of its Main Stem alone (from Baltimore to Wheeling only) had reached the tidy sum of $8,577,692.25; earnings in excess of the preceding twelve-month by $2,067,747.19, and of those for the fiscal year ending in September, 1862, by $4,095,833.27. Yet, the following year —ending September 30, 1865—saw the gross earnings of the Main Stem brought up to $10,096,706.19. This, for a number of years, remained a high-water record; representing a tremendous profit—a large part of which was used to lower the road's funded debt.

There followed the almost inevitable reaction. The lack of the stimulated war traffic—the business lapse that almost always follows a great war—by 1867, had decreased these gross earnings of the Main Stem to $7,442,684.10. Thereafter, they began slowly to ascend once again, this time upon a far sounder basis.

Similarly, in those twelve strenuous months ending September 30, 1864, the business of the vitally important Washington Branch (its statistics still were kept entirely separate from those of other portions of the system) had mounted to $864,480.79; an increase of $161,357.20 over '63; and of $86,064.12 over '62.

As the gross earnings increased, so began the proportion of operating cost to increase in relation to them. Thus, one finds, in this same fiscal year of 1864 (the thirty-third of the actual operation of the road), that this operating ratio was

38.12 per cent for the Main Stem, an increase of 7.93 per cent over the preceding year, and of 6.28 per cent over 1862. The net earnings for the entire system in 1864 were $5,692,680.75; an increase, in turn, of $676,567.04. The Main Stem was able to pay, October 20, 1863, a dividend of six per cent (representing two years) upon its common shares; on April 26, 1864, an additional dividend of four per cent. The Washington Branch continued its semi-annual five per cent payments. And, on the Main Stem, these began to be semi-annual four per cents, to be succeeded a little later by semi-annual five per cents.

.   .   .   .

It is interesting to follow the increase of the operating ratio through these years that immediately followed the peace of Appomattox. That 38.12 per cent of 1864 leaped in the following year to 56.04 per cent. Mr. Garrett must have had something to say to some one about that. In '66 and '67, it was held rigorously to 58.16 per cent and 58.79 per cent respectively. Yet the thing apparently could not be forever held down. In 1868, it took another large step forward— to 66.86 per cent—and in 1869 it was 65.97 per cent. The Civil War had had its inevitable effect of raising wage standards all the way across the land. From these increases, the Baltimore and Ohio could hardly be kept immune. Despite the best efforts of its president.

These presently began, however, to be devoted to the increasing of the volume of the traffic, rather than in futile efforts to hold down the wages of the men. Take the coal business, even today a typical gauge of the prosperity of the Baltimore and Ohio. In 1865, for instance—we still are using the figures of the fiscal year—it handled 408,170 long tons over the Main Stem; of which by far the greater proportion was Baltimore bound. This had represented a tidy increase of 48,609 tons—or about eleven per cent—over the preceding year, and set for the road a new high-water mark. Yet one which was almost immediately to be upset. For the next twelvemonth (ending September, 1866), the coal traffic rose to the mighty figure of 719,711 tons. 'Sixty-seven witnessed a slight recession—to 695,938 tons—but '68 shot the figure ahead once again to a new peak—766,011 tons. Which, again, was to be exceeded immediately. Eighteen sixty-nine saw the enormous traffic of 1,357,990 tons. Baltimore and Ohio at last was beginning to give promise of becoming the mighty coal carrier of today.

.   .   .   .

Of themselves, statistics mean but little. Go back of these figures, if you will; to the concentrated and well directed human effort that was making them possible; that was laying the solid foundations for an important American railroad of today. You will find plenty of evidence of the earnest of that effort in the black-bound reports of the company, which, published annually for a hundred years past, today line the book shelves of its secretary's office.

Taking the last year of the war—for the railroad, the fiscal year officially ending September 30, 1865—, one finds the double-tracking, under great difficulties finally completed on the Washington Branch in the late autumn of 1863, being carried forward on the Main Stem. The report of the roadmaster shows that, in '65, second track was laid on the Pillar Bridge near Martinsburg, between Mariottsville and Plane No. 1, and from Flaggs Mill to Dry Run; while grading and ballasting was well under way for the second track from Dry Run on to Paxtons Cut, eight miles, and between Harpers Ferry and Opequan Bridge, fifteen miles. Mr. Garrett was making his Main Stem ready for the real traffic that was to flow over it, once he had finally bridged the Ohio and perfected his lines to the west of that great stream. The report comments upon the difficulties in laying the second line west of Mariottsville and speaks of the necessities of improving the alignment. This all required much difficult and costly excavation. . . . The report says:

WHEN MR. GARRETT FIRST ESTABLISHED LOCUST POINT.
Ships of steam and sail combined thronged Baltimore harbor.
From a painting by H. D. Stitt.

LOCUST POINT AT A LATER DAY.

An immigrant train preparing to start out from Pier 8.

From a photograph taken in the 'eighties.

Mariottsville Tunnel was not sufficiently wide for two tracks, which increased the embarrassment. The rock was intensely hard, and to allow the free passage of trains, but narrow scaffolds could be used; thus so limiting the space for labor that the men had to work in a reclining and mostly in a painful position. . . .

·   ·   ·   ·   ·   ·

Double-tracking was but one of the progressive steps being taken by the Baltimore and Ohio in those weeks and months that immediately followed the peace. It gave its first attention to repairing the great damage done by the blows inflicted upon it through the war. Furthermore, at Camden Station and at Mount Clare alone, more than $332,000 were being expended upon additions to the structural equipment.[1] The burned roundhouse at Martinsburg was replaced by what was then regarded as not less than a magnificent new edifice and one which has come down to this day as an evidence of the thoroughness of those builders of an earlier one. Framed of giant wrought-iron girders, placed like the sticks of a great Indian tepee, with their foundations in a huge circle and all converging to an apex in a dome, these roundhouses—there are two of them—still form striking landmarks upon the line. Martinsburg ceased long since to be an important operating center, but the old roundhouses are now used for storage purposes and are carefully preserved by the present management of the property.

At the same time that the new roundhouses were being built at Martinsburg, similar structures were going up at Piedmont and at Grafton, which also had suffered more or less heavily from war-time depredations. And new "passenger

[1] At Camden, these took the form of wings to the east and to the west of the main station building; while, at the workshops of the company, were being erected a new foundry, of brick and running 200 feet on Pratt Street, by 200 feet on Carey; a wheel house and fitting-up shop for locomotives; a new scale house had also been put up.

and telegraph stations . . . very pretty and convenient," to quote the language of the report of the master of the road, were being erected at Monocacy and at Glovers Gap.

.   .   .   .

All of these things, however, were but as minor details of the great plan that John W. Garrett held for the post-war development of the Baltimore and Ohio.

In his vision and in his opinion, it was not nearly enough that the road, after so many years of struggle, had finally reached the Ohio; at two points—Wheeling and Parkersburg—with a third tentacle—to Pittsburgh—being put forward toward completion. Not enough even that he should have acquired the Central Ohio and a substantial interest in the Marietta and Cincinnati Railroad. Presently, all these would have to be knitted together, into a fairly compact and singly directed railroad system—a line by which Garrett would try to match the control that the New York Central would soon be getting of the Lake Shore, the Michigan Central and the Big Four; the Pennsylvania, of the Fort Wayne and of the Panhandle; and the Erie, of the Atlantic and Great Western.

If he did not move quickly, Garrett would be outgeneraled by these great rivals to the north of him. No one knew this better than he. He saw the painful possibilities of Baltimore and Ohio shut out, rather effectively, from the fine new traffic-producing centers of the swiftly growing central states. He knew the essential weaknesses of the property that he now controlled; its hard grades over the Alleghenies, as well as the yellow impasses of the Ohio River, over which men and goods and cars must still be ferried, laboriously.

With the growing strength of his holdings in the Central Ohio and the Marietta and Cincinnati properties, he therefore set out toward bridging the Ohio—at Parkersburg and just below Wheeling; as well as completing the double-tracking of his Main Stem—for the immediate moment, as far as Cumberland.

Nor was this all: The choicest prize of all that middle country still remained well beyond reach of his fingers. This was Chicago; which in the 'sixties, by reason of its prettily shaded streets and its abundant green lawns everywhere, had begun to be called the "Garden City of America," but which in that very decade was giving hint of its future metropolitanism.[1]

Even in the mid-'sixties, it was a considerable and a growing railroad center, a manufacturing town of promise, a lake port of increasing traffic. John W. Garrett must have looked at it with hungry desire. True it was that he had his lines well laid for Pittsburgh, for Cincinnati, for St. Louis, too. But Chicago might become as large as any one of these three good cities . . . even larger. . . . The Great Lakes still gave but little hint of the tremendous water-borne traffic that yet was to rest upon their ample bosoms. Nevertheless, there were already many boats. And Cleveland and Buffalo and Detroit and Milwaukee were, like Chicago, smart and pretty lake-port towns, with commerce in them growing year by year.

If Garrett could reach the Great Lakes, even with a single pair of rails, he would be in a position to command at least some of this steadily increasing traffic between the ports of Lake Erie and those of the upper lakes—Huron and Michigan and Superior. Therefore, within this five-year period just following the close of the war, Baltimore and Ohio was to gain control, through its recently acquired Central Ohio property, of the then Sandusky, Mansfield and Newark Railroad Company. Officially, this came to pass February 13, 1869, and of it Mr. Garrett wrote in his report that same autumn:

> . . . This line, now known as the Lake Erie Division of the Baltimore and Ohio Railroad, is 116 miles in length . . . from Newark, on the Central Ohio Division, to the city of Sandusky, on Lake Erie. It extends through five of the

---

[1] First it was to be scourged by one of the greatest fires in all history before it was really to toss off its swaddling clothes and begin its swift rise toward becoming the second city of the continent.

richest and most important counties in the state of Ohio; Licking, Knox, Richland, Huron and Erie. It passes through a number of cities and centers of manufacturing and commercial enterprise. Its terminus, the city of Sandusky, possesses one of the best harbors on the Lakes, which is readily susceptible of such improvement as to furnish great facilities for an extensive commerce. The direct line under the control of the Baltimore and Ohio Company, from Sandusky to Baltimore, is 595 miles in length, over which loaded cars are transported without break of bulk. This additional convenient outlet for the commerce of the Great Lakes and of the extensive intermediate regions to the city of Baltimore will afford such advantages that a large increase of business must result.

Eventually, as will be seen in subsequent chapters, this new line was to be of largest advantage to the Baltimore and Ohio as an important part of its first finger into the rich Chicago pie. For the moment, however, it assumed its importance as a valuable rail connection to the ancient port of Sandusky. Here was a good beginning.

.   .   .   .

Not all of Mr. Garrett's efforts in this five-year period were to be made in extending his rail facilities west of the Ohio. East of the river there still remained much to be done. The important road from Cumberland into Pittsburgh, which for years had languished and at times had all but died, was, under the vigorous efforts of the president of the Baltimore and Ohio, to be whipped into real shape—as a going railroad; even though it was not to be until 1871 that the first Baltimore and Ohio train actually entered the great key city at the confluence of the Allegheny and the Monongahela rivers, which for years had been regarded as the exclusive province of the Pennsylvania Railroad.

East of Cumberland, there were still other lines to be perfected. The citizens of Hagerstown, Maryland, long since fretted by the fact that they were not upon the lines of so important a railroad as the Baltimore and Ohio, sought direct connection with it. So came into existence, right after the war, the Washington County Railroad, twenty-four miles in length, from Weverton, upon the Main Stem, to Hagerstown.

To build and to complete this branch took great persistence and real fortitude. The contractors encountered many difficulties and before they were done—in order to assure the early opening of the branch—workmen from the Main Stem were sent to help them. In addition to all of which, the Baltimore and Ohio subscribed $400,000 for the building of the line. Washington County had managed to contribute $150,000; and its citizens and other private individuals, $220,900. There still remained a deficit, however, and before the branch was opened—December 1, 1867—the Baltimore and Ohio company had given it, in subscription and advances, $762,624.93.[1]

. . . .

A similar branch line, which at about the same time was being incorporated with the parent system, was the former Winchester and Potomac Railroad; running from Harpers Ferry to Winchester, and then on to Strasburg, Virginia. The history of this branch is closely entwined with the building of the Valley Railroad at the very beginning of the 'seventies. All of this makes a chapter in itself. And will be considered at a later time.

. . . .

Another important new link of the system which came into existence at the end of the war was the so-called Metropolitan Branch, making a direct connection between the city of Washington and Point of Rocks; and, so, shortening by some fifty-four miles the previously circuitous rail route between the national capital and the West. In the early 'sixties, Mayor Wallach of Washington had suggested this short line

---

[1] At a later time, Mr. Garrett was to seek, although unsuccessfully, to cut the Washington County Railroad away from the Main Stem. It remains to this day part and parcel of the main system.

and had done his best to bring it into being, but the exigencies of war days had rendered this an impossibility. With the coming of peace, the matter was brought forward once again and, despite many physical difficulties due to the rugged contour of the terrain, it was pushed through to completion. It was opened for through traffic in 1868; and at once became, to all practical purposes, part and parcel of the main line of the system—at least as far as through passenger service was concerned. Today, all of the fine fast expresses of the Baltimore and Ohio continue to follow this attractive route, which brings them directly through Washington and in sight of the great dome of the Capitol. The old main line, between the Relay House and Point of Rocks, much revised and improved as to alignment, now receives most of the tremendous tonnage of the through freight destined in and out of Baltimore, Philadelphia and New York, in addition to a local freight and passenger service adequate for its needs.

.   .   .   .

John W. Garrett's ambitions did not, however, halt at the extension of his rail system toward the west; how to make it reach further east, became to him a matter of consuming interest. With which came, as a most natural corollary, the development of Baltimore—nearly two hundred miles inland from salt water—as a real ocean port.

This last thing he accomplished; let it be said, to his eternal credit. He brought Baltimore, which, nearly a hundred years before had been a seaport of no small importance, sending its graceful clipper ships to the far corners of the seven seas, back into its own once again. He devised favoring rates to the city of Baltimore and Ohio parentage, which became the very foundations of the so-called "differential structure" of today, which still maintains the prestige of Baltimore as one of the very great ocean ports of America.

He did far more than this:

At Locust Point, at the very gateway of the deep inner

harbor, on the Northwest Branch of the Patapsco, where there was, and still is, abundant fairway for the manipulation of the largest ships, he began the erection of a dock and elevator system of real magnitude. The city of New York, always handicapped by highly inadequate port facilities, looked hungrily upon the Garrett development of the harbor of Baltimore: huge wharves, where the largest ships of that day might be berthed; and, directly alongside, long strings of freight cars, of every description, bringing to them the coal and the produce of the inner country and taking in return a vast variety of imports. In addition to which, were erected storage elevators and warehouses of various types.[1]

To better the rail facilities for reaching Locust Point, Mr. Garrett brought about, in the summer of 1867, the construction of what was then known as the Camden Cut-off. . . . For the first decade and a half of the operation of the road from the Camden Station, the line had followed an extremely circuitous route out of Baltimore to Washington and the West. Running almost directly south from the station structures, at the new passenger-engine roundhouse (eventually to be known to all local railroaders as Baileys), it turned abruptly west, then turned again to the southwest. Nor was this all. Thereafter, the line formed an almost precise horseshoe, rejoining the original line of the road, as it ran out from Mount Clare, just east of the historic Carrollton Viaduct. . . . That original line was infinitely more direct.

[1] The dominating structures of this last group were the two storage elevators; with a combined capacity of over 2,000,000 bushels of grain. They contained 331 storage bins, 21 receiving and 11 shipping elevators; in that day the latest word in modern mechanical device for the rapid handling of grains. It was not, however, until 1873 that both of these elevators were finally completed. In that year, the grain exportation at Locust Point, which five years before had been negligible, reached a total of 7,251,717 bushels. Other special warehouse facilities were devised for the handling of sugar and of coffee. But the great strength of Locust Point in those days was in the export coal traffic. Ocean ships came to Baltimore for cheap fuel for their bunkers. And there they found it. The 3600 feet of water frontage in the Baltimore and Ohio terminals there was always well filled with vessels taking aboard coal, either as cargo or as fuel.

The obvious thing to do would have been to stretch a tangent for the new line across the two bases of the horse-shoe. For a long time this logical step was contemplated, and for a long time was fought persistently by the citizens of Baltimore whose personal interests would have been affected by it. After which, the railroad continued for some years its circuitous course for its passenger and freight trains into and out of Camden.

The development of the waterside terminal at Locust Point made this abominable defect in the alignment of the road all the more provoking. Another and a final effort was made by its management to correct it. This one succeeded. On April 15, 1868, the Camden Cut-off, two and one-fifth miles in length, and saving one and a half miles for every train of the Baltimore and Ohio that went over it, was placed in operation. Thereafter, no more passenger trains went over Carroll-ton Viaduct, but crossed Gwynns Falls on a new double-tracked iron bridge, well below, which became known collo-quially as the Bluetop Bridge. Freight trains and work trains in and out of Mount Clare still used the Carrollton Viaduct. And, for a time, in fact, all freight trains continued to use the old line. For those same obstreperous interests that had opposed the construction of the Camden Cut-off in the first place, sought successfully for some months to limit its use to passenger trains.

. . . .

Mr. Garrett was not content, however, to feel that, merely because the railroad that he headed had provided Baltimore with abundant facilities for becoming an ocean port, the thing was then to be called fully accomplished. He felt that definite steps must be provided for establishing modern transatlantic steamship lines into and out of the port, and that this probably could be done by no other agency—at the outset, at least—than by the Baltimore and Ohio itself.

While the country still was in the throes of war, he had

entertained this idea. More and more it appealed to him. He decided to act upon it. So, with the full coöperation of his administration, he purchased from the United States government, at the end of the war, three wooden propellers, which, in 1862, had been built for it at New York. These he named, for Maryland counties, the *Somerset*, the *Carroll* and the *Worcester*. There was also to have been the *Allegany*, but for some reason the deal in regard to this last vessel fell through completely.

These three ships were not large and they were not beautiful. The largest of them, the *Worcester* (formerly the *Nereus*), was only 218 feet long, 35 feet beam, and 20 feet depth of hold—some 1500 tons gross, all told. She was single screw, being driven by two vertical low-pressure engines, of simple type, with cylinders 44 inches in diameter and having a stroke of 48 inches. Her passenger facilities were extremely limited.

Mr. Garrett's knowledge of maritime affairs was extremely limited. Gradually, he had become well versed in many details of railroad management; but the operation of ships in long-distance trades was quite beyond his ken. Otherwise, he never would have purchased such small units—smaller than those in inconsequential coastwise services today—for the inauguration of the Baltimore and Ohio transatlantic service. He afterwards said as much.

Yet, the fact remains that the three staunch little ships did operate; and, for more than three years just following the war, they were the only vessels upon the entire Atlantic to fly the United States flag. They carried the United States mail and they kept alive, even though feebly, the tradition of that glorious American merchant marine which virtually had been swept out of existence by the Civil War. Moreover, they led, even though indirectly, to the establishment and the fulfilment of the Garrett principle: the development of capable transatlantic services that would redound to the glory and to the material prosperity both of Baltimore and of the Baltimore and Ohio—partners in the beginning and partners throughout the long years.

.   .   .   .

The ceremony that attended the inauguration of this little line forms one of the picturesque minor details of the annals of the Baltimore and Ohio. The *Somerset* made the first sailing from Baltimore, Saturday, September 30, 1865. In anticipation of its departure, Baltimoreans read in the *Sun* paper the preceding morning:

The steamship, *Somerset,* one of the vessels about to be inaugurated between this port and Liverpool, and which has been undergoing extensive repairs and alterations, is now so far completed as to be able to start on her first trip across the ocean, as the pioneer of the enterprise, the success of which is of such importance to the mercantile interests of Baltimore. In addition to the elaborate work put upon the hull of the vessel, Messrs. Jas. Clark & Co. of the People's Machine & Boiler Works, have placed a new shaft in her, and her engines have been thoroughly overhauled and refitted. A brief trial trip of the *Somerset* was made a few days since, when a number of gentlemen interested in the enterprise were on board, and after running some sixteen miles expressed themselves perfectly satisfied with the ship in every respect. With fifteen pounds of steam she made thirty-five revolutions per minute, and it was asserted that she can make ten knots with twenty-five pounds of steam, her usual standard.

At noon tomorrow, the *Somerset* leaves this port for Liverpool. She will start from Henderson's wharf, foot of Fell Street. All her cargo is aboard, several persons are booked as passengers. The cargo is nearly as follows: 300 bales of cotton, 100 hogsheads of tobacco, 6000 bushels of corn, 800 sacks oilcake, 40 tons of bark, a large quantity of dye-stuffs, canned fruits and miscellaneous articles. During yesterday about fifty shipjoiners and painters were at work in her, and with this force, by Saturday the repairs and alterations will be completed.

Captain John L. Sanford, an experienced seaman, is the commander of the vessel; Mr. E. H. Sanford is first-mate, assisted by two others. Mr. David S. Frazier is the chief engineer, assisted by three others. Suitable preparations are being made, under the management of Messrs. Wm. P. Smith and W. S. Woodside, officers of the Baltimore and Ohio Railroad Company, to give persons an opportunity not only to see the steamship leave the wharf but to witness her trip some distance down the bay. At and around Henderson's wharf there will be ample room for many persons to congregate at the time of the departure of the vessel, the occasion being one of which Baltimoreans may be truly proud. As the ship leaves the wharf she will be saluted from Fort Federal Hill and by the U. S. Revenue Cutter, and will also be saluted as she passes Fort McHenry. These salutes will be returned by the *Somerset.* The U. S. Revenue Cutter will convey a large party of ladies and gentlemen some distance down the bay. Among these will be Major Gen. Hancock, Hon. Thomas Swann, Governor-elect, Mayor Chapman, John W. Garrett, Esq., and other distinguished gentlemen. It is understood that a steamboat will leave the adjoining wharf, and accompany the *Somerset* as far as North Point, on board of which persons can take a short excursion and witness the departure of the pioneer ship of this ocean line between Baltimore and Liverpool.

The occasion seems to have been fully as auspicious as had been anticipated. . . . The ships in Baltimore harbor were gaily dressed in flags. There were numerous salutes. And in the cabin of the Revenue Cutter (the *Nemaha*) a wonderful collation was served, followed by a flow of oratory of the pre-war type. Among those who spoke were Mr. Garrett, William Prescott Smith, John H. B. Latrobe (now beginning to advance in his years) . . . and others.

The new line started out bravely, even with its small, slow, unbeautiful ships. One finds in the *Liverpool Mercantile Gazette*, in March, 1866, the following advertisement of its service:

Steam to Baltimore;—

Taking goods at through rates of freight to Cincinnati, Louisville and St. Louis. The fine steam ship *Worcester* for Baltimore on the 25th of April. Burthen 1500 tons. This steamer is New York built, of great strength and power and admirably adapted for the trade. The accommodations for passengers are spacious and complete. Captain Eiley is well acquainted with steamers.

For terms of freight or passage apply to: James Browne and Co., 19 Tower Buildings.

Will be succeeded by the following first-class steamers:

Somerset, Wed. 16th May, 1866.
Carroll, Wed. 6th June, 1866.
Worcester, Wed. 11th July, 1866.

Yet, despite the brave beginning, the finish was early. The little vessels could not compete successfully with the foreign lines and, sometime in the fall of 1868, they were withdrawn. . . . The *Worcester* and the *Carroll* were taken to Boston and continued to run for many years between that city and Halifax, Nova Scotia, until literally they were worn out. They were dismantled in the summer of 1894 on Nut Island in the harbor of Boston. . . . Of the fate of the *Somerset*, there apparently is no record.

·   ·   ·   ·   ·   ·   ·

Unsuccessful as was this one attempt of the Baltimore and Ohio to engage in the steamship business, it was by no means inglorious. Not only did it serve to keep aflame the light of the American merchant marine in the darkest years of its history, but it led the road into a powerful alliance with the North German Lloyd Steamship Company, a highly successful and experienced operator of ships upon a large scale. To accommodate these fine German ships better, a splendid passenger and freight wharf, with banking and exchange facilities right on the pier and provision made for the passenger

THE MODERN PIERS AT LOCUST POINT.

Several of them enjoy direct connection by conveyor with the great elevator there and offer every modern advantage for handling export freight.

From a photograph.

LOCUST POINT FROM THE AIR.

With Fort McHenry in the immediate foreground.

From an aerial photograph.

trains being operated into it upon steamer days, was built at Locust Point.

This working agreement between Baltimore and Ohio and North German Lloyd was signed January 21, 1867, and, on the twenty-fourth of March of the following year, the fine new steamer *Baltimore*, which had been expressly constructed for the service, arrived for the first time in the city for which she had been named, and berthed at Locust Point. Her sister ship was the *Berlin*, in later years to be known, most favorably, as the *City of Rome*. . . . These vessels represented a distinct advance over any that had preceded them upon any ocean route anywhere, and their coming into Baltimore was heralded as a distinct advance in the city's progress.[1]

.   .   .   .

A man of real vision, this John W. Garrett! Seeing not alone lines reaching far across the Ohio and well into the mid-West, a through rail line down into the South, in all probability as far as New Orleans (the Valley Railroad, of which much more in another chapter), but a route by water across the Atlantic to a Liverpool terminal . . . eventually, perhaps, rail lines on to Philadelphia and New York. The Baltimore and Ohio became huge, well ordered, self-contained. In the Mount Clare shops, Garrett was building his own sleeping cars and parlor cars; at Relay and Cumberland and Deer Park, he was setting up large hotels for the

[1] Of this arrangement, Mr. Garrett was to write (in his annual report, dated September 30, 1868) after this fashion:

"It is a source of satisfaction that the great, effective and successful steamship company so appreciated the advantages, facilities and economies of the port of Baltimore and of the Baltimore and Ohio Railroad and its connections as to join and coöperate in this most valuable and important enterprise.

"The agreement required the immediate construction of two splendid first-class iron steamships, and embraced provisions for the future enlargement of the line, as the advantages and business of the route developed. It was the conviction of the Board that the subscription made of one-half the capital required for this line was fully justified, especially in view of the increase and impetus that would result to the commerce and growth of the port of Baltimore, and the consequent reactive effects upon the business of the road."

dining and overnight accommodations of his passengers. Self-contained, indeed. The Baltimore and Ohio prepared to establish its own express company . . . its own telegraph line. . . . It was to be—to itself, and to its patrons—all things connected with rail transport; upon the finest scale known half a century ago.

More than all of this, Garrett finally had succeeded in upsetting the political control of the road—a majority membership of the board of directors, representing the stockholdings of the city of Baltimore and the state of Maryland —which, more than once, had all but wrecked the growing, struggling enterprise. Even though both of these governmental organisms still continued to retain their shares. To their own good advantage. To buy them, they had borrowed money, up to six per cent. But the stock began, and for some years continued, to pay ten per cent. There were years when the city of Baltimore reaped an annual profit of more than $130,000 from its holdings in its chief railroad . . . which steadily continued to expand. Garrett's hands were almost upon Chicago; and he had definite plans to assure him an uncontested entrance into both Louisville and St. Louis. But before these are reached, we shall go back—nearly twenty years—to 1853, and for a time take up again the locomotive development of Baltimore and Ohio.

CHAPTER V

THE IRON HORSE IS PERFECTED

Locomotive Development on the Baltimore and Ohio from 1853 to 1876—The Controversy Between Ross Winans and Henry J. Tyson—Thatcher Perkins—And the Building of the 600.

IN the columns of the Baltimore newspapers in the late fall of 1856 and in the spring of 1857, there began a controversy, which, before it was finished, was to have many of the prominent citizens of the town by the ears. Letters in the newspapers were followed by printed pamphlets—hard names were called, much ill-feeling engendered. And all this over the question of the proper type of locomotive for use on the Baltimore and Ohio Railroad. To be specific, whether or not the camel engine devised by Mr. Ross Winans was fit motive power, of the highest possible efficiency, for the road. Mr. Winans had quit the service of the Baltimore and Ohio and had gone to building camel locomotives on his own account, in a well equipped shop of his own, almost directly across the street from Mount Clare. He had sold a few to the Pennsylvania and some other outside railroads. And he was anxious to greatly increase the scope of his endeavors. He seemed to be in a fair way to do this, and the Baltimore and Ohio he had held to be a laboratory ample for the development of his locomotive theories.

Mr. Henry Tyson held otherwise. Mr. Tyson, in June, 1856, had succeeded Mr. Samuel J. Hayes as master of machinery of the road, and he was in a position to enforce his views; particularly so, inasmuch as he was known to be a man of real force and energy.[1]   Yet, Ross Winans could not exactly be called a weakling.   He had a reputation for holding tenaciously to an idea—once he had taken it unto himself.   Having developed the camel engine—by himself and practically unaided —apparently he could see none other; for the Baltimore and Ohio, at any rate.

The camel was a radical development in steam-locomotive construction—no question of that.   Most of the mechanical men of other railroads looked askance at it.   They criticized its hook-motion valve gears; its lack of a forward or leading truck.   Tyson followed these views.   His own inclination was for what had been known up to that time as the "Hayes ten-wheelers," so named from the fact that originally they had been designed by his immediate predecessor in office.

It should be understood that then, as now, the ruling factor in the design of the most efficient locomotive for the Baltimore and Ohio was its great Seventeen Mile Grade, west of Piedmont, rising 116 feet to the mile.   On this hill, engines made their eternal reputation; were either acclaimed good, or definitely and forever relegated to a second-grade rank.   Few there were that could pull a train of any real tonnage whatsoever up this mountain grade without assistance.   Until the coming of Hayes, it had been the practice to try the hill with the road's ordinary four-coupled engines, using the Winans camels as helpers.   This was a makeshift, and a poor one; and Mr. Hayes had sought to overcome it with a ten-wheel locomotive, in general outward appearance very faintly resembling the camel, and yet radically different in its principal features.

[1] Mr. J. Snowden Bell is of the opinion that the importance of Henry Tyson as a locomotive builder has never been fully recognized.   Mr. Bell believes that Mr. Tyson's mechanical ability was of a most unusual sort. . . .   Mr. Tyson was born in Baltimore in 1820 and, in the earlier years of his life, was engaged in milling in Commerce Street in that city. . . .   After his term of service with Baltimore and Ohio, he became, for thirteen years, president of the Baltimore City Passenger Railway; going from that company to the position of mechanical vice-president of the New York and Erie Railroad.   At a later time, he was receiver of the Chesapeake and Ohio.   He died September 8, 1877.

These Hayes engines were generally successful. Seventeen of them were built for the Baltimore and Ohio prior to 1860—three in the company's Mount Clare shops and the others by outside builders—and some of them remained in its service for many years. Twenty years after their introduction, a number of them were made modern by the application of the link-motion valve gear and the widespread truck.

. . . .

Mr. Tyson's first move was to develop and perfect this type of engine; which presently began to bear his own name. He showed no enthusiasm whatsoever for the Winans camel; his designs embodied not one of its essential characteristics. To Tyson, it was as if the Winans engine never had been born. On September 13, 1856, the new master of machinery of the Baltimore and Ohio wrote Winans:

> . . . This company proposes to contract for the building of five ten-wheel locomotive engines, according to designs to be furnished by them. They are to weigh thirty tons with water in boiler and fuel, to have cylinders 18 inches diameter and 24 inches stroke, 50-inch drivers, 30-inch truck-wheels, with link motion and variable exhaust. Inform me at an early date if you desire to make a bid for the whole or a portion of the contract, and at what time the machines could be delivered. Specifications will then be sent you. . . .

Mr. Winans' reply to this note was to call upon Mr. Tyson; to argue with him—unsuccessfully—the superiority of the camel engine; and to hear in return that this type of locomotive would, under no circumstances, be considered. Later, Tyson sent Winans copies of the specifications of the five freight engines. To which Winans replied by submitting a camel design, modified only to the extent that a forward leading truck had been substituted for the front pair of driving wheels. He offered to build these engines for a flat ten thousand dollars apiece.

This offer received scant consideration at Mount Clare. Seven new locomotives—instead of the five originally planned —were ordered from the Baltimore works of A. W. Denmead & Sons, instead of from the Winans works. When they arrived, throughout the following year, they were numbered consecutively from the *222* to the *228*. In the same twelvemonth, Mount Clare itself built two more of the type, the *229* and the *230*.

.   .   .   .

The fat was now in the fire. The Tyson ten-wheelers[1] proved themselves eventually to be fairly good engines, even though it was thought that they had too little weight upon the leading trucks, a fault which, in certain instances, was remedied by adding heavy cast-iron plates, fitting over the frames. But when they first came out upon the line, they were as yet untried; and long before the appearance of the first of them, Ross Winans had taken up his vitriolic and extremely able pen and was preparing a pamphlet on the merits of his camels, as compared with these new ten-wheelers. This pamphlet, when finally it came from the printer, contained not less than thirty-four pages, set in a reasonably fine type.

The inventor of the camel called attention to the fact that 109 of these eight-wheel engines were already in use upon the road, as compared with but seventeen of the ten-wheelers. Of these last, fourteen were in its freight service, the other three in passenger. The passenger engines, in the years 1854 and 1855, had averaged 46 per cent more running than the freight ones and had been maintained at 42 per cent less cost,

[1] "The Tyson ten-wheel engines weighed 61,830 pounds, of which 48,200 pounds were on the driving-wheels. The cylinders were 18 by 24 inches; driving-wheels, 50 inches, with chilled cast-iron tires and boilers of telescopic form, 46 inches diameter of first ring, with crown-sheet radially stayed by $\frac{7}{8}$-inch stay-bolts. The inside firebox was of copper, except the crown-sheet, and was 66 by 41 inches inside dimensions, giving a grate area of 18.5 square feet. . . . These engines were the first on the Baltimore and Ohio Railroad that were equipped with the Gooch or so-called 'stationary' link motion."—From an article by J. Snowden Bell on *Railway and Locomotive Engineering* in April, 1925.

per mile run. This, to Mr. Winans' mind, argued that the ten-wheel type was better suited to passenger service than to freight—this last always the main business of the Baltimore and Ohio. He then confined himself to making a comparison between the fourteen ten-wheel engines in the freight service and the 109 camels similarly employed. He showed that the average cost per mile for repairs to the camels was but 9.31 cents, as compared with 9.47 cents for the ten-wheelers. He, moreover, asserted that the heaviest labor on the line—the bringing of coal trains from Martinsburg to Baltimore, over the heavy grades of the old main line, as they then existed— was reserved largely for the camel engines. They had stood up to it, magnificently.

Mr. Winans argued well for his engines. He stressed particularly the merits of their wide fireboxes and, were he living today, he undoubtedly would have a thrill to see how this fundamental idea has been taken up by the locomotive builders of the present hour. He probably would not be so enthused, however, to find that the leading-truck feature of locomotive design had become practically fixed upon all forms of modern engines, save those designed for the very lightest forms of switching service. . . . He pleaded eloquently for his camels; the strength of their boilers, their steam-generating power, their adhesion, the facility with which they might be fired . . . other distinctive points in which he had an everlasting faith. . . . The pamphlet, once it had come from the press, was given wide distribution. It was reprinted in certain newspapers and in the technical press.

It could not be ignored. It was not ignored.

The directors of the Baltimore and Ohio sat in solemn conclave upon it. When they were done, *they* had evolved a weighty pamphlet—of fifty-eight pages—in which their position in favor of the ten-wheelers was fully set down. This, too, was given wide distribution.

It said sharp things about the Winans camels. It conceded to them very great adhesion, but at the expense of lost speed and an increased fuel consumption.   It alleged that they were roughly and cheaply built and that they were disproportionate in many of their parts.   Looking back from today, it is hard to conceive how any one would see real beauty in the design of the camel engine.   Judged by modern standards, it was an extremely top-heavy and unwieldy thing; in appearance, at least. . . .   The indictment continued: The camel was extremely subject to derailment; hardly a week was passing in which accidents of this kind were not taking place; indeed, within the past week, two had come to pass, with a loss in each case of not less than a thousand dollars.   The road had been much hampered in even attempting their operation.

Mr. Tyson was the author of this pamphlet, finally acknowledged as such.   He turned with enthusiasm to the ten-wheel type.   Of it he wrote:

The ten-wheel engines of which this company owns sixteen [at that particular time] have always proved remarkably safe and reliable.   The passenger service is exclusively performed by them on the third, or mountain, division, and the greater number of them are also kept in freight service on this division, owing to their being considered safer and more reliable on the heavy grades than any other engine.   They are furnished with six driving-wheels connected, to which the power is applied, the rear ones only being flanged; the front portion of the engine is sustained by a vibrating truck.   They have a furnace of sufficient size to generate an abundant supply of steam. They are suited to any branch of the service, and can be run at high speed with passenger trains with entire safety—one of their particular characteristics being their certainty to remain upon the track, except when it has met with a formidable obstruction.

One can fairly see, even at this day, the fine satisfaction with which Mr. Tyson put down his pen when that paragraph was finished.   One also can see a new indignation flushing the already ruddy face of Mr. Ross Winans as he read it for the

THE *Thatcher Perkins, No. 117.*

Carefully preserved at Baltimore is this passenger locomotive of Civil War days, originally built by
Thatcher Perkins at Mount Clare.

From a recent photograph.

THE FAMOUS CAMEL-BACK—*Ross Winans*, *No. 217*.

This type of locomotive for forty years was most typical of Baltimore and Ohio motive-power practice—especially in freight service.

From a recent photograph.

first time; and probably for a good many other times thereafter.
. . . Mr. Tyson had corroborated his opinion with those of
other officers of the road, engaged both in the mechanical
department and in the operation and the maintenance of the
line. You could take it from all of them that there was
no real comparison between the camels and the ten-wheelers;
all odds were so obviously in favor of the latter.

. . . .

Ross Winans is not to be silenced by any broadside of that
sort. Once again he takes his own pen in hand and presently
there comes from the printer a third pamphlet—sixty-four
pages—whose title-page reads after this fashion:

ADDRESS

to the

PRESIDENT AND DIRECTORS

of the

BALTIMORE AND OHIO RAILROAD COMPANY

on the Subject of

LOCOMOTIVE ENGINES,

and the Errors in Relation Thereto, Contained in a Pamphlet Recently Published
by Authority of the Company

By ROSS WINANS

Baltimore

Printed by John D. Toy

1857

Mr. Winans reviews the statements of the document that
he is answering, contradicts many of them, makes further
comparisons of the performances of the ten-wheelers and of his

camels, and concludes with a proposal for the appointment of an impartial "scientific commission" to examine the facts and to report upon them. He makes the issue personal and says to the administration of the road:

> My heretofore prosperous business, in the prosecution of which so many hundreds of persons have been supported, has been so prostrated as to render it not sufficiently encouraging to pursue it further—unless I can counteract the ill effect of Mr. Tyson's abuse of your name and influence, and by a proceeding to which you are parties, establish the injustice to which I have been subjected, and vindicate the reputation of those machines, to whose peculiar properties, I have the authority of the very founder of your Board for saying, you owe the largest measure of your prosperity.
>
> And this result has been brought about at a time when I find myself with a large amount of capital invested in the means of carrying on my business, and a large investment in camel engines, finished and unfinished, without orders or a prospect of sale of them; or the means of turning the large capital invested in my business to account without great loss and sacrifice.

The Baltimore of those days—and for a good many days thereafter—loved a row. Here was fine material for one; nobly started on its way. The habit of writing to the newspapers already had been inculcated in the town, and this controversy made fine fuel for all the volunteer correspondents. . . . Many, many letters were written, much more bitterness was engendered. It made small difference that a considerable proportion of the letter writers knew little or nothing about a locomotive. That was a mere detail. The chief thing was that two fairly well-known citizens of the place, identified with its chief business institutions, had, by some means or other, become embroiled and were washing their linen out in the public eye. That was sufficient excuse.

Mr. Winans lost. One might almost add "of course."

He closed his locomotive works and declared his business utterly ruined.   The Baltimore and Ohio never built another camel engine, although it continued to use the ones it already had for many, many years thereafter.

.   .   .   .

When the Winans works were closed, three of the old type camels remained in them—also the *Centipede*, the curious locomotive in which Mr. Winans had actually tried to combine the leading-truck feature with those of the typical camel, not with overwhelming success.   These stayed in the shops for a number of years.   The Civil War came and, under the great pressure that it put upon the insufficient motive power of the road of that day, Mr. Tyson sought out Winans and tried to buy from him the three camels.   Winans was enthusiastic in his refusal.

"I would not sell them to *you* for a hundred thousand dollars apiece," he said, then turned on his heel and walked off.

In 1863, when Thatcher Perkins had succeeded Tyson as master of machinery of the Baltimore and Ohio, he purchased the old Winans engines, although even then their doughty builder forced the clumsy *Centipede* into the transaction.   This last engine was used for a time in light freight service.   It finally was found quite profitable to scrap her.

.   .   .   .

At this late day, it seems a pity that the differences between Winans and Tyson (in his own way, each an extremely able man) could not have been reconciled and that their great skill in steam-locomotive design could not have been combined, to the benefit of all concerned.   If this thing could only have been accomplished, it is possible that today Baltimore might be one of the greatest locomotive manufacturing centers of all Christendom.   An industry, employing many thousands of men, might have been permanently established; in a city remarkably well adapted for such an enterprise.

In the debacle which followed so extended a controversy, one in which so much of the public had aligned itself, Tyson, as well as Winans, went down.   In the latter part of 1859, that shrewd New Englander, Thatcher Perkins, succeeded Henry Tyson as master of machinery. It was a place in which Mr. Perkins was not on unfamiliar ground. Born down in Maine, in 1810, he had come to the Baltimore and Ohio as long before as 1847, when he had held the same post for four years; but on a Baltimore and Ohio then much smaller and with far inferior motive power. Perkins' ideas succeeded those of Tyson, yet did not supersede them. The camel was dead. The ten-wheeler had come to stay. And Thatcher Perkins was to do his own large part in its perfection.

The "whittling Yankees" everywhere were taking to the perfection of the railroad locomotive, like ducks to water. Down in New England, they were doing tremendous things with it. . . . Hinckley . . . and William Mason . . . and here, now, in Baltimore, was Thatcher Perkins.

There was in Taunton, Massachusetts, in those days, a name with which to conjure—that of William Mason. He became, beyond much question, the father of the modern American locomotive. Just as, in the later day, some genius was to come along and take the crude automobile and make it the magnificent streamline motor car of today, so William Mason labored, successfully, to take the clumsy locomotive of the 'forties and evolve from it a thing of grace and symmetry and power. He gave the steam locomotive the streamline treatment. He simplified its design, evolved the cylinder saddle and made the entire engine strong and compact and simple; with a certain dignified beauty of its own. The influence that Mason exerted upon locomotive design in the United States never has been eliminated; not even in this day, when the builders have been sorely tempted to hang upon the exterior all manner and variety of appliances and excrescences.

The Baltimore and Ohio bought several Mason locomotives, direct from the builder, there at Taunton. The road liked the type.[1] It adopted it; and then adapted it to its own peculiar

[1] The first two Mason engines to be built for Baltimore and Ohio, the 25 and the 26, were placed in service in November, 1856. They differed from the usual

mountainous conditions. With the tremendous demand for additional motive power caused by the Civil War—not only by the vast increases in traffic that it brought, but also by the confiscation and destruction of its engines by Confederate raiders—Thatcher Perkins hardly could keep pace. Mount Clare worked thunderously, night and day, seven days a week. Morning, noon and night, Perkins himself was there at all hours, going over the drawings—a silent, austere, thorough, hard-working man, he was—or stepping out into the shops to energize their forces into fresh endeavors. He was resourceful and he had every need for his resource. Once—in 1865—when he had ordered five engines from Lowell and the works there had complained that they had not the materials from which to build, Perkins had hurried five boilers and the castings for the frames and the wheels up there. Anything to save time. Anything to get more engines, and at once.

Resourceful . . . energetic . . . and yet, as a boy, he had lacked education. He wrote an abominable hand. Once, two of his assistants in the draughting room, which immediately joined his own, puzzled long and hopelessly over one of his memorandums. The word that confused them looked like "ling." Finally they went to their chief. He took a single look at his own writing.

"That is not hard," he commented. "That is *link*, l-i-n-g, link."

Mason practice in having the so-called wagon-top boilers (46 inches in diameter). One of these engines, the *25*, has been retained by the company and by it was shown at both the Chicago and St. Louis world's fairs. With its original balloon smokestack carefully restored, it was exhibited under its own power each day of the Baltimore and Ohio Centenary in the autumn of 1927. . . . Six more Mason passenger locomotives, numbered from *231* to *236* inclusively, were added to the Baltimore and Ohio flotilla in the summer of 1857. The characteristic features of their design comprised the straight boiler, horizontal cylinders, secured to the frame and to a round smoke box through a cylinder saddle; a widespread truck; the elimination of outside frame rails and other excrescences; and a neater and more symmetrical arrangement of the link-motion and the reverse gear. . . . At the outset, all of these Mason engines burned wood, but later they were equipped for the use of bituminous coal.

Mr. J. Snowden Bell, the historian of Baltimore and Ohio locomotives, worked as a draughtsman under Mr. Perkins at Mount Clare, from 1863 to 1865, and well remembers the practice of his chief to have builded for himself full-sized wooden patterns of each new form of casting with which he was experimenting. . . . One day the master of machinery came into the draughting room with a huge wooden box-like thing in his arms. It was a new form of square link that he had devised, to his own satisfaction at least. Yet, when it had been cast, it weighed 434 pounds. Although adopted for a time, it never came into extended use.

That was Thatcher Perkins, every time. If he erred, he erred on the side of overstrength, overweight. His engines were heavier, more bulldog in type, than those of William Mason, which always were to be remarked for their lightness and their grace. But they had great stability. They were fit for the sledge-hammer work of a mountain-climbing railroad.

Take those passenger ten-wheelers which he designed and turned out with great éclat at Mount Clare: Of these, the *117* was the first to come out of the shops and to go into active service—in the spring of 1863. With her brilliant red wheels, her bright band of the same color around the rim of her huge balloon stack, her boiler and her tender of deep maroon, her gay colorings and stripings here and there and everywhere, she was a locomotive to command attention, to be spoken of up and down the line in tones somewhat akin to those of reverence. Perkins saw to it that she was beautifully maintained. . . . The *117* was an engine of which any railroad might be proud.[1]

One of the distinguishing features of the *117* (and those sisters that immediately followed her, the *18*, the *19*, the *29* and the *147*) was her boiler—in the parlance of the locomotive builders—of wagon-top design. These engines were the first

---

[1] With a fine bit of sentiment, the Baltimore and Ohio has refused always to scrap her; in fact, of late, she has been completely restored and made ready for active service once again—after sixty-three years she also ran under her own power at the Baltimore and Ohio Centenary of 1927.

on the road to have combustion chambers. This firebox was unusually long and had a hopper in its bottom, which came to be known as "Horace Greeley's hat." Because of its tendency to leak, this was a source of much annoyance to the engine crews. Afterwards, it was removed, and an ordinary firebox, flue sheet and long tubes substituted. There were 138 tubes, 2¼ inches in their outside diameter, and 12 feet, 4¼ inches long. Their weight complete was approximately 45 tons. The valve gear was of the stationary-link type; and, in order to obtain a sufficiently long radius for the links, "the front ends of the die rods were coupled to arms on a supplemental shaft, journalled on the frame immediately behind the saddle, from which connecting rods extended back to the lower arms of the main rock shaft." At least this was the way that, at the time, it was described, technically. These engines had bar frames of present-day type and their cylindrical smoke boxes at the forward end of the boiler were set in saddles, or "bed plates," as they were then called.

These passenger ten-wheelers were followed by five passenger locomotives of a somewhat lighter type (4-4-0) and numbered consecutively from *237* to *241*. The first of them went into service in January, 1865; the last in December of the following year. There appears to be no accurate record existing of their weight and dimensions, but Mr. Snowden Bell, who made a number of drawings for them, recalls that their cylinders were 17 by 24 inches; the diameter of their driving wheels, 66 inches. Much more closely than their immediate predecessors, did they approach the popular Mason type. In fact, their chief differences from the Taunton engines were in their large cylinders and driving wheels; an increase of six inches in rigid wheel base; and the installation of the then new injectors instead of the time-honored cross-head pumps; those dear, delectable, damnable contrivances, which, in zero weather, used to cause an untold volume of profanity among the old-time enginemen.

· · · · · · ·

Thatcher Perkins used his remarkable ingenuity and his versatility on still another type of locomotive for the Baltimore and Ohio. This was an eight-wheeler (0-8-0) for freight service, which became known, variously, as a "Perkins eight-wheel connected engine" and as a "greenback." The first of these engines, which also were to do their part in establishing Thatcher Perkins' name on the imperishable roll of the real makers of the American locomotive, came rolling out from Mount Clare in February, 1865, as *No. 83.* (Afterwards she became the *No. 32.*) Another of the same class, the *242,* also came from Mount Clare. The others were built outside, although to Mr. Perkins' plans and specifications. The *263* and the *264* came from Reaney, Son and Archbold, of Chester, Pennsylvania (primarily shipbuilders and afterwards to be known as the John Roach plant), and twenty more—*243* to *262*—were from the Grant Locomotive Works, of Paterson, New Jersey. The clever experiment of sending partly finished materials, which the resourceful Perkins had tried out up at Lowell, was repeated in this contract. One complete boiler and practically all the castings and forgings for the Chester engines were furnished from Mount Clare, as well as all the tender wheels for the Paterson engines. A war emergency had justified the additional expense of this sort of method.

In wheel arrangement only, had Thatcher Perkins reverted to the Winans camel type, which these new freighters were built to supersede. The only features of the camels that he took over bodily were the wide fireboxes—of unquestioned value—and the 43-inch drivers. The rest were new.[1]

[1] Mr. J. Snowden Bell, in his *The Early Motive Power of the Baltimore and Ohio Railroad*, has described them as follows:

". . . Their boilers were . . . of the straight type . . . and their cylinders were originally bored out to 19½ inches, but were designed to be rebored to 20 inches. . . . Their frames, which were of the bar type, were very substantial, weighing about one ton apiece. . . . The link motion was of the Gooch type, and a 55-inch radius was obtained for the links by the same means as in the ten-wheel engines. The links were of cast iron, of box form, and weighed 434 pounds each. The draw-bar extended through the ashpan and its front end was coupled to a pin fitted in cross braces bolted to the bottom frame rails. This arrange-

These Perkins engines were the swan song of their builder, as far at least as the Baltimore and Ohio was concerned. Thatcher Perkins determined to return to his greatest love— the building of locomotives for the open market. In the interval between his two terms of employment as master of machinery of the Baltimore and Ohio, he had indulged this desire, as junior partner of the firm of Smith and Perkins, of Alexandria, Virginia. But Smith and Perkins had not prospered and, even before the coming of the Civil War, had been compelled to close down.

This time, Mr. Perkins made his plans more carefully and more fully. He became one of the founders of the Pittsburgh Locomotive Works, located at Allegheny, Pennsylvania—a concern which was not destined to die, but which finally became one of the foundation members of the American Locomotive Works. To it he devoted several years, finally going to take charge of the mechanical department of the Louisville and Nashville Railroad, with which he remained almost up to the time of his death.

.   .   .   .

John C. Davis, who came to the Baltimore and Ohio from the Northern Central in May, 1865, became at once its master of machinery. Capable engine builder that he was, his work at Mount Clare lay along the lines of construction, rather than of design; at least of radical changes in design. The foundations that had been so firmly laid down by Tyson and Perkins were to stay; thereafter, the chief work of the master of machinery of the Baltimore and Ohio was to be of production. The modern American steam locomotive, seemingly, had arrived.

Yet Mr. Davis' work at Mount Clare should not, because of this, be minimized. In the years after he came, the locomotive fleet of the Baltimore and Ohio was tremendously enlarged. Throughout the days of the war, despite the con-

---

ment, by which the boiler was entirely relieved from strains of draft and buffing, has, within a few years past, been brought out as a new and original design."

struction efforts of the company—generally against vast difficulties—this flotilla had barely held its own. It was being too rapidly decimated all the while. It will be recalled that, in the early summer of 1861, no less than forty-two of the road's locomotives and their tenders had been burned there at Martinsburg. Two more engines and their tenders that year were thrown into the Potomac and ruined. And remember, too, that fourteen others were deliberately taken over the highways to Strasburg and to Staunton by the Confederates, for use on their own railroads. Eventually—at the close of the war—the most of these came back; at least, twelve engines complete, one boiler, eleven tenders and two tanks. The fourteenth engine—the *34*—never was recovered.

With these losses to be overcome, as well as a number of antiquated and inefficient engines to be completely scrapped and replaced, the road's locomotive fleet stood at a virtual standstill during the actual years of the war—even though there was much activity at Mount Clare and elsewhere. In 1864, one finds Mr. Perkins reporting 221 engines in that fleet, the precise number that he had reported two years before. Of the 221 engines in service in 1864, but 75 were reported in good condition, 30 in running order, 31 in the shop, 75 as requiring repairs and 10 entirely out of use and ready to be scrapped. The four Ross Winans engines, purchased as a war emergency, were included in this last number.

From this level, the flotilla again began to grow. No longer was there war-time destruction to be overcome; in September, 1865, the Baltimore and Ohio had 243 engines. Twenty-one new machines had been builded in the previous twelve months, and there were the twelve engines returned from "our Southern friends," as Mr. Garrett was once wont genially to call them—before they began raiding his property.

Toward the end of 1866, there were 290 engines; 51 in the passenger and 239 in the freight service. The following twelve-month saw seven more added—of which five had been built at Mount Clare by Mr. Davis and two purchased from the United

BIGGEST IN ITS DAY WAS THIS ENGINE.

The *J. C. Davis, No. 600*, built at Mount Clare in 1875 and in the following year exhibited at the Philadelphia Centennial as the largest passenger locomotive ever built.

From a photograph.

THE FIRST CONSOLIDATION.

With a bright red band around its smokestack, the Consolidation built by A. J. Cromwell at Mount Clare in 1888, and recently named after him, blazed a pathway for heavier motive power.

From a photograph.

States government, which was disposing of its Military Railroad equipment.   Two more came in the next year; and then, in 1869, sixteen were built at Mount Clare, and the total rose to 315.   In 1870, there were 324; in '71, 345; and in '72, 383.   In the following year, Mount Clare made a magnificent spurt and built not less than 42 new locomotives; 48 were bought outside and the fleet total stood at 473.   In the following year, it rose to 549; thereafter, for quite a number of years, this total changed but little; ranging from 549 to 560 engines, or about twice the size of the Civil War equipment, but ten brief years before.

In all of this swift development, Mr. Davis played a most active part.   He had comparatively little time for invention or new design, but he did build a very capable eight-wheel passenger engine (2-6-0 type) for use on the mountain grades west of Keyser.   This, completed in the fall of 1875, was exhibited in the Philadelphia Centennial Exposition the following year, and created a furore.   It was one of the largest, if not the very largest, passenger locomotives built in the United States up to that time.   It was known as the *600*, and so great was its reputation that it too has never suffered destruction but has been carefully preserved by the road from that day to this.

The *600* was one of the noble company, ranging all the way from the Perkins, *No. 117* of war days to the *Lord Baltimore* and the *Philip E. Thomas* (*Nos. 5500* and *5501*) of today, built by the Baltimore and Ohio in its own shops at Mount Clare to handle increasingly heavy trains upon the Seventeen Mile Grade without the aid of a pusher.   In its day, the *600* was a real achievement.   It had a larger grate area than the Perkins engines (in all, 1259 square feet excess of heating surface) and about 8000 pounds more weight on its driving wheels.   It weighed, all told, about 153,000 pounds.   The *Lord Baltimore* type—almost an even hundred feet from end to end—weighs, with its tender, 653,000 pounds.   The *600* had driving-wheels 56 inches in diameter; those of the *Lord Baltimore* are 74 inches in diameter. . . .   There still was quite a bit of progress to be made—within the sharp clearance limitations long before set down for the American railroad. . . . But the *600* represented a distinct step in advance. Times and practices were changing. Few American railroads other than the Baltimore and Ohio were continuing to build their own locomotives; gradually, they were finding it far easier to go out into the open market and buy of builders who were specializing in their construction; and who, by reason of standardized designs and standardized machinery and practices, were making real economies in locomotive production—at least in considerable quantities.

Yet, the fact remains that, in 1925, the Baltimore and Ohio Railroad—then in possession of 2647 locomotives—found it profitable and interesting to build at Mount Clare the largest passenger locomotive ever constructed up to that time—the great *Lord Baltimore*, to which reference has just been made. Which was followed a few months later by its twin, the *Philip E. Thomas*, so named in honor of the first president of the company. The experiment and the engines both were found successful. And this policy, once inaugurated, may now be expected to be brought forward again—at least in the construction of locomotives of an advanced or unusual type.

CHAPTER VI

THE ZENITH OF THE GARRETT ADMINISTRATION

More of the Administration of John W. Garrett—Baltimore and
Ohio Reaches Pittsburgh—And Then Chicago—A Dream of
Southern Conquest—The Valley Railroad and its Early
Beginnings.

THE eighth decade of the last century made much railroad
history for the United States. Things moved rapidly. Not
only did the rail mileage of the entire land more than double
—increasing from 44,614 miles, in 1871, to 92,146 miles, in
1880—with transport facilities of every sort growing in a like
ratio, but whole libraries were to be written of new railroad
laws and new railroad practices. Since the days of the Civil
War, the roads had been at each other's throats. Competition
hardly is the word properly to express their struggle for
business; in many cases, for mere existence. It all was fighting, of the bitterest, truly of the most cutthroat, variety. . . .
Sometimes there would come lulls. Truces . . . agreements
would be made between the roads. Which they would keep
for a time, then as convenience suited them, break. Honor,
seemingly, was not among them. The thing to do was to
keep the business. No matter what the cost. Tariffs were
written, rewritten, and then—overnight, perhaps—destroyed
completely; as a competing road made its appearance with a
far lower sheet.

Through the first seven years of the decade, things went
steadily from bad to worse. The federal report on internal

commerce for 1879 states that, at one time, cattle were hauled from Chicago to Pittsburgh without charge and that, in certain instances, from Chicago to the seaboard for five dollars a car. The rate war spread throughout the entire country. A Boston wholesale grocer found that, having brought lemons all the way across the continent from Southern California, he could send them back to Los Angeles and still reap a profit from them. . . . Passenger rates were proportionately disastrous to the carriers. At one time, a man could go all the way from Chicago to New York for but twelve or thirteen dollars; in fact, there was a very short interval when one could make the round trip for almost that figure. Passenger fares sank to about one mill per mile. In 1876, the great Philadelphia Centennial came and went, and it was not merely the newspaper men and the politicians that could attend it for little or no cost whatsoever.

Out of all this, there had to be relief—or universal bankruptcy for all the roads. Agreements would have to be made; agreements that would stand firmly, that could be enforced. In 1877, came the first of the real railroad pools; the Southern Railway and Steamship Association; in whose formation Albert Fink (of the Louisville and Nashville, but a name imperishably connected with the annals of the Baltimore and Ohio) took the leading part. Later, Mr. Fink turned his talents toward the formation of the so-called Trunk Line Association, embracing the railroads of the United States north of the Potomac and the Ohio and east of St. Louis and Chicago. This association has continued from that day to this; a powerful agent in the settlement of many inevitable disputes to arise among the individual roads themselves, and today a recognized cog in the vast machine of American rail transport.

The effect of the pools and of the standardized tariffs which they brought into being, when enforced, was to check, in part at least, the ruinous competition between the roads. They began to establish definite charges and systems of differential rates—of which, more in good time. But they by no means solved in a moment the grievous problems of the American

railroad throughout the 'seventies. At that time, they did
not even seek to check another highly disastrous form of
competition—overbuilding, the laying down of new lines
ofttimes without rhyme or reason and inspired only by silly
jealousies or vain ambitions on the part of individual roads.

At all these performances, the general public—being the
general public—sat back and applauded. Dear old General
Public! Why worry, it argued, if the roads want to carry our
freight at a starvation price? That is their funeral. What
man unwilling to place himself, and his, on a comfortable train
from Chicago to New York at fourteen dollars apiece? What
community strong enough to refuse to hail with joy the coming
of a new railroad, even though the possibilities of that railroad's making a decent living for itself be so small as to escape
the normal eye?

That these things would have to be paid for at a later time
—and paid for rather dearly—seemingly mattered not. It is
not the habit for most men, or communities, to look very far
into the future.

.   .   .   .

Into this maelstrom, John W. Garrett steered his ship.
Dangerous seas were ahead. Of these, he was not unaware.

More than once, the dangers of the course that he had to
run perplexed him. Whilst the Baltimore and Ohio was
struggling to move men and munitions in the conduct of the
nation's terrible internal war, his competitors, remote from the
scene of the conflict and thus immune from actual destruction
of their property, had tried to set their iron heels hard into his
face. . . . But he was a good fighter, was Garrett. He hit
back. He was filled with resource. Seemingly, he was untiring.
And in this way he began his own march beyond the Ohio and
up toward the Northwest, buying rails and laying them toward
Sandusky . . . toward Toledo . . . toward Chicago.

At which the Pennsylvania Railroad, which had taken the
chief umbrage at what it deemed to be an invasion of its own

particular territory by the Baltimore and Ohio, determined to
carry the fight right back into Garrett's home country. . . .

For a long time, there had been increasing friction between
the Baltimore and Ohio and the other roads with which it
formed the single rail line between New York and Philadelphia,
Baltimore and Washington. Petty local quarrels between it
and the Philadelphia, Wilmington and Baltimore, as well as
the Northern Central (this last road already directly controlled
by the Pennsylvania[1]), developed into serious differences;
differences which apparently could not easily be reconciled.
At the end of the decade of the 'sixties, these had come to a
point where no longer they were secret; but were open and
increasing all the while in bitterness. With a curious disregard
of the public interest, which no railroad administration, to say
nothing of a regulatory commission, would today permit, the
quarreling roads entered into all manner of petty practices,
devised to humiliate and embarrass one another, but which
really acted only to embarrass and delay their patrons. . . .
Train connections at Baltimore were missed, repeatedly and
pointedly. The dreary connection track in Pratt Street, with
its slowly moving horses between Camden Station and President
Street, which gradually became the curse of all through
travelers, hung on bravely, until 1879, when the transfer
steamer *Canton*, running between the Baltimore and Ohio
terminals at Locust Point and the Philadelphia, Wilmington
and Baltimore at Canton, was placed in service. There was,
it will be remembered, similar connection between Camden
Station and the Bolton passenger terminal of the Northern

---

[1] It is interesting to note that there was a time when the Baltimore and Ohio—
in company with the Philadelphia and Reading—actually held control of the
Northern Central. This was at the time when John W. Garrett first became
president. The first election of Mr. Lincoln as President, however, had precipitated a short monetary panic in Baltimore; and it was in the stress of this moment
that Mr. Garrett threw over the control of the road leading north to Harrisburg
and Sunbury. It was then that the Pennsylvania bought its interest, which,
added to some shares obtained in London at a later time, gave it full control of
the Northern Central which later it merged into itself.

Central. With such links, it was easy enough to miss connections, when intentions were of the best. But when intentions were not of the best——

The quarreling increased.

There came a day when the sale of through tickets between the warring roads ceased. If a traveler wished to go from Harrisburg to Washington, he paid the through fare to the agent of the Northern Central at the Pennsylvania capital and received a special form of ticket, which was good actually only to Baltimore. Just before reaching Baltimore, the conductor handed him an envelope containing money for transfer across the city and his railroad fare on to Washington. . . . Similar crude methods prevailed in the other directions. And through passengers cursed loudly at the railroads, and their quarrelings.

In the midst of all of which, the Pennsylvania announced its determination to build its own line from Baltimore to Washington. It scouted about and it found a railroad company, chartered before the war to build a line from Baltimore through Southern Maryland to some point upon the Potomac River in the general neighborhood of St. Mary's City. This company was to be known as the Baltimore and Potomac. . . . The Civil War came and completely blasted the ambitions of the Bowies and the other influential planters of the neighborhood who had planned it; and it was not until several years after the conflict that they had the great good fortune to fall right into the hands of the necessities of the Pennsylvania group. Thereafter, there was to be no lack of money for the enterprise. The Baltimore and Potomac was to be built—and at once. The line into Southern Maryland (eventually terminating at Popes Creek) became a minor factor; the valuable charter of the B. and P. was to be used to gain a new railroad line between Baltimore and Washington—in direct competition with the hitherto highly profitable Washington Branch of the Baltimore and Ohio. The stage was set for real battle.

The necessary legal adjustments for the new purposes of the Baltimore and Potomac were made. Although not without severe opposition on the part of Mr. Garrett and his friends, both at Annapolis and at Washington. But the fundamental popular idea of a new competing railroad was too strong to be overcome. A route, parallel but generally to the south of the Baltimore and Ohio, was surveyed. In the late fall of 1869, construction began and was pressed so rapidly that, a twelve-month later, the roadbed was nearly ready for the rails. A single track was put down and on July 2, 1872, trains began regular service between the national capital and Lafayette Avenue, Baltimore. . . . East of that point there were severe construction difficulties. The entire scheme of the Pennsylvania embraced bringing three main routes from Baltimore (to Harrisburg, to Philadelphia and New York, and the new one to Washington) into a single union station to be built somewhere in upper Charles Street. This would completely avoid the necessity of any sort of transfer across Baltimore. It also necessitated, however, the construction of long and elaborate tunnels, bored through solid rock, both east and west of the new station. These tunnels took much time to construct, and it was not until June 29, 1873, that the Pennsylvania was enabled to run through trains on its own rails between Washington and Baltimore and thence on to Harrisburg. At about the same time, the Philadelphia, Wilmington and Baltimore, running in close connection with the new Baltimore and Potomac, also entered the Union Station.

Mr. Garrett's difficult position was complicated by the fact that the ancient Maryland law, which exacted a toll of one-fifth of every passenger fare taken on the Baltimore and Ohio between Baltimore and Washington, was still very much in effect. In its charter, the Baltimore and Potomac had evaded a similar provision. But its competitor was compelled to turn over to the state treasury of Maryland, twenty cents out of every dollar that it took in on the Washington Branch.

That such a situation was grossly unfair to the older company—a Maryland corporation—must have been apparent to the legislators at Annapolis. These last, seemingly, cared but little, however.   The troubles of a railroad are ofttimes as nothing to your country legislator.   Failing to gain any relief at the State House, the road went to the Superior Court in Baltimore City and obtained (December 10, 1870) a decision that the Maryland tax was repugnant to the provisions of the Constitution of the United States.   Armed with this ruling, it immediately cut its fares one-fifth and ceased to make payments to the state.   It now was in better position to do battle with the Baltimore and Potomac; being rapidly pushed toward completion.   Eventually, the decision of the city court was reversed and then, after threatening to cancel the road's charter, the state authorities set forth to collect the back taxes, as based on the road's statements of its passenger revenues on the Washington Branch. . . .   The thing was thrust back into the courts.   In May, 1875, the United States Supreme Court affirmed a judgment of the Maryland Court of Appeals that the per capita tax—then called the capitation tax —on the Washington Branch was entirely legal.

But so unjust a thing, no matter how legal, could not long continue to stand.   And so, three years later, the General Assembly of Maryland finally passed an act repealing the capitation tax and adjusting all matters of contention between the state and the Baltimore and Ohio in regard to the Washington Branch.   It was specifically ruled that the tax was not due on any passenger on and after the first day of July, 1873 —the day that the Pennsylvania finally began to carry through passengers on its own rails in and out of Washington.   The road having deducted the twenty per cent from every ticket sold on and after the tenth of December, 1870, was out of luck for just that period of time.   It had no way of redress.   And so, for more than two years and a half, through the reduction of fares and the tax it ultimately had to pay, it suffered a lessening of its passenger revenues on a busy stem of the line, to the extent of practically forty per cent.

It all had been a hard-fought battle and when Mr. Garrett drove out to his home at Montebello, in the suburbs of Baltimore, in the March day of 1878, it must have been with feelings of eminent satisfaction stirring within his mighty frame.

.   .   .   .   .   .

He, too, was for carrying the fight right into the enemy's country. Pittsburgh—then, as today, the very center and citadel of the Pennsylvania's best traffic pie—after terrific effort, both financial and constructive, was invaded. Through trains between Cumberland and Pittsburgh, over what was for a time continued as the Pittsburgh and Connellsville Railroad, but which was afterwards absorbed by the parent Baltimore and Ohio company, began in June, 1871.[1] When the first through train from Cumberland and Baltimore poked its nose down to the temporary station on the levee at Pittsburgh, Mr. Garrett again must have felt a sense of very real satisfaction. The enemy's country had indeed been invaded —successfully. No longer could the powerful Pennsylvania feel that it held an important industrial city absolutely in the hollow of its hand and free from any outside interference. While, for the Baltimore and Ohio, there finally had been gained an entrance into a city without a peer anywhere in this world for the production of freight tonnage.[2]

[1] Mr. J. B. Yohe, now (1927) vice-president of the Pittsburgh and Lake Erie Railroad, in 1870, was in the employ of the Pittsburgh and Connellsville, as a telegraph operator at West Newton, Pennsylvania. From there he was sent to the front; to a point east of Connellsville where contractors were finishing the final link of track that would bring Baltimore and Ohio into Pittsburgh. From Ohio Pyle, where young Yohe first was located, he gradually moved up to the head of the completed track, until finally he was located in a work train near Fort Hill. Here it was that the track finally was joined—at Ford Bridge. On April 10, 1871, W. O. Hughart, then president of the Pittsburgh and Connellsville, and Benjamin H. Latrobe, chief engineer of Baltimore and Ohio, together drove the golden spike that connected the line. Telegrapher Yohe sent the news out to the world. Then watched an excursion bound from Pittsburgh to Cumberland pass over the new piece of track. . . . It was a fairly crude piece of track. Brook Tunnel was not yet completed, and so trains had for a time to use a temporary piece of line between Ursina and Fort Hill—right over the top of the tunnel.

[2] Colonel Alexander S. Guffey, of Pittsburgh, writes to the author, saying:
"My grandfather, Alexander Guffey, granted a right of way to the Pittsburgh and Connellsville Railroad across his property at Guffey's landing at the mouth

Yet Garrett was not to be content with the mere conquest of Pittsburgh. Already he was moving on to a still greater goal—Chicago. In a previous chapter has been shown how the "Garden City of America" was already beginning to be recognized as the coming chief railroad center of the continent; how Mr. Garrett, thrusting a long finger of a line northward from Newark, Ohio, to a lake terminal at Sandusky, was at the same time placing himself in a strong strategic position for extension into that selfsame Garden City.

For a time, he had contemplated striking his Chicago line directly west from his new terminus at Pittsburgh.[1] But the extreme roughness of the terrain just west of that city, as well as the fact that both banks of the Ohio—the most logical low-grade pathway from Pittsburgh toward the West—already had been preëmpted by railroads, caused him to hesitate. It was far easier, far less expensive, to build a branch from the Newark–Sandusky line, straight across the comparatively level reaches of Ohio and Indiana, less than three hundred miles to the out-skirts of Chicago.

Accordingly, this was done. At a point 88 miles north of Newark, to be known for many years as Chicago Junction

---

of 'Possum Hollow' on the Youghiogheny River when that road was first constructed. The interesting thing about this right of way grant by my grandfather was the fact that part of the consideration, if not all of it, was the provision that Guffey's Station, as it was afterwards called, should be a 'water stop' for all trains. In the development of service on the Baltimore and Ohio, this provision became a 'thorn in the flesh'; as the family, that is my father's generation, for many years while the old house stood at Guffey's Station, insisted on the original meaning of the words, 'water stop.' As a result, at one time, even in my own early childhood, the very fastest trains on the Baltimore and Ohio had to stop at Guffey's Station. However, the passing of the old home at that point relieved the officials of the railroad company later of much annoyance when it came to the making of the annual schedules."

[1] In this connection, it is interesting to notice that the promoters of the Pittsburgh and Lake Erie Railroad first planned their line largely to bring Baltimore and Ohio freight and passengers out of Connellsville for Cleveland, Chicago and the West. This plan fell through and the road passed into the hands of the Vanderbilt group of railroads, for which it has for years served as the Pittsburgh entrance.

(in recent years, as Willard), construction of a new road began
—almost an air line—which would reach Baltimore Junction
(in the outskirts of Chicago) in just 263 miles. This line
completed, the Baltimore and Ohio would at last have its own
rails right into the strategic railroad traffic point of all America;
by the projected route, 811 miles from Baltimore, and—by the
new Metropolitan Branch—but 784 miles from Washington;
then and now, by far the most direct route between the capital
of the nation and its chief interior city.

Garrett did not hesitate. For the construction of the new
line, he organized what was known at the outset as the Baltimore, Pittsburgh and Chicago Railroad, and work on it was
carried through with great rapidity in the early years of the
'seventies. Despite a bitter winter in 1873–74, the work was
steadily pushed through. Track laying, which was begun at
Fostoria, July 22, 1873, was completed all the way from
Chicago Junction to Baltimore Junction by the fifteenth day
of November, 1874. Eight days later, the regular operation
of the line began. The ensuing winter was even more bitter
than the preceding one—for days at a time the weather ranged
all the way from zero to twenty-three degrees below. Many
construction details remained to be completed—sloping and
widening the cuts and embankments, adding second track and
passing sidings, putting up additional station facilities. But,
again, there was no cessation of endeavor.

Arrangements were made at Chicago to utilize the valuable
terminal facilities of the Illinois Central. Passenger trains
entered the old station of that company on the lake front at
the foot of Randolph Street, while, in the near vicinity, the
Baltimore and Ohio built for itself a commodious brick freight
house, 600 feet long. . . . These facilities continued in use
until two years before the World's Fair, when Baltimore and
Ohio became the prime mover and chief shareholder in the
handsome new Grand Central Station, at the corner of Harrison
Street and Fifth Avenue, which it has since continued to
occupy; in common with the Chicago Great Western, the Pere

THE ROUNDHOUSES AND SHOPS AT PIEDMONT, WEST VIRGINIA.

As they appeared some fifty years ago.

From a contemporary photograph.

THE FIRST BENWOOD BRIDGE.

Built to connect Benwood and Bellaire in the days of the Garrett administration and so forming a connecting link in the through Baltimore-Chicago line.

From a photograph.

Marquette and the Minneapolis, St. Paul and Sault Ste. Marie (the Soo Line properties of the Canadian Pacific). Gradually, it has organized its entire elaborate Chicago terminal properties in a single individual but closely allied company, operating under the legal title of the Baltimore and Ohio Chicago Terminal.

.   .   .   .

Had it been compelled to remain dependent on the tedious and complicated system of ferry transfer over the Ohio River at Wheeling, such a line into the heart of the mid-West would have been of but little value to the Baltimore and Ohio. The construction of modern high-level bridges over that stream, both at Wheeling and further down, at Parkersburg, was all a part of the long-visioned dream of Mr. Garrett for a greater Baltimore and Ohio. . . . Construction of the two bridges began, almost simultaneously, soon after the close of the war.

The first stone of the first pier of the Wheeling bridge (actually builded at Benwood, four miles below that city) was laid close to the Ohio shore, May 2, 1868. The bridge was completed and opened for the passage of trains on the twenty-first day of June, 1871. Its total length, with its approaches, is 8566 feet; the metal work of the bridge itself between abutments being 3916 feet, and the level of the track above low water, 40 feet.

To build the giant structure at so great a height—necessary because of the high smoke pipes of the old-fashioned river boats—necessitated tremendous approaches, to be constructed against terrific natural odds. On the West Virginia side of the river, for instance, there is but a narrow level shelf at the river's edge, before the precipitous hills start straight upwards. Very little opportunity this gave for placing an easy ascent to a high-level bridge. Yet the thing was done—of course. A slight bend of the river and a narrow ensuing "flat" at Benwood gave the opportunity. A loop track, by which trains between Wheeling and the West completely encircle themselves, was the solution. . . . On the Ohio side of the river, the small city of Bellaire nestles close to the bank. The railroad flies high above its roofs; upon the top of a tremendous masonry viaduct which consists of a series of forty-three arches, each 33 feet, 4 inches in width and of an average height of 45 feet. At the rear of the town, the ground is considerably elevated and so the railroad comes to its level, without perceptible grade.

.   .   .   .

The spans of Parkersburg bridge together make an even greater length (4397 feet) than those of the bridge at Benwood, although the total length of the entire structure (7140 feet) is considerably shorter. Its first stone was laid July 9, 1869, and it was open and ready for the passage of trains January 7, 1871. It, too, is a high-level bridge; and, to reach it, the trains pass through the center of one of the main streets of the upper part of Parkersburg, where the main passenger station is located.

The combined cost of these two important bridge structures over the Ohio—both of them originally builded of wrought iron, on the truss plan, and since replaced by fabricated-steel spans—came to $2,237,156.80. . . . They were expensive, but they have been worth every cent that they cost the Baltimore and Ohio, then and now. With their completion, the lines west of the Ohio became closely knit with those to the east of that river. The gauge of the western lines of the system, which formerly had been four feet, nine and a half inches, was changed to the four feet, eight and a half inches of the eastern part of it—today the standard gauge of practically every mile of railroad here in the United States.

.   .   .   .

So it was that John W. Garrett brought his great dream into a highly practical conception. He moved toward a more definite control of the Marietta and Cincinnati—by this time extending from the west end of Parkersburg bridge down to the busy old river port in the very southwest corner of Ohio.

More important, he also changed, at the same time, the chief eastern terminal of the M. and C. from Marietta to Parkersburg.

Since the gala days of its opening, the Marietta and Cincinnati had deteriorated. In the terrific competitive situation which had arisen—in its case complicated by the river boats—it had suffered badly. Gradually, it was compelled to lower its freight rates, until an average receipt of $3.17 a ton in 1868, by 1871, had dropped to $2.08. In 1876, this average went down to $1.13 a ton. And while the quantity of eastbound through freight in 1876 was twelve times as great as that of 1868, the revenue for it was only about four times as much.

Eventually, Mr. Garrett was to obtain this road and make it into what was to be known for many years thereafter as the Baltimore and Ohio Southwestern, but he was not to gain it absolutely until it had gone through the grueling bitterness of receivership. In the meantime, it merely remained a strong western connection.

Similarly, the Ohio and Mississippi, whose opening in 1857 from Cincinnati to East St. Louis has also been noted in these pages already, as a combined triumph of the gustatory and oratorical arts, was yet to come to Mr. Garrett's hands. After similar bitter bankruptcy. . . . Already he had induced the O. and M. to narrow its original gauge of six feet (patterned after that of the Erie and its western link, the Atlantic and Great Western) to four feet, nine and a half inches. . . . Until this had been done, the Ohio and Mississippi was practically limited in freight interchange at Cincinnati to a single road, the Atlantic and Great Western. After it had been accomplished, it had far greater freedom of interchange. Especially with the broad-gauge roads gradually coming to the standard gauge.

Mr. Garrett was to live to see Cincinnati as one of the chief operating centers of the Baltimore and Ohio system. In the later 'seventies, when his hold upon the Marietta and

Cincinnati was much more definite, he greatly improved its terminals in that city; quitting the rails of the Little Miami Railroad (already in the grasp of the Pennsylvania); laying down several miles of brand-new main line right within the community and giving his railroad an entrance that was to be in the years to come, of largest possible benefit to it.   In addition to which, he had shortened the line between Parkersburg and Cincinnati by about thirty miles.

. . . .

John W. Garrett saw south, quite as well as west.

In the days of the Civil War and under stress of the very great military necessities that it created, he succeeded in putting down a street connection between the New Jersey Avenue depot in Washington City and the railroad track that ran across Long Bridge and off over the Virginia lowlands to Alexandria, where it made connection with the railroad on to Orange Court House. . . .   The war finished, he sought to better that connection.   While because, even in the crude and disorderly Washington of that day, there was decided objection to the running of much freight through the city streets—the Washingtonians exhibited definite signs of prejudice against long burden trains passing along the very edge of the Capitol grounds; it was quite bad enough to have the passenger trains go that way—Garrett built a branch road off the Washington Branch, just outside the direct line, which followed the Anacostia Creek down to a long pier in the navigable Potomac, within easy sight and ferriage of old Alexandria.

Definitely he saw south.   He laid hands upon the historic Orange and Alexandria Railroad.   The Baltimore and Ohio began to buy stock in this last company as early as March, 1866, gradually increasing its holdings all the while until, in November, 1872, it was able to announce that it had acquired control of what had then become the Orange, Alexandria and Manassas Railroad.   This, Mr. Garrett proposed to extend through to Lynchburg on the James River, long since an

important industrial and railroad town. From Lynchburg
south to Danville was a matter of a mere sixty miles or so.
(Garrett chartered the company that actually built the railroad
between these two Virginia cities.) At Danville, he would
make direct connection with the Richmond and Danville,
which, with connecting roads, reached all the way across the
Carolinas and down into that growing new town, Atlanta,
destined to become one of the key cities in the railroad strategy
of America. . . . Thus was the Southern Railway of today
gradually being born; even though it was not until 1894 that it
was to attain really definite form and to take for itself the name,
Southern. New Orleans, as a Baltimore and Ohio terminal,
also was in the back of his mind. But John W. Garrett,
nearly thirty years before that, had dreamed the dream of a
second great railroad, which, fifty years later, was to come into the fulfilment of its destiny.

Circumstances finally compelled Mr. Garrett to relinquish
the Southern—or, as it was then known, the Washington City,
Virginia Midland and Great Southern Railroad (for a time,
later, simply as the Virginia Midland). But long after he and
his associates had disposed of the main stem of the Midland,
they hung tenaciously onto that part which, after crossing the
Blue Ridge Mountains, continued from Strasburg to Harrisonburg through the Valley of Virginia, and which was an essential
link of what came generally to be known as the Valley Railroad
—even though only its link between Harrisonburg and Lexington was legally entitled to that appellation.

.   .   .   .

The real beginnings of the Valley Railroad were very nearly
as old as those of the Baltimore and Ohio itself. Long before
the first locomotive of the parent road had reached Harpers
Ferry, the citizens of Winchester and its vicinage, catching the
prevalent railroad fever of the early 'thirties, had formed the
Winchester and Potomac, to link their town with the new road
from Baltimore at the Ferry, twenty-eight miles distant.

Unaided, they planned and financed and built their little road. From England, they imported its first locomotive, the *Tennessee* —one of the very earliest steam locomotives to be brought over to the United States.

In September, 1833, Mr. Moncure Robinson, the first engineer of the company, is found asking for bids for the grading and masonry of its right of way, while less than two years later the *Winchester Republican*, under a heading, "Our Rail-Road, its Progress and its Prospects," says:

> Stockholders and others interested in this important work (and who, in this community, does not feel an interest in it?) will be pleased to learn that the gradation is now finished from Harper's Ferry to Winchester—that a large proportion of the necessary timber is delivered or prepared for delivery— and that arrangements have been made for procuring the iron and locomotives without further delay. Contracts have been closed and are now in the progress of execution for laying the rails and finishing the entire work, out and out, by the 1st. of November next—early enough to affect the price of the growing crop. Nothing is wanted to secure this happy result but attention on the part of the stockholders to the calls of the board. The installments must be paid or the work must necessarily languish. The stockholders will find new encouragements to diligence and punctuality in this matter of paying up, in the fact that the stock of the Baltimore and Ohio Rail-road which, while that work was unfinished, had fallen to one-third of its nominal value, has now, that the road is done, suddenly risen to par—and in the fact that the stock of every finished rail-road in the United States is above par.

To this gentle hint on the part of the press, the stockholders of the Winchester and Potomac must have responded, for it is recorded that, on the ninth of February of the following year (1836), the *Tennessee* came up from Harpers Ferry to Charles Town on her first regular trip over the new railroad, and, after tarrying a few minutes at that county seat, resumed her progress with her train on toward Winchester.

The *Tennessee*, although very small, proved to be a faithful servant to the new railroad. Regularly she covered the line, making two trips daily down to the Ferry and back. Of her, Mr. John Bruce, the first president of the Winchester and Potomac, was to write in his annual report, in that same year of 1836:

> . . . No disappointment has occurred in the regularity of our transportation of burthen and scarcely any has marred the pleasure of travelers who have passed over our road. The depot bell has failed on but one or two occasions—when incessant rains had drenched our fuel—to sound its cheering note at the expected hour of arrival; not one trip, however, has been lost and the mail carried by the Company. . . . The engines have performed uncommonly well—one of them with an amount and continuity rarely known in the history of locomotives [at that time hardly covering a ten-year period!] The *Tennessee* frequently ran over the road . . . four times a day. Since first placed on the track, she has been, on one or two occasions, slightly repaired by the machinist and at an expense of not more than $20. She has continued to run with great satisfaction and with a speed and precision not easily to be excelled—having passed over, with burden and passenger cars combined, not much short of ten thousand miles in 130 days. Engines there are, no doubt, of much greater power, but we question whether any requiring less repair and less fuel—important elements in calculating the value of the engine—are to be found, equal in efficiency with the *Tennessee*.

The first president of the Winchester and Potomac writes his report with much charm. It is worth further exploration. He describes the events that preceded the actual opening of the railroad and then goes on to say:

> . . . On the 14th of that Month [March, 1836] regular transportation and travel commenced, with but one locomotive and less than thirty burthen cars. This very limited supply of motive power, the Board at that moment could command

owing to the unprecedented numbers of orders to be filled by the English workshops, before those of the Winchester and Potomac were received. An agent sent in part for this purpose and provided with funds deemed necessary had ordered three locomotives, and iron work for such a number of cars as was thought sufficient for the first years of transportation. The tried merits of the English engines, as the stockholders were informed at the annual meeting, induced the Board to adopt this course; indeed the machine-shops attached to but few of the Rail-roads of this country are adequate to supply the demands of their own. . . .

With so small an array of machinery it was soon found that the accumulated produce at Winchester and merchandise at Harper's Ferry could not be transported with reasonable expedition, though double duty was often exacted of both engines and cars, the *Tennessee* frequently running 128 miles a day. On the 31st of March, the day on which the road was opened with appropriate ceremony, the Baltimore and Ohio Railroad Company, whose interests are identified with ours and whose experience and zeal have uniformly enlightened and cheered us, promptly loaned the use of a powerful engine— and the timely assistance of the *Thos. Jefferson* will not soon be forgotten in the history of our operations.

Considerable disappointment to traders was the consequence of the limited force of the company. . . . A protracted and severe winter had crowded the early commercial business of the year into a very limited period of transaction—merchandise was thus suddenly accumulated at the various outlets of transportation—and the impatience of merchants was increased with the well-known anxiety of expectant dealers at home for their spring supply of goods. We stood in the breach; urged on the one hand by the Baltimore importer, overwhelmed with business, and eagerly importuned on the other, by the Valley merchant and distant Tennessean, greedy to realize the gain of their purchases. In addition to the unforeseen crowd of business, a difficulty, scarcely to be provided for, presented itself in the portage between the termination of our road and that of the Baltimore and Ohio Company. The room at the East end of the bridge at Harper's Ferry, always contracted,

THE GREAT VIADUCT AT BELLAIRE, OHIO.

Connecting with the bridge over the Ohio, it remains one of the engineering triumphs of the Garrett administration.

From a photograph.

ALONG THE VALLEY RAILROAD.

One of the interesting Bollman bridges, south of Winchester, Virginia, which remained in the service until 1920.

had been still more reduced by the two improvements which unite there; and the wagons which assembled at that point to receive or deliver the neighborhood trade greatly interrupted the drays and other conveyances employed to transport commodities between the Rail-road companies. Had some of these merchants, loudest in the expression of their disappointments, visited that confused spot on those days of scuffle for goods and the laborious turmoil of loading and unloading, they would have found cause to soothe their feelings; while it is readily allowed that the interruption to the trade was in part chargeable to the inexperience of the company's officers suddenly met by an overwhelming business under an arrangement which, we may be permitted to say, was susceptible of improvement by the Baltimore company. A supply of cars, with the engine loaned by the Baltimore Railroad, enabled the company soon to meet with promptitude the demand for transportation. Early in June, grateful for the favor, we returned this locomotive (the *Thomas Jefferson*) and soon after received a new and powerful one (the *Tennessee*) imported on private account from England in anticipation of the two others ordered last year and speedily expected on the road. A very considerable addition has been made to the number of our cars so that entire reliance may now be placed on our ability to transport with despatch, all produce and merchandise consigned to our cars. . . .

.   .   .   .

After that first flurry of excitement, the Winchester and Potomac settled down to the humdrum existence of a small branch line. It was brought into the Baltimore and Ohio system in 1848 and, thereafter, very little attention seems to have been given it. At the outbreak of the Civil War, its rails were so light and its roadbed so neglected that it was of little use to either army in its military operations.

It was after the war that the branch began to loom large in Mr. Garrett's eyes.[1] Before the 'sixties were done, he had

[1] The Valley Railroad Company was incorporated February 23, 1866. A few weeks later a meeting of the subscribers to the capital stock was held at

extended it from Winchester on to Strasburg Junction, twenty miles, where it made connection with the Strasburg and Harrisonburg Branch of the Virginia Midland, to which reference has recently been made here.

At Harrisonburg, the line was, for a time, halted. It might never have reached beyond that quiet old Virginia village, had it not been for the efforts of General Robert E. Lee, who, having laid down the sword, had taken unto himself the congenial occupation of being the president of the Washington College at Lexington—the present Washington and Lee University. Depressed as he was at the outcome of the war, he nevertheless held high hopes for the future of the Valley of Virginia. And when it was proposed that a railroad be builded to thread the length of that valley, General Lee finally agreed to assist the corporation. He eventually became president of the road. In his published life of his father, Captain R. E. Lee says:

In order to induce the city of Baltimore building their railroad from Staunton to Salem, the Valley Railroad Company got together a large delegation from the counties through which it was proposed the railroad should pass and sent it to that city to lay the plans before the Mayor and Council and request assistance. Among those selected from Rockbridge county was General Lee; Lexington at this time was one of the most inaccessible points in all Virginia. Fifty miles of canal or twenty-three of staging over a rough mountain road were the only routes in existence. The one, from Lynchburg,

---

Staunton, Virginia, and Colonel M. J. Harman was elected president of the company. He served until August 30, 1870, when General Robert E. Lee was elected as his successor. General Lee died October 12, 1870, and a few days later Robert Garrett was elected to succeed him.

The ambitious new railroad was aided at the outset by a stock subscription of $1,000,000 from the Baltimore and Ohio Railroad, and another $1,000,000 from the city of Baltimore. Later the Baltimore and Ohio increased its subscription to $1,020,000 instead of the figure originally guaranteed.

consumed twelve hours, the other, from Goshen (a station on the Chesapeake and Ohio Railroad), from seven to eleven. On one occasion a gentleman during his first visit to Lexington called on General Lee and, on bidding him good bye, asked him the best way to get back to Washington.

"It makes but little difference," replied the General, "for whichever route you select you will wish you had taken the other."

General Lee headed this delegation Baltimore bound. While in Baltimore he stopped at the home of Samuel Tagart, who he had met at the White Sulphur Springs. He was invited, with the delegation, to the floor of the Corn and Flour Exchange to meet the citizens of Baltimore. At first he demurred, but at the earnest personal request of John W. Garrett he went there and was given an ovation.

That was in 1869. General Lee gradually became enthused over the possibilities of the Valley Railroad. He came to Baltimore for money with which to build it. Many subscriptions were tendered him. And yet, when all was said and done, the project lingered fearfully. The good general died without seeing one rail laid in the construction of his pet plan.

Slowly, however, the project took form. The link between Winchester and Strasburg had been completed and formally opened, July 28, 1870. Four years later, the Harrisonburg Branch of the Virginia Midland was leased to the Baltimore and Ohio company. Simultaneously, the line of the Valley Railroad—as this portion was, for a time, known officially—was opened between Harrisonburg and Staunton, on the main line of the Virginia Central (the present Chesapeake and Ohio). A little later, it reached Lexington—162 miles from Harpers Ferry. There it halted, for all time.

Mr. Garrett's original plan had been to carry it much further. A right of way through Natural Bridge on to Salem (just outside Roanoke) had been partly purchased for the extension. . . . At Salem, the Baltimore and Ohio would have enjoyed direct connections, not only with the Norfolk and Western, but with the entire railroad system that stretches itself over the face of the state of Tennessee.

Financial difficulties, together with the shrewd machinations of his enemies, thwarted this purpose, however.   Gradually, Mr. Garrett was forced to part with many of his holdings in the Valley of Virginia.   The Norfolk and Western, in the early 'eighties, built—under the name of the Shenandoah Valley Railroad—its own line, from Roanoke straight through to Hagerstown, Maryland, where it connected with the Cumberland Valley, now a branch of the Pennsylvania. . . . Finally, the Baltimore and Ohio relinquished the lease of the Virginia Midland line, between Strasburg and Harrisonburg. But continued to retain the Valley Railroad.   It still holds and operates that picturesque line—a fragment of a dream of shrewd men that never has come into largest fulfilment.

CHAPTER VII

IN WHICH CLOUDS BEGIN TO SHOW

Baltimore and Ohio in the "Black 'Seventies"—Further Expansions of the System—Hotels—The Cumberland Rolling Mills—Rate Slashing—And the Railroad Pools—The Great Strike of 1877.

IN the memorable decade of the 'seventies, it was not alone the railroads that were hurt, and badly. The two notable panics of that decade—in '73 and in '77—cast a financial blight over the entire land. And from this, the railroads, in turn, once again suffered. To starvation rates there now was added a paucity of traffic; at any rates at all. Passenger business, as well as freight, fell to unheard-of depths. And when the railroads struggled, rather helplessly, to recoup themselves by reducing expenses—chiefly wages—they found their rank and file rising up in arms against them. The railroad strike came, right here in the United States, and came to be a very real and a very unpleasant thing.

Mr. Garrett and the company which he headed were again by no means immune. Baltimore and Ohio had come to so commanding a position among the carriers of the land that it could hardly hope to be exempt from the conditions which came to the most of them. When they fought for traffic, it fought, too. When they slashed rates—foolishly and mercilessly—it slashed its own rates. When traffic ceased to come to their gates, it also ceased to come to those of Baltimore and Ohio. . . . Expenditures multiplied; revenues lowered. That was the story of many of the black years of the 'seventies. It was the story of Baltimore and Ohio.   And of almost all its competitors.[1]

Mr. Garrett, at times, was inclined to assume for himself the rôle of optimist; at times, to the intense disgust of those who did not follow blindly his leadership, but openly questioned it. In the annual reports of the company he was prone to paint its past, present and future in rosy colors indeed.   In these documents he did not hesitate to criticise his competitors, openly and bitterly.   He was fond of chiding them upon their capitalization.   Thus (in his annual report, dated September 30, 1881):

> . . . The exceptional and highly conservative system of the Baltimore and Ohio Company, without precedent in America or Europe, by which more than forty-two millions of dollars of net earnings, unrepresented by stock or bonds, have been invested during a long series of years in great and valuable improvements and extensions . . . has enabled the Company to continue the payment of semi-annual dividends of five per cent each on its capital stock, which amounts to only $14,783,300, a sum so limited as to present a marked contrast to that of all competing Trunk Lines, the capital stock of the New York, Lake Erie and Western R.R. being $75,879,-300, that of the New York Central and Hudson River R.R.

[1] In the middle of that decade, one finds Mr. Garrett writing (in his annual report, issued in the fall of 1875):

"In view of the protracted and extraordinary inactivity of every branch of business, and the universal depression of the manufacturing industries of the country, these results will be regarded with satisfaction.   When further considered in combination with the united and prolonged attacks of the great trunk lines upon the business and interests of the Baltimore and Ohio Company, during which time, rates entirely unremunerative were established for the transportation of freight, particularly between the Seaboard and Western cities, the results are not only satisfactory, but gratifying.

"The Pennsylvania Railroad Company offered rates from Baltimore for long periods which were so low as to necessarily involve large losses.   This Company, therefore, declined much business that was tendered to it, in Baltimore and elsewhere, on which the actual cost of transportation would have materially exceeded the gross revenue that could have been earned therefrom."

$89,428,300, and that of the Pennsylvania R.R. $68,870,200.
. . . This very satisfactory condition, under the serious and
prolonged competition and unwise action of antagonistic interests, shows that the Company can, whilst continuing to
effect excellent results for all holding investments in its property, maintain a just policy, protective alike of the interests
of its terminal cities and the regions with which it is connected. . . .

Optimistic as these reports read, they were not always
received by the outer world with the same optimism. They
were freely criticised. It was said, and by shrewd business
men and bankers, that, in proportion to its bonded indebtedness, the share capital of the Baltimore and Ohio was entirely
too low . . . that too many of the road's bonds were in the
personal possession of Mr. Garrett and members of his family.
The president of the road had, close at hand, many enemies, as
well as loyal friends. A brilliant series of attacks upon his
reports, his policies and his railroad was found to have been
penned by Mr. B. F. Newcomer, one of the most respected and
able of Baltimore bankers. No matter which way he turned,
Mr. Garrett found enemies confronting him. He lost some of
his urbanity of earlier years. He ceased to be known as a
particularly genial man, but became a reserved one, while autocratic as of yore . . . absorbed intently in the development of
his railroad property.

He gave all his time—long days and long hours—to it.
Constantly he rode out upon the line. His car, forever and a
day, was being attached to one or the other of the two express
trains that daily made their leisurely way—thirty-six hours—
between Baltimore and Chicago. Sometimes he went out over
the new route, through Chicago Junction and Fostoria, and at
other times by way of Parkersburg and Cincinnati, then north
to Chicago over the Big Four (in those days, a second through
sleeping-car route between Baltimore and Washington and
Chicago). . . . But always the road was first and foremost
in his mind.

The men of the system respected him . . . feared him. In his discipline, he was unrelenting. Once, when out at the far western end of the line, he succeeded in poking his cane through a rotten spot in the wooden platform. Quick as a flash, he turned to his master of transportation, standing close beside him, and scolded him about the possibility of a personal injury and a damage claim coming from such a place. The operating man two hours before had been criticized for his repair expenditures, but said nothing. He knew his chief too well to get into unnecessary argument with him.

And yet, at another time, that same master of transportation was asked to make a list of things that he needed for the line, including new rails. He made his requisition. . . . "Too large," said John W. Garrett, and promptly cut it down, materially. The master of transportation smarted. His face flushed.

"Well, how much can you cut it down?" demanded Mr. Garrett.

"I cannot cut it down one ton," came the reply, "and be responsible for the safety of the road. If you will assume the responsibility, you can name your own figure on my requisition."

He got the iron that originally he had requested.

A one-man road, indeed, the Baltimore and Ohio of those days. With John W. Garrett directing each and every one of its details. Yet, once in a while, giving in, although ever and ever so slightly, to his subordinates. . . . There came to him, there in the 'seventies, a really great railroader as general freight agent. This was Milton H. Smith, whose life work afterwards was to be the upbuilding of the far-reaching Louisville and Nashville system. Mr. Smith had a way of getting down to business, with the least possible delay. On a certain Sunday, a severe flood had stopped all trains west of Cumberland. With a minimum of authority, he took the situation into his own hands and telegraphed an embargo on all freight, until the line could be cleared up and opened once again.

The next morning, Mr. Garrett called Mr. Smith to him. Plainly he was angry. He had only heard within the hour of the freight embargo and had discussed it with other officers of the company. He growled at his general freight agent.

"When do you propose to put such a step into effect?"

Smith took the bit between his teeth.

"It is all done, Mr. Garrett," he replied, coolly. . . . For sixty seconds, Garrett glared at him. . . . But said nothing. Then turned his attention to the papers on his desk.

.   .   .   .

Despite the steady expansion of the road—its president was now preparing to build or acquire connecting lines between Columbus and Cincinnati; between Wheeling and Washington (Pennsylvania) and Connellsville or Pittsburgh; a branch from Cumberland up to Johnstown (the seat of the great Cambria Iron Company and soon to be marked as the theater of the most disastrous flood in the entire history of the land)—Mr. Garrett still handled its infinite details. . . . He it was who brought about the building of more new hotels upon the line— houses, for that day, of great luxury and real beauty. So came into existence that well-known landmark at Cumberland, the Queen City Hotel (in the fall of 1872). In that same year, there was begun a summer hotel at Deer Park, close to the crest of the line's passage over the Alleghenies. . . . This last house was an immediate success. It became necessary, within a year or two after its opening, to enlarge it greatly, by means of wings thrust to the east and to the west of the main structure. But even these were not enough, and a second huge hotel was built by the railroad, at Oakland four miles away. . . . Those were the days when the American summer vacation was just beginning really to come into its own—as a recognized national institution. People were so glad to get away from the humdrum of their ordinary lives that they asked but little of hotels. And both Deer Park and Oakland gave much. Builded at high altitude, they gave assurance of cool nights, the entire summer through, as well as of splendid scenic environment. They offered horseback riding, tennis, croquet, and, to a limited extent, bathing. And quickly became a vogue.

Improved passenger service went as a necessity with the development of such purely pleasure traffic upon the Baltimore and Ohio. Mr. Garrett set about at Mount Clare to build his own sleeping cars and parlor cars, and in his own way. In so doing, he ran amuck of the patent rights, or the patent claims, of the Pullman and the Wagner companies; and the first of these began suing him. At any time he could have ended the suit, simply by placing the Pullman service upon the Baltimore and Ohio; but he very much preferred to run the company in every way as a self-contained and highly independent unit. . . .[1] He even went so far as to set up, at Mount Clare, an elaborate printing plant, to turn out all the many printed forms required in the railroad's business.

Similarly, a rolling-mill plant, closely adjoining the tracks and station at Cumberland, and capable of turning out rails and other heavy iron, became a part of the railroad property. This mill, after its opening in 1872, continued to operate for more than a dozen years. It manufactured the rails for the extension to Chicago and other points and for the double-tracking of the main line from Cumberland on to Grafton, as well as meeting the ordinary maintenance and replacement needs of the property. The day came, however, when the plant was obsolete. It was designed principally for rolling

[1] It was at about this time that Garrett determined to perfect the system of checking baggage upon his railroad. Prior to 1875, the handling of this form of traffic had been under the direction of the general passenger agent. In that year, the office of general baggage agent was created, and Thomas Meehan appointed to it.

At first, there had been no recognized system or control of baggage handling. Trunks, or other pieces of luggage, were marked with chalk to show their destinations. These marks were easily erased or blurred. Then it was that the brass checks first were used. They remained in use for many years—at no little expense. The next step was the use of a pasteboard card in a brass casing. Eventually, this was succeeded by the all-cardboard baggage check of today.

THE HOTEL AND STATION AT CUMBERLAND, MARYLAND.
Built by John W. Garrett in the 'seventies, it still remains one of the landmarks of that brisk city.
From a recent photograph.

THE ROLLING MILL AT CUMBERLAND.

Until the coming of the steel rail it formed a real factor in Baltimore and Ohio operation.

iron rails, weighing approximately sixty-four pounds to the yard.
. . . The company finally found it more profitable to buy the
newer types of heavier steel rail from established manufacturers, and so the Cumberland mill was leased for the manufacture of rails for the expanding coal mine system in the region.

.   .   .   .

Financially, the Baltimore and Ohio tried to make a brave
showing all through the hard years of the 'seventies.   Despite
its depleted income and its tremendous expenditures for the
extension of its lines, it endeavored to keep up its locomotive
fleet and other rolling stock.   It retired obsolete cars and
locomotives and replaced them with others of larger capacity.
By the end of the decade, Mount Clare was turning out consolidation engines, with eight 50-inch drivers, cylinders 20 by
24 inches, and a total weight, without tender, coal or water,
of 102,000 pounds.   These new engines were replacing the
historic camels of Winans and of Hayes on the mountain divisions.   Weighing some forty per cent more, they could easily
handle fifty-two loaded coal cars, as against but thirty on the
part of the earlier locomotives.   Similarly, tonnage was being
added to the box cars and the coal cars.   By the simple device
of raising the hoppers of these last with plate iron, their average
capacity was brought from 20,000 pounds up to 28,000.

All of these things cost, and cost rather dearly.   Against
them the road still struggled to make and pay its dividends.
Relief came only, when, in 1877, the Baltimore and Ohio
succeeded in getting together with its chief fellow railroads in
the northeastern corner of the land and in establishing the
Trunk Line Association, to which reference already has been
made.   Without delay, this new organization went to work.
It established offices in New York and Chicago and began a
quick survey of the entire situation.   It hardly could have
been worse.

In the freight rates between Chicago and St. Louis and
other mid-western centers of traffic, and Boston, New York,
Philadelphia and Baltimore it was at its very worst.   It had

become the supreme object of the northern trunk lines—the New York Central and the Erie and their affiliated roads—to diminish or annihilate the differentials, or the rights to make lower rates to Philadelphia and Baltimore, a lesser distance from the heart of the land, by a considerable number of miles, than either New York or Boston; while the object of the Baltimore and Ohio and the Pennsylvania was, plainly, to uphold these differentials. The issue was clearly drawn indeed. The aim of the new association was to prevent its becoming acute, to avert more open warfare over it. . . . The means finally used for the solution of the problem was the adoption of a percentage of rates, or basis of percentage, between all competitive points in the territory over which the new association sought to assume jurisdiction.

All of these rates were based upon the Chicago-New York one as being 100 per cent. Thus the rate from New York to Cleveland or to Akron, Ohio, took 71 per cent; that to Columbus, 77 per cent; to Indianapolis, 93 per cent; while that to Bloomington, Illinois, was 109 per cent; and that to Cairo, at the southern tip of that same state, became 120 per cent. These percentages, once established, were subject to slight revisions from time to time.

In turn, these rates were based fundamentally upon those set down by the competing water rates of that day (chiefly by way of the Great Lakes, the Erie Canal and the Hudson River). Once these fundamentals had been established, the relative percentages of the different intermediate points were worked out—very largely upon the comparative basis of the actual mileages involved.

The refinement of all this—which was the chief concern to Baltimore and Ohio, and which took nearly two years of discussion before it was set down definitely in the tariffs—came in the granting of differentials against Boston and in favor of Baltimore and Philadelphia. The rule governing this subject was finally adopted in 1879, and, applied to a percentage table similar to that just described, was:

Adjust rates to Boston, Philadelphia, Baltimore, etc., as follows, viz.:

To Boston, and to points taking Boston rates, *add* five cents per hundred to the rates to New York; to Philadelphia and points taking Philadelphia rates, *deduct* two cents a hundred from the rates to New York; and to Baltimore and points taking Baltimore rates, *deduct* three cents per hundred from the rates to New York.

Corresponding arrangements were made for establishing a basis of rates on westbound traffic which originated in all the North Atlantic seaboard cities and adjacent points.

. . . .

The effect of this arrangement upon all the railroads was greatly to clear the air. For the first time in all history, a shipper could sit quietly in his office and, with a printed and definite tariff sheet before him, could figure out for himself the freight rate to any point, almost as easily as he could find the postage on his letters and his small packages. He had but to apply the percentages himself, subject of course to the variants for the six different classifications into which the railroads grouped all merchandise, depending largely upon its actual value. . . . But, best of all, the new arrangement put a dampener on the very iniquitous forms of rate cutting, to which almost every railroad was party, and for which all of them were "paying through the nose"—over and over again.

Oddly enough, the bringing of the passenger rates into similar line and relationship involved much more of a problem than that of the freight. In all probability largely because, while freight goes where it is ordered to go, the railroad passenger is a highly individualistic and independent factor and generally will go where he himself wills to go. And curious small factors ofttimes enter into the exercise of that will. . . .[1]

[1] In speaking of the complicated passenger-rate situation, Mr. S. F. Pierson, commissioner of the passenger department of the Trunk Line Association, wrote (in the *Railway Review*) in 1884:

"Recognizing the difficulties of the problem, the joint executive committee,

Here was the railroad pool in the United States in *aqua pura*. It was a business form long used, and still used, in Europe. The French *syndicat* does not need explanation here. And yet, the railroad pool, which finally fell, almost of its own volition, came to sad abuse, and, perhaps, more than any one other thing, was responsible for the establishment, in 1887, of the Federal Interstate Commerce Commission; which, even at the outset, possessed sharp regulatory power over the carriers. It was preceded in fact by similar organisms in several of the individual states of the Union.

Sometimes, it was Mr. Garrett's will to enter whole-heartedly into these agreements, and, sometimes, he preferred to stand without or against them. You could not rob John W. Garrett of his high individualism. Yet, most times, the Baltimore and Ohio benefited, appreciably, by them.

---

representing most of the important through lines east of Chicago and St. Louis, and north of the Ohio River, entered upon an agreement for the division of certain passenger earnings and traffic, which took effect September 1, 1882, and continued in force until July 31, 1884. The general notion of this movement was to divide all the important competitive business in the territory described, between competing lines in fixed proportions. The object was to secure, by a general partnership in the total traffic to be transported, stable rates of fare between competitive points and better net results by reducing to a minimum the expense of soliciting, advertising, commissions and other fancy expenditures for securing business. It was agreed to submit differences which might arise, and which could not be settled by negotiation, to the adjustment of arbitration.

"This experiment was first applied to business passing between the cities of Chicago, St. Louis and Cincinnati on the west, and Boston and New York on the east. It did not include business passing through either of these points, or any business to or through a number of important gateways in intermediate territory; nor, until a late period, did it include any of the interior cities. Notwithstanding this, stability in the business actually divided under this arrangement was substantially secured. The balances drawn from month to month were promptly paid and, with one or two unimportant exceptions, it was found that roads earning their allotted proportion sought neither to reduce fares nor to pay commissions on business which was secured to them without such expense, and that the roads that were obliged to buy their business under any condition of affairs, secured it at less cost under the protection of the contract. The healthful effects of maintenance of rates between these points were felt in other branches of the business."

The black decade of the 'seventies was passing—good riddance to it. Better times were coming. In the annual report, dated September 30, 1881, Mr. Garrett calls attention to the fact that the tonnage of the through merchandise, both eastbound and westbound, in the twelve months immediately preceding, had risen to 2,014,000 tons; while in the year before it had been but 1,980,397 tons, and in the year before that, but 1,425,629 tons. In 1881, 959,568 barrels of flour had been moved—as compared with but 598,992 barrels in the preceding twelvemonth—and 20,329,858 bushels of grain had been brought down to the port of Baltimore. . . . The passenger earnings of the road were $1,714,922.16. (Compare this with $1,379,990.34 in 1880 and $1,171,033.30 in 1879.) . . . And the gross earnings for the entire system were $18,463,877.26. This represented an increase over the preceding year of $145,-937.16, and over 1879 of the sizable sum of $4,269,696.83.

Baltimore and Ohio seemingly was at a peak of prosperity once again. Even though the year immediately following was to show a decrease in its gross revenues of a little over $80,000. Mr. Garrett, in his annual report in the fall of 1881, again grew optimistic. He said, in part:

. . . The condition of the tracks and engines has been brought to a high standard. New and splendid sleeping coaches, parlor and thoroughfare cars have been added, replete with every modern improvement and convenience, so that the Company now furnishes an equipment unsurpassed for comfort and elegance. The hotels owned by the Company are in superior order, and continue to be managed with exclusive regard to the advantage and enjoyment of its guests. . . .

Unfortunately, Mr. Garrett's optimism was not entirely shared by all who digested his glowing reports. There still were uneasy suspicions about the true financial condition of Baltimore and Ohio. The small amount of capital stock, in comparison with that of its rival trunk lines, of which he still

was wont to boast, was, when you came to consider its high
bonded indebtedness, a very bad thing, the road's enemies still
argued. The Pennsylvania and the New York Central might
have high stock capitalization, but at least they could—if
necessity arose—suspend their dividends for a time. Bond
obligations were things of a different sort; particularly, if a
railroad wished to maintain its credit. And the presence of
many Baltimore and Ohio bonds in the hands of Mr. Garrett
and his family continued to arouse open criticism. To these
holdings had been added those of the late Johns Hopkins, who
had died in 1877, and who left the majority of his Baltimore and
Ohio securities to the foundation of the university which still
bears his name. Through his close association of long years
with the deceased millionaire and philanthropist, Mr. Garrett
exercised an option on these additional holdings of the bonds.

·   ·   ·   ·   ·   ·   ·

The road's fiftieth birthday came and went—practically
unnoticed—in the very blackest year of those black 'seventies.
For, to the general depression that prevailed over the property,
there was to be added labor unrest, riot and destruction.

Together, the eastern trunk lines had decided—at the very
beginning of 1877—that the terrible and widespread commercial
depression in the United States, which was affecting their
revenues most vitally, must be shared, in part at least, by their
workers. In other words, wages must come down. Which always
is a thing more easily said than done. The rank and file of a
railroad is not always responsive to the great financial problems
that are bearing upon the men at the top. Hence it was that
the first rumors of a possible wage cut upon the railroads
brought, throughout the entire land, mutterings and threats of
reprisal.

At that time, almost exactly fifty years ago, there still was
comparatively little organization among the workers of the
American railroad. The four big modern brotherhoods—of
the engineers, the firemen, the conductors and the trainmen—

were hardly beginning to function.   The oldest of these—the engineers—dates back only to 1863.   Most railroad unions, where they existed, were local in character, and there was little correlation or coöperative effort among them.

The Baltimore and Ohio's great competitors to the north —the New York Central and Hudson River, the Erie and the Pennsylvania—anticipated it in the actual wage cut to the men.   As early as May, 1877, the Pennsylvania reduced its pay envelopes ten per cent; at the moment, it seemed without serious objection or resentment on the part of its employés. The Erie followed, then the New York Central.   Still there was no open outbreak.   The Baltimore and Ohio was the last of the four to decide upon the drastic measure.   Mr. Garrett finally was forced into it.   On July 11 he issued a circular which stated that an immediate reduction had been made in the pay of all the officers and operatives of the road whose wage was in excess of one dollar a day.   Five days later, the new order took effect.   It affected every man engaged on the main line and branches east of the Ohio River, the so-called trans-Ohio divisions and all the roads under lease to the company and operated by it.   The notice further stated that the road had postponed its action until its great competitors had made similar retrenchments, in the hope that business would revive and the step could be rescinded.   But business had failed to revive and the wage cut could no longer be postponed.

On the fourteenth of that July, the firemen of the Baltimore and Ohio decided to go on strike.   They said that they could not and would not stand such sweeping deductions from their incomes.   Divisions or sections of the Trainmen's Union (not the present brotherhood, but a national organization then sponsored by Robert A. Ammon, of Pittsburgh) during the spring and early summer had come into being on the system. The locals had been organized by professionals from the Pennsylvania.

The Trainmen's Union made definite statements in return to the circular from President Garrett's office.   It averred that the men were constantly being badly treated by merchants and boarding-house keepers along the line, the latter compelling them to pay inordinately high rates for meals and lodgings and the like.   There was much truth in all of this.   The trainmen stated their troubles, in more detail.   These were not merely while they were out upon the line.   Even at home they suffered from "high rents, extravagant prices for groceries and other supplies and the demands of the money lenders." . . .   These stories had been coming into Baltimore headquarters for some time past.   And when the road had embarked upon its policy of retrenchment, it first had reduced its forces rather than lower wages. . . .   But times had gone from bad to worse. The line still could get a moderate amount of eastbound freight, but it could not get enough to the westward to pay it to load its cars.   It cut the size of the train crews.   Finally, on the longest of the freights, these consisted of but four men; conductor, brakeman, engineer and fireman.   There were, of course, no air brakes upon freight cars at that time, and brakemen frequently were required to set or release the brakes on twenty or more cars.

All these methods failed.   And so, as a final measure, had come the ten per cent wage cut.   And the decision among the trainmen to strike.

Martinsburg, West Virginia, was chosen by them as the scene of their first demonstration.   On the evening of the very day that the reduction was ordered to take effect—July 16, 1877—men began deserting their trains there.   Simultaneously, they also were quitting at the large terminals at Riverside, south of Baltimore; at Cumberland and at Wheeling.   The strikers had notified the crews of all freight trains that no person should move an engine after a certain hour, under penalty of death. . . .   This strike promised to be no laughing matter.

Martinsburg took the center of the stage.   At night that Monday, the sixteenth of July, the train hands who had left Baltimore that morning and those arriving from the west began to concentrate there. Groups of men, hanging about the roundhouses and the station, began to grow in size as evening came on. Every one appeared to be in an ill-humor. . . . There was much talk, and some of it was ugly talk. But, seemingly, no one in command. . . . Until, as at a signal, the locomotives that were accumulating there were detached from their trains and run into the nearby roundhouses. These were all freight locomotives. No one was assuming to stop or interfere with the passenger and the mail trains.

The size of the crowd . . . and the argument increased. The Mayor of the town, Captain A. P. Shutt, was summoned and made a little speech. He counseled against violence. He might as well have talked against the wind. The crowd hooted at him. He told the police to arrest the ringleaders. But they too were impotent. And the civil forces of Martinsburg were finally forced to beat a retreat.

Early in the evening, word of the impending trouble there had gone over the wire to Baltimore. At Mr. Garrett's suggestion, General Master of Transportation Sharp prepared to go by special train to Martinsburg, without delay.[1]

At a little after midnight, Colonel Sharp was on the field of battle. A quick survey of it convinced him that it was no time

---

[1] Colonel Thomas R. Sharp was both railroader and martinet. He was of the old-school type, the sort of man who was wont, upon occasion, to enforce his discipline, rather effectively, first with his tongue and then with his fists. . . . He it was, who, as Captain Sharp, had handled the details of the confiscation of Baltimore and Ohio locomotives and cars by the Confederate army at Martinsburg in 1861. Four years of military service had sharpened his naturally autocratic demeanor.

After the close of the war, when there was much depression in the South, Mr. Garrett had asked Colonel Sharp to come to Baltimore. As he came into his office, the president of the railroad looked at him and said:

"Well, Colonel, your name is pretty familiar to us. A man who can steal a section of railroad, not to mention several million dollars worth [sic] of rolling stock, move the p'under across country on a dirt road and place it on another fellow's line ought to be pretty well up in the transportation business. We have a vacancy in that department and I have sent for you to offer you the position of master of transportation, not doubting your ability to fill it after the demonstration you gave at Martinsburg."

for parleying. He telegraphed Governor Mathews of West Virginia, begging him to send troops without delay to quell the strikers and to keep the road's trains moving. Governor Mathews replied promptly. He ordered Colonel C. J. Faulkner, at Martinsburg, to call out the local militia, the Berkeley Light Infantry, to help preserve order.

Colonel Faulkner—son of the distinguished Confederate general who gave the Union forces so much trouble in western Tennessee during 1862 and 1863—was a bit uncertain as to his instructions. He wired to the Governor, at Wheeling, that the strikers were refusing to let trains pass either east or west through Martinsburg, and asked if his orders extended any further than merely to preserve the peace. The Governor replied, telling Colonel Faulkner to avoid the employment of force, if possible, but to see that the laws were executed, at the same time giving all necessary aid to the civil authorities. The Governor's message concluded:

"I rely upon you to act discreetly and firmly."

All this telegraphing had consumed time. Colonel Sharp, who had watched every detail of it, decided to wait until daylight before starting an offensive against the strikers and set five o'clock as the proper hour. An engineer and fireman were found who agreed to take one of the stock trains through, provided they were given physical protection. Colonel Faulkner, his militia company, the Mayor and his police and the sheriff of Berkeley County were all asked to be present at the proceedings. . . . Colonel Faulkner still hesitated a bit. Again he wired Governor Mathews:

Must I protect men who are willing to run trains and see that they are permitted to go east and west?

An hour later, the Governor replied:

I am informed the rioters constitute a combination so strong that the civil authorities are powerless to enforce the law. If this is so, prevent any interference with the men at work and also prevent the obstruction of the trains.

. . . .

Martinsburg stayed up all night. There had not been so much excitement in the town since a morning in June, 1861, when this same Sharp had been helping himself, rather generously, to the locomotives of the Baltimore and Ohio. . . . In the early morning, the colonel was joined by W. H. Harrison, the master mechanic of the company, who personally helped in firing up the locomotive of the stock train. But when the engineer climbed into the cab and made ready to start, a delegation of the strikers came to him and told him not to touch the throttle or he would be killed. . . . For a time he sat in the cab. Then, with his companion, he slipped off to breakfast.

In the meantime, both the militia and the police had failed to put in an appearance. The day was growing on. Sharp was being constantly goaded from Baltimore to take some definite action. One time when Mr. Garrett had sent him a particularly urging telegram, his eye flashed—he was known to be a man of quick temper—but he kept his head and wired Camden Station:

Tell President Garrett and Mr. King [vice-president of the road] that everything possible for me to do shall be done.

Then, with Mr. Harrison, he went out into the crowd which had gathered around the passenger station and which now numbered several thousand persons. Even from the back country the farmers were getting rumors of the impending trouble and were driving into town. . . . Harrison was personally very popular with the men along the road. He used all his best arguments upon them. But the time had passed when verbal arguments would suffice. The men listened to him, attentively, but refused to change their purpose. Finally, he had to return to Sharp and confess his defeat.

That railroader, in whose heart there still was the indomitable spirit of the grey-coated soldier, refused to acknowledge
downfall. His cold, stern face grew colder and sterner, and
all the while he stroked his beard. He decided, instantly, to fight the thing, to the finish. If no one would help
him, he would do it alone. . . . Sharp frequently had been
accused of being at the bottom of the harsh discipline
system of the road. True as that was, the fact was also true
that he had fought bitterly against the wage cut. But this
was not known among the rank and file of the men. They
had conceived a dislike for him as a bitter disciplinarian and
when he walked toward the engine of the cattle train, to which
the engine crew had returned, many epithets were sent his
way. . . . He ignored these and, climbing part way up into
the locomotive cab, ordered the crew to be on their way. But
again the strikers intimidated the enginemen. And this time
drove them from the cab; after which they disconnected the
locomotive from the train and ran it into the roundhouse.

Nine o'clock came and still no trains in movement at
Martinsburg. . . . But nine o'clock did bring the Berkeley
Light Infantry, gaily uniformed and marching behind fife and
drum, as if it were county muster day. The Mayor and his
useless police preceded them. . . . A hurrah and a shout of
welcome from the strikers and their friends was their greeting.
Behind the soldiery walked the fireman and the engineer who
had been evicted from their cab and who were returning to duty
once again. They too drew a cheer. The crowd was not dis-
cerning in its applause. The engine crew halted at the depot.
Let Allan Pinkerton, who made a careful study of the events of
that notable day, continue the story:

. . . The women threw their arms around their husbands'
necks and frantically embraced them, urging that they refrain from attempting the perilous task. The angry mob
. . . would be sure to do them injury. . . . Their lives
would be lost if they attempted the business again.

But, fairly tearing themselves from the grasp of their

families, the brave fellows started at a swift pace to the round-house, part of the time protected by the militia, and mounted the engine. . . . Soon it moved out and was attached to the cattle-train. Following the locomotive, on either side, were the soldiers, with guns loaded and bayonets fixed. Their progress was snail-like, from the pressure of the close-formed ranks of the strikers, which kept surging against the militia, but indulged in no violent acts, seeming to satisfy themselves with yelling, hooting, hissing and employing harsh and insulting language, principally heaped upon the two men in charge of the engine. When the train was, for the third experiment, made up for starting, the engineer and fireman, protected and guarded in their places by armed soldiers, with still other militiamen upon the tender, the buffers, the pilot and in the caboose, the excitement of trainmen and people rose to a white heat. . . .

Then it was that the civil authorities again grew cautious. How Sharp's fine old military soul must have revolted! Mayor Shutt asked Colonel Faulkner if it would not be best to argue again with the crowd. Colonel Faulkner agreed. Each was an adroit speech maker. But words had no more effect than before. And just before the Mayor ceased making his little speech, the crowd saw the cattle train finally in motion. Let Mr. Pinkerton resume:

. . . As the train . . . drew nigh the switch, a militia-man, named John Poisal, while sitting on the cowcatcher, particularly noticed the position of the switch-ball, which indicated that the train, unless some change was made, would be thrown off the track. Immediately jumping to the ground, musket in hand, he ran forward to the switch. William Vandegriff, one of the striking firemen, stood nigh and had just swung the bar so as to send the engine in the wrong direction. . . .

John Poisal reached the spot in time and put out his hand towards the rod when amid the general confusion, Vandegriff's voice rang out, loud and clear:

"Don't you touch that switch!"

"I'm not going to see the train run on a siding, if I can prevent it," answered Poisal, firmly grasping the iron. He had no time to move it. Vandegriff said no more, but drew a small pocket-pistol from his belt, and before Poisal had time to change the switch, fired two shots in quick succession, full upon the militiaman, one of the bullets ploughing a jagged furrow in the side of Poisal's head, just above the ear, and the other flying wide of the mark. . . . The switch remained unchanged and the locomotive stopped. . . . Poisal, upon receiving the striking fireman's shot, rapidly raised his gun and discharged it, aiming at Vandegriff. Another soldier sent a missile in the same direction and both were well aimed. One bullet struck the young man in the thigh and another penetrated his arm. He fell, mortally wounded. . . . There followed several explosions of small arms but no other persons were seriously injured.

The telegraph carried to the outer world the news of this mêlée at Martinsburg, of the killing of Vandegriff and of the subsequent retreat of the Berkeley Light Infantry from the scene, Colonel Faulkner giving as his explanation that his men simply would not fire upon their fellows. Sharp for the moment was powerless. . . . More telegrams went to Governor Mathews. Finally a company from Wheeling—the Mathews Light Guard—was sent to the scene. It was felt that soldiers from a considerable distance away would awe the strikers, who held absolute sway at Martinsburg and who still permitted only passenger and mail trains to move upon the railroad. . . . It was not until Wednesday morning (the eighteenth) that the fifty militiamen from Wheeling could be landed in Martinsburg. When they arrived, there were still more consultations . . . fresh delays. The militiamen finally were detrained, going into camp near the Court House. In the long run, they seemed no more anxious than their fellows from Martinsburg to quarrel with the strikers. . . . Then it was that Colonel Sharp determined upon his master stroke. He telegraphed President Rutherford B. Hayes, at Washington, of the growing seriousness of the situation and asked that federal troops be sent to relieve it. President Hayes, who had read the alarming telegraphic reports in the newspapers, acquiesced, and that very evening two hundred men of the Fourth United States Artillery, but armed as infantrymen, came into Martinsburg. After which there was no disorder there, nor further attempts to stop the trains. The rioters were compelled to retire. They could not fight the government of the United States.

.   .   .   .

While Martinsburg roared forth in flame, the blaze broke out in Baltimore. The latent fighting spirit of the old town found chance for expression in the trainmen's strike. As to the right or wrong of that strike, the mob spirit did not take the time to ask. It did not care. Very early in the morning of the seventeenth of July, while Martinsburg still remained in open warfare, a train had been wrecked near the gas house in South Baltimore. Some smoke arose and an alarm was sounded, bringing out the fire companies. Slight damage was done but the way was paved for more serious trouble, that very morning. This came first at Mount Clare, where a freight train was blocked, at ten o'clock. And both there and at Locust Point crowds began to gather. . . . In the meantime, the railroad company was using every measure to avoid provoking these crowds. Peremptory orders had gone out from Camden Station, withdrawing all freight trains, and so completely closing all merchandise transportation east of the Ohio River. Only trains or cars carrying passengers and mails were to be permitted to operate.

This move, however, gave the strikers great offense. They were anxious for an immediate issue. . . . For three long days, they nursed their grievances, in increasing wrath. The three long days the railroad officers bided their time. They succeeded in gaining back of them the definite and whole-hearted support of Governor John Lee Carroll, of Maryland, and Mayor Ferdinand H. Latrobe, of Baltimore. The Governor ordered the Fifth and Sixth Regiments of the Maryland Guard to assemble at their armories to be ready for instant service.

On the morning of the twentieth, the storm finally broke. The crowds in the streets and along the railroad tracks grew more excited and nervous. The troops at the armories were ordered to prepare to march to that old-time storm center—Camden Station. Before noon rumors came that the station was being surrounded by an ugly mob. But it was not until seven o'clock in the evening that the orders finally came for the militia to march to its protection.

The Sixth Maryland at that time was quartered in its then new armory, not far from the Shot Tower in Front Street. From their drill hall on an upper floor, the guardsmen looked upon the gathering and noisy mob in the streets below. But when their commander, Colonel Clarence Peters, gave the orders for two companies to march down into and through that mob, the men never flinched. It was a supreme test of their nerves. Epithets —the vilest of insults—flew through the air and so, finally, flew stones and bricks. Some of the guardsmen fell. Their fellows picked them up. The mob pressed in closer. Men of the regiment, who had been left behind in their drill hall, now drew their muskets and fired. A number of the mob were injured. And the body of a young man, named Byrne, who had been killed, was taken away by the police in a wagon to the Middle District Station.

Real street fighting by this time. Desultory, but furious. And increasing all the while. How the old Baltimore did like a real fight! . . . Yet, up through Baltimore Street, the two companies of the undaunted Sixth made steady progress. Men were falling all the way; but for every guardsman that went down, there were three or four of the mob seriously injured. The soldiers, for the main part, kept their heads. Yet they fought back gamely all the while. . . . A newsboy was shot near Frederick Street, and near Calvert two more men of the crowd were killed. But the Sixth pressed forward. And, at the end of a seemingly endless march, joined companies of the Fifth which had just arrived at Camden.

.   .   .   .

That station, itself, now became the seat of battle. To an extent, the militiamen were actually imprisoned within it— with a mob estimated at all the way from twenty to thirty thousand men gathered around its stout walls and barricades. . . . Throughout that evening the siege continued. Many stones and other missiles were thrown through the windows and repeated attempts were made to set the building on fire. . . . Once the crowd did succeed in pretty effectively destroy- ing the dispatcher's office at the Lee Street end of the station, and they burned a fine new passenger coach. But the stout old station stood, like some mighty citadel of feudal days. Even though it was to suffer by fire the loss of a goodly portion of one of its train sheds. Against it the rioters had shown themselves to be impotent. Gradually they wore themselves out. While the threats of Federal troops for Baltimore on the morrow turned them toward other thoughts. Even though it was a full fortnight before desultory rioting all the way along the line completely ceased and train service of every sort was restored upon the Baltimore and Ohio.

.   .   .   .

The strike spread to other roads. The Pennsylvania suffered from it worst of all. Pittsburgh became a more acute storm center than Baltimore. Regiment after regiment of Pennsylvania militia from Philadelphia and other cities at the eastern end of the state were poured in there—with seemingly no effect at all. There were street fights, much bloodshed, freight cars by the hundreds opened and pillaged. After which, wholesale destruction by fire began. Not only freight cars, but passenger coaches of every sort, were burned by the dozens. Then came the shops and roundhouses which were completely destroyed; and, finally, the great Union Station, which was one of the prides of the Pennsylvania system. . . . For six days—from July 21 to 26—Pittsburgh lived in a veritable reign of terror. The full fatalities of that week never will be known. . . . There was fighting also at Altoona, at Reading, at Philadelphia and at both Louisville and Chicago. But Pittsburgh was the great storm center of the entire strike.

In lesser degree, the New York Central and the Erie suffered from the depredations of the strikers and their sympathizers. . . . It was several weeks before the situation had completely quieted down and wage adjustments were completed. After which, there was to remain for a long time that particularly black spot in the history of American railroading.

.   .   .   .

As a contrast it is worth recording that in these same "black 'seventies" the Baltimore and Ohio first instituted its relief department, for the benefit of the injured and needy of its personnel, in accident, in sickness and in death. While this department did not actually come into effect until May 1, 1880, it did succeed in finding, in the first five months of its existence, 595 cases where it was able to be of a very real help. It began with a modest annual appropriation of $6000 a year on the part of the company, a sum which, since that day, has been increased, many times over. But the kindly impulse that prompted a great corporation to lay at least the foundation of a humanitarian and just move for the welfare of its men—a thing none too prevalent in the 'seventies—deserves to be recorded, if for no other reason than as a bright spot in the history of American railroading—a bright spot in a season when it was much needed.

CHAPTER VIII

THE GARRETT SUN BEGINS TO SET

Final Days of that Administration—A Dream of Empire Dissolves—Baltimore and Ohio Loses the Philadelphia, Wilmington and Baltimore—And Proceeds to Build Its Own Line Into Philadelphia—The Death of John W. Garrett.

LIGHTFOOTEDLY, entered the decade of the 'eighties. Business everywhere was better—appreciably better. Once again men smiled more freely. The "black 'seventies" were gone. Thank God for that! Real industrial prosperity again was in sight. Railroad wages had been restored. In Wall Street, shares were up. The railroads may have been overbuilded, but long-visioned men were daring to predict the country was going to grow up to them. There still were many; many sections of this land unrailroaded; and in great need of the iron horse and its trains.

So it was that the ferment to lay new miles of steel still rested upon the country. It was not always in the unrailroaded sections, however, where this fever broke out the most acutely.[1] A new, and sometimes not agreeable, phase of

[1] Baltimore and Ohio marked its return to high prosperity by a large appearance in the one hundred and fiftieth anniversary of the founding of the city of Baltimore, which was held in October, 1880. It was given the right of line in the huge procession that opened that celebration. In the Baltimore and Ohio division of the parade alone, marched five thousand men, thirty wagons, thirty barouches, ten bands of music and a group of interesting tableaux. The road's craftsmen formed the rank and file of the division. The tableaux, or floats, showed a reproduction of the First Stone, the sailing car, the treadmill car, the *Tom*

railroad construction was beginning to show itself. Lines were being put down, closely parallel to one another; not infrequently, without rhyme or reason of any sort whatsoever. Occasionally, there was a reason; and it, too, was not of the pleasantest kind. What became known colloquially as "strike roads"—in other words, lines whose chief real object was to compel their purchase, at a comfortable price, by the prosperous lines to which they were laid parallel—appeared upon the railroad map of the United States. Many others of the same sort were projected.

Today, under the rulings of the federal interstate commerce law, the building of such unnecessary railroads is all but impossible. Yet, in the 'eighties, it became a sort of unofficial, but easily recognized, commercial sport. But a sport that often left real tragedy in its wake.

Such a "strike road" was assumed to be the Nickel Plate (the New York, Chicago and St. Louis), which, for many miles west of Buffalo, had been laid down closely parallel to the Lake Shore and Michigan Southern—one of the richest of the Vanderbilt properties. The Nickel Plate made an even shorter route from Buffalo to Chicago. Yet, in the long run, it failed almost completely in its purpose, if such were really its purpose. Mr. William H. Vanderbilt and his associates finally bought the road, but they paid no fancy price for it. And in the long run did not merge it in the important group of railroads that they were upbuilding.

The so-called "West Shore" was a slightly different sort of story. Incorporated as the New York, West Shore and Buffalo, it was builded to parallel generally the rich New York Central and Hudson River—also known as a Vanderbilt property—all the way across the state of New York. This was to be an elaborate railroad indeed; from the beginning, double-tracked for

---

Thumb, the tobacco rollers and the like. On one of the floats, tickets were being printed and distributed as the procession passed through the streets of Baltimore. For a long time thereafter, these were cherished as souvenirs of a momentous occasion.

its entire length, from Weehawken, New Jersey (just across the Hudson from the city of New York), through to Buffalo, and, at the outset, provided with the finest equipment of every sort that money could buy. No such elaborate railroad had ever before from its inception, been planned and built.

Various motives were ascribed to the promoters of the West Shore. It was said that they were responding to a clamor from the New York State towns for better and competitive railroad service; that they were engaged in investing the surplus profits from another railroad enterprise; and, finally, that they were trying to hector the soul of Mr. William H. Vanderbilt, who in due time would be compelled to buy their property —at a fancy price—in order to protect his own. In due time, Mr. Vanderbilt did buy the West Shore; but that time did not come until after the line had passed into the hands of a receiver and the original promoters had lost most of their investment in it.

A third "parallel" of that day had an entirely different fate. This was the South Pennsylvania Railroad, which was projected to be builded from Harrisburg to Pittsburgh, and which would be not only thirty-seven miles shorter, but of somewhat easier gradients, than the main line of the Pennsylvania Railroad connecting those two cities. In this instance, Mr. Vanderbilt was reported to be on the other side of the fence; to be, with the Philadelphia and Reading Railway, recently emerged from a trying receivership, an important backer of the project. Certain was the Reading's advocacy of the South Pennsylvania. The new line was planned to start right out of its Harrisburg terminals, then to cross the wide Susquehanna on a long bridge, construction on which was begun at once, and some of whose stout stone piers still stand midstream, a pathetic reminder of the futility of some of man's best-laid plans. For the South Pennsylvania, unlike the West Shore, was never completed. It was hardly begun. It died early, and almost painlessly.

.   .   .   .

John W. Garrett, despite his innate conservatism, was destined to build an important, and a lasting, "parallel." True it was, he had both precedent and sound business reason for this radical step. The Pennsylvania Railroad—always his greatest competitor—had furnished both. In the construction of its own Baltimore–Washington line, it had given the precedent; and in the growing aggravation of the Philadelphia–Baltimore connection, it added the reason.

In these pages there has been shown, long since, the growing rift between the Baltimore and Ohio and the Pennsylvania. There has been explained how this came to its worst in the connection situation right at the city of Baltimore. It was quite bad enough at Washington. There the Pennsylvania, acting always through its Baltimore and Potomac company, had located its entrance tracks not only so as to give it an advantageous passenger terminal, but also to gain a practical monopoly of the approach to the historic Long Bridge and the railroad track that led over it to Alexandria and to all points to the south. This competitive advantage Mr. Garrett had endeavored to counteract, although rather ineffectively, by building a branch line from the Washington Branch of the Baltimore and Ohio at a junction just east of Hyattsville, Maryland, to Shepherds Point, on the Potomac, well below the city of Washington and within easy sight of Alexandria, just across the Potomac. He contracted for a car ferry, of ample size and to cost about $125,000, to ply between Shepherds Point and Alexandria and to carry on its broad deck both freight cars and passenger trains. For the latter, there were to be restaurant facilities on the ferry.

All this was while he still held the dream of the control of the Virginia Midland. When that dream faded, there faded, too, the picture of the elaborate crossing of the Potomac there below Washington. Although the branch line to Shepherds Point to this day remains in freight service.

.   .   .   .   .   .

At Baltimore, the situation was even more complicated. The key to the rail route to the north remained in control of the still independent and very rich Philadelphia, Wilmington and Baltimore.[1] This road, which had its own valuable terminals, both in Baltimore and in Philadelphia, had come into the control of a group of Boston bankers and investors. They knew full well that they held a key road. . . . Both the Baltimore and Ohio and the Pennsylvania entered into negotiations with them.

In the meantime, the Baltimore and Ohio, still clinging steadfastly to two trains a day of its own between Washington and Jersey City, cut entirely loose from the Pennsylvania tracks between Philadelphia and Jersey City. It announced that it had acquired running rights over the new combined line of the Reading and the Central Railroad of New Jersey systems between those cities—a through route just as short and far freer from congestion than the pioneer one. To this, the Pennsylvania replied with a fine row over the Junction Railroad at Philadelphia, over which all the Baltimore and Ohio trains must pass, on their way from the rails of the Philadelphia, Wilmington and Baltimore to those of the Reading, by which the Junction Railroad was jointly owned, as well as by the Pennsylvania. The Baltimore and Ohio stood its ground stoutly. Its Washington-Jersey City trains continued to run over the Junction Railroad and thence over the new route to the harbor of New York. . . . It announced the formation, under its control, of the Staten Island Rapid Transit Company, which would afford fine freight terminals, and—at a possible future time—passenger ones as well for the Baltimore and Ohio system in New York harbor. For the present, Mr. Garrett an-

---

[1] The Philadelphia, Wilmington and Baltimore Railroad, at the beginning of 1881, consisted not only of the main line from Philadelphia to Baltimore (95 miles) but the former Philadelphia and Baltimore Central Railroad, extending from Philadelphia to Octoraro Junction, Maryland (46 miles), and the one-time Delaware Railroad from Wilmington to Delmar, Delaware (84 miles), and enough side lines and branches to make a total of 330 route miles of line. It was, indeed, a well located and valuable property.

nounced that he would ferry his through passenger trains intact across the Hudson, to a terminal somewhere on the west side of Manhattan Island; a plan that in actuality never was consummated.

All this time, Garrett and his adversaries struggled for control of the Philadelphia, Wilmington and Baltimore. Mr. Garrett seemed at first to be winning. On February 22, 1881, the eastern newspapers announced that the Baltimore and Ohio, through a syndicate headed by Mr. Garrett's son, Robert, had purchased the control of the P. W. & B. from N. P. Thayer and his Boston associates, at $70 a share (the par value was $50). There was rejoicing in the fine new headquarters building of Baltimore and Ohio, at Baltimore and Calvert streets. But it was a short-lived rejoicing. The other group had far larger resources. A fortnight later, the press wires brought the saddening news that Pennsylvania finally had purchased the Philadelphia, Wilmington and Baltimore from Mr. Thayer and the Boston committee that he headed—at $80 a share.

.   .   .   .

To John W. Garrett this must have been a staggering blow —the loss of this highly important Baltimore-Philadelphia link. In turn, a link of his most important Washington–New York line. Yet he received the blow in fighting spirit, and decided to return another for it. He would "parallel." He would build for Baltimore and Ohio its own line from Baltimore to Philadelphia; if necessary, right on to the harbor-side of New York. Things were ripe for such a step. Smashing prosperity was upon the land; Baltimore and Ohio shares were quoted at $225 each; the road was doing an astounding volume of business, and all at a good profit. He would have— and did have—but little trouble in financing the ninety-five-mile extension up to Philadelphia. The intermediate towns would welcome a competing road. The Philadelphia, Wilmington and Baltimore had been not only independent, but frequently indifferent.

THE SUSQUEHANNA RIVER BRIDGE, 1886.

Designed for single-track operation, it performed faithful service for nearly twenty years, when it was replaced by the present modern double-track structure.

From a contemporary photograph.

JOHN W. GARRETT'S GREAT PRIDE

Was this fine central headquarters building at Baltimore and Calvert streets, Baltimore. It was destroyed in the great fire of February, 1904.

From a contemporary photograph.

So came, in June, 1881, the definite determination of the Baltimore and Ohio to build its own line on to Philadelphia; to its already established Reading-Central Railroad of New Jersey connection. At the end of that month, the Philadelphia, Wilmington and Baltimore was formally turned over to the Pennsylvania. For it, was paid $16,675,692; of which $14,949,-052 went to the committee of Boston stockholders.

The Pennsylvania did not at once order the through Baltimore and Ohio passenger trains entirely off the P. W. & B. For more than two years, the transfer steamer, *Canton*, continued to carry them across the inner harbor between Locust Point and a slip near the old President Street Station; but, in October, 1884, it served notice on the Baltimore and Ohio that it would no longer carry these trains, and would charge its local fares to all Baltimore and Ohio passengers east of Baltimore.

This edict raised ire in the new Calvert Street headquarters. The Baltimore and Ohio immediately withdrew from all passenger pools in its territory.   It would fight its own battles, and in its own way.   The fat was indeed in the fire.   C. K. Lord, the general passenger agent of the Baltimore road—he had come from the Atchison, Topeka and Santa Fé to be the first of that title on the Garrett property—remonstrated with the Pennsylvania.   He called attention to the fact that the two trains each day on the Philadelphia, Wilmington and Baltimore, which were furnished it by the Baltimore and Ohio, carried, on an average, more through passengers between Philadelphia and Baltimore than the four other trains operated by the line. Acting President Robert Garrett stated that, in the twelve months previous to September 1, 1883, the Baltimore and Ohio had given traffic to the P. W. & B. to the extent of more than $930,000.   He further charged that the Pennsylvania was actively engaged in buying the shares of the city of Baltimore, so that it might actually control the Baltimore and Ohio and shut out the Garrett family from its administration.

To all of this, the Pennsylvania said nothing.

In November of that same year (1884), a telegraphic dispatch, sent from Baltimore to certain New York newspapers, read:

> No confidence is placed in the rumor that the Pennsylvania Railroad and Vanderbilt are going to oust Robert Garrett from the presidency of the Baltimore and Ohio Company. The Garrett block of stock is from 40,000 to 50,000 shares. Trustees of the Johns Hopkins Hospital own 17,000 shares. Gregg Brothers hold 7,500 shares. The total stock of the road is 147,000 shares. The Baltimore and Ohio stock is scarcely on the market. Since September 9, there have been 649 shares sold, at from 178 to 167, the present figures. The firm of Robert Garrett and Sons is buying all it can get, at 167.

. . . .

While these rumors, the most of them unfounded, filled public attention, Baltimore and Ohio was redoubling its efforts to complete its Philadelphia line. Early in 1883, the first actual contract—for the approaches and masonry piers of the great wrought-iron bridge to be builded over the Brandywine at Wilmington, 104 feet high and 800 feet long—had been awarded. It was quickly followed by others. The road, as far as the state line which separates Maryland from Delaware, was actually being constructed by the parent company, under its Maryland charter; through Delaware and Pennsylvania, the Baltimore and Philadelphia Railroad Company had been incorporated to build the extension. The bonds of the latter company had been placed in the hands of trustees as security for a loan of £2,400,000, which had been negotiated at par in London by the Baltimore and Ohio, and 4½ per cent bonds issued against it.

The bridge over the Brandywine, although the first to be put under actual contract, and in itself a most sizable structure, was hardly to be compared in size with that which would have to be builded over the broad Susquehanna. Many soundings and surveys were made, before this giant structure finally was located, about a mile above Havre de Grace at the mouth of the river. Advantage was taken of a large island, lying in the middle of the stream, to vary the method of construction to be followed. At the best, it was all a huge undertaking.[1]

In every way, the new Baltimore–Philadelphia line was to be of the highest type. Grades were reasonably low, curvature easy. From the outset, it was planned to be double-tracked, for its entire length, and laid in heavy steel, in rock ballast. At the more important intermediate towns along the route— Newark, Wilmington and Chester—handsome passenger and freight stations were being erected. The site of the passenger terminal in Philadelphia was fixed at Twenty-Fourth and Chestnut streets, at the bank of the Schuylkill River, a location of very real value, the wisdom of whose selection has been shown increasingly in oncoming decades. The Phila-delphia station, for that day, was particularly elaborate. Advantage was taken of the high level of Chestnut Street, as it

---

[1] In President Garrett's report for 1884 there appears the following reference to this important new bridge:

" . . . It . . . will be one of the largest and most remarkable structures of its class in the world. It is the determination of the company that it shall be of the most substantial, safe and durable character. It will be 6346 feet in length, 94 feet above mean low tide, and will rest on eleven granite piers, having their found-ations on the bed-rock of the river. . . . The foundations for six of the piers have been difficult, reaching, as they do, a depth of 85 feet below low water, and necessitating the use of caissons, with air chambers, in which the men, engaged in removing the debris in order to reach bed-rock, have worked under a pressure of 37 pounds per square inch. Much of the masonry for the foundations and piers has been placed and all will be finished about the time the superstructure is ready. The pneumatic caisson work will be completed about the 1st of December. The superstructure will be of steel. It has been let to the Keystone Bridge Company for delivery and erection in the early spring and will consist of seven deck, and two through spans. The length of the deck spans will be: one of 520 feet, four of 480 feet each, one of 375 feet and one of 200 feet. The two through spans will be of 520 and 375 feet respectively. There will be 2288 feet of iron viaduct, averaging 67 feet in height, for the construction of which, in the shops of the company, arrangements have been made. All the other bridges on the line between Balti-more and Philadelphia will be of iron, and will be built at the shops of the company. . . . "

crossed the river at that point, to work out a very ingenious two-level head house, flanked by an iron train shed, 100 feet in width and 300 feet in length.

From the Chestnut Street Station to the main line tracks of the Reading was a gap of about a mile, and this it was planned to bridge by a new connecting railroad—the Schuylkill River East Side Railroad—which, entirely free from rival or competitive influence, included a sizable tunnel under a corner of Fairmount Park, and which thus afforded easy and picturesque connection between the Baltimore and Ohio's own line and its trackage route from Philadelphia on to Jersey City and New York. This connecting railroad was put into construction simultaneously with the new passenger station and its approach tracks from the south.

.   .   .   .

There was some delay in bringing the passenger trains into this new central passenger terminal. Petty influences, which steadily had opposed the building of the Baltimore and Ohio extension into the City of Brotherly Love, took their last stand in the Philadelphia City Hall.[1] The Baltimore road had ex-

---

[1] This opposition was shown in many ways. It lifted its head in the State Capitol at Harrisburg, when Baltimore and Ohio attempted to obtain certain necessary rights and easements, where the right of eminent domain was not sufficient, and at Trenton, where permission was sought to bridge the Arthur Kill. This last also brought a battle before the House and the Senate in Washington. . . . All these fights, the railroad won. . . . Philadelphia was much more difficult. For a time it looked as if the Councils of that city would absolutely bar the new railroad enterprise. Then it was that the brilliant general counsel of the Baltimore and Ohio, John K. Cowen, brought out his famed pamphlet, *Here and There, or a Tale of Two Cities*, which blazoned the question, "Is Philadelphia finished, and ready to be fenced in?". . . . The result of this pamphlet and Cowen's impassioned personal appeals was to reverse the position of the Councils. John Bardsley, who followed the matter most closely, afterwards remarked that after that, if the Baltimore and Ohio had wanted to run down Chestnut Street and put its station in Independence Hall, Philadelphia would not have objected. . . . Nevertheless, it was to be noted that canny Philadelphia had insisted, in all its ordinances, that all passenger trains of the new railroad should, for all time, make station stops within its boundaries.

treme difficulty in getting the necessary municipal authority to build its drawbridge over the Schuylkill River, two miles below the station. But it set itself hard to the task and eventually achieved it. The enabling legislation was passed and the bridge was begun.

All this took time—much time. Yet, by the twenty-fifth of May, 1886, enough of the new line had been completed to enable the transfer of the Baltimore–Wilmington sector of it from the construction to the operating forces of the company, and the inauguration of regular train service, both freight and passenger. On July 11 of that same year, a Baltimore–Philadelphia freight service was begun; and, on September 19, through passenger service between the two cities was established. All of this came into instant popular favor. And almost immediately it was necessary to add three suburban trains in and out of Philadelphia to accommodate this form of business, which showed a real desire to make use of the new road.

Rumor those days carried the Baltimore and Ohio much further than Philadelphia. It was being said that it would lay its own tracks into Jersey City—one Newark, New Jersey, newspaper related solemnly that the roadbed of an uncompleted railroad between that city and Bound Brook was to be rehabilitated for such a line; another journal just as solemnly averred that the Southern New Jersey (today the long south arm of the Central Railroad of New Jersey) was to be taken over bodily by the Baltimore and Ohio, which would establish train connection with it by a car ferry across the Delaware, some forty-five miles below Philadelphia.

But there was naught to any of these rumors. For the moment, Baltimore and Ohio had about spent its energy. The Baltimore–Philadelphia line, well builded as it was, every mile of its length, had cost a rather pretty penny. Moreover, it will be recalled that the road had entered into excellent trackage arrangements with the Philadelphia and Reading and the Central Railroad of New Jersey to carry its trains on to Jersey

City and New York. . . . After nearly fifteen years of struggle, it was again in strong strategic position against the machinations of its great rival.

.   .   .   .

To keep pace with its important new eastern additions, the rest of the system was being brought into good condition. The most important construction on the western end of the system was between Pittsburgh and Cincinnati, where, slowly but very surely, a new direct line was being evolved. "Friendly and coöperative interests," to quote a current report of the company, were building a road seventy-one miles long, across the level Ohio country from Columbus, through Washington Court House to Clinton Valley (now Midland City) on the Cincinnati, Washington and Baltimore, as the Marietta and Cincinnati, already under Garrett control, had been renamed. From Wheeling, east to Washington (Pennsylvania) the Hemp-field Railroad had long been held. It was proposed to connect this with Connellsville by a link, forty-five miles long, which presently was incorporated as the Ohio and Baltimore. This road, once completed, would have given a short line between Washington and a large coke country to the east. It never was completed. It began to be foreseen that the coke industry was dying, that in future years commercial coke was to be chiefly a by-product of the huge plants producing artificial gas in the larger cities of the country.

With the Ohio and Baltimore project definitely abandoned, it then was planned to build a direct road between Washington and Pittsburgh. A small local property—37½ miles long, the Pittsburgh Southern Narrow Gauge Railroad—was purchased, and for 17¼ miles—between Washington and Finleyville—was straightened and widened to the standard gauge. For the remaining distance—between Finleyville and Glenwood, just above Pittsburgh—an entirely new line was laid down; a good standard railroad it was, laid in sixty-pound steel. . . . It was opened for regular traffic in August, 1883.

Now it was that the Baltimore and Ohio had at last a fairly direct line from Pittsburgh toward the West. Eventually, it was to better this original route greatly. But the system finally was in a position not only to move coke and other products west out of the Pittsburgh district, but to bring into that great industrial territory iron ore from Sandusky and grain and other foodstuff from its Chicago gateway.

.   .   .   .

As Mr. Garrett steadily enlarged and linked his system together, he gave due attention to improving the service on its earlier lines. Trains were being added to the schedules, both freight and passenger. A fast service, with two passenger trains daily, was inaugurated between Chicago and Niagara Falls, by way of Auburn (Indiana) the Wabash and the Grand Trunk Railway. . . . Mount Clare was busy, not merely turning out more locomotives and more freight cars of every description, but many new passenger coaches; in addition to parlor cars and sleeping cars and dining cars of the finest and newest types. The running time of existing trains was being shortened. In May, 1880, the Baltimore and Ohio ran a trial trip of a new locomotive from Sandusky to Newark, Ohio, 116 miles, in two hours and forty-five minutes. The new engine was the smart *296* and C. L. McEwen was the engineer. . . .[1]

In 1884, another remarkable run was made upon the road. Upon the adjournment of the Republican National Convention, which had named James G. Blaine as its candidate for President out at Chicago, a group of Washington news-

---

[1] This remarkable record (for that day) was soon to be surpassed, in a rather dramatic fashion. William Galloway, one of the oldest and most revered of the road's employés, a man who in the 'thirties had operated one of the original "Dutch engines" on the Washington Branch, in 1882, in the seventy-fifth year of his age, ran a passenger locomotive a long stretch at a sustained speed of over a mile a minute. His son acted as his conductor on that trip. His grandson —Charles W. Galloway—is the present (1927) operating vice-president of the system. Working for the Baltimore and Ohio in the case of the Galloways is more than a mere family tradition.

paper men had announced their desire to get to the
capital just as soon as was humanly possible. They turned
toward the Baltimore and Ohio. The road said that it would
take them to Washington in record time.

That meant something—even in 1884. The American
railroad already had hung up some very good speed records.
The Pennsylvania, for instance, had one for having covered
the 444 miles between Jersey City and Pittsburgh in a flat ten
hours. That went down, when the Baltimore and Ohio ran
its newspaper special back from the Chicago convention
and, upon the western end of the system, made a distance
of nineteen more miles in fifty minutes less running time.
The newspaper special at one place actually went six miles
in less than four minutes.

The entire distance between Chicago and Washington—at
that time 812 miles—was run in twenty-two hours and thirty
minutes actual time (standard time had just come in upon the
American railroad and railroaders still spoke of "actual time"
as they figured these records). The special, consisting of a
combination car, a dining car, two Baltimore and Ohio sleeping
cars and the Mann boudoir car, *Adelina Patti*, left Chicago at
2.10 o'clock in the afternoon, passed through Garrett at 5:25 P.M.,
Chicago Junction at 8:35 P.M., Newark at 11:08 P.M., Bellaire at
1:31 A.M. and reached Washington at 1:40 P.M. (Chicago time)
—Baltimore, thirty-nine minutes later. It was handicapped in
various ways. For instance, on the eleven miles of Illinois
Central tracks that it used in coming out of the Chicago
passenger station, it was forbidden to exceed fifteen miles per
hour; while, on the stretch of the line across Indiana, there
were then seventeen railroad crossings at grade, at each of
which a full stop was required. . . . It had not been the
intention to make speed east of Grafton; in fact, it had been
planned to add the newspaper men's cars to one of the through
expresses bound east from Cincinnati. But, at the last minute,
plans were changed and the newspaper special was sent on, as
an advance section of the regular express, and so permitted

to lower the record still further.[1] . . . When word of the performance of the newspaper special was carried to Mr. Garrett at his home out in the suburbs of Baltimore, he expressed real gratification at it; and ordered the time reduced on the regular trains.

. . . .

What of Mr. John W. Garrett in these brisk days at the beginnings of the 'eighties?

Truth to tell, the veteran president of the Baltimore and Ohio was not coming to his downtown office so often nor so regularly as in days of yore. Nearly a quarter of a century of responsibility for the road was at last beginning to tell upon him. The great new headquarters building that he had caused to be erected at the corner of Baltimore and Calvert streets, with its vast high-ceilinged offices and its two "patent hydraulic passenger elevators," knew his firm tread but little. He showed an increasing preference for working at his home—in winter in his town house, which still stood in Mount Vernon Square; and in summer at his lovely suburban residence, Montebello, three or four miles out North Charles Street way. At his home, he received such officers of the road and other persons as he was pleased to summon to him. He had purchased two or three one-horse carriages and these performed a constant ferry service between headquarters and his house.

A few folk from the outer world came actually to see him, but these were very few indeed. Mr. Garrett, with three telegraphers close beside him and reading every dispatch that went over the railroad's line, as well as personally scrutinizing every voucher that paid out its money, cared less and less to r.ceive callers, unless they were old or close friends. . . . He preferred to be all the while with Mrs. Garrett. She it was who began to stand as a sort of buffer between him and the

[1] In connection with this, it is interesting to note that the *Capitol Limited* on the Baltimore and Ohio of today daily makes the run from Chicago to Washington, 786 miles, in just nineteen hours; yet she is not considered more than an ordinarily fast train.

outside world.   She received callers; in most cases, not merely received but dismissed them.   If they managed to convince her of the necessity of talking with her husband, she generally sat in the conversation, frequently joined in it.   Her comments and her questions were apt, and to the point.

When this remarkable woman died, in November, 1883, her husband refused to be comforted.   Her death seemed to take away most of the interest in life for him.   He sickened. He took no further interest in business.   His son became acting president of the road.   And when, on September 26, 1884, in the sixty-fifth year of his age, Mr. Garrett's death at his cottage at Deer Park was reported on the streets of Baltimore, the men who had stood close to him were not astounded.

Nevertheless, the death of John W. Garrett had a profound effect upon the community.   He was sincerely mourned; not merely within it, but far without.   Great leaders of finance, such as William H. Vanderbilt and Junius S. Morgan, at once bespoke his praise.   They had feared him ofttimes; but always they had appreciated him.   While, from the rank and file of the road, there came the most sincere tributes to his memory. Autocrat that he was—unmistakably—he unquestionably was loved for that very quality.   For that was the way and manner of that day and generation.

The directors of the Baltimore and Ohio—as well as many other institutions with which he had been more or less directly connected—passed resolutions upon his death.   For twenty-six years he had been president—the unquestioned guiding force—of their railroad.   He had found it a penniless, politics-stricken line, still lingering on the east bank of the Ohio, and he had made from it a mighty railroad system, reaching from the shores of the Delaware to those of the Mississippi and the Great Lakes.   The resolutions, after providing for the closing of the company's offices and shops on the day of his funeral, as well as the customary respect of their being draped in mourning for thirty days, stated that the directors deplored the loss of their president:

. . . because it has fallen upon a community, to develop which, he devoted all the powers of a great intelligence and a persistent energy which, deterred by no obstacle, had but one purpose, the giving to Baltimore the unequalled advantages of its geographical position and placing it as one of the greatest entrepôts of the world, between the mighty West of our country and the transatlantic nations. . . .

Many were the resolutions passed, the epitaphs written in token of the exit of this very real captain of American industry. But, perhaps the finest was one that he, himself, had written; in one of the few statements that he had ever made to the press. It took the form of a credo for the railroader; and it is as pithy and as much to the point as when Mr. Garrett first penned it. It reads:

Time is longer than speculation. Sell nothing, restrict dividends, for the sake of the long credit of the stock; all wait together, stockholders and officers. Invest the surplus in the system. Let politics alone. Neither conciliate it or antagonize it. Particularly do not corrupt it, or you will get its appetite on edge and it will gnaw you all your days. Responsibility in the working force; conservatism in the management; patience in the stock list. Do not fool with weakisms. Side branches must construct themselves. Push for large terminal points and the side places must build toward the stems, or extend in their general direction.

After forty years, this remains sound railroad doctrine.

.   .   .   .

Of the administration of Robert Garrett—son of John W. Garrett—little is to be said here. The younger Garrett was a man much loved and not a little respected. Into his hands was entrusted the important task of the completion of the new line into Philadelphia. He did not shrink from that trust.   But gave his every effort toward the finishing of the road.

Yet, at the time he ascended to the presidency of the Baltimore and Ohio, Robert Garrett was a sick man—physically and mentally. Before his two years in office were ended, he had broken, completely. In that brief time, there was opportunity for him to contribute comparatively little to the prestige of the property.

CHAPTER IX

HARD TIMES RIGHT AHEAD

Baltimore and Ohio Drifts Into Heavy Seas—The Short Administration of Samuel Spencer—Charles F. Mayer and His Struggles
to Right the Craft—Increasing Difficulties—And, Finally,
Receivership.

LIKE a rudderless bark, Baltimore and Ohio now floated out
upon the bosom of a sea, pregnant with dangers. Drifted,
without destination, or without course. Her captain had been
called from the bridge, suddenly and forever. For the moment, there seemingly was none to take his place. . . . Yet, so
great a ship, one so deeply freighted with human hopes and
responsibilities, could not be permitted so to drift, indefinitely.
Quick survey was made of her company. From it, one, a
mate, was brought to the tiller of the craft. He was a Virgin-
ian; a man who had had a training on the railroads of the Old
Dominion. His name was Samuel Spencer, and he had shown
a considerable aptitude for all the details of railroad operation.
In 1872, as a supervisor of trains and engines on the old Valley
Division, between Harpers Ferry and Strasburg, he first had
been discovered by Mr. Garrett. Later, he went for a time to
the Virginia Midland.

According to an anecdote told to this day, the intimate
acquaintanceship between John W. Garrett and Samuel
Spencer began on a trip to Europe which the two men took upon
the same steamer, in the early 'eighties. Their meeting at
the wharf in New York had been more or less accidental. . . .

Spencer had again become affiliated with the Baltimore and Ohio. He had gone to the New York pier in the hope of saying good-bye to his chief. But Mr. Garrett would not have it so.

"You must get on this steamer, Spencer, and go to Europe with me," Garrett had insisted. "You know Baltimore and Ohio and I have to have more money for the property. You are the very man to talk to those bankers over there."

Spencer went.

He must have argued well, for the railroad got the money, and he received for himself the post of its vice-president. In this, he improved his opportunities. He became, more than ever, familiar with its resources and its possibilities. While in negotiations with other railroads, ofttimes involving highly delicate matters of tariff and other adjustment, he showed himself adroit, resourceful, sound.

The administration of Samuel Spencer as president of the Baltimore and Ohio was short—barely a twelvemonth—but it was most creditable. The road was in capable hands, no doubting that. Yet the reaction of the Garrett days was strong. There were factions—factions within factions. Much discussion, and bitter, as to matters of policy. Some of these factions were personal, others were political. Maryland is a state rather fond of politics—sometimes fond of it as a sort of difficult and serious game. It will be recalled that upon the board of directors of Baltimore and Ohio there sat, at all times, four members appointed by the state of Maryland and seven members by the city of Baltimore,[1] in addition to the twelve elected by the other shareholders of the company.

.   .   .   .

When Samuel Spencer first came to the presidency of Baltimore and Ohio, there had accrued a floating indebtedness

---

[1] These political members held office, not by virtue of business training nor an especial value in the operation of a railroad, but automatically, because of the extension of aid to the Baltimore and Ohio by both city and state in times well past. The political directors often were a source of much irritation to the actual directing heads of the road.

ROBERT GARRETT.
President of the Baltimore and Ohio, 1884–1887.
From a painting.

SAMUEL SPENCER.
President of the Baltimore and Ohio, 1887–1888.

From a photograph.

of roundly $8,769,000, a staggering sum for those days; especially so when viewed in comparison with the capital of this particular company. Mr. Spencer, with the aid of a committee of the board, sought means by which this burden might be lightened and the old-time credit of the company reëstablished. He insisted upon a rewriting of the book values of the property. He felt that they were being set at far too high a figure. Ancient locomotives, long since become practically obsolete, were being figured at their original costs—at least thirty per cent too high, it was said. . . . In those days, railroad accounting was a weird and uncertain thing. Those great modern gods of accurate finance, obsolescence and depreciation, had hardly begun to show their heads within it.

Yet, even in that day, Spencer realized the great economic truths for which they stand. Backed by the powerful banking house of Drexel, Morgan and Company, he continued to insist upon writing down the book values of the physical properties of the road. He did much more. It will be recalled that, under the Garrett administration, Baltimore and Ohio had established its own express, telegraph and sleeping-car services. Spencer disposed of these features now coming to be rather extravagantly expensive, to the United States Express Company, the Western Union Telegraph Company and the Pullman Palace Car Company. Through the funds released by these sales, he was able to make reductions in the floating indebtedness of the company; although not without opposition from those who continued to consider the absolute ownership of these affiliated railroad services as highly desirable adjuncts of the operation of the system.

Spencer steadily continued to insist upon a reappraisement of the equipment and the steady writing down to conservative values the company's investments in bonds, stocks and accounts. In all, these modifications were to result in a reduction of about $22,000,000 in profit and loss—still leaving that account, however, with a credit balance of something over

$23,000,000.[1] That Mr. Spencer was conservative in the matter of revaluation of equipment is indicated by the further charge of over $600,000 by the succeeding administration; "upon the completion of the revaluation."

.   .   .   .   .   .

Samuel Spencer spoke always with great simplicity—and great honesty. For his sincerity and his honesty at Baltimore, he paid—with his high position. His attempts to straighten out the now somewhat befuddled finances of Baltimore and Ohio aroused bitter opposition; within the official ranks of the company, as well as without. He became, in certain high quarters, decidedly *persona non grata*. Finally, on December 19, 1888, he tendered his resignation as president. It was promptly accepted. He had occupied the highest executive post of Baltimore and Ohio just one year and nine days. . . . Later, Mr. Spencer became the first president of the Southern Railway. He, then and there, was given the opportunity that had been denied Mr. Garrett—of building up a great railroad in a reconstructed South. . . . The Southern Railway truly is Samuel Spencer's monument. Upon it, he died, in a train collision, whilst riding in his office car. After which, that railroad, with real sentiment in its soul, erected, in front of its large Terminal Station at Atlanta, a statue of him—a memorial to his genius and his foresight.

.   .   .   .   .   .

Mr. Spencer was succeeded as president of the Baltimore and Ohio by Charles F. Mayer, a merchant and lifelong resident of Baltimore. Mr. Mayer had been brought up in the

[1] That the reduction in the value of bonds and stocks owned by the company was a radical one indeed, is indicated by the attitude of Mr. Spencer in his report for the year ended September 30, 1888, that "the reductions in the values of the stocks and bonds owned by the company need not be regarded as permanent, as future developments may, and probably will, render some of them interest-bearing securities." . . . Subsequent experience showed this prediction to be a true one.

countinghouse of his uncle. He developed a keen and accurate business insight and later traveled extensively in both North and South America, visiting the latter in the capacity of super-cargo in clipper ships running out of Baltimore. As such, he was charged, not only with disposing of outbound cargo, but with the acquisition of a return load. Eventually succeeding to his uncle's business, Mr. Mayer became a merchant, and a successful one. He rose to be president of the Despard Coal Company (developed when the West Virginia gas coals first came into the market and largely owned by Baltimoreans) and later was elected to a similar post by the Consolidation Coal Company, then controlled by the Baltimore and Ohio and the Garrett interests, and at that time one of the world's largest producers and shippers of bituminous coal. It was the signal ability that Mayer demonstrated in expanding this coal busi-ness, as well as in firmly establishing the credit of Consolidation, that marked him as a logical successor to Samuel Spencer.

. . . .

At this fairly recent date, it is quite impossible to place a fair estimate upon the administration of Charles F. Mayer. Certain it is that, within its seven brief years, Baltimore and Ohio sank to depths that few men had deemed even possible. Financially, the road walked in the valley of despair. There came a time—early in the decade of the 'nineties, when great financial depression was upon the land everywhere—when it seemed no longer able to carry even the moderate traffic thrust upon it. The entire property sank into disrepair. Yet, there is every evidence that this pathetic situation was not because of a lack of effort, but rather in spite of a most earnest and energetic and prolonged attempt to sustain the property, and to place it on a proper competitive basis.

Commencing vigorously, the Mayer administration had arranged for the refinancing of the floating indebtedness (previously carried by the Morgan interests, which had withdrawn their support of the property after the retirement of Samuel Spencer), as well as for the purchase of additional equipment and the making of many improvements in line and roadway. So vigorously did this Mayer plan work at the outset, that, after its first two years, a special report from the president to the board showed such real expansion of facilities and business as to encourage the hope that the credit of the company would be securely reëstablished. A hope that, unfortunately, was not to be realized.

First of all, Baltimore and Ohio needed a genuine expansion of its working facilities. In the final days of Garrett control, it had fallen somewhat behind its active competitors.[1] The property needed large extensions and improvements, even within the somewhat limited areas which it had chosen for its more immediate development. Mr. Spencer, in his one annual report—dated September 30, 1888—had called attention to some of the most pressing of these: additional docks and piers at Philadelphia; the enlargement and rearrangement of the Locust Point Terminal at Baltimore; a new passenger station at Washington, together with a probable relocation of tracks there; the completion of the double-tracking of the Metropolitan Branch and the abolition of the difficult double curve at Harpers Ferry. All this, and much more, needed to be done. Pittsburgh stood in need of a proper passenger station, and the road that connected it with Wheeling had grades and curves that needed immediate correction, if not elimination; while, in the city of Wheeling itself, the track arrangement was so very bad as to demand instant attention. . . . In Pittsburgh, only, was anything definite being done with this program. Here the new passenger station actually was being erected; a fine sub-

[1] Coal long since had become the great tonnage factor of the road; it ranked high, too, in its average proportion of the annual receipts. But the steady industrial progress of the United States was causing the opening of still other bituminous fields in West Virginia—these last located chiefly upon the lines of the Chesapeake and Ohio and Norfolk and Western railroads. Baltimore and Ohio soon was to be compelled to look to its laurels in the battle for this traffic.

stantial brick building upon the Monongahela levee at Smith-field Street, with a train shed, 80 by 412 feet. Washington did not get its new station—not at least in the Mayer adminis-tration of the Baltimore and Ohio,—although the old one was rebuilt and extended. A two-storied brick addition was made to the New Jersey Avenue depot, and, for more than a decade, this had to suffice until, under the directing guidance of Presi-dent Theodore Roosevelt, the present magnificent Union Station was built, and the older passenger stations of the city entirely demolished. But this was not to come until about 1907.

A far more serious situation was that at Baltimore. In its chief city, the Baltimore and Ohio was a railroad with its main line all but completely severed. In other words, the new road that Mr. Garrett had builded into Philadelphia, in his dis-appointment and chagrin at the loss of the Philadelphia, Wilmington and Baltimore, had no direct track connection with the older part of the system. Across the busy fairway of the inner harbor, there plied ferries which carried the trains, both passenger and freight, between the new Philadelphia line and the old line from Camden Station to Washington and the West. This arrangement was, to a degree, clumsy and time-taking. Yet, there seemed to be no easy way of bridging the gap. Baltimore long since had become a closely builded city of metropolitan pretensions, and to thrust a new main-line rail-road across it, obviously, was no sinecure. When it last had been attempted, nearly twenty years before, by the powerful Pennsylvania, the thing had been accomplished only by the construction of elaborate and expensive tunnels.

Still the need was acute. And eventually it had to be, and was, met—by the construction of more elaborate and ex-pensive tunnels underneath the closely builded portions of the city. Of all of which, more in good time.

.   .   .   .

Not long after his election to the presidency of the Balti-more and Ohio, Mr. Mayer had conducted some of the members of his board on an extensive trip into the mid-West; the greater portion of which was made upon the road's own tracks. His account of this trip, as set down in the annual report of 1891, gives an accurate account of the physical position of Baltimore and Ohio at the beginning of the final decade of the last century.

At Cumberland, the inspecting group saw the new consolidated shops, which were to replace the inadequate and somewhat ineffective ones at Keyser, at Piedmont, at Connellsville, and also right at Cumberland itself. It rode on toward Connellsville and Pittsburgh. Of what was seen on that part of the journey, Mr. Mayer wrote:

> The directors who accompanied us were astonished at the numerous industrial enterprises along the line of this division and the prosperity there was evidenced on all sides. . . . The Baltimore and Ohio Railroad Company contemplated some years ago constructing a line from Connellsville to Wheeling, via Washington, Pennsylvania; the line from Washington, Pennsylvania, to occupy the location of the present Wheeling, Pittsburgh and Baltimore Railroad. The undertaking was abandoned, after a heavy expenditure for grading, bridging, etc., between Connellsville and Washington. The present administration had put in operation about nine miles of the line west from Connellsville, to develop some very large coke industries recently opened.

At Pittsburgh, the party inspected the new passenger and freight stations, as well as the extended terminals there. They also traveled over the Pittsburgh Junction Railroad, connecting the Baltimore and Ohio with the Pittsburgh and Western, which ran north and west from the former city of Allegheny, on the north banks of the Allegheny and Ohio rivers, and which was being acquired by Baltimore and Ohio as a needed link in a direct through route from Pittsburgh to Chicago and the West. The pathway via Washington (Pennsylvania) and Wheeling already had proved woefully roundabout and inadequate.

The party rode out from Allegheny over the Pittsburgh and Western, leaving the main line of that road at Warren, Ohio, to go to Fairport, upon Lake Erie. Let Mr. Mayer resume:

> At Fairport, an independent company, the Fairport Warehouse and Elevator Company, in which the Baltimore and Ohio Railroad Company owns an interest, has erected two large warehouses, 650 feet by 100 feet, and an elevator with a capacity of two millions of bushels. The receipts of merchandise and grain at this port have been governed in the past season by the ability of the Baltimore and Ohio to carry east the freight that has offered.

Just here was the problem, steadily extending all the while in its magnitude, that had confronted, not merely Mr. Mayer, but many other presidents who had preceded him in the administration of the road. Yet, most of these predecessors, handicapped as they had been, unquestionably, by lack of proper funds, had not felt the extreme financial restrictions that were gradually being tightened upon him. . . . Let him go ahead, once again:

> You are aware that until the purchase of a control in the Valley Railway Company of Ohio, and in the Pittsburgh and Western Railway Company, the Baltimore and Ohio had no terminal on the lake, excepting Sandusky, the use of which for lake shipments was confined chiefly to coal. It was of no avail for lake business eastbound. . . .

Under the Mayer administration, the Baltimore road was entering Cleveland; in 1890, this attractive lakeside community was already giving promise of becoming the huge industrial city that it is today. A terminal property, with about 3000 feet of river front for the docking of ships, had been purchased by Baltimore and Ohio, and plans were being prepared for the construction of the necessary freight and passenger stations, and the like. . . . The Valley Railroad ran south from Cleveland, to Akron (in those days giving no indications of its coming manufacturing importance, even though it already was a pretty and brisk small city). At Akron was the western terminal of the Pittsburgh and Western. To make this newly acquired line part of the Baltimore and Ohio's new and efficient short route from the seaboard and Pittsburgh to Chicago, it would be necessary to build an entirely new stretch of railroad, seventy-five miles in length, to Chicago Junction (now Willard, Ohio). This, Mr. Mayer was already preparing to do. . . . Return for a final paragraph or two of his report to his board. After describing in further detail the excursions of the special party of inspection, he concludes:

As I stated to the Board in November, we readily can do thirty millions of business annually. [In the preceding twelve-month, the gross of the road had been $24,000,000.] We need not seek it; it is seeking us. We are refusing business now because we have not the facilities to handle it properly. The difficulty is this: Locust Point is now the measure of what we are able to do. It is up to its fullest capacity as at present laid out. Locust Point will be relieved by the completion of the terminals in Brunswick and Benwood, both of which will be done practically in June. We then require an additional number of sidings on the Main Stem and Philadelphia Division, orders for which have already been given, for completion by the first of July. We require, in addition to that, some forty locomotives, the orders for which will shortly be placed, and, say, 1500 additional cars, which are being ordered.

I think that it is safe to say that, by the first of July, the company will be in condition to do business at the rate of thirty millions a year. We will feel the good effects of these enlarged capabilities only to a limited extent this year, but, with the prosperous condition of the country, there is no reason why we should not reap the benefits of our increased facilities next year.

I think, with such a statement as this, you will agree with me that you have ample cause to congratulate yourselves upon the condition of the company.

CHARLES F. MAYER.
President of the Baltimore and Ohio, 1888–1896.

From a photograph.

THE PITTSBURGH PASSENGER STATION.

It stands on the levee of the Monongahela in the very heart of the city.

A roseate picture it was, indeed, that Mr. Mayer had thus painted for his board. There were other details to it; one of the most important of which was the completion of a valuable new route from Pittsburgh down into the rapidly developing West Virginia country. The purchase of the erstwhile Pittsburgh and West Virginia Railroad, extending from Clarksburg, on the old Parkersburg Branch, to Richwood, had been cleverly supplemented by the construction of new connecting lines, between Clarksburg and Fairmont (on the original main line), and between Fairmont and Connellsville; this last link passing through Morgantown and Uniontown. This cross-country line, running, in a general way, at right angles to the Main Stem of the system, bade fair to become, of itself, an important traffic route. It also opened new coal fields to the road. . . . In more recent years, it has more than justified the foresight of Mr. Mayer and his associates in establishing it.

A roseate picture, indeed. . . . And when one comes to consider the difficulties—the vast and all but overwhelming difficulties—under which it had been painted, there can be naught but admiration for the man who had conceived it.

From the very beginning of his administration, Mr. Mayer had known not for a day—hardly for an hour—what it was not to be handicapped and harassed. No sooner had he succeeded Mr. Spencer, before Mr. Morgan, smarting under the defeat of his lieutenant upon the Baltimore and Ohio, called a loan of $5,000,000 which he had made the road shortly before. Moreover, the property finally was divorcing itself from the weakening hand of state and city partial control (this control ofttimes interference), which had, in the past, so many times pressed down upon it. Yet, to rid itself of this political hand, the railroad required still more money. It became necessary to float stock, to pay both Maryland and Baltimore for their stock holdings. This was done; chiefly overseas. But so completely that, finally, there remained only a preferred stock holding by the state in the Washington Branch—which, in time, was also to be wiped out. Because of this holding, the state still continued to appoint two members of the board of directors of the railroad; the other ten were elected by the stockholders. This was a considerable change from the first year of the Mayer administration, when there had still been eleven political appointees to the board (seven from the city and four from the state) as against but twelve elected directors.

These things were—decidedly—steps forward. So was the issue of another $3,000,000 of securities to provide necessary new rolling stock for the road, as well as to complete the double-tracking of the Baltimore–Philadelphia line and still other highly necessary improvements.[1] Incidentally, in the rolling stock alone, Mr. Mayer accomplished one highly practical and progressive development. In truth, he may be called the father of the modern gondola car, for the transport of coal.[2]

Mr. Mayer, from the outset, had attacked the situation boldly. That was ever his way. He called back into the service of Baltimore and Ohio as vice-president, Thomas M. King, who formerly had held the same position with the road, who was known for his constructive ability and who was familiar with the needs and possibilities of the property. At the same time, he found, up in the Northwest, a most capable and practical railroader in John T. O'Dell, who until his death (in February, 1926) was generally regarded as one of the foremost transportation officers the American railroad has yet produced. Mr. O'Dell was made general manager of Baltimore and Ohio. Acting under Mr. Mayer's instructions, he abandoned—at once and for all time—the hopper type of car. He succeeded in developing the type of modern gondola, which

---

[1] All of this difficult financing—the securing of money for a company whose reputation (and, consequently, whose credit) had descended to a low point—was necessarily accomplished piecemeal; the last notable feat of the Mayer administration being the financing of a so-called "terminal mortgage bond" of $8,500,000 on the Baltimore Belt Line and several new yards along the system.

[2] Until then, on the Baltimore and Ohio and most other roads, the so-called "hopper car" had been generally used. In appearance, this quaint carrier resembled nothing quite so much as three or four tin ash cans set in a row upon the deck of a flat car. . . . Its extreme capacity was about thirty tons, although its average was much nearer twenty. It was far from efficient.

was built first in wood, and then in iron, and all the while with steadily increasing coal capacity. In this step, the keen early experience of the president of the Baltimore and Ohio in the coal trade was of large value.

Yet, in the long run, it was the coal situation that was to prove a large part of his undoing as the chief executive of the historic Baltimore railroad. He had, as has just been shown, begun to ramify the system in West Virginia, steadily increasing its tentacles into the bituminous fields. . . .

Baltimore and Ohio, at the very beginning of the Mayer administration, still occupied a proud and a leading position in the soft-coal traffic. With its great Locust Point terminals at Baltimore, its foreign trade and its domestic, it handled, in 1889, some 31 per cent of the Eastern tide water coal traffic in the United States. (This is coal passing out of the capes of the Chesapeake and the Delaware, bound to New York and other domestic ports.) Its nearest competitor was the Pennsylvania, handling about 29 per cent.

Gradually, however, the scales were to turn. In 1890, it was the Pennsylvania that handled the 30 per cent, and the Baltimore and Ohio between 28 and 29 per cent. All the while, new names were coming into the lists. One first began to hear —as serious coal competitors—of Norfolk and Western, and Chesapeake and Ohio. Even the New York Central, far to the north, by means of an increasing interest in the Fall Brook Railroad (which eventually it was to purchase), running from Lyons upon its main line down into the Beech Creek region of Pennsylvania, was becoming an active factor in the situation.

Not only was competition thus very greatly increased, but, under it, the soft-coal rates began to decline. They went to sickening depths. . . . Baltimore and Ohio was in no position, at just that time, to withstand such an onslaught. It quickly lost both its prestige and its position in the soft-coal trade. For, while the actual tonnage each year did not decline appreciably, the relative tonnage did. From a position, where in 1889 it had handled 31 per cent of the total tidewater coal traffic, it had

descended, by 1896, to a point where it handled but 4 per cent.
From that time forward, however, there was to come a steady
ascendance once again in these percentage totals for Baltimore
and Ohio.

.   .   .   .

By the year 1892, the Mayer administration, despite all
these great handicaps, so many of them inheritances from its
predecessors, reached its pinnacle.   Then it was that under
it the great picture of Baltimore and Ohio reached its most
roseate hues.   The things that its president had outlined for
his board began to take actual shape.   Work had been begun
on the Baltimore Belt Line Railroad, connecting the loose end
of the older Main Stem, at Camden Station, with the Baltimore–Philadelphia line at Bay View, on the eastern outskirts of
Baltimore (of this, very much more in the succeeding chapter),
and the particularly bad curve upon the bridge at Harpers
Ferry was finally, after all these years, being wiped out.
Progress to make Baltimore and Ohio a really efficient modern
railroad was being made.[1]

---

[1] Epitomized, it might be said that the physical achievements of the Mayer
administration consisted of a tightening of the hold of Baltimore and Ohio on the
Staten Island properties; the beginning of the completion of the extension to
Philadelphia through the construction of the Belt Line through Baltimore; the
building of new yards and terminals at Brunswick, Cumberland, Glenwood and
Benwood; the acquisition of the lines from Clarksburg to Pickens and Richwood, together with the construction of connecting lines from Clarksburg to
Fairmont and Morgantown to Uniontown and the securing of control of the
Pittsburgh Junction road and the Pittsburgh and West Virginia Railway; the
building of the link between Akron and Chicago Junction, which gave the system
a new through low-grade route between Baltimore and Chicago, by way of
Pittsburgh; the buying of the lines into Fairport and Cleveland; and the con-
solidating and securing control of a connecting route from Parkersburg through
Cincinnati to St. Louis.   So was grouped the main structure of the Baltimore
and Ohio of today.   It was an ambitious structure indeed, and, if times in
general had been more propitious to Mr. Mayer, it might easily have been
regarded as his monument; a monument of which to be passing proud. . . .
In all, there had been added: in new construction, 178 miles; in additional lines
acquired, 743 miles; in the direct ownership secured of what is today the South-

Then, within the twelvemonth, came the great panic of 1893, which really started with the Baring failure in London. For many years, the Barings had been bankers for, and loyal supporters of, Baltimore and Ohio. Yet it was not their failure in itself, but rather the widespread international disasters that followed in its wake, that was to prove the slow but sure undoing of the Baltimore road. For a long time, it fought bravely to ward off the inevitable, fought a steadily losing fight. It cut expenses at every turn. It reduced its dividends, then abandoned them. But all to no avail.

Yet, in the remarkable World's Fair at Chicago, in the summer and autumn of 1893, it sought courageously to show the world its prestige and its position. Its tremendous exhibit at that show—in truth, a detailed and comprehensive representation, not merely of the development of the railroad in the United States, but of transport everywhere since the earliest days of civilization—still is recalled by many, many visitors to the Fair. This exhibit was, almost entirely, the work of one man, Major J. G. Pangborn, a traffic officer of the road who devoted much of his life to assiduous personal study of its early history. He it was who collected and restored the remarkable assortment of the line's early locomotives, and builded full-size reproductions of many other famous engines, the whole world over. To which, finally, was to be added the Baltimore and Ohio's crack new locomotive of 1893, the *Director-General*, which had attained a speed record of ninety-six miles an hour. Although it has long grown obsolete, this greyhound locomotive still is retained in one of the roundhouses of the company.

. . . .

Gay shows at world's fairs, however, could not hide oncoming tragedy. The handwriting was upon the wall. Deep

---

western Division of the system, another 925 miles. . . . In the same administration, the company's locomotive fleet had been increased from 755 to 890 engines, its car totals from 27,108 to 27,320.

as Baltimore and Ohio had descended into the valley, there were still lower depths for it to reach.

Charles F. Mayer saw these—in advance. He was a man of vision. But he was helpless. He was an indefatigable worker. Early and late he was at his office in the Baltimore headquarters. He himself handled a tremendous volume of affairs. Sometimes, it seemed as if he would never quite get abreast of that constant tide. Important men sat a day, two days, three days at a time in his outer office, awaiting the opportunity of personal speech with him. He did not mean to be discourteous to them; he was at heart a gentleman, a man filled with culture and with a desire to be of largest help to all with whom he came in contact. But the details of his position gradually became quite too much for him.

More than John W. Garrett even, he attempted to absorb the minutiæ of his work. Alarmed all the while by the growing deficits in the road's operation, he, himself, sought to examine carefully into all contracts for new work, and personally approved the requisitions even for the material and supplies required in the everyday operation of the road; at the same time, zealously watching the income and outgo through the company's treasury . . . an all but impossible task. It was hard for him to delegate these things to others. Once, when a wheel chair was needed for handling invalids at Camden Station, Mr. Mayer went over to Howard Street and bought the appliance himself.

No wonder then that the days were not long enough for this president of Baltimore and Ohio; that gradually he lengthened his daily stay at his office, until eight o'clock in the evening became his regular hour for closing his desk and going home.

There is a story told of him in those days that shows the driving energy to which the man forced himself.

Mrs. Mayer, in the years that her husband was president of Baltimore and Ohio, was far from well. One day as she lay abed in their home, Mr. Mayer sitting beside her, she summoned his personal porter and aide, one David, a negro who waited upon his master with the devoted attention so characteristic of his race.

"David," she said, "Mr. Mayer has agreed that at five o'clock each afternoon, no matter who may be in the office nor what unfinished work upon his desk, you are to bring him his hat and coat and escort him out to his carriage which will bring him home to me. . . . Do you understand?"

David understood. That very evening, he sought to place the new scheme into effect. Upon the minute of five, he brought to the president his hat and coat. Mayer laughed, but put them on and went home. But the next day, when, at just five, David again brought him hat and coat, he merely smiled—and went on working. The scheme was dropped, then and there. Mayer plunged, harder than ever, into his work.

.   .   .   .

Yet, in vain, all these endeavors.

Black days were growing blacker still. The storm broke hard upon Charles F. Mayer. Quarrels and dissensions broke out among the stockholders and among members of the board. The road seemingly had but few friends left. It stood alone, deserted. In Baltimore, almost everywhere within its territory, it long since had become a byword and a jest. Few there were to lend it aid, of any sort.

Charles F. Mayer finally stood alone, all but deserted. The storm broke personally upon him. He was forced to resign. On January 24, 1896, he ceased to be president of Baltimore and Ohio. Thirty-five days later, the property entered into receivership.

CHAPTER X

The Baltimore Belt and the Howard Street Tunnel—Mount Royal
Station—The Royal Blue Line Inaugurated—Travel Magnificence—Staten Island Terminals and the New Station
in Chicago.

IN the autumn of 1889, it began to be rumored in Baltimore that a connecting railroad tunnel was about to be built,
under the entire length of Howard Street. First rumors connected the projected enterprise with the Maryland Central
Railroad, a somewhat unstable venture, which, a number of
years before, had pushed its narrow-gauge line out from the
city toward the northeast, first reaching the lovely shire town
of the county of Harford—Belair—and then, after many
vicissitudes, achieving York, in the neighboring state of
Pennsylvania. This railroad (today known as the Maryland
and Pennsylvania), toward the end of the 'eighties, had come
under the control of two promoters, William Gilmor of Baltimore and John Henry Miller of Pittsburgh. These men had
a large plan for the Maryland Central. They proposed, first,
to establish for it a tidewater terminal on Baltimore harbor,
and then to push it north through Pennsylvania to a connection with the Lehigh Valley Railroad.[1] At the same time,

---

[1] The Lehigh Valley was unable to fulfill its plan to extend its system to
Baltimore over the Maryland Central. It was leased in 1891 to the Philadelphia
and Reading, and then, quite naturally, the scheme fell through. Even the abro-
gation of its lease to the Reading—in 1893—did not revive it. With the exception
of some construction in the valley of Deer Creek, looking forward to a crossing of
the Susquehanna River, the Maryland Central remained the purely local line
that it is today.

the road would be changed from narrow gauge to standard. It was proposed to call it the Baltimore and Lehigh.

In the long run, the road had the standard gauge. But it never progressed beyond York. Yet its terminal plan developed into a scheme of very great interest to the Baltimore and Ohio. In fact, the promoters of it had been greatly encouraged in the enterprise by the friendly advice and active assistance of John K. Cowen, general counsel of the Baltimore and Ohio.

.   .   .   .

It will be recalled that the Garrett administration, failing to obtain for itself the Philadelphia, Wilmington and Baltimore, expended much money and effort in building a brand-new link of its railroad from Baltimore to Philadelphia; but that, when this new line had been completed and opened to traffic, it still lacked actual rail connection with the rest of the property; cars and trains, of necessity, had to be ferried across that busy (even though fairly narrow) navigable branch of the Patapsco that forms the inner harbor of Baltimore. . . . At the best, this transfer business was awkward; time-taking. At its worst—in times of bad weather or unusually heavy traffic— it became almost unspeakably bad.

The elder Garrett had considered the possibilities of building a direct line across the center of Baltimore, to unite these two disconnected, but most important, elements of the property that he headed. Those who followed him gave even more thought to this solution of the problem.

A real problem, it remained. One not capable of easy solution. To build an efficient railroad, of at least two parallel tracks, across the heart of a city, already approaching metropolitanism and a half million of population, is never a sinecure. True it was that the Pennsylvania had done that very thing— in Baltimore and less than twenty years before. But twenty years in the progress of our American cities is a long time indeed, and there had been much criticism of the Pennsylvania's tunnels.   It was said that they were dirty, poorly ventilated and, much of the time, smoke-filled.   Baltimore and Ohio's first thought was that it could not follow into a similar error.

So it was, that, for a long time, the administration of the road seriously contemplated building an elevated connecting railroad across the town; between Camden Station and the Philadelphia stem.   Such a line, modeled upon the lighter structures already in use in New York and Brooklyn, or, more precisely, the new elevated line of the Pennsylvania through Jersey City, would run over private right of way for much of its length, parallel, but very close, to Pratt Street.   In this way, it was hoped to save much in property damages. But the final location of the proposed elevated railroad, entirely on private property, save for street crossings, also promised many damage suits of this sort.   And even after much land had already been acquired for the new line and some of the steel for its construction placed on order, the work was halted. That line was never built.

.   .   .   .

The Howard Street Tunnel suggestion of Gilmor and Miller made great appeal to President Mayer and his associates. For one thing—and a most important one—it had been planned, from the beginning, to have its southern terminal in the Camden Station yards of the Baltimore and Ohio, which would, in this way, become a terminus of the proposed Baltimore and Lehigh.   The northern end of the new link railroad would be at North Avenue, where the Maryland Central already had acquired a terminal, in the valley of Jones Falls.

If the new route—which was incorporated as the Baltimore Belt Railroad Company—could be extended from North Avenue and the Falls north and east, it could be brought easily to a junction with the Philadelphia line of the Baltimore and Ohio at Bay View, in the extreme northeasterly corner of the city.   The construction of this part of the link would be—in

MOUNT ROYAL STATION.

Standing in a fine park, its tall clock tower long has been a dominating landmark of uptown Baltimore.

From a photograph taken some years ago.

THE FIRST ELECTRIC LOCOMOTIVE, 1895.

Built originally for service in the Howard Street Tunnel, Baltimore, it still is retained as the first electric locomotive to be operated upon a standard steam railroad.

comparison at least with Howard Street Tunnel—comparatively inexpensive.   The territory through which it would run
was, as yet, little developed.

.   .   .   .

So was born the Baltimore Belt Railroad, with the great
Howard Street Tunnel of today—not, at first, a Baltimore
and Ohio conception, but gradually becoming a most important
link of the system, as well as affording, in Mount Royal Station,
one of the most convenient and handsome passenger terminals
in all the land.   The Baltimore Belt was incorporated with
Mr. Gilmor as its president; and Samuel Rea, who had joined
the project of the Maryland Central Railroad, became its
chief engineer.[1]

Mr. Rea's talent in tunnel construction was brought to
bear (in 1889) upon the Baltimore problem.   Swift progress
was made in the preliminaries.   On December 2 of that year,
the *Sun* announced that surveys had been completed both for
the tunnel—from Camden Station to Richmond Market; then,
as now, at the north end of Howard Street—and for the open-
cut sections on to the Bay View connection; for Baltimore
and Ohio's interests already were recognized as being para-
mount in the new enterprise.   The Baltimore and Lehigh
scheme was beginning to fade out of the picture.

In that same issue, the *Sun* averred that the new line would
cost about $5,000,000 to build (as a matter of fact, Howard
Street Tunnel alone cost more than $2,400,000) and that this

---

[1] To any student of American railroading, Mr. Rea needs no introduction.
Skilled railroad engineer and operator, born and bred of the Pennsylvania, he left
that system for a few years only; later—in 1892—to return to it, as assistant to
the late President Roberts—himself an engineer.   Under President Roberts and
his successors, Mr. Rea was charged with the study and development of many
engineering projects. The most notable, carried out under his supervision and
direction, being the New York tunnel extension of the Pennsylvania, together with
the great new station in that city and the Hell Gate Bridge of the New York
Connecting Railroad. . . .   A little later, Mr. Rea became president of the
Pennsylvania.   But for tunnel work he always has had an especial flair.

figure would include the construction of a handsome new station on the north side of North Avenue, just west of Jones Falls (at Oak Street). This structure was to be shared by the Maryland Central and the Baltimore and Ohio. The real estate for it, as well as for shafts for the construction of the Howard Street Tunnel, was rapidly being purchased. That tunnel would be more than 7000 feet in length, and, under a popular, busy city street, probably one of the longest "soft dirt" tunnels ever dug.

Much of downtown Baltimore rests upon a vast gravel bed, of tremendous depth; and, to bore the tunnel, it was thought by some that shields and compressed air would have to be used—in the manner long before perfected by Greathead in boring for wagonways and the Underground under the Thames and the streets of London. But the able contractors finally completed the tunnels, by ordinary methods.

Another new station—even larger than that at North Avenue—it was announced would be built into the tunnel at Lombard and Liberty streets. This was to cover an entire triangular block and the first plans provided that it be surmounted by a huge tower that would bid fair to become a landmark of Baltimore. At the track level of this new station—29 feet below that of the street—there would be a very long center platform, 500 feet in length, between the two tracks of the tunnel, and reached by stairways and by elevators. This was not planned to supplant Camden Station, but rather to supplement it. . . . The construction, somewhere in Howard Street near Monument, of a third or intermediate station, was also—somewhat vaguely—discussed.

.   .   .   .

Baltimore received this colossal plan with keen interest. But not without criticism. Some folks wrote to the newspapers reminding the town what an upset its downtown sections had received at the time that the Union Station had been built; upon what was then regarded as an extremely uptown part of

Charles Street; there was the usual nervousness displayed about the construction of any large tunnel and there were the "constant readers" who cited the gas and smoke of the Pennsylvania's tunnels as an argument against any more bores of that size and type. Some folk wanted the Baltimore Belt charged sidewalk easements on the new tube, and suggested that the thing be made retroactive and so applied to the earlier tunnels of the Pennsylvania. While others suggested that, in accepting the new rights of way, the Baltimore and Ohio and the Northern Central—very remotely connected with the inception of the new enterprise—should relinquish their valuable tax exemption privileges in the state of Maryland. This last was formulated into a bill at Annapolis. Which, in course of time, was defeated.

In the long run, common sense prevailed. The easement matter was forgotten and the Baltimore and Ohio announced that, in the new tunnel, electric power would be used for the haulage of the trains. This gave the project a new and a highly important status. Up to that time, electricity—then barely come into general use even upon the street railways of the American city—had not been used to any real extent upon any of the standard railroads. Great tunnels, both in the United States and in Europe, still clung to the steam locomotive. Its vapors filled the Hoosac and the Mt. Cenis . . . the long bores under New York and under Baltimore . . . all, alike. Yet the broomstick trolley already had come far enough to begin to hint of the possibilities of this great new undeveloped god of transport—electricity. And the Baltimore and Ohio was soon to show to the world its immediate possibilities in solving the disagreeable tunnel problem for the railroad; not merely as motive power, but for lighting and signaling purposes as well.

An electric power station was built—in Camden yard—and the current taken out over the line in a curious overhead contraption—two light Z-rails laid parallel to one another, with their feed wires and breakers supported upon a substantial construction of multiple steel arches placed at regular intervals. Upon these rails there traveled a sliding shoe or trolley.[1]

When the tunnel finally was finished and ready for traffic, but one electric locomotive was under construction, although two more were under contract; all from the General Electric Company, which coöperated with the American Locomotive Company in building these stout pioneers. It was at first arranged that the tunnel be used for passenger trains only—and freight continued to be transferred from Locust Point to Canton by barge until ample electric locomotives were available to handle the entire traffic of the road through the new tunnel. . . . A real innovation was the complete electric lighting of the bore. It also was planned to place lighted clocks along the tunnel walls, for fear that the electric currents would disturb the engineers' watches. . . . These fears, too, have long since proved to be utterly groundless. But they are interesting today as showing how very little was then known about electric traction of any sort.

There was yet another reason for feeling that the freight trains could still be handled easily by the ferry transfer between Locust Point and Canton. The original arrangement was that the Baltimore and Ohio should pay the Baltimore Belt a certain definite sum for each and every car of any sort that should be handled through the new tunnel route. This being so, it was felt to be good business to send as few cars by that pathway as was possible.

Eventually, this rather archaic scheme of payment was abandoned; the Baltimore and Lehigh scheme, as a through route and an entrance to Baltimore for Lehigh Valley, having failed to materialize, the Baltimore and Ohio took over the

[1] At the time of its installation, the overhead construction was thought to be the only really safe method for conducting the current out over the line. After seven years of use, however, it was abandoned on the Baltimore Belt and taken down, in favor of a far simpler and more practical under-running third-rail system, so insulated and otherwise protected as to offer no danger whatsoever to any who might chance to brush against it. The record has shown virtually no accidents arising from this source.

entire ownership and control of the Belt, first guaranteeing the five per cent annual interest on the $6,000,000 bonds already issued by the tunnel company.   That done, it became in every way more advisable to send practically all traffic through the tunnel, doing away completely with the rather cumbersome ferry transfer across the harbor.

.   .   .   .

All this anticipates.

Before the tunnel could be operated, even after charters, easements and franchises had been safely obtained and the project completely financed, there remained the grave problem of the actual construction of the bore.

The difficulties here were not to be easily overestimated. From North Avenue on to Bay View—the greater part by far of the seven miles of the Belt—the construction was to be comparatively easy, such few tunnels as were used being short. The longest of these, 892 feet, was from Oak to Charles streets, passing under both of these thoroughfares, as well as Maryland Avenue.   A 445-foot bore ran under and from St. Paul to Calvert streets.   There were some fairly heavy cuts; but all of this was as nothing to the Howard Street Tunnel.

A short portion of this tunnel—in the neighborhood of Pratt Street crossing—ran so close to the surface that it was dug as an open cut and girders set to carry the replaced street overhead.   All the rest of Howard Street Tunnel—as completed, 7341 feet long—is a brick masonry arch, 21 feet, 3 inches in extreme height, and 27 feet in width.   It was built of the so-called "invert type," the floor being a flat reverse arch, to give additional strength to the side walls.

.   .   .   .

To dig the tunnel, seven shafts were sunk along the route. With these, in addition to the headings near Preston Street and just below Camden Street, it was possible to employ, simultaneously, a number of gangs and tunnel shields.   More-

over, with fine meticulousness, the city of Baltimore insisted
that three shifts of men, each shift working eight hours, should
be kept at the work twenty-four hours a day; that not more
than 400 feet of unlined tunnel should remain open at one
time; and that these uncompleted sections should not be in
two contiguous blocks. Fear was felt for the safety of the
stores and other business places along Howard Street. But,
again, these proved groundless. For the most part, the householders and storekeepers along that important thoroughfare
were quite unconscious of the huge construction that was
going on under their very feet. Even after the tunnel had
been fully completed and was receiving heavy traffic, the pro-
fessors of Johns Hopkins University (at that time located in
Howard Street) reported no disturbance whatsoever to their
delicate scientific instruments.

For one thing, the major part of the Howard Street tunnel
rests from 50 to 65 feet beneath the surface of the pavement;
and, for another, the general contractors, Ryan and McDonald,
knew how best to go at it. They had had some previous
railroad experience, building the easterly end of the Philadelphia line of the Baltimore and Ohio along and through
Fairmount Park, where some fairly difficult construction
problems had been met and solved. Afterwards, Mr. Mc-
Donald was to gain an even wider fame as the chief contractor
for the original New York subways.

The main contracts, as well as the sub-contracts, were
awarded September 12, 1890. The work was divided into
four main sections: from Bay View Junction to Belair Road;
from Belair Road to Guilford Avenue; from Guilford Avenue
to a point near Mount Royal Avenue; and from this last point
through the great tunnel to Hamburg Street, just below
Camden, and within the Camden Station yard, into which the
tunnel tracks would debouch by means of an easy upward
grade. . . . In the tunnel itself, the grade was all in one
direction, rising on a steady .8 per cent ascent all the way.
This long grade, while necessitating a pretty steady pull on

the part of the electric motors bringing northbound trains
through the tunnel, has compensated for itself by permitting
the southbound ones to coast through it, all the way from
Mount Royal to Camden, without attaching electric locomotives, the steam ones remaining as inert as when they are
being pulled up the tunnel.   This all has long since become a
matter of very precise and comparatively easy railroad operation.

.   .   .   .

Work on the first three sections of the new line went
through with comparative ease and rapidity.   But there was
no hurrying the large tunnel.   At times, the rate of progress
upon it was exasperatingly slow.   The gravel bed which forms
so much of the foundation of Baltimore proved difficult at
many points.   Occasionally, veins of quicksand presented themselves and each of these was a fresh problem, in itself.   There
was much trouble with water, with seepage, and with hidden
streams.   This was the probable reason for building the invert
arch, which, at the outset, had not been contemplated.   Even
after the tunnel had been completed and placed in use, it was
necessary, at one point, to open a section of the terrain beside it
and to grout it thoroughly with cement before it was made
perfectly safe.

.   .   .   .

The stations presented real problems in themselves.
From the beginning, there had been a general public feeling
that the main station of the Belt—the future main station of
the Baltimore and Ohio in its home city—should be at or
near Baltimore Street.   The intersection of that street with
Howard was, and still is, one of the important industrial hubs
of the entire city.   The elaborate structure with the great
tower planned at German Street (to which reference has just
been made) was designed in deference to that demand and
feeling for a passenger terminal within the very heart of
Baltimore.

But, in the long run, that particular station was never builded; even though a great deal of time and effort was spent in excavating for it. The open area, which would have been filled by its subterranean platforms, still exists under Liberty and Howard streets; a great space, unlighted and unseen—a sort of secret basement of Baltimore.

Instead of having two entirely separate stations within three blocks of one another, it finally was found to be far more practicable to combine their facilities in a rebuilt and enlarged Camden Station. For a time after the completion of the tunnel, the through passenger trains which traversed it still backed in and out of the old train shed of Camden; just as they had done in the days of the ferry transfer. In 1897, the present low-level station in the cut at Camden was built, with its train shed, its fine long platform, its stairs and elevators; all between the main eastbound and westbound tracks of the tunnel. At the same time, the train shed of the upper level was torn down and completely rebuilt; into a fine steel house for locals and all other passenger trains originating or ending at Camden. The ancient building was refurbished to continue as one of Baltimore's chief passenger terminals.

·   ·   ·   ·   ·   ·   ·

The problem of an uptown station on the Belt was not so easily solved.

It will be remembered that the east end of the North Avenue bridge over Jones Falls (at Oak Street) had been considered an ideal location for this station, one into which the trains of the Maryland Central also could come. The stretch between Charles and St. Paul streets also was considered; but this was rejected, largely because of the extreme low level of the Belt Line tracks at that point. Moreover, Baltimore had not swept out quite so far. Oak and North seemed far more advisable. This site would involve the building of a new North Avenue bridge, but that was deemed as nothing; the old one was so far gone as to be almost unsafe.

The Pride of the Royal Blue.

Engine *No. 1310* with its fine lines and its great drivers thought nothing of the Washington–Jersey City run in five hours flat.

From a recent photograph.

A PASSENGER COACH OF THE ROYAL BLUE LINE—1886.

The brilliant blue, the gay stripings and the Maryland crest on these cars made them splendidly conspicuous.

From a recent photograph.

In the end, however, the location at North and Oak also was rejected. . . . The Pennsylvania Railroad, which, quite naturally, had looked upon the building of the Baltimore Belt with none too friendly an eye, and its objections, coupled with some rather intricate real-estate problems, was responsible for the rejection.

The Oak Street site would have permitted of an easy and a logical approach from both directions; particularly from the portals of the Howard Street Tunnel, a short distance to the south. It would have been much better than the ungainly double curve in the vicinity of North Avenue that finally it was necessary to install.

But this logical line would have crossed the Pennsylvania's tracks at the very throat of its Union Station yard. That road raised a protest against the constriction that an overhead railroad bridge, with its necessary piers, would place upon the future development of the Union Station facilities. It threatened to take the matter into the courts. A dreary and long drawn-out legal battle loomed.

In the long run, the entire matter was compromised. The Belt Railroad was bended through the so-called Bolton Lot, the historic outer depot of the old Northern Central and its still more ancient predecessor, the Baltimore and Susquehanna, and was brought over the Pennsylvania's Washington line tunnel just within the portals of that bore. Even then, the four tracks of the Belt Railroad were not to be permitted to rest upon the top of the Pennsylvania tunnel. An elaborate bridge-arch construction, which in effect carries one tunnel over another without resting upon it, was finally installed— at no small cost. . . . The Northern Central and Maryland Central tracks were crossed upon the same viaduct that passed under the new North Avenue bridge and over Jones Falls.

．　　．　　．　　．　　．　　．　　．

No wonder that, with all this intricacy of construction to be accomplished, time passed and that it was May 1, 1895, before the first regular passenger train ran through Howard

Street Tunnel. This was Train 514, of the Royal Blue Line, northbound; and, the electrical equipment still being unready, it was hauled by a steam locomotive up the steep grade. . . . The engine, which had come through from Washington, was nearly out of water by the time it had reached Bay View Junction, and it became necessary to stop the train there five minutes before its tank could be refilled. . . . This process had formerly been accomplished during the crossing on the transfer ferry. It was provided for in the future by the installation of track tanks a few miles east of Baltimore.

.   .   .   .

The steam operation of the tunnel did not last long. By the first of June, the first of the electric locomotives was on its way to Baltimore from the Schenectady shops of the General Electric Company, and on Thursday, the twenty-seventh of that same month, it was given its official trip; easily hauling a steam locomotive up through the tube from Camden Station to the crossover at North Avenue in an even seven minutes. William Cooper, one of the electrical experts of the General Electric, was at the control switch of the motor, which had replaced the traditional throttle of the steam locomotive.

In this simple way, did the first practical electric locomotive, not only upon the lines of the Baltimore and Ohio, but upon the lines of any steam railroad in the United States, come to the system where, forty years before, probably the first experimental electrical locomotive ever built had been given its trial (the Page locomotive, which, in 1854, had been run for a while between Washington and Bladensburg). Once again, did Baltimore and Ohio show itself a real pioneer in modern traction.

The engine was a nine days' wonder for Baltimore. As it lay upon a siding in the Bolton Lot—the site of the future Mount Royal Station, not yet begun—waiting for a clear track for the return to Camden, a great crowd gathered roundabout it. The usually keen journalistic ear of the *Sun* paper noted:

. . . Bellowing bullfrogs, croaking foghorns and shrieking steam-whistles would have to form a syndicate to beat the toot from electric locomotive *No. 1*. It is as loud as the whistle on an Atlantic liner. The mightiness of this voice is explained by the fact that there are carried on the locomotive, great reservoirs of compressed air, which is used for the operation of the train airbrakes. The air is compressed by a pump driven by an electric motor. . . .

Compared with the most modern electric locomotives of today, used on the Baltimore and Ohio and other progressive railroads the world over, old *No. 1* (still carefully preserved by the company in Baltimore) now looks like a mere pygmy. But, in 1895, newspaper paragraphers referred to the strange newcomer as a "giant." Compared with the steam locomotives of that day, it was hardly less. It weighed 96 tons and, with a total length of but 34 feet, 8 inches, it had the astonishing drawbar pull of 56,000 pounds. It was said that it would run sixty miles an hour while hauling a train, and, while the line of the Baltimore Belt offered no opportunity for actual tests, there was no doubt but that, on open road, it could easily have reached this speed.

.   .   .   .

The uptown station of Baltimore and Ohio finally went upon the Bolton Lot and became known as Mount Royal. Thus was a historic rail terminal perpetuated. Where the tall clock tower of Mount Royal rises today, trains from the north have been coming into and out of Baltimore since 1832. For that was the year that the Baltimore and Susquehanna began the operation of its trains, to the Pennsylvania state line—thirty-two miles to the north.

Much care and thought were given to the design of the new station. The Bolton Lot, which at one time had been suggested as the location for a permanent exposition of the products of Baltimore industry, was large enough, not only to provide for a roomy passenger terminal, but also to permit of handsome parking in every direction. This last was done, and has always been beautifully maintained, by the city. Through travelers on the Baltimore and Ohio remember Mount Royal, not only as the station which is forever immaculate, but which gives out from under its train-shed eaves vistas of greenery, of flowers and of trees and shrubs and close-cut grassplots.

After more than thirty years of steady use—it first was opened for passengers September 1, 1896—Mount Royal remains today a sturdy thing of granite, handsome, imperturbable and impressive. A station of much dignity—always. With its chief feature, that tall commanding clock tower, by day and by night a landmark of modern Baltimore; by day, a sheer granite shaft of Romanesque, by night its bright clock faces surmounted by a great and glowing electric "B & O". . . . While handling, in an average year, far less passengers than old Camden, Mount Royal's business increases steadily all the while. For each year sees Baltimore climbing steadily northward; markers that but a few years ago stood close to the edge of open country are today part of the closely builded community. The wisdom of the men who long ago located Mount Royal Station has been, in these recent years, fully justified.

.   .   .   .

With the completion of the Mount Royal Station, that interesting Baltimore and Ohio creation of a quarter century or more ago, the Royal Blue Line, took a fresh spurt forward. The Royal Blue came as a direct and a most natural sequence to the completion of the Philadelphia Division and its direct connection to the through New York line of the Reading and Central of New Jersey railroads. It was first inaugurated on July 31, 1890, and, from the outset, it was a popular success. It was *de luxe* in a day when the fullness of that phrase had hardly been recognized. As its bright crown, it boasted an all-Pullman train—the *Royal Limited*—

which swept back and forth between Washington and Jersey City daily, in an even five hours. Swift riding was not unknown on the Baltimore and Ohio of that decade. Just a few weeks before the opening of the Belt Line, Baltimore was astonished to read that a Raymond and Whitcomb party had been carried from the Canton ferry landing, over the Philadelphia Division to Chestnut Street Station, ninety-five miles distant, in an hour and thirty-seven minutes. And this had included a stop at Wilmington.

The Royal Blue endeavored to build its reputation through swiftness as well as through the luxury of its equipment. This last was all that the car builder of that day might possibly create.   From without, its deep blue color—hence the name of the new line—with its richness of Royal Saxon gold striping and its gaily emblazoned state crests upon the car sides, made the trains stand out most definitely in sheer beauty. Within, the magnificence of the equipment kept pace with its shining exterior.   Parlor- and sleeping-car decoration was, here in the United States, at its apotheosis. From the club cars, through the dining cars—the two finest of them named the *Waldorf* and the *Astoria*, after Mr. Boldt's tremendous new hostelry in Fifth Avenue, New York City—to the brass-railed observation cars, the Royal Blue represented the last word in train equipment and service.   It commanded attention and brought much traffic to the new line.

It has been gone a number of years now. In the craze for standardization which spread over our railroads not long after the beginning of the present century, the Royal Blue trains passed out of existence, but the name and reputation still linger.   The modern trains that run today over the Baltimore and Ohio are not less comfortable than these historic ancestors. They are, however, heavier and safer, and the simplest of them have many conveniences unknown in even the finest of the *de luxes* of that day.   But, assuredly, they are not more colorful.

.   .   .   .

With the Royal Blue putting its best foot forward as a bid for the immensely valuable passenger traffic between New York and the West and the Southwest, Baltimore and Ohio was making equally strong efforts to capture the more remunerative freight business. It had acquired the Staten Island Rapid Transit Company—an elaborate scheme launched but a few years earlier by Erastus Wiman—and this system it began to develop, as a freight terminal for the entire New York metropolitan district.

To make the Staten Island property available in this fashion, it became of course necessary to link it to the main property. This was done by the construction of a comparatively short stretch of railroad from a point on the Central Railroad of New Jersey, near Cranford, to and over Arthur Kill (separating Staten Island from the mainland of New Jersey). The Baltimore and Ohio's newly established running rights over the Reading and the Central of New Jersey made this a perfectly efficient and practical link and saved the vast expense of building a brand-new line all the way across New Jersey from Philadelphia, or some point just below that city.

.   .   .   .

The bridge over the Arthur Kill was completed and placed in service in 1887.[1] Simultaneously, two broad ocean piers, side by side and 350 feet in length and extending into a portion of New York harbor most easily reached by the largest of ocean ships, were made ready for business. Warehouses and elevators were opened. And traffic began to flow to them—without delay.

No longer was Baltimore and Ohio dependent upon but two ocean gateways—and those from 150 to 200 miles in from the open sea—for the development of its foreign traffic. It now had a triple gateway—with a tentacle at Locust Point,

[1] The Arthur Kill bridge, as originally constructed, was single track and was composed of a through-truss, pivot-swing central span, 496 feet in length, a west approach, 83 feet long, and an east approach, 147 feet in length.

READY FOR THE DAY'S RUN.

A Baltimore and Ohio local of the 'nineties ready to set out from the old Washington station.

From a contemporary photograph.

GRAND CENTRAL STATION, CHICAGO.
For many years past, the handsome and commodious passenger terminal of
Baltimore and Ohio in the heart of Chicago.

From a photograph.

Baltimore, a second at Philadelphia, and the third at Staten Island, New York; each equipped with direct track connections and capable of being expanded to handle increasing volumes of business. With the Staten Island arm ready to handle, not merely traffic to and from overseas, but the great volume of freight originating in New York, in Brooklyn and in the many, many communities roundabout these cities, as well as from the rail and water connections off toward New England and the North.

.   .   .   .

As these developments were being reached at the eastern end of the system, similar ones were coming to pass at its western end. Baltimore and Ohio, after twenty years of tenancy, was quitting the Illinois Central station in Chicago— for a more advantageous and centrally located structure.

The Illinois Central, after having maintained, for many years, its chief Chicago passenger terminal at Randolph Street, upon the lake front, now was moving it to a larger site at Twelfth Street. The World's Fair of 1893 had furnished it the excuse to build in a far more generous fashion than had ever been possible upon the cramped Randolph Street site. It created for itself, at Twelfth Street, the present dignified Romanesque structure, which at some time in the near future is to disappear in favor of a still larger terminal.

Baltimore and Ohio never ran its trains into the Twelfth Street Station. It found for itself an even better location— one far closer to the heart of the city—within almost a stone's throw of the famous "Loop," the criterion by which, since the 'nineties, all downtown Chicago has been measured. This was in the new Grand Central Station, at Fifth Avenue and Harrison Street; which was being financed and built by a number of railroads, in which the Northern Pacific, the Wisconsin Central and the Chicago Great Western were the leaders.

The Baltimore and Ohio's passenger trains first began using the Grand Central December 1, 1891—a date almost coincident with that of the opening of the new through route to the West by way of Pittsburgh and the recently acquired and partly rebuilt Pittsburgh and Western.   They have been using that same terminal ever since.   It remains, handsome, commodious, centrally located.   Its tall tower, like that at Mount Royal, dominates a great central portion of an important American city, and also in electricity nightly flashes out "B & O" to a whole world of potential travel.

CHAPTER XI

A SHORT RECEIVERSHIP

Dark Clouds Roll Up Again—John K. Cowen and Oscar G. Murray
Appointed as Receivers—Baltimore and Ohio Comes to New
Pinnacles of Business—Foreclosure is Avoided—And the Penn-
sylvania Buys Control.

LET no one, after reading the pages of the preceding chapter,
paint for himself too glowing a portrait of the Baltimore and
Ohio of the 'nineties. True it was, that in that important
decade, the system had expanded itself, tremendously; that it
had added to and perfected itself in many, many ways—the
Belt Line enterprise in Baltimore was but one of a number of
its large and far-seeing projects. On the other hand, the
administration of Charles F. Mayer—who remained seated
firmly in the saddle through the first half of the decade—began,
as has already been seen before it was well advanced, to run
into increasing storm. The staunch old Baltimore clipper
awaited heavy seas just ahead.

Its skipper began—as all properly minded captains always
do begin—to meet oncoming darkness by trimming ship.
Untoward expenses, of every sort, were cut, to the limit. In
some cases, the economies were accomplished even at the expense of the proper upkeep of the property. . . . Finally, the
Belt Line project was the only one being pushed ahead. It
was so well advanced before the worst times came to the road,
there was such urgent and immediate need for it, and it had

been so well financed, that there was naught to do but to see it through. So its completion did not lag.

But, elsewhere upon the property, not only were all improvements abandoned, but even maintenance was skimped and neglected. The lines of the Baltimore and Ohio fell into very poor condition; its motive power and its tracks and stations became a laughingstock and a byword. It had been a number of years since there had been any large additions to its fleet of locomotives. Many of the engines in service, hauling freight and passenger trains, had become obsolete and were no longer fit for the burdens being put upon them. Cars, too old and too worn to run upon the rails longer, were left, battered and forlorn, abandoned along the right of way. To journey west upon the Baltimore and Ohio was not only to take a degree of personal risk and to incur certain and many train delays, but to see, with one's own eyes, a picture of a once splendid railroad property, rapidly going to rack and ruin.

A brave effort was made to maintain the service to the character already established—even though there were shortage of equipment of nearly every sort. Particular effort was made to keep the New York. Washington passenger service up to the high standard set for this new route.

Here, then, the obverse of that brilliant picture that we saw but a moment ago. Here, behind the scenes, the broken-down equipment and—far worse—the shattered morale of the rank and file of the line.

. . . .

Financially, the picture was hardly better.

It is not necessary to recount here the severe monetary and industrial troubles that were precipitated upon the United States in the year of grace, 1893. The disastrous and overwhelming failure of the great banking house of Baring Brothers in London—stout friends always of Baltimore and Ohio—is ofttimes credited with being the beginning of the financial debacle that was to be visited upon the entire nation. Other causes, however, worked with an equal import. In many lines of American industry, there had been over-expansion—times had been just a little too good to be true. Under much prosperity, men, ordinarily cool and shrewd, had become a bit giddy-headed. Balance—always the firm foundation of business—had been lost; the commercial structure was wabbly; the Baring failure was merely the push that sent it tottering, and scattered some of its wreckage over the face of all the nations of the world.

There had been times when the Mayer administration of the Baltimore and Ohio had held every confident hope for an ultimate tremendous success for itself. But, events placed themselves too stoutly against it. Freight and passenger rates, reduced by one cause or another to terribly low levels, the almost utter lack of any sort of coöperation between the individual roads—in fact all but ruinous competition, —had placed the American rail carriers in a weak position generally. The crashing blow to the commercial life of the country, the industrial stagnation that followed in its wake, meant traffic lowered to the very lowest point. To which was added very great unrest within the labor ranks of many of the roads. To such clouds there were few silver linings.

Wonder it not, then, that the earnings of Baltimore and Ohio sank to low levels indeed. In the fiscal year, ending in 1892, the gross for the system (excluding always the Baltimore and Ohio Southwestern, still operated as a separate railroad) had reached a high point of $26,034,167. Then it was that Mr. Mayer's hopes were also at the highest. The effect of the few months of general financial depression included in the fiscal year of '93 had been to lower this gross to $25,877,357. In the next twelve months, it sank to rock bottom—to an appalling $22,502,662. The following two years showed slight improvement—$22,817,182 in 1895, and $23,944,781 in 1896. But the mischief had been done. No amount of trimming the ship—of bringing expenses of every sort down to the traditional bone—

could offset that tremendous loss in traffic revenues. . . .   The
great bark of Baltimore and Ohio was headed straight for the
shoals.

It struck on the last day of February, 1896—a leap-year
twenty-ninth, that came partly as an omen of ill fortune for
the old road, and partly as one of eventual good.

On that final day of February, 1896, the Mercantile Trust
Company of New York, recovering a judgment of $924,470.83,
filed its creditor's bill against the company in the United States
Circuit Court for the District of Maryland.   The creditor's
bill set forth the insolvency of the Baltimore and Ohio and
prayed for the appointment of receivers.   The Court, in the
person of Judge Goff, granted the petition and appointed
John K. Cowen and Oscar G. Murray as receivers.   And a
portion, at least, of conservative Baltimore had one of the
most miserable hours of all its recent years—its pride and its
pocketbook had been touched, to the quick.

.   .   .   .

With this sharp stroke, two important figures came
forward upon the stage of the Baltimore and Ohio—men who
are bound, ineffaceably, with its history.

Of the two, Mr. Cowen was no stranger to Baltimore.   Nor
to the railroad which bore its name.   Long before, he had
made his impress upon the property.   His power in it had
grown steadily.   Until, but a short time before the receivership, he had been elected to its presidency; succeeding Mr.
Mayer, who retired to nurse a very sick wife back to health.
Unfortunately, he failed in this.   Mrs. Mayer died, late in
March, 1896.

John K. Cowen came of Maryland stock.   Born in Holmes
County, Ohio, October 24, 1844, his family had, but a few
months before, migrated there from Rising Sun, in Cecil
County, Maryland, not far from the banks of the Susquehanna.
Cowen sought out, and received, a thorough general education;
ending at Princeton, where he was a college mate and intimate

friend of Robert Garrett. Mr. Cowen was graduated from Princeton in the summer of 1866, and, after two years of hard study at his home, using law books borrowed from a family friend, was admitted to the Ohio bar. He began practice there, but pickings at first were few and far between. He was wont to say, laughingly, that he had come out of college "with a good education and a good constitution, but without much money."

Robert Garrett did not forget his college friend. In 1872, he sent for Cowen and placed him in a responsible post in the law department of the Baltimore and Ohio. There he rose, rapidly. He became general counsel of the company—succeeding the distinguished and venerable John H. B. Latrobe—and very soon was recognized as one of the foremost citizens of Baltimore. He took a prominent position in civic affairs and, shortly before his selection as president of the railroad, he was elected from the Fourth Maryland District to Congress. This post he resigned soon after his appointment as co-receiver of the Baltimore and Ohio. But, in the comparatively few months of his political service at Washington, he came to know very intimately, Grover Cleveland. He had a tremendous admiration for Cleveland; a man whom he resembled in more ways than one; not the least of them in his straightforwardness, his marvelous aptitude for hard work and his dogged determination.

.   .   .   .

Oscar G. Murray, on the other hand, had arrived in Baltimore but a few months prior to the receivership. His training had all been in a highly practical end of railroading. He was a Connecticut Yankee who had drifted down to Texas and had found his first railroad job there; selling tickets at Galveston for the old Galveston, Houston and Henderson, now a part of the Southern Pacific system. Murray was the sort of man who, wherever he goes, makes friends, and warm friends. He did not long remain a ticket agent. By 1880, he loomed up as the general freight and passenger agent of the Santa Fé lines in Texas. Five years of that, and again he advanced— this time to be traffic manager of the Missouri Pacific properties in that same state. After this, his progress was eastward. November 1, 1888, found him freight traffic manager of the Big Four at Cincinnati. His next progressive step was as vice-president in charge of traffic of the Chesapeake and Ohio Railway, at that time closely affiliated with the Big Four. . . . From the Chesapeake and Ohio, he had come to the Baltimore and Ohio—in December, 1895—also as vice-president in charge of traffic.

Oscar Murray was the most spectacular president that the Baltimore and Ohio ever knew. Big, good-natured, immaculately dressed always, he became, in a town ever rather famed for its good living, a most distinguished *bon vivant*. A bachelor, he lived in a suite that took almost a half floor in the fashionable and then new Stafford Hotel in Mount Vernon Square. He was a man of meticulous elegance. The good taste of his carriages and—in a slightly later day—his motor cars equaled that of his always immaculate apparel.

With all of this magnificent exterior, Mr. Murray was large-hearted and large-minded. Genial always, he was kind and generous, to a fault. His largess was famous. The older employés at the Stafford still remember the tips he gave. He entertained; frequently and superbly.

Yet, back of all this, there were the brain and the intelligence of a thoroughly trained railroader. He was shrewd, tactful, patient. And he possessed an almost uncanny faculty for going straight to the heart of any subject that came his way. . . . He was among the last of the old-school railroad officers, men who accomplished their ends very largely through personal contacts, of one sort or another. After them, was to come the generation of executives who worked through methods and a carefully coördinated corps of subordinates. The older generation went a good deal by the rule of a well schooled thumb.

This, then, was the partnership that undertook the steward-
ship of Baltimore and Ohio in one of the darkest chapters of
all its existence. Working together, and with a remarkable
singleness of purpose, Cowen and Murray were bound to
achieve something definite.

.   .   .   .

Throughout the first two months of 1896, Mr. Cowen had
been struggling to avert the calamity of receivership; with all
the potential dangers that forever lurk in its shadows. He had
tried to comfort and to assure Baltimore and the important
centers that the road served. He endeavored to appease the
purveyors of the most necessary railroad supplies. And, all
the while, he was struggling—an almost hopeless task—to find
funds. The fact that the company long since had outgrown
the financing resources, even of so considerable a city as
Baltimore, and was, for the moment at least, without a close
and confidential banking-house connection in New York, was
an additional handicap.

Up to the last moment, refinancing syndicates were attempted, but all of these were of no avail. The floating debt
steadily increased—over $4,325,000 already was due, for
materials, traffic balances and the like—creditors became all
the while more insistent and more disagreeable, and the company itself finally found that it had exhausted all available
assets upon which it could hope to raise funds to meet even its
most pressing needs. It was like a dog driven into a corner.
It had even gone so far as to mortgage its home—the preten-
tious Central Building at Baltimore and Calvert streets that,
but a few short years before, had been John W. Garrett's
particular pride and delight. When it took this step, cautious
investors lifted their eyebrows.

John K. Cowen, wearily trudging the streets of New York,
called upon one banker after another. Courteous was his
welcome always; but always emphatic the refusals to do business with Baltimore and Ohio. Sometimes—not often—they

laid out tentative syndicates with him—on paper. One of
these was to raise about $1,500,000 in cash, to meet the road's
most immediate and pressing needs, and later to add between
$11,000,000 and $13,000,000, taking a collateral trust mortgage
for which it was to find a market. But the syndicate found
that it could not raise even that first $1,500,000, and the thing
died, a-borning.[1]

.   .   .   .

Hard days, indeed.

Andrew Anderson, the venerable personal secretary to
John W. Garrett and for many years afterwards secretary of
the company itself, used to tell about walking down through
the Charles Street gardens one bright spring day there in the
early 'nineties, and having a local banker overtake him and
walk along in step with him.

"I happen to have an extra fifty thousand dollars on my
hands this morning," the banker had remarked, rather casually.
"Do you think that the B. and O. could make use of it?"

Mr. Anderson did not think. He knew. But he also
knew that it would show poor credit if he accepted the banker's
proffer too quickly. He replied in a most guarded way, saying
that he would talk with his fellow officers and, if they could
use the fifty thousand, they would let the banker know. . . .
They decided that they could use it.

.   .   .   .

Gradually, during those winter days of '96, the footing became harder. An important loan of nearly a million dollars
to the Mercantile Trust up in New York was due on March 1,

[1] J. Pierpont Morgan felt that he could do the thing. But the terms and the
concessions that he proposed were just a little too much for Mr. Cowen. They
involved principally the domination of the road in the interest of the "Main
Line" mortgages, to the exclusion of lateral liens, such as existed on the Philadelphia, Chicago, Pittsburgh and the Southwestern divisions of the system.
In justice to his company, Cowen felt that he could not possibly accept such
terms.

and a million dollars, always sizable, was, at just that moment, an immense sum of money to Baltimore and Ohio. Mr. Cowen, who had gone to New York in the last week of February, was trying to keep a stiff upper lip as he hurried from one banker to another; but it came hard. In the morning newspapers of the twenty-eighth day of that month, he was quoted as saying:

> So far from there being foundation for the adverse reports made in New York in regard to Baltimore and Ohio affairs, the facts are that experts have finished their examination and find the condition as represented to the new board of directors, that the securities in hand against the floating debt are ample and the plan for the rehabilitation of the property has progressed so far as to meet the approval of the directors and will be ready for announcement in a short time.
>
> There is no truth in the rumor that the Baltimore and Ohio will default March 1. The negotiations for the collateral trust loan intended to take care of the floating debt and provide new capital for the needs of the company have progressed favorably. . . .

No one who ever knew Mr. Cowen might doubt his sincerity, even in the face of such an eleventh-hour statement as this. The truth of the matter was that the president of the Baltimore and Ohio—no unseeming optimist, but a hardheaded business man and lawyer—actually expected to avert the receivership crisis. Up almost to the very moment of the signing of the decree by Judge Goff, he was hopeful that some way might be found—must be found—to avoid the receivership. The final necessity, resulting in the granting of the judgment, came as as great a shock to him as to any other citizen of Baltimore.

·   ·   ·   ·   ·   ·   ·

The dramatic twenty-ninth day of February fell upon a Saturday. In the morning of that day, General Louis Fitzgerald, president of the Mercantile Trust Company, sent for Mr. Cowen, Edward R. Bacon—president of the Baltimore and Ohio Southwestern and an important director in the parent Baltimore and Ohio—and some other bankers, and announced what he was going to do. . . . Cowen, Bacon and one or two of the junior financial officers of the company left on the 11:30 flier from Jersey City to Baltimore. . . . All the way down the line, they signed a certain issue of bonds—five hundred of them in all—in order to make them valid before receivership. . . . Arriving in Baltimore, Cowen and Bacon hurried to Judge Goff's chambers. Murray joined them there. The signing of the necessary papers took but a few minutes. When it was done, John K. Cowen as president of the Baltimore and Ohio Railroad Company was impotent; but as receiver of that company—in truth, a federal officer—great, new, valuable power was in his hands.

.   .   .   .

The effect upon Baltimore was profound. . . . The news of the coup did not reach all the corners of the town until the following Monday morning—the men who had planned it had arranged to place it as great a distance as possible from the opening of the stock exchanges.

Yet, even their forethought could not prevent a debacle in the shares. But thirty days before (January 31), these had sold on the New York Stock Exchange at 42½. . . . Some of the wise and far-seeing ones in Wall Street, knowing the inwardness of the situation and anticipating that the company was going to have trouble with those March-first obligations, began selling early in February. On Saturday, the twenty-ninth, even though the news of receivership was not to escape until long after the closing of the market, Baltimore and Ohio common had fallen to 21⅝, a drop of 13¾ for the week. The worst was yet to come: the news of the actual receivership drove the stock still further down. On Monday, March 2, it sold in New York at 16½; on the following Thursday at 15½;

and on the next day at 13. This was the lowest point. From that time forward, the financial world seemed to gain confidence in the men who were handling the situation. The stock advanced—but very slowly.

That 13 was almost the low point for all time. Certainly since the dark days of 1838, when there is a record of the sale of forty shares at 23. . . . In the late 'twenties, when the company was hardly born and struggling fitfully for life itself, it is said that its shares sold as low as six and nine dollars. But that was a long time before. In 1881, Baltimore and Ohio had been quoted on exchange at 210; there were known to be private sales at 220. That was the highest point ever reached for the stock.

.   .   .   .

Sunday, March 1, was no church-going day for Cowen and Murray. Literally, they took off their coats and dug into the great task right ahead of them. They had found Judge Goff both able and willing to coöperate with them—to the fullest extent. They informed him of their intention to place the property at once in the best possible physical condition for the handling of a traffic tide that already was beginning to rise once again. The Federal judge told them that he would support them, to the limit.

So it was that, the very next morning, it was announced in the newspapers that the 4500 shop workers of the Baltimore and Ohio of that day (about a thousand of them were employed at Mount Clare, which for long months past had been limping along on a part-time basis) would go to work at once upon a ten-hour day. For weeks before, these men, except when they were not working at all or upon an eight-hour day, had been upon the nine-hour basis. . . . This move on the part of the receivers gave some assurance, not only to Baltimore, but to Cumberland and Grafton and Wheeling and Pittsburgh and other shop centers of the road.

Baltimore, especially, needed this assurance. The *Sun* on

the morning of Monday, March 2, was saying in its editorial columns:

> The appointment of receivers for the Baltimore and Ohio Railroad does not come as a surprise to the business community, but the general regret will be no less keen on that account. The company is the largest Maryland corporation, and the most important. Its history goes back to the time when Baltimore was a small town. It received enormous benefits and grants from the state of Maryland, but it has been the child of the city of Baltimore. . . . The stock and other securities of the company are largely held in this city. The city, itself, is a creditor for a large sum, though happily it disposed of its holdings of stock some years ago; the Hopkins University has a large block of its common stock, beside some thousand shares of the preferred, and the large floating debt of the company is doubtless partly owing to our citizens. There are other business interests all over the city which may be affected and about which there is a natural anxiety.
>
> But there appears no occasion for undue alarm. The receivership is designed solely, as it is stated, to give the company protection from importunate creditors, while it can be rehabilitated. There has never been any lack of business for this great railroad. It has, it is said, been more embarrassed for equipment to handle and transport the traffic offered than by the lack of business. In short, the Baltimore and Ohio is a magnificent property, with abundance of business offered and with full capacity to earn splendid revenues. Its friends believe that, with the wise and conservative management promised by its receivers, the company only needs a few years respite from its creditors to become rehabilitated, and in the meantime, the holders of its shares and securities should not become unduly discouraged by the present conditions which may, in fact, lead to their redemption or restoration.

The kindly soul who penned that editorial was more of a prophet than perhaps he ever had opportunity to realize.

JOHN K. COWEN.
President of the Baltimore and Ohio, 1896–1901.
From a photograph.

"RUSSIA."

The ancient engine sheds back of Mount Clare will awaken many memories amongst older Baltimore and Ohio men. They disappeared in favor of highly modern roundhouses.

All of the comment that ran through the streets of Baltimore that March day was not so kindly. One local banker—very wisely he did not permit his name to be used—expressed himself very definitely on the situation to a *Sun* reporter. He said:

Now that it is all over, we can review some of the mistakes which, in my judgment, led up to the financial crisis of the Baltimore and Ohio.

Of course, it may be ancient history, but it is interesting history. I was closely affiliated with Mr. John W. Garrett for many years and advised him to aid in the construction of the Union Tunnel, at a cost under $1,000,000. He declined and I told him the Baltimore and Potomac and the Philadelphia, Wilmington and Baltimore roads would construct it. They did so. The tunnel which the Baltimore and Ohio, after many years, has been forced to construct, has cost nearly $10,000,000.

I beseeched Mr. Garrett to buy the Philadelphia, Wilmington and Baltimore road. I got him in the notion to do so but the opportunity to purchase was lost. He told me he could parallel the P. W. & B. for $8,000,000. The cost was in the neighborhood of $25,000,000 but Mr. Garrett was not an engineer and his estimate was only guesswork. The Baltimore and Ohio has absorbed many other roads and in doing so has assumed obligations far beyond the values of the roads. Notably was this the case with the Pittsburgh and Western, which has been a burden upon the Baltimore and Ohio ever since its purchase.

The banker did not prove to be half so good a prophet as the editor. For the day was to come—and not long thereafter —when the Pittsburgh and Western alone, as part of the important main Chicago stem of Baltimore and Ohio, was to prove itself well worth all that it had cost—and more besides.

.   .   .   .

One of Mr. Cowen's first moves, to which Mr. Murray and the court gave cordial approval, was to bring in the dilapidated old freight cars from along the right of way, and to place them in good running order once again. Paint gangs went out along the line. And the passenger trains, for the first time in recent years, began to run on time, or nearly so. While Murray turned his immediate attention to getting loadings for the freights.

More important still was the announcement, within the first week of the receivership, that a thousand brand-new box cars and coal cars were being ordered for early delivery. Before the receivers were to lay down their work three years later as finished, 15,350 box cars, 6750 wooden gondola cars, 6000 pressed-steel ones, 310 passenger and miscellaneous cars and 216 locomotives were to be added to the road's rolling fleet. Enough equipment, in itself, for a good-sized railroad. And all in addition to extensive repairs to the older rolling stock. In the comparatively dull summer of '96, Cowen and Murray gave what was said to be the largest steel rail order ever given in America, up to that time, and at the lowest price per ton. They purchased 123,010 tons of rail, at a total cost of $2,142,-132; and had the satisfaction of seeing steel advance from six to nine dollars a ton, before they were done with their tenure of office. [1]

With the new rails, went $1,200,000 for cross ties and more than $500,000 for ballast. A tidy item of $750,000 was expended upon new bridges and a huge one of $12,000,000 upon the labor that installed all these improvements. Over $35,000,000 in all was expended. . . . Mount Royal Station was completed and opened, and Camden, with its fine new steel train sheds, completely rebuilded. Cleveland had a new depot . . . and so did many other cities on the system. A physically new Baltimore and Ohio was being created. For the receivers were not content merely to relay the lines—in many cases they straightened and corrected the alignment, radically and

[1] In that brief thirty months, locomotive prices advanced from two to three thousand dollars over those under which they had contracted for their motive power.

materially. While miles of brand-new railroad were graded and laid down.

. . . .

Yet, far more important even than these great endeavors, was the successful accomplishment of the great goal of the receivers—the saving of the company from a foreclosure upon its property and a complete reorganization. In this point, very much more was at stake than might appear upon the surface. It will be recalled that the state of Maryland, in chartering the Baltimore and Ohio, had conferred upon it valuable tax exemption privileges. . . . Afterwards, the commonwealth, more than once, had repented of its generosity and had gone into the courts to recover taxes from the railroad company, but the stout charter that John V. L. McMahon had obtained for the railroad in the very hour of its birth firmly stood against these raids. There seemed to be no question at all in legal minds that foreclosure and reorganization would forfeit this ancient charter. And so force Baltimore and Ohio to begin life again; on an entirely new and far less satisfactory basis. So that charter was the one essential thing to be saved —at any reasonable cost.

In the end, company and charter stood—as firmly as that old rock of Gibraltar. For one of the few times in all history, a great railroad was forced into bankruptcy and, within three brief years, emerged from it; with its honored name and charter alike unchanged, its shares and other securities higher in value than they had been for years before. Receivership for the Baltimore and Ohio had been changed from tragedy into victory.

. . . .

At the beginning, it was not so easy.

Baltimore—all the other communities through which the road passed—was frankly skeptical of the situation. In some of the smaller places, local sheriffs got out executions against whatever property they might lay their hands upon. In at least one instance, a locomotive was attached legally, and physically was chained to the track. In Baltimore, there was a great deal of suspicion and unrest. A local protective committee was formed among security holders. There were bitterness, recriminations and suspicions.

Gradually, the bitterness and suspicions were alleviated. Cowen and Murray—suave, diplomatic, capable—created confidence; first in themselves, and then in the property that they were guiding. Moreover, business was coming in upon the line again—in a volume that it had not known for years. In April, 1896, it was known that the earnings were running $3000 a day ahead of what had come to be considered as normal for the road. Even in March of that year, the total earnings of the property were $42,000 over March of the preceding year, which had been considered rather good. The $23,944,781, which already we have seen as gross earnings for the fiscal year of 1896, rose in 1897 to be $25,582,122; took another jump in 1898 to $27,722,787, and in 1899—the year when the receivers were dismissed and the property returned to its owners—this had become $29,260,000. The following year, the gross was over $35,877,500. The great crisis had been turned successfully.

.   .   .   .

Yet, at no time was it as easy as it may read upon these pages.

At the beginning of the receivership, it had been hoped that the affiliated Baltimore and Ohio properties—Baltimore and Ohio Southwestern; Pittsburgh and Western; Pittsburgh, Cleveland and Toledo; Valley Railroad of Ohio; Staten Island Rapid Transit; and Pittsburgh and West Virginia; all of these then operated as separate roads, but, with the exception of the Staten Island property, since then merged into the parent company—might be saved a similar embarrassment. The very able general counsel of the road at that time, Hugh L.

Bond, Jr., had succeeded, but a short time before, in saving the Baltimore and Ohio the Chicago Terminal, by thrusting it into a receivership and then having the parent Baltimore and Ohio buy it in on foreclosure, before a rich western road, whose mouth watered for that treasured terminal, could place its hand upon it. . . . It was not possible, however, to save these other smaller roads. Receivers were, in turn, appointed for them; and soon after they, too, emerged from their receiverships, they were closely absorbed in the reincarnate Baltimore and Ohio.

.   .   .   .

At the time of the appointment of the receivers, the capital stock of the Baltimore and Ohio consisted of a par value of $25,000,000 in common stock (of which the Garrett family still owned some 60,000 shares) and $3,000,000 in first preferred, and $2,000,000 in second preferred. The company emerged from the receivership—June 30, 1899—with a capital stock of $45,000,000 common and $60,000,000 in four per cent noncumulative preferred, in addition to a funded debt of $141,000,000 at an average interest rate of but something over three and one-half per cent.

The thing seems astounding.

More than $35,000,000 had been spent upon the radical betterment of the line in the preceding forty months, and the only assessment upon the stockholders had been one of twenty dollars a share, for which each of them had received preferred stock which had accrued in value before the certificates could be printed and sent them.

So ended one of the most phenomenal receiverships in all railroad history.

.   .   .   .

The old ship had come through hard seas and shallow waters, had touched bottom, but had not foundered upon it. While she had rested upon the shoals, she had been refitted and was in a better position than ever before in her history to sail forth once again. Cowen and Murray, aided by some of the ablest financiers in the land—amongst them William Salomon, James Speyer, Jacob H. Schiff, E. H. Harriman and Charles Steele of New York and Alexander Brown of Baltimore—had set her firmly upon her keel. There was a significant group of new names in her ownership—amongst them, those of Philip D. Armour, Marshall Field, Norman B. Ream and James J. Hill. . . . Mr. Hill, in particular, was showing a kindly eye to the property. He sent one of his brilliant young lieutenants, Frederick D. Underwood—who had made a remarkable record in the construction of the Soo Line—to the Baltimore and Ohio, to become its vice-president in charge of operation.

Mr. Underwood did not remain many months with Baltimore and Ohio. He left the company soon after, becoming president of the Erie Railroad, a property with which he remained as its undisputed head for a quarter of a century; in which time he rebuilded and well reëstablished that historic property. Almost coincident with the departure of Mr. Underwood from the Baltimore and Ohio, very early in 1901, the "Chicago group," as it became known, sold its sizable holdings to the Pennsylvania Railroad. The sale these gentlemen made to the Pennsylvania was not at a sacrifice. The syndicate had purchased its common stock at 26 or thereabouts; it sold at a point close to par. . . . The Pennsylvania seemingly was glad to pay any reasonable price for the shares of its competitor. When the coup had been executed, it could afford to sit back in its great offices in Broad Street Station, Philadelphia, and laugh. . . . It had swallowed the canary.

. . . .

There was little laughing in the headquarters of the Baltimore and Ohio those days.

Mr. Cowen, with his property thoroughly rebuilt and rehabilitated in every way, with its constituent roads more firmly welded to the parent than ever before in its history, with traffic pouring in upon them all in unprecedented volume and all the while steadily increasing, could see but little future for

Baltimore and Ohio as a Cinderella for the powerful Pennsylvania. He was in a most unpleasant plight—which presently was to be increased, immeasurably.

There came a morning—in May, 1901—which brought a letter from a high officer of the Pennsylvania to his desk, and to his personal attention. He tore it open. It was brief, and to the point. The high officer of the Pennsylvania "regretted" —very much regretted—that it had been found advisable, necessary in fact, to have an operating man, rather than a legal one, at the head of Baltimore and Ohio. While they had every confidence in Mr. Cowen's great ability and in his loyalty to the property . . . etc. . . . etc. . . . they, "regretfully," would be compelled to ask for his resignation as president of Baltimore and Ohio. In token, however, of his able service and his great abilities, they would be pleased to have him continue, indefinitely, as general counsel of the road, at the same salary that he had received as president.

Cowen read that letter, again and again; each syllable burned its way into his very soul. . . . All day long he sat at his desk, answering questions that were put to him, absent-mindedly and only in monosyllables. . . . That was the last day he ever sat at that desk.

He went away from it, not to return. The same cruel fate that had been allotted to his college mate and friend, Robert Garrett, was to be dealt to him. From that very moment, he was to break; first mentally, then physically. A really great mind was to be overclouded by the shadows. . . . He traveled far to regain his health—to South America, to Europe, all the way around the world. But it was too late. The thing that was taken from him was never to be returned. When he came back to Baltimore—not so many months later—it was to return to a sick bed, from which he was never to arise. He died April 26, 1904.

.   .   .   .

On June 1, 1901, Leonor F. Loree became president of the

Baltimore and Ohio. Mr. Loree, then and now a most distinguished American railroader, not only as a practical operating man and executive head, but a skilled student and writer upon the theoretical phases of transport, had spent eighteen years in Pennsylvania service, rising all the while in the ranks of that railroad from the post of an assistant engineer to be vice-president of its western lines, with his headquarters at Pittsburgh. In those eighteen years, he had become well schooled in Pennsylvania practice and tradition. An indefatigable worker, a brilliant executive, he was fitted to be chief lieutenant of Broad Street Station in Baltimore. As such, he began to apply himself, manfully, to a man-sized task.

CHAPTER XII

THE TURN OF THE CENTURY

Baltimore and Ohio in the Southwest—Early Troubles of the Ohio and Mississippi—General George B. McClellan as Its President —Resigns to Enter the War—Construction Difficulties—A Change in Track Gauge.

THE beginning of the present century found the Baltimore and Ohio Railroad in far stronger position than ever before in its history. In the entire seventy-five years of its progress, the company had never before enjoyed such a flow of traffic. For this, it was largely indebted to the energy and the resourcefulness of its traffic vice-president, Oscar G. Murray. Mr. Murray made vigorous use of traffic methods then much in vogue everywhere in the land, but which were not always reflected in the tariffs. The revival of business following the Spanish-American War was another factor. In addition, Baltimore and Ohio had never before been in such excellent physical condition to handle heavy business. With lines straightened and grades reduced, with new track put down and new bridges put up, locomotives and cars purchased (or rebuilded) by the hundreds and the thousands, Baltimore and Ohio finally was coming toward a position to take its rightful place among the railroad giants of the land. On January 1, 1901, it consisted of 3221 miles of main line, of which more than 800 miles were double-tracked. Upon these, there were in operation 1034 steam locomotives and four electric ones, 696 passenger cars and 50,983 freight and service cars. The total earnings of the system for the year which ended June 30, 1901, had reached the sizable figure of $47,971,223.99; of which, $35,553,871.87 had been earned by the freight traffic of the company; $9,054,601.53 by its passenger service.[1]

These earnings for the first full year of the present century now included, for the first time in the history of the company, those of the Baltimore and Ohio Southwestern. The beginnings of this latter company we saw in these pages long ago; how, toward the end of the 'fifties, the somewhat successful Marietta and Cincinnati and the distinctly unsuccessful Ohio and Mississippi were completed and linked; and, after a mighty celebration in '57, had become the long permanent southwestern arm of Baltimore and Ohio; by which it reached both Cincinnati and St. Louis, and, at a little later time, Louisville also.[2]

The peculiar and extended financial troubles of the Ohio and Mississippi—and, to a lesser extent, the Marietta and Cincinnati—are not to be recounted again in detail in this record. It is enough to say that, once the celebrations and the junkets

---

[1] This ratio of four to one between the freight and passenger revenues of the company became, year after year, so little varying as to be an almost standardized figure.

[2] The original Baltimore and Ohio Southwestern Railroad was an outgrowth of the Marietta and Cincinnati (first incorporated as the Belpre and Cincinnati) and the Hillsborough and Cincinnati railroads, both chartered with the intent of constructing lines of railroad between Cincinnati and other Ohio River towns; Wheeling being the objective point in the case of the former and Parkersburg in the case of the latter, to connect at these points with eastern lines under construction.

The Hillsborough and Cincinnati constructed that part of its projected line between Hillsborough and Loveland, Ohio, 37 miles; 16 miles of which, between Blanchester and Loveland, form part of the main line of the Baltimore and Ohio Southwestern. Under a contract of union made in 1854, the Hillsborough and Cincinnati corporation was absorbed into the Marietta and Cincinnati and its property acquired by purchase in 1861.

The Marietta and Cincinnati constructed its line from Blanchester to Harmar, (Marietta) Ohio, opening this line through for traffic April 4, 1857, connection with the Northwestern Virginia Railroad (Parkersburg Branch) being made through ferriage of nine miles from Harmar to Parkersburg. Access was first gained to Cincinnati through use of the Little Miami Railroad from Loveland to Cincinnati.

that had announced the completion of the "American Central Line" through from the upper Ohio to the Mississippi had been entirely finished, and the last noisy guest returned east, the promoters of these linked railroads faced a practical situation, without much balm in it.   Theirs was destined to be no bed of roses.

Particularly was this true of the Ohio and Mississippi. Within three years after the great Cincinnati celebration, its Eastern Division, extending from that city to Vincennes, Illinois, was in the hands of a federal receiver.   Two years later, the Western Division, connecting Vincennes with East St. Louis, was in a similar plight.   For five years, trustees struggled with the problem of making profitable a railroad, heretofore unprofitable.   And it was not until November 4, 1867, that these men were able to combine the Eastern and Western divisions—which, up to that time, had been operated as two separate railroad companies—into what was to be known as the Ohio and Mississippi *Railway*.   Under this title it was to have a new try at life.   The first organization had been the Ohio and Mississippi *Railroad*.   A slight change in terminology not infrequently may indicate a large change in organization.

.   .   .   .

In these few paragraphs, there is but little reflection of a terrible struggle being made through long months, and even years, to operate properly a new railroad, top-heavy with financial obligations.   To the men who attempted the task, must be given a large due of real praise.   Among them was George B. McClellan, who, a very little later, attained a real eminence in the Civil War.   For a very short time, he was president of the Ohio and Mississippi, Eastern Division.   As such, his name appears signed to its annual report for 1860-61. When the next report appeared—a year later—the office of president was vacant.   General McClellan was at the head of the Army of the Potomac.   He did not return after the war to the Ohio and Mississippi.   By that time, the road was again

becoming involved.   The report of William D. Griswold, made
September 9, 1867, to Allan Campbell as chairman of the
trustees, gives a fairly accurate picture of it at the end of the
war.   In part, this reads:

> . . . The condition of the Ohio and Mississippi Railroad,
> from Cincinnati to St. Louis, was such, in the spring of 1864,
> that nearly all that has been done and furnished in work,
> labor and materials upon the track, and upon engines and
> cars, has been simply an expenditure for construction.   The
> grade, bridges, culverts and other structures appurtenant to
> the track had been so imperfect in their original construction
> and were so dilapidated from that imperfect state that the idea
> of repairs cannot be attached to the work required upon them.
> The extraordinary repairs upon them during these three and
> a half years has been a work of construction and reconstruc-
> tion, and in that time has amounted to a million and a half
> of dollars.

But, Mr. Griswold opines, the roadbed and track and
structures from Cincinnati to Vincennes are now (1867) in
generally good condition.   "As compared with other western
roads," it is in excellent order.   Much bridge work has been
done, and, at Seymour, Indiana, there is a new "good and
substantial enginehouse and machine-shop."   But the Western
Division has not been improved so rapidly; there has been a
distressing lack of ballast.   It had been, he says, "in so
wretched a condition in the spring of 1864 that it could hardly
be called a railroad."   Since then, despite the difficulties, there
had been considerable ballasting done and 500 tons of new iron
laid down, in addition to about thirty miles of rerolled rails.
Still he believes that many, many miles of new rail are still
needed—urgently.

Difficulties, indeed!

One has but to read carefully the report of that general
superintendent of the early Ohio and Mississippi to gain a faint
idea of some of them.   At one point he says:

THE EADS BRIDGE ACROSS THE MISSISSIPPI RIVER AT ST. LOUIS.
It was the first bridge to span the Father of Waters at that important point.
From a photograph.

THE ROUNDHOUSE AT MARTINSBURG, WEST VIRGINIA.
For years a landmark on the Main Line of Baltimore and Ohio.

... We have been seriously injured by several disastrous floods. Twice our track has been overflowed by the swell of the Ohio River [then, as now, it followed the river for more than 25 miles west of Cincinnati], subjecting us to serious expense and delay as well as loss of business. In August, 1866, an extraordinary and sudden swell of the small streams which flow into the Ohio swept out a large culvert under the road, making an enormous chasm. All the loss and damage occasioned by this catastrophe cannot be justly estimated at less than $75,000. In the following month, another and similar flood swept away in an hour, the bridge over the Miami of four spans, of 210 feet each, with its piers of masonry.

Since then, the ruined bridge had not yet been replaced, although Griswold was making steady attempts to finance it. The new structure would be builded of masonry and iron and would cost not less than $350,000. In the meantime, the Ohio and Mississippi (still a broad-gauge line) laid a third rail along the standard-gauge line of the Indianapolis and Cincinnati Railroad (now a part of the Big Four) for the nine miles between North Bend and Lawrenceburg, and for five weeks it detoured its trains over this route. All of this was not an inexpensive piece of business. The detour arrangement cost $9000 a month, and Mr. Griswold was sure that the entire expense of the disaster would not be less than three quarters of a million dollars.

Yet, he was not entirely pessimistic about the situation. He says, a little later:

... Our cars are, generally, in first-rate condition. Since I took the road we have increased the stock, by building at the shops more than 200 new cars, and have rebuilt all the old ones, saving of them such parts only as were sound. . . .

Of the road's eighty locomotives, all but six or eight were serviceable. Superintendent Griswold had rebuilt a number of engines, and had purchased six new ones. He wished to make other improvements to the property; bettering its terminals and putting a fence along each side of the right of way for the entire length of the line.   "The large amount of stock killed by our trains makes this an imperative and pressing necessity," he warns.   He also pleads for the construction of a tunnel at a point on the road known as Willow Valley, where such a bore —which will cost, he estimates, about $100,000—will not only straighten and improve the line, but will also shorten it, a full two miles.

But a hundred thousand dollars is a hundred thousand dollars.   Do not forget that.   And the Ohio and Mississippi has not a financial reputation that renders it particularly easy at this time to borrow money.   Yet, Mr. Griswold shows that the financial condition of the property is by no means so bad as has been generally felt.   To quote him again:

> . . . The incumbrances by mortgage or otherwise resting upon this road are less than $11,000 per mile of its length, and when the corporate reorganization now in progress shall be consummated, it will be entirely free from embarrassment, free from every form of debt except by mortgage, and the incumbrance by mortgage will be less than $18,000 per mile. . . . In this condition, with a present annual earning of $3,400,000, no road in the country can furnish a bond of more solid and reliable security than the Ohio and Mississippi.

At no time does Griswold's faith in the future of the road lag.   He firmly believes that, by its position and general course, it offers great promise.   It traverses a country over a distance of 340 miles as yet thinly populated, and not one quarter developed.

> It points westward to regions, vast in extent and fertility, which already, for a thousand miles, are traversed by railroads, over which will rapidly pour into them increasing populations whose enterprise and thrift will react eastward and over this line of road. . . .   Its situation is such that no competition

between its terminal cities will ever be created against it, other than by Indianapolis and Terre Haute which already has existed for several years.

Mr. Griswold closes his report by urging certain special lines of extension for the property; particularly, the construction of a branch south to Louisville, an important city with its own extensive railroad ramifications; the building of a cut-off, twenty miles in length, from North Bend across to Hamilton and on to Dayton, there to connect with the broad-gauge Atlantic and Great Western (the present-day Erie), to save an hour and a half in the running time of through trains between New York and St. Louis; and the laying down of a third rail for the sixty-five miles between Odin and East St. Louis, so as to enable the standard-gauge trains of the Illinois Central to enter the latter city and so form a better competition with the Mississippi River steamboats, still in the high heyday of their glory. . . . A slight complication of trackage, to be sure. What a peck of trouble that variance in gauge used to make!

· · · · · · ·

Only one of these things finally was done:

The line from North Vernon, Indiana, for fifty-three miles to Jeffersonville—just across the Ohio from Louisville—was constructed under the charter of the Fort Wayne and Southern Railroad Company, and was first opened for operation in April, 1869. In 1888, an extension of this branch, seven and a half miles long and connecting it with the great new Kentucky and Indiana Bridge over the river from New Albany to Louisville, was put into service.[1] Thereafter, Baltimore and Ohio trains touched the soil of Kentucky and had direct entrance into the city of Louisville.

The present-day Springfield Division, crossing the main line of the Ohio and Mississippi at right angles and running from Beardstown to Shawneetown, Illinois, a distance of 228 miles,

[1] This extension was chartered as the New Albany and Eastern Railway.

was constructed under the charters of the Illinois and South-eastern and the Pana, Springfield and Northwestern railroad companies,[1] and was put into service March 27, 1871. . . . The little Bedford Branch, twelve miles in length, did not come into full use until 1893.

By that year, the Ohio and Mississippi was becoming but a memory. Yet it had had its other years of vicissitude. Another receivership was to be undergone. It was to spend the eight years between November 17, 1876, and April 1, 1884, in receivers' hands, although without a foreclosure being achieved against it. . . . It seemed, for a long time, as if all the efforts of the men who were handling it could not make it profitable. Not even the reduction of its broad-gauge track to standard gauge.

This, of itself, was a task requiring nicety and skill. . . . There was published, a few years later, an account of this difficult piece of railroad engineering which is not without its interest here. This account reads, in part:

The line, as originally built, was six-foot gauge and it was later determined to change it to standard [sic] four-foot nine-inch gauge. This change was made on the main line between Cincinnati and St. Louis on Sunday, July 13, 1871, the Louis-ville Division having been changed the Sunday previous. At daylight three gangs of men began work on each section of about three miles in length, the first gang drawing spikes and throwing rails, the second gang spiking and the third gang setting rails to gauge and lining up track. Some sections had their work completed by noon, and others by about 2 or 3 P.M. The first train passed over the track at 3:40 P.M., the change of gauge of the entire 340 miles, Cincinnati to East St. Louis, having been made in about eight hours.

About eight or nine months previous to this change, work was begun cutting down engines and trucks to cars. The former were white-leaded and stored at Cochran shops until a day or two prior to the change. When the gauge was changed,

[1] Consolidated in 1869 as the Springfield and Southeastern Railway.

trucks were changed to cars very rapidly by means of hydraulic jacks, and there was little or no interruption to traffic on account of the change having been made.

Three years later, a step only second in importance to this was made when, James B. Eads having finished his remarkable bridge over the Mississippi at St. Louis, Ohio and Mississippi passenger trains were permitted to pass over it and through its adjoining tunnel into the Union Station and the heart of one of the greatest traffic centers in all America. Freights were still halted at the waterside at East St. Louis, however; which, in common with other eastern trunk-line systems, still remains the practical commercial terminal of the Baltimore and Ohio Railroad at St. Louis, even though all of its passenger trains, through and local, come into and out of the huge terminal station there, today crossing the river either by the old Eads Bridge or the newer Merchants one.

．　　．　　．　　．　　．　　．　　．

The original Baltimore and Ohio Southwestern Railroad will be recalled as an outgrowth of the Marietta and Cincinnati, whose easterly stretches had long since been relocated so as to bring it into Parkersburg over the Ohio River bridge and a direct connection there with the parent Baltimore and Ohio. When the Ohio and Mississippi was formally taken over by Baltimore interests and (November 1, 1893) merged with the first B. & O. S. W., the name of the consolidated line was changed to the Baltimore and Ohio Southwestern Railway Company, and the Ohio and Mississippi then ceased to have a corporate existence. . . . In turn, the Baltimore and Ohio Southwestern Railway was to be brought into the Baltimore and Ohio Railroad, although its separate corporate existence was not to cease. But this was not to be until several years later. For a number of years, the Baltimore and Ohio Southwestern continued to be operated as a distinct railroad; although by many of the same officers as the parent company.

CHAPTER XIII

A NEW MASTER AT BALTIMORE

Leonor F. Loree Becomes President of Baltimore and Ohio—Many
Additions and Improvements—The Pennsylvania Overlordship
—Mr. Gould Enters Pittsburgh—And Baltimore and Ohio
Buys, and Sells, Coal Properties.

A REAL railroad it was, indeed, that Baltimore and Ohio
that confronted Mr. Leonor F. Loree and the Pennsylvania
control behind him there at the turn of the century. Within
a half-dozen years, much had been done to it. Yet, not all had
been achieved that was possible. On the contrary, although
a great deal had been accomplished in the rehabilitation of the
property, much of this was yet to be classed as mere beginnings.
As foundation work, Loree, in the two and a half years of his
tenure of office, was to go ahead steadily with this work of reconstruction. A highly practical operating man and engineer,
he studied carefully, along his own lines of thought and
method, the possibilities for the development of Baltimore and
Ohio, and prepared a twenty-year program for its improvement and expansion. At the very outset, the problem was
to develop the property adequately for the handling of a business, which already threatened congestion; to the point where
the disagreeable freight embargo might have to be invoked.

The greatest immediate necessity of the road, Loree felt,
was a system of intermediate interchange freight yards. With
these properly installed, there could be handled, without
increase of main-trackage facilities, a far heavier traffic and

much delay eliminated and cost reduced. Accordingly, he built five of these yard equipments—at Keyser and Fairmont, West Virginia; at Holloway, Ohio; and at Connellsville and New Castle, Pennsylvania. These were highly modern yards, each with the newest type of well lighted, well ventilated and well tooled roundhouse. They cost approximately a million dollars apiece, but, in Mr. Loree's opinion, they were, because of the fact that they had been placed upon the periphery of a great circle of Baltimore and Ohio trackage in the heart of the system, worth several times that sum. Each of these new ganglia, operated in conjunction with its fellows, gained a greatly added value. . . . New yards were also built at Demler and at Try Street, Pittsburgh. A highly modern engine house, power plant and shop layout were installed at Glenwood (Pittsburgh); engine facilities at the greatly congested terminals of Brunswick, Cumberland, Grafton and Newark (Ohio) were substantially improved; a new boiler shop was erected at Mount Clare; new shop machinery and tools provided at all classified and running-repair points; while plans were prepared for a large central locomotive repair and manufacturing shop to be erected near Wheeling, the center of gravity of the entire system, as well as for new engine terminal facilities at Philadelphia, Baltimore, Brunswick, Grafton, Newark, Cleveland, Cincinnati and elsewhere. All of these, except the proposed plant at Wheeling, gradually were built.[1]

In addition to all of this, the new president of Baltimore and Ohio worked out important grade reductions, line revisions and double-tracking; thus greatly improving the road movement of equipment. Between Relay and Brunswick, this revision work eliminated not less than 1700 degrees of curvature. At the same time, the rather mean grades over

---

[1] As a matter of fact and of record, many of these improvements were planned and some of them were started under the administrations immediately preceding Mr. Loree's. Mr. J. M. Graham, the distinguished chief engineer of Baltimore and Ohio at the beginning of the present century, himself planned many of these works. His foresight and vision in these matters cannot be overestimated.

Mount Airy were reduced, substantially.   Loree built a low-grade (.3 per cent) line around the end of South Mountain, and an interchange yard at Cumbo.   This last gave a second pathway of car exchange with the Philadelphia and Reading, and so expedited freight movement. . . .   Grades on the Chicago Division were cut in half.   The same thing was done on the former Cleveland, Lorain and Wheeling.   In both of these places, the maximum grade now was brought to .3 per cent.

Double-tracking excited Mr. Loree's attention.   Baltimore and Ohio stood gravely in need of it.   He built, just to the south of Cumberland, the Patterson Creek Cut-off; which, with a tunnel, 4120 feet in length, shortened the main line between Baltimore and Cincinnati by more than ten miles.   Cut-offs were built on the Cleveland, Lorain and Wheeling at Pigeon Run and at Medina.

On the Chicago Division, 52 miles of double track were laid; on the Connellsville Division, 38 more; on the Pittsburgh, another 38; between Connellsville and Braddock, 48 miles of third and fourth track were completed.   Between New Castle Junction and Struthers, 14 miles were built; while, between Niles and Cuyahoga Falls, 41 miles of improved double track were laid down. . . .   In fact, an actual new line, with 14 miles of tangent in it, was constructed between Youngstown and Akron, eliminating many grade crossings and other operating difficulties.[1]   In this last arrangement, the Pennsylvania shared.   It was endeavoring at that time to better its Pittsburgh–Cleveland line.   To accomplish this, it had decided some time before to build a cut-off of its own, west from Youngstown. It went so far in its project as to buy a right of way, parallel to

---

[1] Minor pieces of double-tracking at this time were at Chicago Junction, 23 miles, and at Holloway, 27 miles.   From Cherry Run to Harpers Ferry, 32 miles of new lines were completed, as well as 13 miles from Lemley Junction to Buckhannon.   In coöperation with the Pennsylvania, a practical double-track operation was created between Massillon and Sterling, Ohio, 24 miles. . . .   Other pieces of constructive work done under the Loree administration comprised the fine new passenger station at Wheeling and a radical reconstruction of the great bridges over the Ohio at Benwood and at Parkersburg.

LEONOR F. LOREE.
President of the Baltimore and Ohio, 1901–1904.
From a photograph.

The First Mallet in America—Baltimore and Ohio *No. 2400.*

Now known as the *John E. Muhlfeld*, after her designer, this fine piece of motive power went into service on Sand Patch Grade, at the beginning of the century, and is still (1927) in steady use.

From a photograph.

and adjoining that of the new Baltimore and Ohio line beyond
that city.   But it never laid down tracks upon that right of
way.   It found itself able to make an arrangement advantageous to itself to run its Pittsburgh–Cleveland fast trains
over the new route of the Baltimore road.   Much money was
saved to both railroads by this arrangement.   Yet, it is doubt-
ful whether it ever could have been accomplished without the
Pennsylvania domination of the Baltimore and Ohio.   Put this
down, therefore, as a beneficial result of that domination.

The purchase of the Ohio River Railroad might not be so
accredited.   Preparations for it had begun before the coming
of Mr. Loree.[1]   This last line, running parallel to the river for
208 miles southwest from Wheeling, was a comparative newcomer upon the railroad map of the land.   Standard Oil
interests promoted and built it.   For a number of years, the
late H. H. Rogers was its president.   It was incorporated in
1881 as the Wheeling, Parkersburg and Charleston (the name
was changed the following year), and, two years later, actual
construction was begun on the line, the gangs working south
from Benwood.   At no time was the road embarrassed for
funds, and work progressed rapidly.   Smart little towns in the
Ohio Valley—Sistersville was one of them—that never before
had seen the locomotive nor heard the sharp call of its whistle,
but had been accustomed all the years to the sonorous call of

---

[1] The arrangement to purchase this important link of railroad was one of the
final acts of Mr. Cowen's administration; although the special committee to report
on the feasibility of the transaction did not render its report until Mr. Loree had
been president for more than a month.   It reported that an agreement had
been reached (with H. H. Rogers and Charles Pratt and Company) to purchase
30,171 shares (51 per cent) of the outstanding stock of the Ohio River Railroad
Company and the entire line and property of the West Virginia Short Line Railroad Company, as constructed from New Martinsville to Clarksburg, West
Virginia, including also 204 acres of land at New Martinsville, for $7,500,000.
Other shares of the Ohio River Railroad Company were to be sold to Baltimore
and Ohio at $50 per share.   In payment for all of this—and some minor proper-
ties—Baltimore and Ohio arranged to issue notes for one year, from July 1, 1901,
at an interest rate of 4 per cent. . . .   The entire arrangement was ratified by
the board of the Baltimore and Ohio very early in July, 1901.

the steamboat as she poked her nose around the bend, were at last to be reached by the railroad. They welcomed it gaily. . . . On January 16, 1884, operation of the Ohio River Railroad began between Wheeling and Parkersburg, and both of these towns had once again the thrills of thirty years before, when the railroad first had come to them.

From Parkersburg, construction went steadily forward to Point Pleasant, which was reached late in 1886; the first regular trains running over the extension on the eighth day of January following. . . . Within the next twelve months, the line had been completed through to its announced terminal—a connection point with the Chesapeake and Ohio Railway near the new town of Huntington, West Virginia. When this had been done, the Ohio River had been closely paralleled by railroads along its banks, all the way from Steubenville to Cincinnati; in fact, to Aurora, Indiana.

The chief traffic of the Ohio River Railroad, at its inception, was oil. Which was logical, inasmuch as it had been builded, at the outset, almost as a direct accessory of the Standard Oil enterprise. Gradually, other business developed. A passenger traffic flowered; frequent and regular trains were better than the infrequent and highly irregular steamboats; faster, too, even though it was written in an early report of the company:

> . . . The practice of stopping so many trains on signal at farm crossings and wherever a passenger desired to alight has been discontinued; thus the wear and tear to the equipment by reason of these numerous stops has been done away with. . . .

The same report announces the securing of two new Pullman parlor cars for the passenger trains. Eventually, there were parlor cars on four day trains and sleeping cars on the night ones, finally running not only out of Wheeling but out of the Union Station, Pittsburgh, over the tracks of the Pennsylvania. . . . Gradually, this last road gained hand over the Ohio River Railroad, until the day came—at about the beginning of the century—when it was bruited about that the Pennsylvania finally had acquired it, for its very own.

Yet, if the Pennsylvania did at one time actually control, if not own, the Ohio River property, it did not long hold on to it. A tacit agreement was reached between it and the Baltimore and Ohio that the former should not strike its lines directly south; nor the latter, directly north. With this truce in mind, the Ohio River Railroad was transferred to the Baltimore and Ohio, of which it has since become a connecting link and a very valuable integral part.

. . . .

Mr. Loree also acquired for Baltimore and Ohio the remaining outstanding shares in Pittsburgh and Western, additional shares of the Cleveland, Lorain and Wheeling, and a large interest in the Philadelphia and Reading, which held—and still holds—the stock control of the Central Railroad of New Jersey. These last two roads formed—and still form—the entrance line for Baltimore and Ohio into the New York metropolitan district. . . . The Reading shares, purchased in 1901, have greatly increased in value.[1]

. . . .

At about this time, Baltimore and Ohio was threatened with invasion by a new competitor; apparently, a very serious one. The so-called Gould interests were preparing to enter its territory. Mr. George Gould, acting through the Wabash,

---

[1] The Philadelphia and Reading, one of the large coal distributing systems of the East, was the owner of 53 per cent of the stock of the Central Railroad of New Jersey, which held extensive terminal facilities in New York harbor. With Baltimore and Ohio, it will be recalled, these two companies long had maintained active traffic relations, including the operation of the Royal Blue Line trains over their tracks between Philadelphia and Jersey City. Mr. Loree felt it most desirable that these relations be made permanent. Therefore, Baltimore and Ohio purchased, for $22,231,313, Reading preferred and common stock of a par value of $27,555,000. A similar amount of stock was purchased at the same time by the New York Central interests.

which already he controlled, had purchased the Cleveland and Wheeling Railroad and he actually was extending it into the very heart of that great traffic center, Pittsburgh. This involved tremendously heavy construction, the building of great embankments, the driving of long tunnels and the construction of a mighty bridge over the Monongahela, almost at the very point where it enters the waters of the Ohio. All of this did not deter Gould. He not only prepared to build on this large scale, but he actually completed his project; even to the finishing of a sizable passenger station close to the historic Point.

For this enterprise, he had reorganized the Cleveland and Wheeling into the Wabash-Pittsburgh Terminal Railway (now the Pittsburgh and West Virginia). Next, he purchased the long-existent Western Maryland, which in its inception also had been aided financially by the city of Baltimore and the state of Maryland. He then announced his intention of connecting these two companies by a link of railroad. This caused much apprehension in the offices of Baltimore and Ohio. When it was further found that Gould actually was preparing to buy the properties of the Fairmont Coal Company as an aid to this plan, Loree secured the purchase of that property, the Somerset and the Clarksburg Coal companies by the Consolidation Coal Company. For many years, Baltimore and Ohio had held a very substantial interest in the Consolidation, and now Mr. Loree purchased 13,701 additional shares of that company, so that the road owned 53,532 shares out of a total of 100,000 shares. It now found itself in possession of what was then perhaps the largest acreage of unmined coal held at that time in one ownership in the entire country. Later, as will be seen in a moment, it was compelled to sell its control of the Consolidation.

In ways similar to this, Mr. Gould soon began to find himself blocked, at nearly every turn. Unsuccessfully, he fought his stout opponents. Gradually, his imposing dream of a single transcontinental railroad (to be composed of Western

Maryland, Wabash, Missouri Pacific, Denver and Rio Grande and Western Pacific) under a single management faded. . . . His eastern properties slipped out of his fingers; then followed, in due course, the westerly ones.   He retired from active railroad management, and the name of Gould became merely a part of the dramatic railroad history of this continent.

·   ·   ·   ·   ·   ·   ·

An outstanding feature of Mr. Loree's administration of Baltimore and Ohio was the introduction upon the road, in 1904, of the first compound articulated Mallet locomotive ever built and operated in the United States. This engine was designed by John E. Muhlfeld, general superintendent of motive power of the road, in conjunction with the American Locomotive Company. It was of the 0-6-6-0 type and weighed, with its tender, 477,870 pounds; having a tractive power of 71,500 pounds—at that time, an almost unheard-of figure.   This engine also incorporated the then new and novel, but now often used large boiler, firebox and grate area; long boiler tubes; high steam pressure; multiple expansion of steam in cylinders; piston valves; and Walschaert valve gear and power reverse gear.[1]

This pioneer Mallet was first placed in service on the Sand Patch Grade of the Pittsburgh Division.   It gave such a good

---

[1] Clifford S. Sims at that time was general manager of Baltimore and Ohio. At Mr. Loree's suggestion, he had taken a house in Eutaw Place, just across from the home of the president.   This enabled the two men to walk downtown together many mornings.   On one of these matutinal jaunts, Loree turned suddenly to Sims and asked him what he knew about the then new Mallet type of locomotive. The general manager replied that there were some in Russia and some in Switzerland; none in the United States.   "Find out about them for me by tomorrow morning," said Mr. Loree.   Sims found out.   A little later, arrangements were made with the American Locomotive Company to build one of the new engines; at the same cost per pound as the other engines that it was then turning out for Baltimore and Ohio. . . . This first Mallet, *No. 2400*, since named the *John E. Muhlfeld*, is now in regular service for the company.   First shown at the St. Louis Exposition in 1904, it was operated at the Fair of the Iron Horse in the autumn of 1927.

account of itself there that eventually others were ordered; for the hard grades of the Main Stem as it crosses the Allegheny Mountains. This, however, was in the Willard administration.

The heavy locomotive, as well as the machine advanced in all its details, always has interested Mr. Loree. For many years, the heaviest engines in the country had carried about 135,000 pounds on the drivers. Before leaving the service of the Pennsylvania, he already had built locomotives of 160,000 pounds on the drivers, which was about the limit of the capacity of the bridges. . . . Other roads were doing likewise. The economies of the large engine were too obvious to be ignored long. . . . The new president of Baltimore and Ohio did more. Shortly before coming to that post, he had journeyed to Mexico, and while there he had ridden on the remarkable Fairlie locomotives then in use upon the steep 5 per cent grades of the Mexican Railway. A little later, he heard of the Mallet and —Selah!—the Mallet came to the Baltimore and Ohio, first of all the railroads of America. Today, there are more than 2050 engines of this type in use on the roads in the United States. Long since, it ceased to be an experiment.

· · · · · · · ·

Cars also interested Loree. The freight car, originally built upon the Baltimore and Ohio to carry about 7000 pounds, up to the time of the Civil War, still carried only about 10,000 pounds. Right afterwards, this capacity was increased, to 20,000 pounds. By 1880, this had reached 40,000 pounds; by 1890, 60,000 pounds. The next five years realized large advances in the carrying capacity. The 100,000-pound car came into universal use and a good many railroads found that a large part of their equipment had been rendered obsolete. . . . During the two and a half years of the Loree administration, the freight cars owned by Baltimore and Ohio increased from 62,992 to 83,532 in number, but this by no means represented the increase in the freight carrying capacity of the property. That story was better to be told in the increased capacity of the individual car units themselves. This it was that made the real addition to the haulage capacity of the road's freight fleet. . . . Similarly, the much increased hauling power of the individual locomotive unit was far more impressive than the increase of the mere numbers of these units (from 1361 to 1839 during the Loree régime).

.　　.　　.　　.　　.　　.　　.

All these things—others, too—are to be placed to the credit of the Loree administration. But some other things—more definite and more concrete—were open to some question. For instance, in the long run, the Pennsylvania compelled the Baltimore and Ohio to sell its large holdings in the Consolidation Coal Company—this was long before the interstate commerce laws had ruled against the ownership of collieries by the railroads—although it found plenty of reasons for keeping its own coal properties. . . . More than this, it had moved with leaden feet in supplying the Baltimore road with modern cars. At the end of the Murray administration and toward the termination of the regency, the controlled property possessed not a single steel passenger car; it was still purchasing wooden passenger coaches, although the Pennsylvania was buying modern steel coaches—by the hundred. Despite the increase of its freight fleet, both in numbers and in capacity, the Baltimore road had but 38 per cent of steel freight equipment, against a much larger percentage upon the lines of the Pennsylvania. . . . Baltimore and Ohio, in no small sense, was Cinderella.

But, worse than all these things, was the blow to the morale. Baltimore and Ohio men, seemingly, had lost the ability to think for themselves. They had become so used to orders and suggestions—direct or intimated—from Broad Street, that their initiative was greatly impaired. In the selling end of the organization, this was particularly noticeable. The traffic officers of the Baltimore company—even a long time after they were freed from Pennsylvania domination—seemed unwilling to take stands, especially in inter-company matters, that would oppose, even in the slightest degree, Broad Street Station. . . . It took long years of effort to bring them out of this mental attitude. In spirit, the Pennsylvania overlordship over Baltimore and Ohio extended a long time after it had, in fact, expired.

·   ·   ·   ·   ·   ·   ·

How came this overlordship to be terminated?

It is an interesting story, and one that can be told within a comparatively short space:

It was ended just before the long-dormant Sherman Act, under a vigorous Rooseveltian influence, began to be exerted against a policy of the railroads all the way across the land to consolidate themselves; in many cases, without regard to public interest or public necessity. . . . Yet, it is but fair to say that it may have come about in an entirely different manner.

The late Logan G. McPherson in his book, *Railroad Freight Rates*, gives this picture of the movement that led to the original acquisition of Baltimore and Ohio by the Pennsylvania. He wrote:

. . . The amalgamation of different railroads, that had been predicted when pooling was abolished by the Interstate Commerce Law, proceeded [this was at the very end of the last century] upon an enlarged scale. To the solid front of the great shippers seeking rate concessions, the railroads found it necessary to present a compact line. This led to the purchase by one railroad company of the stock and securities of another, and the appearance of the same men on the boards of competing companies. This plan, designated as the "Community of Interests," in great measure accomplished its purpose. The cutting of rates was practically obliterated. The giving of rebates was almost entirely abolished. The credit for this achievement belongs to Alexander J. Cassett in higher degree than to any other one man. As general manager and then as vice-president of the Pennsylvania Railroad Company during the period of chaotic competition that brought the "pool" into being, he became entirely familiar with the pressure that the great shippers brought to bear upon the railroads for rebates, and with the vulnerability of the railroads, especially the longer and weaker lines, to their onslaughts. During the seventeen years of exemption from the burdens of routine administration, he remained, as a director of his company, in touch with the progress of events, and conceived and matured the far-reaching plans which he proceeded to work out when he returned to the active service of the Pennsylvania Railroad in 1899, as its president. This was the very time when the extension of the industrial amalgamations gave warning of the increasing power of their managers to force the railroads to their terms, and when, as a result of the intervening legislation, the practice of rebating had become vicious because no longer general, but special, and no longer done as a matter of course, but secretly and carefully concealed. With the great resources at his command, interests to give a voice in the management were purchased in the Baltimore and Ohio, Chesapeake and Ohio and Norfolk and Western railroads, lines extending to the North Atlantic seaboard. The coöperation of the New York Central lines was next secured. It was then announced that rebates would no longer be accorded to any shipper, no matter how important. . . .

Larger shippers, accustomed for many years to concessions from the railroads, could not adapt themselves quickly or easily to this new policy. The Carnegie Steel Company was particularly rebellious. It threatened reprisals. It threatened also to build its own railroad to the seaboard, and in the end did build one from Pittsburgh to Lake Erie. In the meantime, it solaced itself by diverting its traffic, whenever and wherever it was possible, from the Pennsylvania.

But Mr. Cassatt stood firm. With the powerful New York Central in full and actual coöperation with him, with the other important lines reaching the soft-coal and steel districts in his control, he could—and did—laugh at Mr. Carnegie and the other protesting manufacturers. The giving of rebates—a malicious practice which the Interstate Commerce Commission for twelve ineffective years had been endeavoring to stop—was ended; seemingly, for all time. . . . And this was to be recorded as one of the very greatest achievements of Alexander J. Cassatt.

.   .   .   .

If this then actually was the chief reason for the acquisition of Baltimore and Ohio by Pennsylvania, once it had been accomplished, there was no further reason for Broad Street Station holding tightly to the Baltimore property. But there will be few who will believe that the throttling of a steadily rising and an increasingly dangerous competitor was a thought that was entirely absent from the minds of the gentlemen who were dictating the policies of the Pennsylvania. . . . A public protest—more or less outspoken—against any hit-or-miss consolidation of the rail carriers, without national plan or program of any sort, was beginning to make matters a bit uncomfortable in certain high railroad circles. Remember again that the very outspoken gentleman by the name of Theodore Roosevelt was expressing his frank opinion of rail consolidations, dictated by selfish interests without any regard for those of the general public. . . . The so-called Sherman Act, passed a few years before, in an effort to prevent unwholesome consolidations of capital, was brought out, dusted off and successfully invoked. . . . Some of the western carriers were to be the first to feel its teeth. The Burlington learned that it could not be a single company with the Great Northern and the Northern Pacific. Later, the Union Pacific was to be ordered to divest itself of its control of Southern Pacific. The great popular god of transportation—competition—was not, here in the United States at least, to be so rudely thrust aside.

.   .   .   .

It is possible that news of this may have filtered into the

THEY STRAIGHTENED THE OLD MAIN LINE.

One of the achievements of the Loree administration was the bettering of this very early
road through the picturesque valley of the Patapsco.

From a photograph.

THE PASSENGER STATION AT WHEELING.

Built twenty years ago, it remains one of the handsomest on the entire system.

inner places of Broad Street Station. At any rate, it was not long after the first moves in this federal program that the Pennsylvania began to divest itself of its Baltimore and Ohio shares. In 1906, it was holding 820,878 shares of common and preferred stock of the Baltimore company; or something less than forty per cent of its total capitalization. In that year, having accomplished its rebate purpose, it began ridding itself of Baltimore and Ohio (also of Chesapeake and Ohio). It sold to the Union Pacific Company (at that time, Mr. Edwin H. Harriman was influential upon the board of Baltimore and Ohio, which he was serving as a director) 395,406 shares of the Balt'more road, with a par value of $39,540,600.

The Pennsylvania system continued, however, to hold 425,472 shares, with a par value of $42,547,200. It held these for seven more years. Before that time had completely elapsed, Washington had spoken again; this time through the sharp decision of the Supreme Court, ordering the Union Pacific to divest itself of its holdings of Southern Pacific, under which it had held a working control of the latter company. A plan for the disposition of this offending stock was approved by the court, June 30, 1913; under it, the Union Pacific exchanged with the Pennsylvania system lines $38,292,400 par value of Southern Pacific shares for $21,273,600 common and $21,273,600 preferred stock of Baltimore and Ohio. This cleaned out completely the Pennsylvania holdings of Baltimore and Ohio and all of its interests in the property. A little later, its representatives on the board of the Baltimore company retired.

Inasmuch as the stock of the Southern Pacific was paying six per cent at that time, it was, in the words of the annual report of the Pennsylvania Railroad for 1913, "deemed advisable to make the exchange." It was a good trade—in more ways than one. A good trade, for all parties concerned. For, a little later, the Union Pacific distributed to its own stockholders its Baltimore and Ohio shares as a pro rata dividend. A better thing for the Baltimore road could hardly have been imagined. It had had, at a single fell stroke, more than twelve thousand individual stockholders added to its roster; the distribution of its shares had been placed upon a broader basis than ever before in its history.

.   .   .   .

Mr. Loree's active connection with Baltimore and Ohio had, however, terminated long before this. For some time, he had been looking for wider fields of conquest. In the mid-West he found them. The Rock Island called to him. He accepted its call. And a virile president of Baltimore and Ohio stepped out of its ranks.

One accomplishment of Mr. Loree's administration is particularly remembered—and with a very pleasant feeling—in the headquarters of Baltimore; this was in the matter of office salaries.

Baltimore, up to that time at least, had not been known as a city generous in salaries. This held true on its railroad. The Garrett administration, in this regard, had been particularly parsimonious. . . . When Oscar G. Murray had come to the head of the traffic department of the road, he had fought for —and had succeeded in obtaining—a general salary raise in that department, which had enabled it to compete with other high-grade railroads for the best of human material in the market. But the other departments of Baltimore and Ohio had been permitted to shuffle along in the same old fashion. With what heartburnings and envies, can be easily imagined.

Loree changed this. He brought the salaries of the operating and engineering and maintenance ends of the property up to the level of those in the traffic department. . . . He did more. Like Charles F. Mayer, an incessant worker, he was at headquarters early and late each day. Gradually, there was forced upon his attention the fact that a great many of the offices were lighted, evening after evening. He investigated. He found that it had become an all too common practice for the clerks to work after supper and late into the night. Loree stopped this. He introduced much labor-saving machinery into the offices—duplicating machines and the like—and so was able practically to end this night work. This meant a distinct cash saving to the company—in overtime and in supper-money allowances. With such a saving made, Mr. Loree was enabled, during his thirty-one months of office, to raise the average salary of the headquarters clerk from about sixty-five to ninety dollars a month. While the raise in individual efficiency far exceeded this proportion.

His tenure of office as president of Baltimore and Ohio ended January 1, 1904. On that day he retired, to become, after a season on the Rock Island, president of the Delaware and Hudson Company. He was succeeded at Baltimore by Oscar G. Murray, whom we have already seen coming there but eight years before, as vice-president in charge of traffic, and, with John K. Cowen, making a brilliant record in handling the property through the trying days of its receivership.

CHAPTER XIV

MR. MURRAY SUCCEEDS MR. LOREE

Baltimore Terminal Problems Once Again—The Washington Station, and Its Predecessors—Oscar G. Murray as President—The Cincinnati, Hamilton and Dayton Joins the Baltimore and Ohio Family.

FOR the Howard Street Tunnel, Mr. Loree never entertained a high regard. His keen engineering mind began to seek its elimination, not so much from the point of view of best utility to Baltimore and Ohio alone, but also as a step in a large program that he held for the unification of the railroad-passenger facilities in the city of Baltimore. The overlordship of Pennsylvania over the Baltimore road rendered this an ideal time for such a consolidation. And so Loree had his engineers draw up elaborate plans for it.

They returned to the earlier plan of the Garrett days for some sort of elevated structure in Pratt Street, either over or parallel to that thoroughfare. Only the Loree elevated-railroad plan was for a much larger affair; with six parallel main-line tracks extending from Canton on the east to the main line of the Baltimore and Potomac on the west. Both the Baltimore and Ohio and the Pennsylvania would thus have easy connections with it, east and west; while the Northern Central, the Western Maryland and the Baltimore and Lehigh (the present Maryland and Pennsylvania) would reach it from the north by means of an elevated line over Jones Falls—in almost precisely the same location as the present Fallsway.

A splendid union station—a real union station for every
passenger train entering or leaving Baltimore—was the focal
point of this scheme.   This structure, it was planned to locate
near the inner harbor of the city, probably in close proximity to
Charles or Calvert streets. . . .[1]   Modern freight terminals of
every sort were also a part of the plan, although it was expected
that much of the through freight, of the Pennsylvania (if not
of both roads), would pass through the tunnels of that line,
finally abandoned for passenger service—probably to the relief
of many thousands of passengers.   The Howard Street Tunnel,
Mr. Loree proposed to turn over to the electric-railway interests
of Baltimore; to be the main stem and the beginning of a real
rapid-transit system north and south through the city.

.   .   .   .

At this day, it is needless to say that the ambitious project
died a-borning.   The Pennsylvania, as we have just seen,
slowly relinquished its hold of Baltimore and Ohio, and the
opportunity for the building of such a union station—if such
it was—was forever lost.

Yet there soon came another, somewhat like unto it.   On a
quiet Sunday morning in February, 1904, there began in Baltimore a fire which presently was to be a conflagration and a holo-
caust; and, before it finally was checked, to cause vast property
destruction.   In that devastating blaze, the Baltimore and
Ohio central headquarters building at Baltimore and Calvert
streets (that lordly structure which had been the especial pride
of John W. Garrett) was completely destroyed.   While many
of the oldest records of the company were saved from the oncoming flames, others, quite as valuable, were burned.   And the
loss to the company was not easily to be estimated in dollars
and cents.

As Baltimore slowly dug herself out of her ashes and began

---

[1] In this way, the passenger docks of the various steamers plying the Chesapeake Bay would be close at hand.   In recent years, this has been the only large
passenger interchange for the railroads entering Baltimore.

the construction of a new business heart, the question of a new station near the south end of the Howard Street Tunnel—this time for the exclusive use of the Baltimore and Ohio and to replace Camden Station—again showed itself. This time it was suggested that a broad plaza be created in Howard Street, just below Baltimore Street, and that the station, comprising also the general offices of the company, embrace both sides of the widened street, for several blocks. . . . In the long run, this ambitious project went the way of the first.

But the railroad company did replace its central headquarters, although not on the same site as the burned one. It moved two blocks further west on Baltimore Street, and, at the most important intersection of that throughfare with Charles, it erected the fine fourteen-story office building that has served as its chief headquarters ever since. . . .

.   .   .   .

More important and more vital by far than the passenger-terminal problem in Baltimore, was the similar one in the neighboring city of Washington. Here has always been a real interchange point for passenger travel of every sort.

In a much earlier chapter, the completion of the Washington Branch (in 1835) into the capital city of the nation was related. How, at the outset, the Branch found a terminal for itself—unpretentious in the extreme—near the rear of the Capitol; at Pennsylvania Avenue and Second Street, N.W., where the Baltimore and Ohio Company had purchased two lots for $9500, and upon them had adapted a station building, out of two small brick houses which closely adjoined one another and faced the avenue. A small train shed had been erected at their rear.

James G. Berrett, an early Mayor of the city of Washington, arrived over the still new railroad in 1839 and, in his reminiscences, he afterwards wrote of the experience:

There was but one public mode of transportation north of the Potomac leading into Washington, that was the Washington

Oscar G. Murray.
President of the Baltimore and Ohio, 1904–1910.
From a photograph.

A WELL-KNOWN WASHINGTON LANDMARK, THIRTY YEARS AGO.

The New Jersey Avenue Station of Baltimore and Ohio

Branch of the Baltimore and Ohio Railroad. The train of cars consisted of one passenger car, a portion of which was devoted to the storage of baggage, and the engine.

We approached the depot, which was formed of a dwelling-house which had been utilized for the purpose by removing the interior up to the second story. The engine brought us within a short distance of this old house and we were pushed in, by the engine switching down and driving at the other end. This depot was located on the north side of Pennsylvania Avenue, about 150 feet from what was then called the Tiber [Creek]. . . .

Not far distant from this first depot in Washington, was a once-famous tonsorial emporium, which (in the city directory of 1850) advertised itself, in this fashion:

WILLIAM WASHINGTON

HAIR DRESSER, BARBER AND SHAMPOONIST.
4 DOORS WEST OF RAILROAD DEPOT.

Gentlemen having 5 minutes to spare before the departure of the cars for Baltimore may be shaved and dressed immediately.

.   .   .   .

This curious first station in Washington was gradually outgrown. In that very year when William Washington was inserting his advertisement in the city directory, the District Councils of the capital were authorizing the Baltimore and Ohio to erect a new local passenger station; an edifice in keeping with the steadily growing dignity and importance of the town. The railroad company accepted the plan. Its new structure was built in the fall of 1850 and the spring of 1851; substantially, of brick, and in the Italian style of architecture, having a tall tower as its chief external feature. This tower contained a clock and a bell—the latter ringing before the departure of each train.[1]

[1] In his excellent small history of the three stations of Baltimore and Ohio in Washington, Mr. Washington Topham states that this second station faced 119

This station was first put into service Wednesday, April 9, 1851. For fifty-five years thereafter, it served Washington faithfully as a gateway—much of that time as the sole railroad station of the town. Through its broad doors, history marched, again and again. Lincoln strode through them, and so through them also came the Sixth Massachusetts, the Seventh New York and many of the other regiments from the North that were to do their part to keep the Union intact. . . . Throughout the four years of the war, the New Jersey Avenue Station continued to be a great focal center. Camps sprang up roundabout it. Day and night, it never closed its doors. There was not an hour when it was not thronged by the boys in blue—their fathers, their mothers, their sweethearts. . . . Then, in '65, the hegira reversed itself. Through the doorways of the yellow brick building, the boys went scurrying back home again—north, east, west. Not all of them went back—but hundreds and thousands and tens of thousands did, each day, each week. . . .

Traffic at the Washington station increased steadily after the war and the day came when radical enlargement to its head-house facilities was absolutely essential. The waiting-room level was then placed at that of the C Street sidewalk (which, in the course of the steady improvement of Washington, had come to be raised some fifteen feet) and it became necessary to use a long flight of stairs to reach the level of the train shed floor.

It was the steady improvement of Washington that compelled the Baltimore and Ohio, in days not long after the end of the Civil War, to make more material changes in its terminals there than mere additions to its passenger station. The road had succeeded, just before the war, in making a track connection through the middle of First Street and Maryland Avenue from its New Jersey Avenue terminal to the Long

feet on New Jersey Avenue (at the intersection of C Street) and that its covered train shed was 340 feet in length and 62 feet in width. The roof of this train house rested firmly upon thirty-four solid granite columns.

Bridge and the railroad that ran over that structure and beyond; to Alexandria, to Orange and (later) to Danville and many, many other southern points. During the war, this connection track was of incalculable value to the Union. But, after the conflict, it began to be increasingly regarded by Washingtonians as an eyesore.

The vigilant eye of Alexander R. Shepherd—the Mussolini-like personage who rescued the L'Enfant plans and upbuilded the magnificent Washington of today—finally fell upon this offending track down the center of two important streets. He demanded its removal. When John W. Garrett, his mind on other matters, hesitated, Shepherd waited—ten days; and then, on a November evening, in 1872, he marched two hundred workmen into the streets and had them tear up the tracks—a matter of but a few hours. Washington Topham stood in the street—at about the site of the present-day Peace Monument—and watched the track come up.

The Baltimore and Ohio would have been embarrassed considerably by this summary act had it not been for the fact that it had just completed its new branch road to Shepherds Point, whence it enjoyed a short connection by car ferry with Alexandria, Virginia, and the railroads leading out from that place. . . . Truth to tell, its entire entrance into Washington was upon thin ice; it hung far too much upon the whimsical favor of politicians; of that of the District Councils or Congress, or both. True it was that the original Act of Congress of March 2, 1831, which had first permitted the Washington Branch to enter the District, had given Baltimore and Ohio certain valuable easements and rights of way through Washington streets as well as the right to occupy certain public squares. These were to run until 1910. That year finally approached. There was some apprehension in the offices at Baltimore, which finally resulted in the passage of another statute by Congress, extending for a time the easements and rights. Yet, even before the passage of this bill, Baltimore and Ohio, in response to a definite sentiment in the

city of Washington, was preparing to build new terminals there;
tentative plans already had been drawn for a handsome
Normanesque passenger station at Delaware Avenue and
C Street.

.   .   .   .

That station also was destined never to be builded.   One
wonders how many of these monumental enterprises have been
planned, all the way across America, never to progress beyond
the embryo of the architect's drawings!

A new factor was thrusting itself into the situation.

When the Baltimore and Potomac (a long, slender finger of
the Pennsylvania) had reached into Washington, there in the
late 'sixties, it had builded for itself, in the Mall at Sixth Street,
a sizable brick passenger station and train shed.   This terminal, which, a little later, was to attain a tragic distinction as the scene of the assassination of President
Garfield, also served the railroads leading south from Washington.   It was, for its day, a fairly attractive building, but it
occupied a site which it had no business to be holding.   For,
since the days of L'Enfant, the Mall had been destined to be,
in its final development, a truly magnificent esplanade or
broad parkway, leading from the Capitol past the Washington
Monument—almost in its precise axis—right through to some
other monumental feature (which, eventually, became the
Lincoln Memorial). . . .   A long lean station and train shed
placed squarely across the Mall made the realization of this
ideal seem to be a long distance indeed in the future.

Generations of Washingtonians railed, ineffectively, against
this condition of affairs.   The station remained.   It remained
for more than a quarter of a century—in fact, nearly thirty-
five years—a blot and a bar to the development of the
Washington Beautiful.

Then there came to the White House the remarkable
Theodore Roosevelt.   Mr. Roosevelt achieved as one of his
great dreams, as a triumph for his administration, real progress

in the making of the Washington Beautiful. In the most brilliant season that the White House had ever known, he brought to its hospitable board such great civic dreamers as Burnham and Olmsted and McKim . . . many, many others as well. Gradually, the modern plan for the development of the city—along the same general lines that L'Enfant had originally used—evolved itself.

But the Pennsylvania station still stretched its bulk squarely across the Mall.

Roosevelt saw it there, and raged. When he complained to the railroad officers, they laughed or ignored the matter. Then the Big Stick waved. In the direction of Capitol Hill. Congress awoke, and, like a troupe of subdued small boys, fell in line with the master's wishes. It began to legislate. . . . A splendid new union station became part of the plan for the Washington Beautiful. But a union station would be as nothing without the full coöperation of the railroads that were to use it. And they were indifferent. The Baltimore and Ohio had definite plans for a Delaware Avenue station of its own, which presently were succeeded by drawings for a similar edifice in Stanton Square, at the intersection of Maryland and Massachusetts avenues. The Pennsylvania also hinted at plans for a new Washington station for itself. . . . Fortunately, none of these schemes ever came to anything.

Both the Baltimore and Ohio and the Pennsylvania preferred to remain in their respective locations and to develop their existing facilities separately, believing that from a railroad standpoint there were advantages in so doing which they regarded as more important to them than any possible from a joint station project. And the various municipal and congressional committees recognized that there was at least much to be said in support of the view of the two railroads that they could not be compelled to surrender their rights in their locations. Certainly not without some adequate compensation.

The proposal for a union station had however been conceived and urged with the idea that Washington was the national capital and that its development should be considered and proceed upon a broad basis consistent with that fact. In order to permit of the city's development along such lines the two railroads agreed to forego their own plans and to acquiesce in the plan for a union station of a character suitable for the capital of the nation.   Incident to this project it was necessary that each of the two railroads surrender their existing rights and incur very substantial expenditures in changes of line and elimination of grade crossings, in addition to the large expense involved in the construction of the new terminal proper.   And it was in consideration of such matters that Congress appropriated to each of the two railroad companies the sum of $1,500,000.   The negotiations for so vast a project had naturally extended over a considerable period, but with the passage of the Act of Congress of February 28th, 1903, entitled, "An Act to Provide for a Union Railroad Station in the District of Columbia, and for other purposes," the way was open for the building of this very fine union terminal.

This they now proceeded to do.

.   .   .   .

The question of a proper site was a matter, not only of first consideration, but a most important one.   The fact that the two existing chief railroad stations of the city were situated, not actually so far apart from one another, but on opposite sides of the Capitol Park and the Mall, was a very large complication. . . .   For a time, a plan was considered, whereby all the trains of Baltimore and Ohio would enter the proposed Union Station—then to be somewhere on the south side of the Mall—by using the Metropolitan Branch and the so-called Metropolitan Southern, entering and leaving the city through a small corner of Virginia.   While this, undoubtedly, would have resulted in placing the station nearer the business heart of the city than finally was done, it made, with a double

crossing of the Potomac, an extremely roundabout route for
Baltimore and Ohio; particularly so, for its trains to the north
and east.   When this scheme finally was definitely abandoned,
a sigh of relief was breathed in Baltimore.

.   .   .   .

About a half mile to the north of the Capitol, there had
existed, since there had been any Washington at all, an ungainly
and unhealthy swamp tract.   Delaware Avenue led from the
Senate Wing direct to it, and then, in its bog, disappeared.

When it was announced that this swamp—twenty feet below
tidewater level—was to be the site for the monumental Union
Station, Washington lifted its aristocratic eyebrows.   But the
decision remained.   "Impossible . . . to build a fine station
in that hole," suggested old Washington.

But there it was that the station finally was builded; on
firm ground forty feet above tidewater level.   What scraping
and filling and movement of earth this entailed, only the men
who built the structure will ever know.   Millions of cubic yards
of dirt went into the site for the building and its approaches.
Of these, a considerable number came from the long tunnel
which was bored from the front of the station under Delaware
Avenue and the front of the Capitol tract to the existing lines
of the Pennsylvania and its through connections to the south
(about a mile, all told).

.   .   .   .

Today, no one doubts the wisdom and the farsightedness
of the choice of the site of the Washington station.   Conforming
to the original L'Enfant plan of the city—the scheme to which
there has been a more or less faithful adherence all these years
—it stands upon the north side of Massachusetts Avenue, at
the precise point of its intersection with Delaware Avenue—a
natural hub or axis point.   Wisely it was determined to place
the giant structure on the far side of Massachusetts Avenue, so

that that great thoroughfare (160 feet in width from curb to curb) should not be crossed in any visible way by a railroad yard.   More wisely still, it was placed in keeping with the splendid architectural scheme of Washington; one of the most carefully designed cities in all the world.

To such a well advised site, there presently was added the genius of an outstanding American architect: David H. Burnham, of Chicago.   At the outset, Mr. Burnham tossed away all fantastic architectural schemes.   Norman, Romanesque, Flemish, he would have none of any of them.   Neither would he accept brick for a building material.   Only enduring granite would do.   With his skilled pencil he evolved gradually a highly classic building, long and broad and low; a structure in dignified keeping with the nearby Capitol, as well as the other finer buildings of Washington.   With its simple and splendid façade, 630 feet in length, its tremendous waiting room and other public apartments, it quickly became known as one of the handsomest railroad stations ever built, as well as one of the most convenient in its use.

The plan of the station is simplicity itself.

At the rear of the head house, 630 feet in length and 210 feet in width, there is a giant concourse, 760 feet long and 130 feet wide.   The arched roof of this apartment has no pillared support.   It is said to be one of the largest rooms in the world. It is estimated that 25,000 persons could be brought into it at a single time.[1]

This concourse, in turn, gives to the passenger-train tracks, which lead out at right angles to it.   There are twenty-two of these, for arriving and departing trains, parallel to one another and served by broad platforms running alongside them. Sixteen of these tracks, at the west side of the station, are at

---

[1] The proportions of the Washington station were influenced, to no small degree, by the great crowds that come to the capital for the inauguration of the President each four years.   Other events from time to time attract visitors by the thousands.   While, at certain seasons of the year, the tourist traffic comes to a high tide indeed.

THE UNION STATION, WASHINGTON.

Regarded as one of the handsomest in the world, it is used by every Baltimore and Ohio passenger train that enters or leaves the capital.

From a photograph.

A MODERN TERMINAL, FROM THE AIR.

This aerial photograph of the Union Station at Washington shows clearly its ingenious arrangement of passenger tracks and platforms, as well as the "throat of the yard."

the level of the concourse and waiting room and are used chiefly by trains to and from the north and west.   The other six, leading into the connecting tunnel under the Capitol Park, are on a lower level, but are reached by easy stairs and elevators. These tracks are designed for trains to and from the south. East of them, just outside the station, are six others, chiefly for express services.

In order, it was said at the time, not to interfere with the proper architectural dominance of the Capitol, no vast spreading train shed was to be built over the tracks and platforms of the new station.   These are protected, to an extent, by narrow roofs or pavilions running the length of each train platform. They lead into the great concourse.

.   .   .   .

This mammoth station was constructed by the Washington Terminal Company, whose capital stock is divided evenly between the Baltimore and Ohio and the Pennsylvania Railroad (as inheritor of the Philadelphia, Baltimore and Washington). The executives of each of these two railroads alternate annually as president of the Washington Terminal Company. The roads share the expenses and the incidental receipts of the station—these last coming from news stands, restaurants and the like.   The other railroads entering Washington— the Southern, the Richmond, Fredericksburg and Potomac and the Chesapeake and Ohio—are tenants and pay for their use of the station and its other facilities on a rental basis.   But the station is, at all times, a great financial liability to its owner roads.   They estimate today (1927) that it costs them thirty-four cents each time they haul a passenger in or out of it.

The original modest estimate of $4,000,000 for the cost of the building itself was, as had been freely predicted, far exceeded.   When it was all done, it was found that the building itself, with its immediate approaches, had cost $11,440,301. (To duplicate it today, however, would probably cost more than twice that sum.) . . .   The entire enterprise had meant an expenditure of $20,725,774. Of this sum, Baltimore and Ohio paid $11,392,144; the Pennsylvania, the balance.

Wonder not that the experienced railroad regards the possibility of building a "monumental" station anywhere upon its line with a deal of apprehension.

.   .   .   .

Throughout the first six years of the present century, swift progress was made upon the construction of Washington station and its elaborate approaches. So rapid was the work that, in the fall of 1907, the structure was announced as practically finished, and ready for use. . . . The last train of the Baltimore and Ohio to pull into or out of the historic old station in New Jersey Avenue was the *Duquesne Limited*, which departed for Pittsburgh at 2:52 o'clock in the morning of Sunday, October 27. After that, the ticket sellers closed their cases for the final time, and they themselves departed for the great white stone structure over on the freshly filled heights a quarter of a mile away. Into that station, four hours later, came the first train. To Baltimore and Ohio was to be given the honor of dedicating the structure. Its Train No. 10, eastbound, backed into the station at 6:50 o'clock that Sunday morning, discharged its passengers and their luggage and received others, before departing on its course to Baltimore, Philadelphia and New York. . . . A month later, the Pennsylvania and the southern roads began the use of the new station, and the old structures which it superseded were being turned over to the hands of the wreckers. Old Washingtonians watched with no little regret the demolition of the picturesque old station in New Jersey Avenue. There were few, however, to weep over the passing of the ungainly structure in the Mall. Again, that open space was really open. Every stick and stone of the station was torn away. Washington smiled. And so smiled the Man with the Big Stick up at the White House.

.   .   .   .

The completion of the Washington station project may, perhaps, be set down as the chief single achievement of the administration of Oscar G. Murray as president of the Baltimore and Ohio.   As an engineering enterprise, however, it had, in its earlier stages, demanded much thought and effort on the part of J. M. Graham, then the chief engineer of the system,[1] and his associates.   Several miles of busy main line had to be completely relocated and rebuilded; many facilities, incidental to any great terminal, provided.   With a heavy traffic being handled all the while.   Yet, the thing was done—with much dispatch and with a minimum of interference to trains, either freight or passenger.   And, when it was all completed, Baltimore and Ohio in Washington was in a far better position than ever before in the history of the road.   For not only had it acquired splendid new terminals, both passenger and freight, but it now had what it had entirely lacked before: a practicable and a direct track connection with the various important railroads leading south from the national capital.   Thereafter, the branch to Shepherds Point lessened in importance; it became chiefly valuable as a purely local-freight facility.[2]

.   .   .   .

[1] James M. Graham is to this day regarded as one of the most eminent engineers who ever worked on the upbuilding of Baltimore and Ohio.   Born in Crawfordsville, Indiana, in 1850, and educated at the Kentucky State University, he began his railroad career as assistant engineer on the former Grayville and Mattoon Railroad (now a part of the Illinois Central).   In September, 1891, he entered the service of Baltimore and Ohio, as superintendent of the Ohio and Midland divisions.   Seven years later, he was made general superintendent of the trans-Ohio divisions.   On February 1, 1899, he was appointed chief engineer of the Baltimore and Ohio Railroad, a post which he held for five years, resigning to become vice-president of the Erie Railroad. . . .   He planned in detail and built much of the low grade and new line-revision work between Baltimore and Cumberland.   The revised old main line between Baltimore and Brunswick is his railroad monument.

[2] With the completion of the new Washington station and the approach tunnel leading into it from the south, there came a readjustment of the ownership of one of the two railroad systems reaching from the Federal capital in that direction. The Washington Southern Railway and the Richmond, Fredericksburg and Potomac Railroad, together forming the sole railroad line between Washington

Some other large construction work was finished in the six years of the Murray administration: New roundhouses and yards were erected at Philadelphia and at Baltimore; and, in the latter city, extensive additions were made to the shops at Mount Clare. In Wheeling, the historic western terminus of the original Baltimore and Ohio, there was much track reconstruction and a handsome new passenger terminal was erected. Other fairly large improvements were made to the property.

Yet, after the virile administration of Mr. Loree, that of Mr. Murray was, in contrast, fairly quiet and tranquil. Never dramatic, it was, however, most of the time, progressive. Mr. Murray continued to exert his great genius as a traffic-getter. Of railroad transportation, he was a supreme salesman. He knew how to get the business, and he went out and got it. There were few tricks of the trade that he did not know—and he possessed a few of his own in addition.

In the earlier years of his administration, the result of this salesmanship showed itself in steadily increasing receipts. In the twelve months of the fiscal year which had ended June 30, 1906, the Baltimore and Ohio system, including its controlled or affiliated lines, earned a gross of $82,508,719; and this represented a sizable increase over the preceding fiscal year (the first of Mr. Murray's command of the property), which had returned, from the Baltimore and Ohio property alone, but $67,689,997 (as compared with $77,392,056 from the same properties in 1906). The following year—ending June 30,

---

and Richmond, were consolidated into the Richmond-Washington Company, of which the Baltimore and Ohio Railroad became a one-sixth owner; the other five shares being evenly divided among the Pennsylvania Railroad, the Southern Railway, the Chesapeake and Ohio Railway, the Seaboard Air Line Railway and the Atlantic Coast Line Railroad. . . . There had been some talk of the Seaboard building a line to parallel the R. F. & P. between Richmond and Washington, also of the Baltimore and Ohio building its own bridge across the Potomac to meet such a new line. . . . With the new joint ownership of the existing line, and its double-tracking and other improvements which immediately were begun, all such duplication plans were abandoned.

1907—there was still further increase; a total of $88,552,924 from the system, including its controlled or affiliated lines.

But this last was, for a considerable time, to remain a peak figure. Nineteen hundred and seven is recorded in the business annals of the nation as a very bad year, generally. There were financial depression and panic, followed by a period of industrial stagnation. All of this resulted in a greatly lessened traffic for the railroads, in which Baltimore and Ohio took its share. Its total for the year which ended June 30, 1908, was but $79,377,351. The following twelvemonth was worse. The gross again fell—this time to $76,412,856. . . . Thereafter, however, the tide turned. Earnings began again to show a steady increase.

.   .   .   .

If Mr. Murray were alive today, he probably would point to the acquisition of the Cincinnati, Hamilton and Dayton for Baltimore and Ohio as the chief achievement of his administration. By so doing, he not only gained for the Baltimore road important new fingers into the coal districts of southern Ohio, but a valuable linking line, north and south, between Cincinnati and Toledo and (by trackage rights) into the heart of that rapidly growing American industrial city, Detroit.

The Cincinnati, Hamilton and Dayton was a historic American railroad, once proud and comparatively rich, which had become a football between politicians and railroad promoters. Once an extremely well maintained property, it had been permitted to deteriorate, sadly. Its cars and its engines, as well as its 900-odd miles of main-line track, were in bad condition. While its financial position was well-nigh hopeless. No longer could it take care even of its most pressing money needs.

Originally (in 1851 and 1852), it had been built north from Cincinnati, through the busy industrial Mill Creek Valley, to Hamilton, and thence, along the banks of the Miami, to Dayton, just sixty miles distant from the Ohio. In the huge old barnlike brick station at Dayton, it had had direct connections with the Mad River and Lake Erie Railroad—the first railroad ever to be builded in Ohio, and now a part of the New York Central Lines—which extended on to Sandusky and to Cleveland. Its arrangements with the Mad River road contemplated for the C. H. and D. an interest in the receipts, as well as in the expenses of its passenger and freight steamers, plying between those two Lake Erie ports and Buffalo.

But, during the first decade of its career, the Cincinnati road had quarreled, repeatedly, with the Mad River road. Seemingly, there was no reconciling their differences. Finally, the managers of the C. H. and D. determined to sever, for once and for all time, their mutual arrangements with the Mad River and Lake Erie and to strike out independently. They decided to create at the brisk new village of Toledo, at the head of Lake Erie and the mouth of the Maumee River, a port of their own. The gap between Dayton and Toledo would be covered by the Dayton and Michigan Railroad, already building.

A green-covered and much yellowed pamphlet tells in detail of this plan. At one place, it says (referring to the Dayton and Michigan):

. . . It is already [1858] completed as far as Lima—130 miles from Cincinnati and 70 miles from Dayton. Its eventual terminus will be Toledo. . . . The completion of the D. & M. Road to Toledo (which, from the present condition of the work, it is believed may be effected in the course of the current year) with such running arrangements with this company [the Cincinnati, Hamilton and Dayton] as to make the two roads in effect identical, would secure to this company an amount of business which it would be difficult to estimate. The entire line from Cincinnati being made shorter than any other to the Lake, and the expense of transportation up and down the Lake between Toledo and Buffalo, being the same as between Cleveland and Buffalo, would, during the navigable season, have a preference in connection with Eastern freighting business, in both directions over every other competing line. The road from

THE CENTRAL HEADQUARTERS BUILDING, BALTIMORE.
Built at Charles and Baltimore streets by the Murray administration after
the great fire of 1904. It is still in use.

From a photograph.

THE BRANDYWINE VIADUCT, WILMINGTON, DELAWARE.

This stone structure of Baltimore and Ohio, one of the finest bridges in the United States, is another monument to the Murray administration.

From a photograph.

Toledo to Detroit, also, being 56 miles in length, and now in full operation, forms with the C. H. & D. and the D. & M. roads, a continuous line of 256 miles from Cincinnati, which, there being no rival line, must necessarily command all the trade between that city on the south and the whole of southern Michigan on the north. The further junction at Detroit with the Great Western Railway of Canada, opening a route from Detroit to Niagara Falls and Montreal, within a few miles as short from Cincinnati as that of any other existing line, and passing through one of the most beautiful countries in the world, insures a certainty of passenger business from Cincinnati to the East which must ultimately give it equal, if not superior returns of profit, as compared with other lines. The junction of the line also at Lima with the Pittsburgh, Fort Wayne and Chicago road cannot fail to yield a good share of eastern through business by way of Pittsburgh, and of western, by way of Chicago. . . .

When one realizes the diminutive size of the Cincinnati, Hamilton and Dayton in that year of 1858, he feels that here was an ambitious program indeed. It *was* a small road, then. It had but twenty-two locomotives, all of them wood burners. Two of them, the *Jenny Lind* and the *Tom Thumb*, with their bright colorings, were the pride of the boys who dwelt along the line.

Yet, the Cincinnati, Hamilton and Dayton, unlike a good many of its small compeers of that day, was not to be doomed to an early absorption or extinction. It completed its traffic affiliations—one of the best of them was with the Atlantic and Great Western extension of the broad-gauge Erie, which it accommodated by means of a third rail laid all the way from Dayton to Cincinnati—and remained for years a profitable and independent small railroad.

It was not until early in the present century that it began to run upon financial shoals. . . . The details of these difficulties are not germane to this narrative. It is enough to say that, in 1905, the Cincinnati, Hamilton and Dayton, together with the Pere Marquette, which it then guaranteed and controlled, was purchased by J. P. Morgan and Company and offered to the Erie Railroad. It was given out that the Erie had purchased the two roads. F. D. Underwood, then the president of the Erie, was in Europe at that moment. When he heard of the transaction and came hurrying back, he made an inspection trip of the property. He was not satisfied with the roads and quickly refused to accept them. Mr. Morgan took them back; personally—not through his banking house—expending between seven and eight millions of dollars to keep faith in the situation. He immediately placed the property in a receivership. A little later, he offered it, through Norman B. Ream, to the Baltimore and Ohio. The directors of that road appointed a special committee to consider the proposal. After much consideration, and under the urging of Mr. E. H. Harriman, one of their number, it was decided that the Baltimore and Ohio would accept it—on a seven-year trial. In the meantime, it was to be operated strictly as a railroad in every way separate from the new proprietor road.[1]

This experiment was not successful. Times were hard, freight rates were very low, and the roads (C. H. and D. and Pere Marquette) could hardly earn their fixed charges. They remained in receivership until a year or two after the coming of Daniel Willard as president of Baltimore and Ohio. Under his general charge, and the immediate supervision of Mr. William Cotter as president of the two roads, they emerged from their receivership. But, in the case of the C. H. and D., only for a short time. In 1913, there came the terribly disastrous floods throughout all Ohio, and the Cincinnati, Hamilton and Dayton was one of the chief sufferers from these. Again it went into receivership—under the skilled hands of the late Judson

---

[1] In his report of 1909, President Oscar G. Murray says:
". . . Negotiations pending during the year have been concluded recently and made effective July 1, 1909, whereby your company will acquire, at the expiration of seven years, at a price then to be agreed upon or determined by arbitration, the controlling stock of the Cincinnati, Hamilton and Dayton Railway Company. . . ."

Harmon, former Governor of Ohio. When it again emerged, it had been divorced completely, not only from the Pere Marquette, but also from the branch running due west from Hamilton, Ohio, through Indianapolis to Springfield, Illinois.[1] While preparations were being made to abandon and tear up many miles of hopelessly unprofitable lines; the most of them in western Ohio.

.   .   .   .

Gradually, this former rail Cinderella has become a prosperous, as well as an essential, railroad. Its direct and well located main line, north and south across Ohio, its wonderfully valuable terminals in both Cincinnati and Toledo, its entrance to such highly prosperous industrial towns as Hamilton and Dayton and Lima, gave promise of its future value to the farsighted railroaders who first approved of its acquisition. To buy it, Baltimore and Ohio reappraised its requisition in 1916, wiped $11,000,000 off its profit and loss account; at a time when it could none too well afford such a reduction. To-day, to its present owners, the rail property alone is worth more than the $61,000,000 paid and assured, while miscellaneous assets taken over at less than $2,000,000 now have appreciated to nearly the entire amount written off in 1916. Under good management, this old Cincinnati line has become a real asset. Oscar G. Murray did not err when he approved its purchase.

[1] This branch took the name, Cincinnati, Indianapolis and Western, and, for more than a dozen years, was operated as a completely separate railroad. Together with the Monon, it formed a direct and busy through rail route between Cincinnati and Chicago. . . . In 1927, it again lost its identity, then becoming, in every way, a portion of the steadily growing Baltimore and Ohio system.

CHAPTER XV

Mr. Daniel Willard Becomes the Executive of Baltimore and Ohio—
Changing Problems in Railroading Bring New Types of Rail-
roaders—Expansion on the System—The Magnolia Cut-Off—
New Bridges, Tracks and Cars.

ON January 1, 1910, Daniel Willard became president of the
Baltimore and Ohio Railroad. He was the fourteenth and—
for the period of the first one hundred years of its history—
the last president of the company. In that same first century,
he achieved the second longest term of office in the road's
history—his eighteen years as president being overshadowed
only by the twenty-six that John W. Garrett served in the same
post.

Mr. Willard's advent as president upon the property was in
keeping with a general policy that, at the turn of the century,
was beginning to show itself upon all the railroads of the
United States. The time had been, and was gone, when a
railroad president was apt to be something of a figurehead. A
certain remote magnificence, not to say pomposity, had been
shrouded about the post. There was a penumbra of greatness.
Frequently, the railroad president was a lawyer, or a banker;
not infrequently, he acceded to the head of a carrier property,
almost automatically, by reason of a dominating or a heavy
ownership in its securities.

The coming of a new century changed much of this.
Economic conditions were a powerful leaven. The end of the

Spanish War had witnessed the prices both of luxuries and necessities in America starting upon a long upgrade; seemingly, with no end in sight. The average railroad executive began to be faced with grave new problems. With his tariffs, for the haulage of both freight and passengers, more or less firmly fixed by custom and mutual understanding, his revenues were remaining year in and year out at a comparatively motionless figure; whilst his outgo—expressed in labor costs and expenditures for fuel and other materials needed for construction, as well as for operating—began to rise, alarmingly. Swiftly the margin between income and outgo—in many cases, already none too wide—narrowed. It faced utter obliteration. The old-time railroad executive, as well as the old-time railroad owner, was beginning to have a really hard time of it. . . . The situation gradually went from bad to worse. There seemed to be no end at all to that upgrade.

Then it was that, upon the American railroad, the typical operating executive began to come into his own. If he knew his trade; if he was a genuinely good railroader; if, with his ingenuity and his experience, he was capable of finding new economies or making better use even of old ones, he was apt to find himself rising pretty rapidly in his chosen profession. The old generation of railroad presidents began to step down and out; in its place there came the new generation—men who had lived long years in the hard-headed romance of train movement and locomotive maintenance and cost sheets and all the rest of that sort of thing. These men, with a knowledge acquired close to the hard top of the steel rail itself, proved themselves worthy leaders. With their economies, they generally kept that narrow margin open—sometimes, at costs which only they themselves knew.

.   .   .   .

Of this generation was Daniel Willard.

It is not meet that in this book there should be praise of the living executives of Baltimore and Ohio—their time is

yet to come. Yet, facts are facts. And no chronicle of the
first hundred years of Baltimore and Ohio may close with an
omission of the record of the last eighteen years of that cycle—
these last in some respects, the most important period in the entire history of the property. The object here will be to set
down these salient facts in the simplest fashion possible; yet,
with a full realization of the large part that they have
played in the present-day development of the property.

Hence, it becomes essential to know that Mr. Willard was,
from the outset, a thoroughly trained railroad operating man.
Born in the village of North Hartland, Windsor County,
Vermont, from a good New England parentage, he had his
first job on a railroad—the old Central Vermont. Later,
he was firing an engine—on the Connecticut and Passumpsic
—and then, in due course, he was driving one; later on the
Lake Shore, and afterwards on the Soo. On the Soo, he
came to do other things; he was master mechanic in a winter
when the road was new and poor, and he had to be both
boss and the entire force working at the roundhouse. Later,
he rose to higher positions in its operating forces.

These things gave Willard knowledge of the beginnings of
his craft. Always, too, he has loved railroading; both as a fine
science and as a highly practical profession.

When, in 1901, Frederick D. Underwood, who had helped
upbuild the Soo, came east to become vice-president and
general manager of the Baltimore and Ohio, he brought Daniel
Willard with him and gave him the post of assistant general
manager. Willard's job, during the three years that followed
in Baltimore, was to have charge of the maintenance of the line
and its rolling stock. It gave him opportunity to make a close
study of the property. He did not neglect that opportunity.

Underwood went, it will be recalled, from the Baltimore
and Ohio to become president of the Erie, and so to put that
historic railroad well on its proper foothold. He took Willard
with him, making him vice-president of the Erie. . . . After
a few years, Willard increased still further his practical operat-

DANIEL WILLARD.
President, 1910–
From a photograph.

ON THE MAGNOLIA CUT-OFF.

Where the new freight cut-off of Baltimore and Ohio crosses the Potomac and the o
Main Stem—this last now chiefly reserved for passenger trains.

From a photograph.

ing experience, by becoming vice-president of the Burlington. From this post he went, at the very beginning of 1910, to become president of Baltimore and Ohio. He has remained in that post from that day to this. . . . So runs, as simply as it may be told, the personal record of the fourteenth president of the Baltimore road.

.   .   .   .

Daniel Willard came to the presidency of Baltimore and Ohio with but few firmly fixed notions as to how he would operate the property. His mind was open. With a keen understanding of the road, he knew that, first of all, it would have to be thoroughly rebuilt, and substantially enlarged at many places, to make it an effective modern carrier—to enable it to take its right place with its fellows in the northeastern field. For a number of years past, it had failed to hold its own with its principal competitors. Headed by a highly expert traffic man—Mr. Oscar G. Murray (who, upon Mr. Willard's election as president, was made chairman of the board of directors, an office especially created for his occupancy)—it was skilled in the solicitation of traffic, yet many times it failed in the handling of it. . . . Blockades of cars and of trains were all too frequent on the system. These were, quite naturally, at their worst in the hard months of winter. Yet, those are the very months when the traffic runs flood high upon our railroads of the northeast; when, most of all, they must be girded and ready to handle their business, promptly and adequately. . . . A freight embargo is not a nice thing. During the first decade of the present century, it began coming, with unpleasant frequency, on Baltimore and Ohio.

That the Baltimore road would have to be made fit— and that at once—for the burden it should be handling, quickly and economically, soon fixed itself in Willard's mind as the prime problem. He prepared to do that very thing. How well he succeeded may be judged, perhaps, from the fact that the gross receipts of the road, which during the fiscal year of 1910 (when first he came to the property as its head) were $90,223,401, in the calendar year of 1927 were $246,078,510.[1] That, of itself, tells a rather considerable story.

.   .   .   .

Within six months after first he came to Baltimore, Mr. Willard had arranged for convertible bond issues which would bring into the company's treasury a needed $62,000,000, for immediate extensions and repairs.   With this sizable sum in hand, he was prepared to go ahead with rebuilding certain portions of the road upon a large scale and under definite plan. Since the days of the receivership, there had been far too little expenditure toward bringing Baltimore and Ohio into full line and pace with its competitors.   It was lagging behind; it was behind in its trackage, in its motive power and cars, in terminals, in almost everything that pertains to an absolutely first-class and well-rounded railroad.   As a result, it functioned in a way that was far from ideal.

.   .   .   .

The worst place on the system was at one of its most critical points—between Cherry Run, West Virginia, and Patterson Creek, just east of Cumberland.   Along fifty-seven miles of double-track main line between these two places, passed, and still passes, a very large portion of the through business of Baltimore and Ohio.   Into Cumberland there come the two

[1] It is but fair to state that the $246,078,510 of earnings in 1927 represent, to a considerable degree, certain large advances in freight, passenger and other rates granted to the railroads since 1910, as well as increase in traffic due to acquisition of other railroads; for example, properties formerly operated as the Cincinnati, Hamilton & Dayton Railway, now operated as a part of the Baltimore and Ohio under the corporate name of the Toledo & Cincinnati Railroad, also a number of smaller railroad properties absorbed from time to time and now operated as a part of the Baltimore and Ohio system.   If the business moved in 1927 had been carried at rates in effect during 1910, the gross revenues would have amounted to about $147,000,000; however, of this amount, after giving proper consideration to the merged companies, approximately $45,000,000 reflects increased business which is not to be lightly ignored.

chief stems of the road to the west; the line through Pittsburgh to Chicago, and the one through Grafton to Cincinnati and St. Louis. Each pours its generous meed of traffic into the Main Stem. East of Cherry Run, the traffic fans out once again; a good part of the eastbound freight is diverted there and sent north over the Western Maryland and the Reading. But, between Cherry Run and Patterson Creek, there was, these many years, a veritable bottle neck. . . . One of the worst places on this bottle neck was at the Doe Gully Tunnel. Daniel Willard, in the early days of his office, riding over the line, once noticed as many as six miles of freight trains tied up at each end of this bore, awaiting the passage of passenger trains, so that they might finally make their slow progress through the near-impasse.

Today, Doe Gully Tunnel no longer exists. They blasted off its roof and in its place there is now a fine four-track line; through a deep and almost gradeless cutting. . . . Instead of but two main-line tracks between Cumberland and Cherry Run, there are now not less than three all the way; in some places, four parallel pairs of rails. All of which are in addition to the Magnolia Cut-off—a fine piece of double-track freight railroad, and but eleven miles in length, in comparison with the seventeen miles which it has superseded, in part. But those eleven miles of relief line, crossing the Potomac twice and piercing one of its jutting mountains by a sizable tunnel, cost upwards of $6,000,000; just as it took another million dollars to tear the roof off Doe Gully Tunnel. . . . These improvements were completed prior to the advent of the World War. What they would cost today is, to an extent, problematical. Certain it is that the expense would be much increased; by some millions of dollars.

.   .   .   .

The fifty-seven-mile stretch between Cherry Run and Cumberland was by no means the only bottle neck on the Baltimore and Ohio of the beginning of the century. Similar near-impasses, only relatively less important, existed upon each of the main stems stretching west from Cumberland. Each was choked, definitely, by a long single-track tunnel. On the line to Grafton, Wheeling and Parkersburg, the historic Kingwood Tunnel was the bottle neck; on that to Pittsburgh, Sand Patch Tunnel, more than a mile in length, was a stretch that made operating men grow grey before their time. It quickly became part of the Willard plan to change these tunnels into double-track bores. A parallel double-track tube was placed next to Kingwood, the original tunnel still being used for a single-way movement; but at Sand Patch, an entirely new double-track concrete-lined tunnel was cut through; the timber-supported old bore then being completely abandoned and suffered gradually to fall into decay.

This done, the double-tracking of the entire main line from Philadelphia and Baltimore to Chicago, by way of Pittsburgh, was pushed through to completion. In the very nature of things, it was not a speedy job. As a matter of fact, it was not until the autumn of 1917 that Willard had succeeded in accomplishing it, for every mile of the distance; even though, several years before, he had reduced the few remaining single-track stretches across Indiana to such short lengths as to be almost negligible factors in the operation of the road. The thing to do in cases of this sort—the thing that was done upon Baltimore and Ohio—was first to double-track those stretches of the main line which experience had shown to be most in need of immediate relief. After that, it was a comparatively easy matter to fill in the intermediate portions with second main-line track.

In matters of this sort, Mr. Willard's practical experience was of real help to him. . . . He showed it once when he was advising with his people in regard to the first of the double-track stretches up on the Parkersburg Branch.

A profile of this particular and important link of the Baltimore and Ohio system shows it to be full of ups and downs —not unlike the so-called roller coasters at amusement parks.

only with its heights and its depths much less marked. . . .
A road, crossing the highly mountainous country of West
Virginia almost at right angles to the mountain ranges, could
hardly have avoided grades—and many of them.

"Be sure," cautioned Willard to his engineers, "that you
get these additional passing tracks up on the tops of the hills,
not down in the valleys.   In other words, I want the location
of every one of them to be a real help to the train to get under
way once again."

His practical experience in the cab of a locomotive had
taught him that.

.   .   .   .

Next to tunnels, bridges are apt to rank in the railroad
operator's mind as near-impasses.   Particularly is this true
when economy and the great length of a bridge have induced its
original builders to make it only wide enough for single-track
operation.

Such a bridge had been, unfortunately, the impressive
original structure over the Susquehanna on Mr. Garrett's
Baltimore–Philadelphia line.   Shortly before Mr. Willard's
accession to the presidency of the road, there had already
been begun a complete reconstruction of this structure; no
longer was it heavy enough for the rapidly increasing weight
of the cars and locomotives that demanded passage over it. . . .
While the workmen were busy upon this reconstruction, one
of the spans near the eastern end of the structure collapsed,
and so complete was the wreckage, that it was then and
there decided to abandon any efforts to rebuild the old bridge,
but to replace it at once with a fine modern double-track
structure.   This was in the beginning days of the Willard
administration.

It may seem easy enough to decide to build a new bridge
and then to go ahead and build it; but, in the case of even a
fairly busy trunk-line railroad already in operation, there are,
to put it mildly, complications.   Some provision obviously

must be made for handling the unceasing traffic during the period of reconstruction and replacement.

American bridge engineers have some remarkable performances to their credit in this very sort of thing. They have, between trains, torn out and replaced whole bridge spans. But these have been—relatively—small bridges. The high-set Susquehanna structure, nearly a mile and a half in length and eighty-five feet above the surface of the river at low tide, gave no opportunity for such measures.

In the excitement that had followed the unexpected collapse of a span of the original structure (fortunately, it went down under a freight and no one was seriously hurt), immediate plans were made to detour all Baltimore and Ohio trains over the nearby Pennsylvania (the former Philadelphia, Wilmington and Baltimore) between Wilmington and Baltimore. But this stretch of parallel railroad is also a congested line, and there was much delay to the trains of both roads. The emergency brought forth one of the ablest of the younger Baltimore and Ohio lieutenants, Arthur W. Thompson, at just that time in charge of the maintenance of the road. . . . Thompson took the first train to the spot, and by means of herculean labors succeeded in building, in sixty brief hours, a short stretch of double-track railroad (over fairly rough terrain), which connected the Pennsylvania and the Baltimore and Ohio, just west of Havre de Grace. A similar connection already existed near Perryville, on the opposite side of the Susquehanna. By use of both of these links, the detourage of Baltimore and Ohio trains over the rails of its competitor was thereafter limited to a brief two miles, including the new double-track low-level bridge of the Pennsylvania, close to the mouth of the river. This emergency movement continued for about two years. But when its splendid new double-track high-level Susquehanna Bridge of today had been finished, with a bettered approach at its western end, Baltimore and Ohio had relieved itself of a most disagreeable bottle neck on the easterly part of the system. "Slow orders" for Susquehanna Bridge had long

THE TWIN TUNNELS UNDER KINGWOOD.

The portal of the second one may be seen at the left of the original bore.

From a photograph.

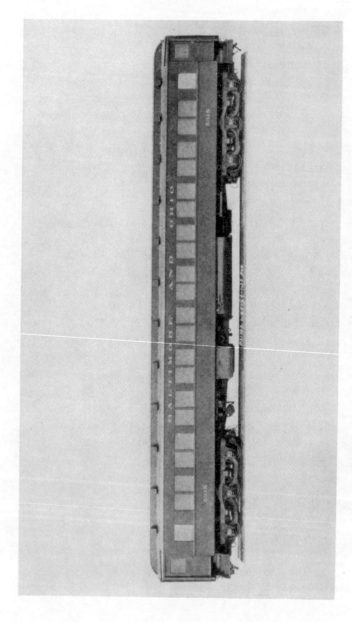

A MODERN PASSENGER COACH ON THE BALTIMORE AND OHIO.

All steel, and with six-wheeled trucks, it is the standard equipment on the system today.

From a photograph.

been the bane of the dispatchers upon the Philadelphia Division. Upon the new bridge, trains might pass one another at any point, and at a speed hardly less than upon the land.

.   .   .   .

At the same time the new Susquehanna Bridge was being finished, work was being pushed through upon a similar structure across the Brandywine. The beginnings of this also preceded Mr. Willard's administration. It had been planned in the days when the Pennsylvania still had a large hand in the operation of Baltimore and Ohio, and in its design it reflected, in no small degree, the taste and practice of the controlling road.

A slight change in the location of the line just north of the passenger station at Wilmington enabled the builders of this new bridge to do their work without reference to the daily traffic of the road. Thus, they were able to toil in at least a degree of leisure, and this they needed—for the bridge that they were building was no fabricated structure of steel to go up almost in a matter of days and of hours. It was constructed in a generation when the parent Pennsylvania was still inclined to favor the stone arch, for use in permanent bridge structures; particularly, those builded to carry an unusually heavy burden.

So it was that the new Wilmington bridge became a stone-arch structure from end to end—and one of the handsomest ever built in America. With its seven evenly placed and rounded arches standing in an exquisite city park and rising 114 feet above the waters of the narrow Brandywine, it typified the highest ideals of bridge construction; of all time or place. The fact that the man who had contracted to build it bankrupted himself upon the operation, is not germane to the beauty nor to the rugged strength of the great masonry structure. The essential fact is that the Wilmington Bridge is one of the very few in the United States builded for all time and for all conditions of service. That it may fairly be expected to live to this promise, may be gained from the fact that the Thomas Viaduct, which Latrobe built at the Relay House in 1835 to carry 10-ton locomotives and their small cars, today carries 300-ton locomotives and 5000-ton trains without a single addition of any sort to the original structure.

.   .   .   .

Two additional large bridges were both planned and builded by the Willard administration.   Each involved an expenditure of close to $2,000,000.   One of these is over the mouth of the Big Miami River, a few miles west of Cincinnati; the other is over the Allegheny within the city limits of Pittsburgh. Each represents a last word in bridge construction.

Two smaller bridges also are worthy of momentary attention:

The first of these was at Lumberport.   There came a spring, soon after Mr. Willard had assumed the presidency of Baltimore and Ohio, when winter lingered late.   Willard began to grow uneasy in anticipation of the large problem of getting the West Virginia coal up to the Lake Erie ports for the annual movement up the Great Lakes.   He felt that the road might fail to do its part and that some homes up in the Northwest possibly might be without fuel the following winter; an unthinkable condition of affairs.   He called some of his aides in on the problem; yet, the best advice that he gained from them was to go ahead with more double-tracking.   In the heavy mountainous country of West Virginia, the expense of such procedure was apt to be all but overwhelming; moreover, the time factor was coming sharply into the question—extensive double-tracking, with new tunnels to be bored, bridges builded and all the rest of it, is a matter of long months and years. . . .   Willard rejected that solution.

There was brought to his attention, however, a far simpler plan.   By taking the old Main Stem from Grafton to Wheeling— long since reduced to the status of a branch road—and the so-called West Virginia Short Line—from Fairmont through Lumberport to Brooklyn Junction on the Ohio River line and practically parallel, although a number of miles removed, from the old Wheeling main line—and by putting an articulated one-way movement of coal trains upon both of them (empty coal trains up the one line and the loaded trains down the other), what was the real equivalent of a double-track operation would be at once attained.

Only one obstacle to this plan presented itself: There was, due to the position of the overhanging mountains, a difficult switching movement at Clarksburg, a compulsory sort of back-wards and forwards drilling in the yards there that was bound to congest trains and prevent their prompt handling. It was quickly seen that only a new bridge across the Mononga-hela at Lumberport could obviate this clumsy movement.

Ergo: Such a bridge must be builded, at once.

Willard called his engineering assistants to him. They told him that the thing could be done, but that it would take time—much time. There were many details to be worked out. Some one would have to see the Secretary of War (the Monongahela is a navigable river) . . . soundings would have to be made . . . etc. . . . Willard then turned to Arthur W. Thompson, at that time chief engineer of maintenance of the company.

"I shall see the Secretary of War," said he. "You build the bridge."

Thompson built the bridge. He built it within ninety days, which, for a seven-span double-track steel bridge, 800 feet in length, is something of a record. On the night that he received the assignment, he was aboard a train bound for Lumberport. . . . Ninety days from the day that he received his orders to build Lumberport Bridge, it was ready and in service. There was no coal blockade that summer, the next winter no coalless houses in the Northwest.

Similarly, there was built a short but important bridge at Grafton that brought the branch leading southwest from the busy junction point (toward Pickens) into better working consonance with the main line. Because of the peculiar prox-imity of rushing river and steep mountain sides, it had always been said that the Grafton bridge could not be built. . . .

Willard and Thompson built it; in a matter of weeks, rather than months.   They also built a fine new passenger station at Grafton.   But their chief pride, forever and a day, was that new bridge, well hidden from the main-line track, which transformed the hitherto awkward Grafton yard into one of the most efficient on the entire system.   It cost money, but not a great deal of it.   Compared with some other expenditures of the Willard administration in the days when it first was putting the Baltimore and Ohio house in order, it was as nothing at all.

·   ·   ·   ·   ·   ·

All in all, Mr. Willard's administration expended for additions and betterments to the right of way, in the eighteen years from 1910 to 1927, inclusive, $145,563,200.   This sum went not alone for bridges and tunnels and additional main-line trackage. A good part of it was expended in added yard facilities, in grain elevators, and storage warehouses and shops and their equipment.   Of these last, two, of the most advanced type, were builded; at Cumberland and at Glenwood, just outside Pittsburgh.   In addition to which, the other and older shops of the company were revised and vastly improved; both as to buildings and to machinery.

"Make sure first that you are doing the best that you possibly can with your existing equipment," said Mr. Willard to his mechanical forces.   "Then, if you are in real need of it, you may come to me for additional equipment."

Historic Mount Clare—today one of the oldest railroad shops, if not the very oldest, in continuous service in all the world—received its full meed of attention.   Once attuned to an output of from sixty-five to seventy repaired and rebuilded locomotives a month, it had fallen in its average output to between thirty and forty.   Mr. Willard, within a few months, had it on its way to turning out three completed locomotives a day; soon its output will be four engines each twenty-four hours—and for longer and more complicated machines than those of former years. . . . Modern methods, including the use of the so-called "spot" system, have done as much to accomplish this advance as have modern machines. Mount Clare, long since cramped in its area by the steadily onrushing growth of Baltimore, has been kept forefront in the ranks of American locomotive and car shops only by the most intensive development of its facilities, of every sort.

In the first eighteen years of the present administration of Baltimore and Ohio, some $9,157,125 were expended in new shop facilities alone. Which compares with the $11,187,215 spent for rights of way and station grounds; the $16,477,480 for bridges, trestles and culverts; the $9,498,564 for terminal yards and tracks; even with the $25,647,281 for main-line trackage.

.   .   .   .

Yet, the track of a railroad (using the word in the broadest possible sense) is only the beginning of its physical problem. Given the line on which to run, in proper condition, there comes next attention to the problem of the vehicles to run upon that track—both those that pull and those that are pulled.

When Daniel Willard first came to the Baltimore and Ohio, he found its engine fleet once again considerably depleted in its efficiency. There had been a rather long-drawn-out strike on the part of the shop workers, and the maintenance of both the locomotives and the cars had fallen to a point well below a fair normal. . . . Moreover, there was a real insufficiency of engines. The road possessed, on January 1, 1910, 1886 locomotives (as compared with over 2500 at the present time), and these were of a type far inferior to those of today in strength and efficiency. The difference can best be expressed in the total tractive power of the locomotive fleet of Baltimore and Ohio—just 58,130,121 pounds in 1910, and over 126,000,000 pounds at the present day.

As in the matter of track expansion, Mr. Willard sought first to meet the most pressing needs of the road. To meet the immediate emergency his judgment, supplemented by that of his mechanical engineers, went to the Consolidation type of locomotive, with a tractive force of about 40,000 pounds at the drawbar.   The Mikado engine, particularly, took Mr. Willard's eye.   Of the 187 locomotives ordered during the first eighteen months of his administration, the greater number, by far, were of this type.   One hundred and five engines were purchased in the following twelve months—also chiefly Mikados.   Baltimore and Ohio kept right on buying these sturdy engines until it finally possessed a fleet of nearly 600 of them alone. . . .   Gradually, the road swung to the Mallet type, as well; until it had 135 of these great loco-motives.   The Santa Fé type became another favorite. There are now 154 of these in its locomotive forces.   And 219 Pacifics.

Yet, these mere figures do not tell the entire story of the motive power; of, for instance, 1576 locomotives furnished with superheaters and so, not so much increasing their tractive power, as accomplishing savings in fuel and water, running from 20 to 26 per cent.   Eight hundred and sixty-five of the engines have been equipped with stokers.   It is considered practically impossible to work a locomotive of 55,000 pounds tractive power to its full capacity with hand firing.   The automatic stoker comes to its own on the biggest engines.

.   .   .   .

After locomotives, cars.

When Daniel Willard came to the Baltimore and Ohio as president, there was not a steel passenger coach on the system, nor an electrically lighted one.   Only 38 per cent of the freight equipment was either steel-frame or all-steel.   Heavier engines brought, as a natural corollary, far heavier trains; and far heavier trains, obviously a far greater strain upon the structure of the cars.   Here, then, was another limitation of the wooden car.

Today 98.9 per cent of the freight equipment of the road and

MODERN PASSENGER COACH—INTERIOR.

Showing the individual seats which already (1927) have become a highly popular feature.

From a photograph.

INTERIOR OF A BALTIMORE AND OHIO DINING CAR.

These so-called "Colonial cars," named after distinguished American women of early days, show the good taste and charm of Georgian furniture and decoration.

From a photograph.

64.8 per cent of its passenger cars are all-steel.[1] The freight cars of the system have increased from the 79,883 of January 1, 1910, to 104,623; the passenger cars from 1154 to 1704. But, again, the increase is not best expressed in the mere units of cars —the total capacity of the car fleet best tells the story. In the eighteen years from January 1, 1910, to December 31, 1927, the total freight-car capacity of Baltimore and Ohio increased from 2,921,110 tons to 5,065,545 tons—or over 73.5 per cent. The average capacity of the individual car in that same time came from thirty-seven tons up to forty-eight.

Similarly, the passenger cars grew longer, bigger, in every way better. Each new car today is, automatically, an all-steel car. Very recently, many of the newest coaches on the fast main-line trains have been radically changed in their seating arrangements from the time-honored plan so long in vogue upon our American railroads; comfortable individual chairs, patterned largely on those in parlor cars and in the long-distance motor busses, have been introduced. A great stride has thus been made toward providing for the full comfort of the traveler, without reducing an iota the capacity of the car. . . . At the same time, new lights, brightly painted ceilings, and carpets down the main aisle of the cars have also contributed to his further comfort.[2]

While the supplying of sleeping cars, parlor cars, club cars and other passenger-train equipment representing the height of luxury in our American travel on the Baltimore and Ohio

[1] The slightly lesser showing of the latter type is due to the retention of some wooden coaches, light and clean and well maintained, upon branch lines and purely local passenger trains where the demands upon them are not rigorous in any way. Today the road possesses sufficient new steel passenger coaches to equip all its through passenger trains; from 75 to 80 per cent of its patrons ride in equipment of that sort.

[2] One of the things in which Baltimore and Ohio has a modest pride is in the fact that nothing but six-wheel trucks are used under its passenger cars. Many local passengers on the system ride upon the same sort of trucks as the president's business car—nothing less.

is the exclusive province of the Pullman Company, the road, in common with practically all its compeers in this country, owns and operates its own dining cars. From modest beginnings, this armada of rolling restaurants has come to consist of not less than seventy cars, which operate at all hours and from almost every corner of the system.

These cars have been kept constantly in the forefront of American car design, not merely from the mechanical point of view, but from the artistic as well.   They are simple, dignified, handsome. . . .   Quite recently, the policy has been adopted of naming them after women identified with the colonial progress of America.   This type of car—the so-called Colonial type —in its interior, with its leaded windows, gleaming white sides and ceiling, its Heppelthwaite chairs, and the rest of its correct appointments, represents the purest type of Georgian decoration that is found in the fine homes of early America. The first to be builded was the *Mount Vernon* (later renamed the *Betty Zane*).   Since then have come in quick succession the *Martha Washington, Dolly Madison, Betsy Ross, Betsy Patterson, Molly Pitcher, Nellie Custis, Priscilla Alden, Mollie Stark, Abigail Adams, Margaret Brent, Virginia Dare, Rebecca Rolfe, Margaret Corbin* and *Ann Bailey*.

.   .   .   .

Given good track, good locomotives, good cars; the next problem—and it is a very real one—that confronts the railroader is that of the proper correlation and operation of all these factors.   The best equipped railroad in all the world is as nothing without an intelligent scheme of operation.

Again, the answer is in the facts.

Because the story of the Baltimore and Ohio's operations during the past eighteen years is so intricate and so dramatic a one, it will not be told within this chapter; but must take its proper place in the pages of the succeeding ones.

CHAPTER XVI

DIFFICULT PROBLEMS OF OPERATION

Early Years of the Willard Administration—Upbuilding a Railroad Morale—The Terrific Ohio Floods of 1913—Widespread Disaster—Quick Steps Taken to Place the Road in Service Again—The Road's New Financial Structure.

TRACKS and trains are, in themselves, real railroad problems. Yet, large as these are, they are overshadowed, always, by that of their proper usage; of their correlation, if you prefer to put it that way. The railroad operating executive must have good right of way, including terminals and all the rest that goes with it; he must be provided with efficient engines and cars, in generous plenty; all these are his tools. But a real master workman regards his tools as but accessories to the real end to be accomplished. Over tracks, trains must be operated—here is the very soul and essence of the railroad. But it is in the manner of the operation that one finds the real efficiency with which its business is, or is not, being conducted. On this thing, it stands, and stands well; or falls, and falls miserably.

Before the construction gangs were well at work upon Doe Gully or Kingwood or Sand Patch or the other large improvements that were the beginning steps of his large program for the reconstruction of Baltimore and Ohio, Daniel Willard was giving his chief thought to this problem of precise administration. Unquestionably, the road had gained a little of a bad name. No denying that. Many times its trains were late, very late; there were occasions when freight congestion became intolerable. Baltimore and Ohio had its friends among the shippers, and they were loyal ones; but it also had its enemies, and some of these were bitter. To win this latter class to his support was just one of a thousand very real problems that confronted Willard at the very beginning of his administration. . . . Before he was done, it might be said—fairly—that Baltimore and Ohio had no enemies. It had ceased to be used as a butt in minstrel and variety-hall jokes. . . . Its patrons were its friends; and they were all loyal ones.

To work such a transformation meant a plan—meant something very much more than plan alone. It meant thought, patience, endeavor—much of each. It has meant, for eighteen years past, the cultivation of cordial and understanding relationships between the road and three types of folk—its employés, its patrons and its neighbors; the citizens of the many communities, large and small, through which it passes. "To be a good neighbor," long since became a Baltimore and Ohio slogan; recognized as such the country over.

.   .   .   .

Of the three types of folk whom he had to cultivate and to understand, Willard placed his fellow employés first.

He had come to a road famed among its contemporaries for the long service and the loyalty of its workers. For two and three and four generations of a family to work for the road is no unusual experience for Baltimore and Ohio. Certain Maryland families—Galloway and Spurrier and Beaumont are typical of these—have been upon its pay rolls almost since the first small horse-drawn train began its daily pilgrimages between Baltimore and Ellicotts Mills. Today, there are over 1500 men—out of a total of 68,907 in the company's employ—who have been working for the road for forty years and upwards. One hundred and fifty-nine men have a record of fifty years or more of faithful service.

With such human material with which to mold, Mr. Willard was able to develop a group of railroad workers, which, for spirit and loyalty and morale, today is without superior anywhere. Always he has fostered promotion within the ranks of the company; yet, never to the extent of using mere seniority as the only test for a man's advancement. The record of his eighteen years shows but few men brought to the road from the outside for executive positions. On the other hand, the road's records are filled with almost countless instances of men rising from train crew or machine shop or trackside or office force to positions of steadily increasing executive importance. Baltimore and Ohio has not only found men in its own ranks for its official posts, but it has trained them for other roads. At this time, the presidents of two important eastern railroads —the Lackawanna and the Central Railroad of New Jersey— are recent Baltimore and Ohio graduates.

．　　．　　．　　．　　．　　．　　．

The best answer to such an intelligent policy, intelligently administered, is in the result. Measuring 1910—the beginning year of the Willard administration—with 1927, one finds some rather striking results. For instance, one discovers that, in the fiscal year of 1910, Baltimore and Ohio hauled in its freight traffic, 12,675,482,892 tons one mile; while, in 1927—in accordance with present-day American railroad practice, the calendar year is used—this traffic came to 22,528,749,584 ton miles. The passenger traffic also showed an increase—from 763,448,759 passenger miles to 902,306,942; but this was not so vital nor so large. It is important, however, to know that an operating ratio of 71.64 per cent in 1910—which, at one time, in the days of the government operation of the road, reached as high as 97.56 per cent—in 1927 had become 75.65 per cent; due largely to steady wage advances to the men. It is worth noting that an average trainload of 466 tons in 1910, by 1927 had become 942 tons, with the average carload raised from 24.1

to 32.1 tons.[1]   These are the figures by which the trained rail-operating man measures the performance of any given property. For them, in its own case, Baltimore and Ohio has to offer no apology whatsoever.

Yet, back of these statistics, is the story of a consistent and steady and well driven human effort. In due time, there will be shown in these pages a few pictures of highly specialized effort in the company—such as pensions, relief associations and the like, some of which, within recent years, have assumed large proportions. All of these things are very good. They have been of tremendous help in the gradual up-building of Baltimore and Ohio. Yet, back of them, always has been the achievement of the rank and file of the road in its everyday job—and this achievement is the result of human understanding between the road's officers and their sub-ordinates; at almost every corner of the property and at almost every possible time.

.   .   .   .

If it had not been for this achievement—even in the first three years of the present administration—it is possible that the road might not have been able to cope with the great Ohio floods of March, 1913.

That far-flung catastrophe was the most dramatic incident, or series of incidents, in the annals of Baltimore and Ohio since the days of the Civil War; or at least since the strike riots of the dark hours of the 'seventies.

It came to the property, unheralded. For several days it had rained steadily all over the East; an unrelenting, heavy rain, which gradually assumed the proportions of a veritable Biblical deluge. The officers of the railroad company in their

---

[1] All of this, despite the lowering of impressive main-line averages by the many, many branch lines of Baltimore and Ohio. Upon the main stems, the 5000-ton freighter long since became too common to be especially noteworthy; but the branches neither require nor can they even fill long trains, and heavy.

offices at Baltimore had watched the rain dash against their windows, hour after hour; had listened to reports of rivers to the west steadily rising in their courses. . . . Yet, had given no great concern to any of this. In March, protracted rain storms are not unusual.

.   .   .   .   .   .

The floods, as such, commenced with the long rain storm, which began in Ohio, at eight o'clock in the morning of Sunday, March 23. This rain continued, almost unremittingly, throughout that day and the three that followed. Gradually, many of the rivers throughout Ohio—chief amongst them, the Muskingum, the Scioto, the Little Miami and the Great Miami—began rising. As, hour after hour, the downfall persisted, the rate of the rising increased. By noon of the twenty-fourth, the rivers already were at flood heights. At Zanesville, for instance, seventy miles from Marietta (where the Muskingum finally pours its waters into those of the Ohio), the water rose steadily, until it came to a crest height of fifty-one feet, eight inches, which was at least fifteen feet higher than ever before in the records of the town. The famous "Y" bridge at that point—the solid concrete structure at the precise intersection of the Muskingum and the Licking rivers, which, a few years before, had replaced the earlier wooden bridge of the National Road—was completely overflowed. To the eternal credit of its builders, it did not go out. The stout wrought-iron structure of the Baltimore and Ohio was not so fortunate. Three of its four spans finally yielded to the onrush of the waters.

The situation at Zanesville was repeated a few miles further west—at Columbus. Here it was the Scioto that was on the rampage. The Big Four Railroad, over which the Baltimore and Ohio enters the Ohio capital from the West, gave early notice that it could no longer be responsible for the safety of its Scioto bridge. A rerouting of trains, by way of Chillicothe and the Norfolk and Western tracks, was immediately arranged. This was of short duration. Soon, there was trouble at Chillicothe (further down the Scioto), and much of it. The river was piling itself back of the Baltimore and Ohio embankment across the end of the park there. And, before the waters were done, there was no inconsiderable property damage—and twenty-five lives lost.

Further down the Scioto—at its mouth, at the old river town of Portsmouth—the trouble was being repeated. The mighty Ohio itself was coming into flood. It could not much longer withstand the tremendous influx of water that was being poured into it from its many tributaries. True it was that the two uppermost of these—the Allegheny and the Monongahela—had contributed but little to the debacle. (In fact, at no time was the Monongahela to go into the March flood. It had held the center of the stage two months earlier. The Allegheny went higher. But the Pittsburgh levees in March, 1913, never reached the flood stages that they had seen in the preceding January.)

But the Beaver River, most easternmost of all the important streams in Ohio, was in high flood; and Wheeling finally saw the waters come to within two feet of the record high water of 1884, which still is remembered, with a shudder, throughout the entire Ohio Valley. Yet that earlier flood, in its damage to the railroads, was not to be compared with the deluge of 1913.

Cincinnati often has caught its full share of the historic floods of the interior of the country. It did not escape the 1913 catastrophe. The water, which had stood at about a thirty-foot stage on March 25—rather low for that season of the year—that evening began to rise. It rose a foot an hour during that night and the day and night that followed; until it came to a crest of fifty feet. After that, the rise was slower. But it was steady. The Ohio is a river notoriously slow to wrath. But when it begins to come, it comes inevitably. . . . The morning of the first day of April saw men in rowboats scanning the high-water mark of '84, firmly painted high on one of the stone piers of the old suspension bridge. March, 1913, came within one foot and one inch of that record; which meant, at Cincinnati, seventy feet; the high-water stage of the most destructive flood that America has ever known.

Curiously enough, the water stood twenty feet higher at the Cincinnati levee than it stood at Mayville, Kentucky, sixty miles further up the Ohio. This anomalous condition, it was finally discovered, was due to the setback of the waters emerging from the Great Miami at its confluence, fifteen miles below Cincinnati. The Great Miami was breaking all records. It poured its flood into the Ohio, much more rapidly than the larger river could possibly carry it off. Poured its waters with such a sweep that the pilot of a large packet steamer saved himself from being dashed into the opposite shore only by heading his vessel straight into the current. By something very much like a miracle, he saved the boat and its passengers from destruction.

. . . .

West of Cincinnati and the Ohio state line, the flood situation continued—almost at its worst—all the way across Indiana and into eastern Illinois. The West Fork of the White River, which crosses under the Baltimore and Ohio just west of Washington, Indiana, went on a rampage of its own. Here was a peculiarly troublesome stream. It began its mischievous capers well up on its course—at Anderson, and again at Muncie and at Indianapolis—and, by the time it had come to the southern part of the state, it had changed mere mischief to stark tragedy. At its crossing under the Baltimore and Ohio, it managed first to wash out the so-called Blue Hole Trestle, which carried the railroad track over a great slough, or overflow opening, for the river, 284 feet in width. This occurred at 10:50 o'clock on the evening of March 27. Fifteen minutes later, the main bridge of the railroad over the river two miles further west—a two-truss steel structure, 420 feet long—also went out.

Real tragedy there was in the first washout. Upon the

Blue Hole Trestle, there had been standing, in the blackness of the rain-filled night, a light locomotive; attached to it, a string of flat cars, upon which a work gang was standing. . . . Without warning, the cars and the track upon which they stood began to give, with a crackle which gave place to a sullen and deafening roar, above the racket of the rain.   The train master, G. C. Stevens, called to the gang to jump, for their lives. Some of them jumped.   Some of them stayed by the work train. It seemed to make but little difference.   When, in the feeble flickerings of lanterns and of torches, they were able to count noses once again, it was found that four men were gone—Engineer Theodore Garst, Fireman Reason Jackson, General Yardmaster D. L. Shafer and Night Yardmaster C. McLemore. All of these men were residents of Washington.   When, after a time, their bodies were recovered, they were given state funerals.   All deaths of heroism are not those of the battlefield. The railroad has its own roster of honor.

Other casualties were to be recorded from the system, but none so far-reaching as this Indiana one; none where men had so bravely and so helplessly faced death; to be compelled, finally, to pay the full price for their surpassing courage.

.   .   .   .

The railroad is a living thing.   It is, if you please, a system of throbbing, pulsing arteries.   But cut one or more of these important arteries, let it remain severed, and the railroad, to the extent that it remains severed, is a dead thing—of little value whatsoever. . . .   In those hard March and April days of 1913, many Baltimore and Ohio arteries were severed; not once, but repeatedly, and in widely separated portions of the system. . . .   Sometimes, it was hours—even days—before headquarters could know of these individual disasters.   Alongside the arteries of the modern railroad, there run also its nerves —the delicate copper strands of the telegraph and the telephone which sensitively bind it together.   When Baltimore and Ohio arteries were severed in those trying days, nerves went also. Sometimes, they went more quickly than the tracks—a final résumé showed that the company had lost in the floods more than 3500 telegraph poles and the lines that they held into the air. . . .

Without those nerves, it was hard to get any news of the disaster; harder still, to get relief to the beleaguered points. The first thought of the men at Baltimore and at other head-quarters points upon the system was to get relief trains through; —bearing food and clothing and other supplies, along with doctors and nurses and volunteer workers—to the folk resident in the inundated and wrecked towns, or to passengers and train crews marooned upon long miles of stalled trains. . . . In the case of an ordinary train wreck or similar disaster blocking a single line of railroad, the procedure usually is simple; trains may be sent forward by the lines of the nearest parallel or adjacent railroad. The process is called detouring.

But the Ohio floods devastated almost all roads in the inundated territory about equally. An exception was the Lake Shore and Michigan Southern (now the New York Central), running along the extreme northerly edge of the state. The management of the Lake Shore turned over its facilities to the disabled roads to the south. Over its tracks, there poured for several days the chief trains of the Baltimore and Ohio, the Pennsylvania, the Erie and the other lines to the south, whose bridges were down and whose tracks for miles were lost under the yellow flood waters.

The Lake Shore was indeed the exception. And it was only in the northernmost part of the blocked Baltimore and Ohio system that detouring was possible for any length of time. In the other portions of the flood territory, bridges must be replaced and tracks, turned and twisted, must be made true and straight once again. Which, when one considers that more than three thousand miles of the Baltimore and Ohio system had been directly and seriously affected by the flood, was no small problem.

From all far corners of the property, men and machinery were garnered and sent to the front for action—whenever and wherever it was possible over the gnarled mass of railroad wreckage that extended for miles.   When Baltimore and Ohio's resources had been exhausted, aid was asked of other roads; outside the afflicted zone.   Systems, such as the Burlington, the Northwestern, the Soo, the Milwaukee and the Rock Island, gave, and gave generously, of their crews and equipment. . . .   Yet, for some days after the flood had attained its peak and had begun, ever so slightly, to subside, the rain continued, almost daily.   The working gangs—hard at it night and day and under all conditions of weather—saw the work that they had so carefully accomplished washed out again and again from under them.   And set forth cheerfully once again to repair the wrecked lines.

.   .   .   .

A typical situation was that at Zanesville.   Already there has been shown how the Muskingum, which at that point receives the waters of the Licking River, went out of control in the early stages of the disaster.   The flood swept through the streets of the small Ohio city.   Ten inches of water stood in the lobby of the Zanesville Hotel.   The guests were mealless. The kitchens were under water and the head chef was barred out from the flooded area by the militiamen who had been brought in to help control the situation.

At 9:45 o'clock in the morning of Wednesday, March 26, Span No. 2 of the Baltimore and Ohio bridge went out; Nos. 1 and 3 followed about an hour later.   Span No. 4 remained in place.   It was protected by a gristmill from the full force of the waters. . . .   All traffic ceased.   Telegraph and telephone wires were down.   For long hours, Pittsburgh and other Baltimore and Ohio operating centers knew naught of the vast extent of the damage that had been wrought.   Finally, the news began to filter through.   And, as soon as there could be any train service whatsoever, aid began to find its way.   At

WHEN THE WATERS ROLLED OVER ZANESVILLE.

The crest of the tide has been reached and recession begun.

From a photograph taken from Putnam Hill, March 28, 1913.

CLEARING UP FLOOD WRECKAGE.

Through the sole remaining span of the Baltimore and Ohio bridge over the Muskingum at Zanesville, Ohio, Engineer Paul Didier prepared to build a temporary trestle.

From a photograph taken at the time.

Zanesville, this aid came in the person of Paul Didier, then the resident engineer of the company at Pittsburgh.[1]

Didier put on his top boots and his oldest clothes and left Pittsburgh at a quarter of nine Sunday morning, the thirtieth. At CD tower, twelve miles east of Zanesville, the train stopped. It could go no further. There was no more track ahead. . . . Didier got out and walked that dozen miles through the thick mud to Zanesville. He reached the beleaguered town at six o'clock. He noted that the river still stood nineteen feet above the ordinary high limit. He took a good look at the ruined bridge. There was nothing else that he could do.

On Monday, there was nothing that he could do; except to note that the waters were slowly falling once again. Late that afternoon, he fastened three thirty-three-foot rails together and plumbed for the bottom. He was figuring all this time on building a timber-bent trestle across the Muskingum, just as soon as the waters would give him the least fighting chance. The camp trains began rolling in to aid him; with men and materials, from Pittsburgh, from Cumberland, from as far off as Baltimore. Railroad trains were coming a little closer to Zanesville, from the west as well as the east. By Tuesday, a rough sort of bus connection was being arranged between them.

Tuesday, there arrived in Zanesville the president, the operating vice-president and the chief engineer of the Baltimore and Ohio. They asked Didier many things. They did not *ask* him how long it would take him to rebuild the bridge. They *told* him that it *must* be ready in the shortest possible time. Didier replied that he would do it in two weeks. He actually did it in eight days.

That sounds simple. It was not simple. To build, across a swollen and a mud-filled river, a bridge capable of carrying

[1] Mr. Didier is a rare personality. Even in the Baltimore and Ohio family, which has many rare personalities. Frenchman born, he studied under Victor Hugo in Paris and fought for his country in the Franco-Prussian War of 1870. For many years he has lived in Pittsburgh; serving also as the Belgian Consul in that city.

heavy passenger or freight trains in perfect safety, is no child's task.[1]   Didier so found it.   It was not until Sunday, the sixth, that the waters of the two rivers had receded to a point where he was willing to risk the lives of the workmen on the difficult construction job.   (Even as it was, one life was lost upon it.) On Monday, the fourteenth, the regular operation of trains began over the temporary bridge.   No longer was the railroad severed at that point.   And the stout trestle bridge was to remain in place for many months—until a steel one could be fabricated to replace it.

Mr. Didier has written a memorandum of just how he began his difficult job.   It is a short and extremely modest document. It reads:

One of the most salient features to the handicap of the rapid placing of the skeleton bents was the bringing of the bents from the west shore framing park to where the bent was to be lowered and this was handicapped by the west span not being carried away by the flood waters.   This span, which was similar to the other three spans washed away, was a through-truss bridge and, in order to speed up the work, no time could be lost by lowering and hoisting the boom of the derrick-crane to and from the work; this span was rather a hindrance to the work and to obviate this I removed the portals, top-struts, wind-bracings, etc., leaving the trusses unprotected against any possible wind pressure; thus allowing the derrick-crane free and unobstructed speedy but cautious movement across the bridge to and from the work.   It was the great time-saving scheme of the whole work, risky but successful.

Wherever there were such situations, there seemed to be Didiers to rise up and to meet them, successfully.   It is traditional of Baltimore and Ohio that, whenever a real emergency has arisen, a real man has arisen to cope successfully with it.

[1] The situation was complicated for Didier by the fact that, a few inches below the mud brought down by the flood, the Muskingum had a hard, almost impenetrable rocky bottom.   This gave the engineer the worst possible opportunity for the placing of his wooden trestle bents.

Where important bridges—such as those at Zanesville, at North Bend (over the Great Miami) and at Washington, Indiana—had been washed out, it was necessary to send at once to the steel mills to prepare to roll and fabricate new spans and members.   Because this process took time, temporary wooden trestles, similar to that at Zanesville, were put up at once.   All this cost much money; but, to a railroad, time is money, always, and no effort and no expense too great to restore, in some fashion at least, a severed line.

.   .   .   .

The longest that any single link of the Baltimore and Ohio remained completely severed was on the main line between Cincinnati and St. Louis, where, for twelve days, regular train service of every sort was suspended.   Conditions on this important link were such that it was particularly difficult to get aid and supplies through to the work gangs.   Its many miles of single track, and the fact that it ran through a territory without many feeding or parallel roads—and such as were, largely occupied with their own troubles—delayed greatly the replacing of this part of the road.   But the men who labored upon it did not falter.   The wonder is that they were able to reknit it, in twelve days, instead of taking double or triple that space of time.

.   .   .   .

When the last of the flood waters were receding and the lines all had been reunited, even though in temporary form, it was time for headquarters at Baltimore to make some accounting of the damage that had been wrought.   Despite desperate efforts to save them—including the running of loaded cars and engines out upon their threatened spans—seven sizable steel bridges had been washed out and completely destroyed.   Of these, the largest by far was the structure over the mouth of the Great Miami.   It took long months to replace this bridge, and then—within the next two or three years—it was again destroyed; this time by a terrific ice jam in the Ohio. . . .

When the bridge was replaced that time, it was rebuilded upon a scale that, as far as experts might judge their remotest possibilities, would amply admit all flood waters, without the slightest bit of damage to itself.[1]

Thousands of feet of pile-and-frame trestle upon the system also had been washed out; yet this was as nothing, compared with the miles of ballast and track that had been completely wiped out of existence by the flood waters. Stations and other small buildings, along with passenger cars and freight cars, had gone racing and swirling down the enraged streams; in many cases, never to be found and regained. . . . The localities most seriously affected, aside from the Cincinnati–St. Louis line, were at Zanesville, Marietta and Hamilton, where large bridges had been washed away; and at Dayton and Chillicothe, where the yards were badly damaged. The Ohio River line, particularly as it neared Kenova, suffered most seriously. And there was much track, as well as some small bridges, lost on portions of the system throughout western Pennsylvania, Ohio and Indiana.

It was estimated that the property damage to the Baltimore and Ohio was something over $2,750,000. This did not include a loss in traffic estimated to be somewhere around $1,500,000. In addition to this, the Cincinnati, Hamilton and Dayton, which already had become a part of the Baltimore and Ohio system, had a property loss of $1,450,000, and an estimated traffic loss of $350,000. Six million dollars—much more— was the price that a helpless railroad paid for a single devastating storm in the very heart of its area.

. . . .

To provide equipment for a railroad—even in normal times, let alone those of widespread disaster—takes money; generally,

[1] The present bridge over the Great Miami was completed in 1921. It is double-tracked, 1417 feet in length, and consists of six through-truss spans and four girder spans. It cost to build the not inconsiderable sum of $2,100,000. . . . It is placed high above the river and there is every reason to believe that it will remain in place for many years to come.

a very great deal of money. To the Baltimore and Ohio, money has not always come either quickly or easily. There has been shown in these pages how very difficult it was for the company at times to raise even enough cash to keep itself in the barest form of operation. . . . In recent years, however, this has changed. Baltimore and Ohio credit never stood at a higher point than upon the centennial anniversary of the birth of the company; nor its securities in more favorable demand, not only from individual investors but from conservative banks, savings banks, insurance companies and the like.

At the time of the reorganization of the company (between 1898 and 1901), several separate and distinct mortgages were created upon its property. The two largest of these—the Prior Lien and the First mortgages—being secured mainly by liens upon the main line and the more important branches; the other mortgages—the Southwestern Division, the Pittsburgh Junction and the Middle Division—were, as their names would indicate, divisional in their scope.

These were all inelastic, being tightly fixed as to interest rates and maturities and restricted as to the amount of bonds reserved for the future capital requirements of the company. The reserve bonds proved inadequate and soon were exhausted. Still more money was needed for capital purposes. The road —it now was in the Loree administration—was rapidly being expanded in many of its physical requirements. All of them took money, and most of them took a good deal of money. So there was created (in 1901) the Pittsburgh, Lake Erie and West Virginia Mortgage. This, like those it followed, was divisional, tightly fixed as to terms and amount. . . . In 1901, the company also issued and sold $15,000,000 of convertible bonds, which subsequently were converted into common stock. The following year saw an additional amount of common stock —$65,000,000—marketed. . . . After this, there was a pause for four years—when $27,750,000 in common shares were issued and sold.

It began to grow increasingly difficult for even the best of our railroads to market common stock. Continued political attacks upon them and the failure of either the states or the federal government to relieve their rate structures, despite their much increased operating costs, at last began to tell upon them in the money marts. Other methods of financing were sought. In the case of Baltimore and Ohio, recourse was had to short-time loans—until March, 1913, when bettered conditions enabled the company to issue and sell $63,250,000 in convertible bonds. These were used to fund the short-time loans and to retire them.

. . . .

These methods of financing, while squarely meeting every expediency, were unsatisfactory alike to the company and to its investors. Its officers sought a better way out. Over $126,000,000 in mortgage bonds, created at the time of the reorganization, were due to mature in 1925, and these would have to be met. That was but one phase of the problem. Another was to have, for all time, some comprehensive and reasonably elastic plan of permanent financing—a sort of underlying and forever dependable financial foundation for the entire property. Gradually this plan was evolved.[1] It took the name of the Refunding and General Mortgage. Here was a

[1] The man largely responsible for the development of this great financial structure and who took the brunt of its creation on his shoulders is none other than George M. Shriver, the present (1927) senior vice-president of Baltimore and Ohio. Mr. Shriver had made the road and its problems a lifelong and affectionate study. He came to it, in 1886, as a clerk in the accounting department, but two years later found him as private secretary to the president, Charles F. Mayer. When Mr. Mayer retired and was succeeded by John K. Cowen, Shriver retained the same office. He applied himself most diligently to the affairs of the road and L. F. Loree raised him to the post of assistant to the president. . . . One year after the election of Daniel Willard as president of the company, Mr. Shriver was elected a vice-president; in 1916, this title was changed to senior vice-president. His interest in the property has been unflagging. While he has specialized in its financial and accounting arrangements, as well as in its welfare work and its public relations, there has not been a single phase of its operations that has escaped his attention. With a passion for detail, he also keeps a fine grasp on the broader outlook of vision and of policy.

financial reserve for the property, for all time; a railroad company in the eighty-fifth year of its life putting out a security that could appeal—and did appeal—to the most conservative investors.

This new mortgage was designed to become, ultimately, a first lien upon the entire system of the company, through the refundment, under its provisions, of all underlying prior liens, including those of the mortgages created during the reorganization and thereafter, aggregating at the time approximately $282,350,000; and, in addition, the $63,250,000 convertible bonds of 1913.

.   .   .   .

The Refunding and General Mortgage of Baltimore and Ohio contains a number of provisions, which, at the time of its creation, were unique and which, while giving maximum protection to the security holder, afforded the company permissible latitude in the issuance of bonds at various interest rates, maturities, etc. The authorized issue of the bonds is limited to an amount, which, together with all the prior debts of the railroad company, after deducting the bonds reserved to retire prior debts at maturity, shall not exceed three times the then outstanding capital stock of the company, with the additional limitation that, when the aggregate amount of the bonds outstanding and the bonds reserved to retire prior debt shall be $600,000,000, no additional bonds shall be issued—except those reserved to retire prior debt—without the further consent of the stockholders of the company. Such additional bonds may be issued only to an amount not exceeding eighty per cent of the cost of the work done or the property acquired.

.   .   .   .

Here then, in brief, is the entire bond policy of the Baltimore and Ohio Railroad of today. Its absolute soundness is attested by hosts of bank presidents and other critical investors of every sort.

In 1924, it was deemed prudent to anticipate the refunding of a part, at least, of the $131,125,280 face amount of bonds maturing in 1925. Taking advantage of the money conditions then existing, the company, in August of that year, issued and sold $75,000,000 face amount of its First Mortgage Bonds, maturing in 1948 (which had been reserved for the purpose of retiring an equal amount of its Prior Lien Bonds, maturing July 1, 1925), and also sold $35,000,000 of Refunding and General Mortgage Bonds in order to make payment at maturity of various divisional mortgages—and for other capital purposes.

In 1925, arrangements were made for the extension of the time of payment of the $45,000,000 Baltimore and Ohio Southwestern Division Bonds until 1950. With the extension of these securities, the company successfully concluded the refinancing of the $131,125,280 of mortgage bonds maturing in 1925, and also provided some $24,000,000 required for betterments to its property.[1]

.   .   .   .   .   .

By 1927, its Centenary year, the credit of Baltimore and Ohio had improved to such a remarkable extent and financial conditions in general were such, that the company was enabled to issue and sell—very largely to its own shareholders—$63,242,500 of additional common stock, at 107½. The rights to subscribe to this new issue were put out at a ratio of one to four of the already existing shares. They were eagerly sought. Which, in view of the long term of years in which practically no American railroad had dared put a new issue of stock upon the market, was something of a compliment to the condition of Baltimore and Ohio in the one-hundred-and-first year of its life.

[1] In 1917, Baltimore and Ohio had created another divisional mortgage, the Toledo–Cincinnati Division, in the acquisition of the Toledo and Cincinnati Railroad Company (formerly the Cincinnati, Hamilton and Dayton), all the outstanding bonds of which are redeemable under the Refunding and General Mortgage. . . . Due to conditions existing during and directly after the war, it

ACROSS THE GREAT MIAMI TODAY.

Three times the floods and ice have swept away Baltimore and Ohio bridges at the mouth of that turbulent stream. The present bridge, built in 1921, is far longer and stronger than its predecessors.

From a photograph.

THE BALTIMORE AND OHIO BRIDGE OVER THE ALLEGHENY RIVER AT PITTSBURGH.

A fine example of modern steel-bridge construction on the system.

From the proceeds of the sale of these new shares, the company retired $35,000,000 in ten-year six per cent bonds, which were called for redemption on January 1, 1928; the balance going to property additions and betterments. By this step, it not only reduced its annual fixed charges by $2,100,000, but it made a real improvement in the relationship of its stock and mortgage debts to its total capitalization. A proportion of 26.64 per cent of stock to 73.35 per cent of mortgage debt was changed to one of 33.48 per cent of stock and 66.52 per cent of mortgage. In other words, instead of a proportion of one of stock to three of bonds, one was created of one of stock to two of bonds. This much improved relationship it was expected would be reflected in the future in a broader market for the company's securities and a cheaper financing of its monetary requirements. [1]

was deemed inexpedient to sell long-term bonds for capital purposes.   Instead, the company issued and sold $35,000,000 in ten-year bonds.

[1] At the end of its Centenary year (1927) the capitalization of the Baltimore and Ohio Railroad Company was as follows:

First Mortgage Bonds..................	$156,995,100
Refunding and General Mortgage Bonds..	125,000,000
Divisional Mortgages...................	98,965,200
Convertible Debenture Bonds	63,250,000
Other Bonds, Equipment Obligations, etc.	95,970,723
Unassumed Obligations of Owned and Operated Properties...............	6,762,200
Total Secured Debt...............	$546,943,223
Capital Stock Outstanding:	
Preferred 4%........................	$ 58,863,181
Common...........................	215,187,853
Total Capital Stock	$274,051,034

CHAPTER XVII

BALTIMORE AND OHIO IN KHAKI

War Breaks Out Overseas and Traffic Multiplies Upon Our Rail-
roads Here—Their Steadily Increasing Burdens—The United
States Enters the Conflict and the Railroad War Board is
Created—Its Work and Its Achievements.

BALTIMORE and Ohio rebounded quickly from the all but
overwhelming disaster of the Ohio floods.

The United States is so very great, so very far-reaching
indeed, that even such a widespread catastrophe does not often
produce a serious or a lasting effect upon the nation as a whole.
In fact, this disaster in the central portion of the land,
itself, presently began to make traffic for the railroads. Dayton and the other cities that had suffered chiefly from it began
to reconstruct themselves, upon a much better scale than ever
before. Building materials and other supplies began rushing
in—by the hundreds of trainloads. And, in consequence,
freight traffic benefited very largely thereby.

Moreover, hardly fifteen months were to pass before a
new disaster was to be visited upon the world—in every way
incomparably greater than any flood imaginable, and yet,
in turn, bringing tremendous new tides of traffic to the railroads of America.

In distant lands—far across the Atlantic—men were spring-
ing at each other's throats. In Central Europe, a great war—
a world war, one yet to attain dimensions almost unbelievably
great—had begun. At the outset, the United States was to

stand only as a spectator; shocked and dazed and not fully realizing the final import of the conflict to her. . . . In its next phase, we were to assume the rôle of purveyors to certain of the warring nations—as the maker of thousands of tons of ammunition and other munitions of war to be shipped overseas. At the outbreak of the war, traffic on many of our railroads was suffering a considerable diminution. Upon the Baltimore and Ohio, there had been achieved in the calendar year of 1913—a record high up to that time in gross earnings—$101,760,757. In 1914, this had dropped to $91,895,912. It was not to reach this low figure again.

The tremendous impetus given to industrial America in the late autumn of 1914 showed itself clearly upon the earnings of all the railroads in 1915—upon the Baltimore and Ohio alone, the gross earnings jumped upwards to $100,717,667. . . . America was indeed hard at work. Shipyards, long since abandoned, or practically so, were thriving with work; every factory was being expanded, to its limits; new ones, by the dozens, were going up in each important industrial city in the nation. Freight traffic—passenger traffic, too—multiplied, amazingly. . . . In 1916, the total gross earnings of the Baltimore and Ohio were $116,968,881; in 1917, they were $133,613,322; in 1918, they were to reach the almost unimaginable figure of $174,191,446; which, afterwards, was to be known as but a rung in a ladder reaching much higher.

Before these totals of 1917 were ever reached, much was to happen to the eventful course of Baltimore and Ohio. After long months of anxiety and of doubt, the United States was finally to enter the World War; as an active participant. On the sixth of April of that year, it cast its lot irrevocably with France and Great Britain and the other Allied Powers. . . . It became a soldier. It took off its coat, rolled up its sleeves and prepared to do its own full part in the winning of the most eventful conflict in world history.

Which meant that its railroads must do their part. No longer was theirs to be a commercial adventure alone; now they, too, were soldiers, enrolled for the fullest duty to the land that had made them possible. They did not wait to be told their duty. On the rainy night in April, 1917, that Congress formally declared war against Germany and her allies, the executives of several leading American railroads—including Baltimore and Ohio—already were in communication with one another, looking forward toward the establishment of some workable plan of unified coöperation with the authorities at Washington. It was decided that there must be set up immediately, at the national capital, some form of centralized agency, with full authority to coördinate the activities of all the steam carriers, so that they might render collectively the greatest possible transport service in aid of the war program. Such an agency—the Railroad War Board—was brought into being.

.   .   .   .

Woodrow Wilson's signature was hardly dry on the Declaration of War before the attention of official Washington was upon the inland transport problem. Instantly, it was recognized that, upon the ability or the failure of the railroads of the United States to function properly, might easily rest the winning or the losing of the war.

Phases of the rail situation arose quickly on all sides.

The first one that came to the attention of the troubled men at Washington was a naval one. Our fleet in the Pacific needed Pocahontas coal, from West Virginia; must have Pocahontas coal, at once. Ordinarily, a movement of collier ships through the Panama Canal would have met this necessity. But already our ships were being withdrawn; for even greater, more immediate necessities. The Secretary of the Navy sent for the president of the Baltimore and Ohio, in his capacity as chairman of the Advisory Commission of the Council of National Defense, to which he had just been appointed by President Wilson. . . . The crisis was explained to him. Mr. Willard found just how many coal cars would be needed each day; and arranged to get them from railroads which already had agreed, informally, to coöperate in the situation. He worked out direct routes across the continent upon which a preferred movement of coal might best be established.

Certain influences at Washington interfered. These began to demand that the railroads that had had governmental assistance of one sort or another be given the preference. These influences had to be met, quietly argued with, and overcome. It all took time, and a great deal of energy. But it had to be done.

Even before, food shortages began to show themselves. There was a serious drought down in Texas. Two thousand carloads of cattle had to be moved up into Nebraska, and that at once. No time to be lost anywhere. This time, the Secretary of the Interior sent for Mr. Willard. He made the very valuable suggestion that the railroads would be compelled to organize, and that Daniel Willard, himself, would have to head the centralized organization. To the last part of this suggestion, the president of the Baltimore and Ohio demurred; but to the first part of Mr. Lane's plan, he enthusiastically acceded.

"I shall call a conference of the railroad executives with the Council and see if we cannot do this very thing."

It was done. That night, Mr. Willard sent hundreds of telegraphic calls to the presidents of the leading American railroads to come to Washington, there to formulate a definite program for their coöperation in the war. . . . Some seventy railroad executives, representing the chief companies in the United States, responded to the call and met in a Washington hotel on April 11. The grave urgency of the situation was explained to them, and they were asked to appoint a committee of five of their number to form a central war board. This was done. For the Railroad War Board, there were designated: (as chairman) Fairfax Harrison, president of the Southern Railway; Julius Kruttschnitt, chairman of the board of the Southern Pacific Company; Howard Elliott, president of the Northern Pacific; Samuel Rea, president of the Pennsylvania; and Hale Holden, president of the Chicago, Burlington and Quincy. To these, there were added as ex-officio members Edgar E. Clark, of the Interstate Commerce Commission, and Daniel Willard, who, as has just been said, already had been appointed by President Woodrow Wilson as chairman of the Advisory Commission of the Council of National Defense.

Five hours it took to form this all-powerful central committee.[1] Within the next week, 635 railroad companies—including all of the sizable railroads in the land—by official vote of their boards of directors, had given the Railroad War Board power of attorney over their several properties. It had been suggested that the federal government exercise its sweeping war-time powers and take over the railroads and operate them, itself. The roads believed theirs to be the better method. And it was given the first opportunity.

Under this new centralized administration, there now came more than $17,500,000.000 in railroad property; some 260,000

---

[1] Its first and most significant step was to pass and place upon the public record, the following resolution (written by President Fairfax Harrison of the Southern Railway):

"Whereas, This meeting has assembled in response to an invitation from the Council of National Defense, and has had laid before it a resolution by that Council as follows, viz.:

"'Resolved, That Commissioner Willard be requested to call upon the railroads to so organize their business as to lead to the greatest expedition in the movement of freight';

"Therefore, be it

"Resolved, That the railroads of the United States, acting through their chief executive officers here and now assembled and stirred by a high sense of their opportunity to be of the greatest service to their country in the present national crisis do hereby pledge themselves, with the government of the United States, with the governments of the several States, and one with another, that during the present war they will co-ordinate their operations in a continental railway system, merging during such period all their merely individual and competitive activities in the effort to produce a maximum of national transportation efficiency. To this end they hereby agree to create an organization which shall have general authority to formulate in detail and from time to time a policy of operation of all or any of the railroads, which policy, when and as announced by such temporary organization, shall be accepted and earnestly made effective by the several managements of the individual railroad companies here represented."

route miles of line, together with terminals and other appur-
tenances; 2,500,000 freight cars; 56,000 passenger cars; and
over 66,000 locomotives; to say nothing of 1,750,000 railroad
men. No other American industry had ever given itself so
whole-heartedly and so unselfishly to a patriotic cause. While,
in the entire history of the world, no other one railroad organization, even approaching this in size, had been created. The
thing to do was to make it function, effectively. This thing
was done; and with an amazing speed.

.   .   .   .

Now there was given a new duty to the Baltimore and
Ohio and its fellow railroads: Almost overnight—so it seemed
—vast army concentration camps, or cantonments, sprang up,
here and there and everywhere across the face of the land. In
truth, these were more like cities than mere camps. For
thirty-five thousand men to be fed and housed and trained
in one of them was as a mere nothing. They were builded
upon a scale of immensity hitherto unknown.

Three of the largest of these cantonments—Meade, in
Maryland, halfway between Baltimore and Washington;
Sherman, at Chillicothe, Ohio; and Taylor, at Louisville,
Kentucky—were located directly upon the lines of Baltimore
and Ohio. While Camp Benjamin Harrison at Indianapolis,
Camp Dix, near Trenton, New Jersey, and Camp Merritt,
just outside New York City, were within what generally is
regarded as Baltimore and Ohio territory.

The very first task was the upbuilding of these army cities—
from virgin territory. To the vast traffic burdens of the railroads, there was now added another. Lumber must be
fetched down from out of the Northwest and up from the
South, to go into the fabricating of hundreds and thousands
of barracks structures. . . . Presently, there was added still
an additional burden; by early September of that eventful
1917, the cantonments were practically completed, and into
them was being poured the raw human material which pres-

ently was to become units of one of the finest fighting armies the world has ever known. . . . The troop train, which had had its inception on the Baltimore and Ohio during the Civil War more than half a century before, swung into existence once again.

Across the land these troop trains moved, swiftly, silently, unannounced. In many cases, to the same general destination —the ports of embarkation from which the boys took ship to Europe. . . . Every precaution was taken to conserve their comfort and their safety. And, to the eternal credit of the American railroad, it was to be said ever afterwards that in the entire vast movement, involving the handling of many millions of men and their effects, there was not one single serious troop-train accident. Put that down, if you will, as a real achievement of our American railroads.

Such movement did not come as a matter of chance. It came as a matter of careful planning; of an active coöperation between the War Department, the Navy Department and the railroads—always as represented by their self-constituted War Board. It came, against tremendous handicaps.

The moment of our entrance as a nation into the World War had begun to pile new obligations upon our railroads. Hardly an industry there was across the nation that did not feel a war-time impetus—which quickly was translated into a need for increased rail service. There began to be severe shortages of cars. And of locomotives. The railroads sought to purchase more of every sort of rolling stock for themselves. But manufacturers were busy in a vast variety of war productions, and neither cars nor locomotives nor the steel nor other materials from which they are fabricated could be obtained quickly.

The roads sought to conserve their energies to meet the unforeseen situation. They cut all frills from their operation. They consolidated many of their trains; removed from their schedules all that could not show good reason for their existence. The most of these were passenger trains. Yet, it was not possible to remove more than a fraction, even of these. For the war proved itself a maker of greatly increased passenger riding—folk on war business bent. It became a war-time duty of the railroads to move, as quickly and as efficiently as possible, those who came and went in the service of their country—no matter in how remote or how humble a capacity.

All of this was accomplished, despite the actual lessening of the resources of the roads. They gave, and gave generously, both of their money and their men. They contributed to the various Liberty Loans, as well as to the Red Cross and other similar activities; while out from their ranks there marched forth railroaders of many ages—to actually take up arms in their country's service. Many thousands of these went into the regular branches of the Army and the Navy. In addition to these, several special railroad regiments were created, whose chief duty it was to be to see to the proper movement of the American Expeditionary Forces and their munitions in the lands overseas.

Many of these activities came under the more or less active administration of the railroads' War Board. It worked simply, effectively. It quietly expanded itself to meet the steadily increasing demands made upon it. It took unto itself, as a wing, the long-established Commission on Car Service of the American Railway Association. It established committees for other special functions. It sent its well trained representatives, clothed with authority, to the cantonments and other points of especially heavy train movement. These men did much to expedite the movements of troops and of munitions. Unceasingly, the War Board worked. Without it, it is difficult to know how the railroads of the United States ever could possibly have carried their great war burdens. An increase of nearly 120,000,000,000 ton miles in 1917 over 1915—greater than the entire ton mileage of any year in England, France, Germany, Austria and Russia combined—gives fair idea of the size of these.

Car shortages came, and they were serious. Locomotive

shortages came as well, and they too were serious.   The railroads, through their central agency at Washington, endeavored
to combat all of these.   More passenger trains were removed—
or consolidated.   Embargoes—temporarily suspending freight
service for this commodity or that—were put into effect.
Gradually, these embargoes grew more stern, more far-reaching.
In the name of war-time emergency and backed by the strong
arm of federal authority, much could be done along these lines.
But not everything.

.   .   .   .

In all of this mighty effort, Baltimore and Ohio took its
full share.   As has just been said, at the very moment of our
entrance to the war and at the earnest insistence of President
Woodrow Wilson, it contributed, its own president, to assume
the important office of chairman of the Advisory Commission
of the Council of National Defense.   Its boys marched off to
war—both in the regular arms of the service and in the railroad
regiments.   Men left the engines and cabooses and the telegraph keys in the valleys of the Potomac and the Ohio and the
long stretches that lie in between and beyond them, to run the
engines and the trains and pound the keys in the valley of the
Loire in far-off France.   Not all of these came back.   On the
honor roll of Baltimore and Ohio, there are 93 gold stars for
the boys that still rest overseas.   Some 103 more were injured.
And a total enlistment of 6795 men—about one-tenth of the
entire working force of the road—was to be recorded, both
for overseas service as well as the necessary military work
to be done right within this country.   For its record, in this,
the third great war in which it has participated Baltimore
and Ohio has no apologies to make.

Back of human offering, back of financial contributions to
patriotic funds and loans of every sort, was the unceasing
effort in the proper operation of the road itself.   A total of
14,174,302,157 revenue ton miles in 1915—one of the lowest
years of the second decade of the present century—rose, in

1917, to be 17,163,578,902 ton miles—or more than twenty-one per cent. Passenger miles in that same period increased from 700,811,968 in 1915 (the lowest in many years) to 950,-274,669 in 1917; 1,170,699,747 in 1918. . . . Likewise the expense of conducting the road grew—out of all proportion to its traffic and its earnings. Forced to compete in the open market with shipyards, munition plants and other prosperous "war brides" for both labor and materials, it found its operating ratio rising from 67.17 per cent in 1915 to 77.11 per cent in 1917, and to 92.19 per cent in 1918. Which meant that a net earning of $33,065,064 in 1915, by 1918 had descended to but $13,599,267—a really appalling figure. But Baltimore and Ohio kept right on. Like many and many another good soldier, it had to ignore its empty and its gnawing stomach.

.   .   .   .

But this could not last forever.

In the closing days of 1917, when hard oncoming winter weather and long months of unceasing peak-load activities of every sort were beginning to take toll of the spirit and the strength of railroaders of every sort and degree, there came, relief, in a new and rather unexpected fashion.

On the twenty-eighth day of December, 1917, President Woodrow Wilson, acting with the authority vested in him by Congress, exerted the fullness of his war-time powers and, in the name of national defense, took over the Baltimore and Ohio and its fellow railroads and placed them all under the direct operating control of the federal government. To work out this tremendous plan of control, Mr. Wilson appointed William G. McAdoo, already Secretary of the Treasury, as Director-General of Railroads. Mr. McAdoo thereafter filled both posts. His authority was absolute; to it the railroads submitted—as a man . . . as a good soldier. Theirs was not to question, but to obey. And so, to immediate obedience, they proceeded.

CHAPTER XVIII

THE END OF GOVERNMENT CONTROL

A Period of Readjustment—Labor Difficulties—Coöperation Becomes the Watchword—Human Relationship Upon a Railroad—Physical Improvement—Baltimore and Ohio Enters Upon the Second Century of Its History.

OF the period of the government control of the railroads of the United States, little is to be written in these pages. Suffice it to say, that is a time that many a railroader recalls with feelings of sadness. In the name of the winning of the war, some curious things were done; not the least of which was the creation of a huge bureaucratic organization; even though the experience in Great Britain, in an even greater emergency, had been that a war-time operation of her railways could be, and actually was, accomplished with a force of approximately twenty-five persons. . . . All these things are now history. Many of them are being forgotten. The fact remains, however, that, in twenty-six months of government control, our railroads suffered almost incalculable damage to their morale; while even their physical loss was not a thing lightly to be estimated. At the end of the period, many of them, in their physical upkeep and their traffic, were back to a period from ten to twenty years before the beginning of the World War.

In all of this, Baltimore and Ohio took its own fair part. It was a good soldier; and, as a good soldier, it obeyed orders. Its president, in common with the president of the neighboring Pennsylvania, relieved from the actual management of the property, from the side lines, as an observer, watched others conduct it. Fortunately, these others were, for the most part, men of the Baltimore and Ohio family; long trained in its traditions, its practices and its ideals. To a man, they strove to hold the property together, without in any way lessening its war contribution; to keep it as an operating unit; to retain, as far as was humanly possible, its traditions and its fine and carefully nurtured morale.

Yet, despite all of this, real damage was done the road. Not, in all instances, physical damage. It was not easy to see, at first sight, the traffic streams, long since become well adjusted to Baltimore and Ohio channels, in the name of war emergency, diverted to other pathways. Yet, such was the case. To all of which was to be added the serious physical deterioration of the property; its right of way, its buildings and its rolling stock. It took six years after the termination of federal control to bring the physical condition of the road, in all its phases of maintenance, back to the standards reached in 1914.

Only one of these war-time moves might have been interpreted as having been really helpful to Baltimore and Ohio; and, in the long run, even this was to be found as being actually detrimental in its final result: One of the early acts of the Director-General was to arrange to have Baltimore and Ohio passenger trains, entering or leaving the city of New York, use the Pennsylvania Station in Seventh Avenue in that city; as well as to make the tickets of the two roads, between points reached in common by both of them, interchangeable on all trains.

The first feeling of the man who lived in Baltimore and Ohio territory, and who was a steady user of its passenger trains, was that a great service had been done him by this drastic move of the Director-General. His own convenience had been served, appreciably. But the fact that the Pennsylvania had possibly been done a real injustice probably did not so quickly appear to him. It had invested its money in its New York City station as a competitive feature in its fight for passenger traffic. It did not enjoy the forcing of tenants upon and within its stronghold; even though large rentals were to be paid for the privilege.[1] It grew increasingly restive under the arrangement, even though it permitted it to continue for several years after the expiration of the period of governmental control. Finally, in August, 1926, it ended the contract under which Baltimore and Ohio had occupied the station.[2] Which, the patrons of the tenant road having become fully accustomed to the many privileges of the centrally located great station, was a distinct injustice to the road, as well as to these passengers. But with such injustices are the records of all wars fill

.   .   .   .

Baltimore and Ohio, in common with the other important railroads of the country, having been returned to its owners for direct operation, upon the passage of the so-called and far-reaching Transportation Act early in 1920, the stage was set for a patient reconstruction of the property once again. The damage of the twenty-six months of government control, to things both seen and unseen, had to be repaired. To make full reparations was to be a matter of many more than twenty-six months. To this large task, President Willard and his group of loyal co-workers at once began to apply themselves.

[1] In addition to the Baltimore and Ohio, the Lehigh Valley, reaching to Rochester, Buffalo and other points, chiefly non-competitive with the Pennsylvania, was brought at the same time into the Seventh Avenue station.

[2] Baltimore and Ohio met this crisis cleverly. It retired to its former rail passenger-terminal facilities at Communipaw (Jersey City) and, taking advantage of a highly modern form of transport, correlated with its trains in that roomy terminal a complete system of motor busses, operating into and out of the heart of Manhattan and Brooklyn. In this way, these communities were given a railroad service to the South and West superior to any that they had before enjoyed; and Baltimore and Ohio was enabled, not alone to hold for itself its large passenger traffic into and out of the metropolitan district of New York, but to increase it appreciably.

THE WATER-TUBE FIRE BOX ARRIVES.

Shown at the Fair of the Iron Horse last autumn (1927) was this highly modern Baltimore and Ohio freight locomotive, No. 4045, which has as its outstanding novelty feature, a water-tube fire box.

From a photograph.

THE MALLET OF TODAY.

No. 7151 of the Baltimore and Ohio freight fleet. It weighs, with tender, 351 tons and has a tractive power of 118,800 pounds.

The fever of industrial activity, which continued throughout the war and for some long months after the Armistice, had brought greatly swollen gross revenues to the road.   The total earnings of the calendar year of 1918 were $174,191,446; those of 1919, $182,620,015; of 1920, $231,944,446.   Each, in its turn, was record breaking.

It was, however, when one scanned the sheet for net earnings that one began to see the real story of those hectic years. Net in 1917—the twelvemonth just prior to governmental operation—had been $30,589,111; a high figure for that decade, although not quite a record one.   In the twelve months of 1918, the "net"—the thing by which railroaders rise and fall—had dropped woefully, to but $13,599,267.   Not in many years had so low a net revenue been recorded.   Dividends upon the common stock ceased entirely.

The following year—the second of government overlordship—was even worse.   Despite steadily increasing gross revenues and drastic internal economies, the net declined still further; to $12,750,891.   Yet, even this was not the worst. The very next calendar year—1920—was to find the profits of the road down to $5,660,396; for a great, well located railroad property like Baltimore and Ohio, a mere nothing.   And this, despite the gross return, for the same twelvemonth, of $231,-944,446—up to that time, a top record for the system.

Something in Denmark was rotten, indeed.   By examining the operating ratio of those troublous years, one can see the story even more clearly.   In 1917, this had stood at 77.11 per cent—a very high figure, yet perhaps to be excused by war-time conditions, chiefly the high cost of labor and of materials.   But 1918—the first year of governmental operation —found this ratio bounding up to 92.19.   'Nineteen-nineteen was even worse; with 93.02 as its percentage.   While 1920 was 97.56.   Baltimore and Ohio was rapidly coming to the point where it actually was going to cost the road more to operate than it took in—with all of its swollen revenues.

True it was that ten months of 1920 were under private

operation again; the old hands were back at the helm.   But it was to take many times those ten months to undo the damage that had been done.

It took careful pruning, real diplomacy, to bring costs down to a figure where the railroads, even with the newly advanced freight and passenger rates which the Transportation Act of 1920 finally brought them, were to be able to display profit again on their books; to overcome the patches of red-ink figures that had begun to show themselves—increasingly—on those pages.   This was not, of itself, enough.   Not only did salaries have to be readjusted, but—equally important—the working forces had to be reduced, in actual numbers. Economy became the order of the day.   On the Baltimore and Ohio, a working force of 72,257 men on March 1, 1920— the day that the road was handed back to its private management—had, twelve months later, become but 58,862 men. By these radical moves, the road did not lose in efficiency; but, on the contrary, greatly gained. . . .   From this low figure, partly due to a slump in traffic, the employment rose by 1923 to a total of 65,483.   Since then, it has remained nearly stationary.   At the end of 1927, 68,907 persons were on the pay roll.

.   .   .   .

By 1921, there had come to pass in America the inevitable slump that follows, sooner or later, the over-stimulus of a great war.   Once again, Baltimore and Ohio shared the problems of its fellows.   Its gross revenues fell off, sharply.   In the twelve calendar months of 1921, they dropped to $198,-622,373.   But the net rose; to $32,165,350.   It continued to rise until 1926, when it reached a grand total of $50,163,850. In 1927, in common with the net incomes of most American railroads, it dropped somewhat; to $44,817,227.   In the same year, the gross of Baltimore and Ohio was $246,078,510, as compared with $257,573,386 for 1926.   In the case of Baltimore and Ohio, this comparatively slight drop was ascribed largely to labor troubles in the coal fields which temporarily lessened their output.

One other thing fell, and for several years continued to fall—the operating ratio.   From the all but impossible figure of 97.56 per cent of 1920, it fell in the following year to 83.80, and the men at headquarters began to breathe more freely once again.   In 1922, it fell again—slightly—and stood at 82.16.   In 1923, it was 77.98; and in 1924, 77.01; in 1925, 75.40; and in 1926, 73.83 per cent.   In 1927, a slight rise, due to wage advances, brought it to 75.65 per cent.   A healthy ratio had been reached once again.   And without any serious disturbance of wages (although there had been many raises) or of the morale of the road.   This last, in fact, steadily improved.

From the outset of the present administration of Baltimore and Ohio, it has sought ever to work with its men; never over them.   From the difficult adjustment situation with its shop workers—another problem which it faced in common with the other important rail carriers—it emerged triumphantly.   Baltimore and Ohio long since determined to work with the established unions, not against them.   As sound financial policy, it sought, singly and collectively, to coöperate with them. In all of this, it has been preëminently successful.   Among its fellows of the North American continent, it has stood out boldly in employé coöperation.

.   .   .   .

A very delicate and difficult situation with the shop crafts came to a crux on July 1, 1922, when the shop workers of the Baltimore and Ohio, in common with their fellows of many other large railroads, went on strike.   The road was much embarrassed by this.   Hoping all the while to make a definite and reasonably permanent settlement with its own men, it still made efforts to replace them, *in toto*, at its

various shops.   It got along, as best it could.   Throughout
that trying summer, President Willard at no time lost hope
that the situation might be adjusted, without losing the road's
long-time workers; the men who had been upbuilded in its
morale, and thoroughly trained in its working practices.   He
sought all the while to find the solution to the problem.

It so happened that, just before the strike, Mr. W. H.
Johnston, president of the erstwhile Machinists' Union, in
connection with Mr. O. S. Beyer, Jr., an efficiency engineer
of established reputation, had called at Mr. Willard's office in
Baltimore and had stated that they would be glad to coöperate
with the officers of the Baltimore and Ohio Railroad in an
attempt to develop a practical plan under which workmen in
the shops might help in improving the efficiency of the plant
operations. . . .   The president of the Baltimore and Ohio
had then welcomed this general proposal.   But before anything could be done toward putting it into effect, the nation-
wide railroad shop strike, into which Baltimore and Ohio was
drawn willy-nilly, broke upon the country. . . .   Yet, throughout the ten trying weeks that followed, Mr. Willard never lost
sight of the Johnston-Beyer proposal.   All the while, he kept
turning it in his mind, and this was the thing that stimulated
him toward not merely a fair but a generous settlement with
his own shopmen; which, in the long run brought the workers
very largely back to their old places.   The value of all this to
Baltimore and Ohio cannot easily be overestimated.   What it
might expend in increased wages, would be more than made
up in the increased efficiency—both single and collective—of
its shop workers.

On the Baltimore and Ohio, the shop-crafts strike ended
September 15, 1922, almost as abruptly as it began.   It had
been, as such things go, an orderly affair, in which there had
been at any time only a minimum of bad feeling. . . .[1]   When

---

[1] While train service, as on the other railroads that were affected by the
strike, had suffered, no passenger or shipper had been very greatly embarrassed
during the period of its existence.   The strike was settled September 15, 1922.

it all was a matter of history, Mr. Willard renewed the discussions with Johnston and Beyer as to the bettering of the employé relationships in the company's shops. A definite procedure was planned.

For the first experiment, the shop at Glenwood was chosen. Glenwood is located just outside the industrial city of Pittsburgh, where the labor situation is, almost always, difficult. So difficult had it become for Baltimore and Ohio there, that the road had more than once considered closing those particular shops, transferring their activities elsewhere. At the behest of Pittsburgh merchants, it tried, however, to keep them open.

From the very outset, the plan worked. It worked better all the while, as it went along. More and more, the men themselves came forward, with many small (a few rather large) but practical suggestions, which went toward the better working of the shops. After a year, it was decided to adopt the plan in all the principal shops of the system—about forty-five in all, and employing, all told, some 25,000 workers. A formal agreement was entered into between the railroad company and the Federated Shop Crafts in its services, by which coöperative committees were set up in each of these forty-five shops and arrangements made for these committees to meet at least twice each month. This plan has since continued.

In the first eight months of its working, some 657 meetings, with an average attendance of twelve men at a meeting, were held. Just 5272 suggestions, ranging all the way from the proper handling of a locomotive in the back shop down to the need of a new sidewalk across to a roundhouse door, were received. Of these, 3810 were adopted.

That was an eight-months' trial period. The most recent figures at hand cover a forty-six-months' period. In these forty-six months, 4615 meetings have been held, 20,247 suggestions have been received and discussed, 17,158 adopted.

Slightly curtailed passenger service was restored immediately; while, by October 9, all freight embargoes had been removed. The road functioned normally again.

No longer is the plan considered experimental [1] It has now been followed by many other railroads in the United States; in Canada, the Canadian National Railways, the largest single system upon the continent, has adopted it, with a large degree of success.

.   .   .   .

Mere statistics cannot give the value of such a far-reaching plan as this; the upswing to the morale of the road's workers, their keener interest in its problems and their solutions, the actual money savings accomplished—in a thousand different ways. When asked some time ago what was the value of such an understanding and such a relationship, the president of the Baltimore and Ohio replied:

. . . It seems to me that there can be only one answer to that question: It gives to every employé an enlightened and enlarged view of his own worth and importance as a part of the great organization known as the Baltimore and Ohio Railroad. It emphasizes to each man the importance of the work which he himself is doing and the responsibility which goes with his job or position, and which rests upon him personally to do good work, to do honest and dependable work, not just because it is really his duty as an honest man to give good work in return for good wages paid in good money, but because, realizing the responsibility which he shares with the management for the safe and proper operation of the railroad, he wants to do good work; he wants to do thorough and dependable work in order that he may fulfill the enlarged conception which he has of the responsibility which properly rests upon him as a part of the railroad organization. In fact, I think that it has come about that the workmen themselves in greater degree than ever before are doing and doing happily the best that is in them, not just because they feel *obliged* to do it, but rather because they *want*

[1] The success of the plan among the shop workers led, January 1, 1925, to its extension to the transportation and maintenance of way employés of the company. The percentages of meetings, attendance and results in the shops crafts have been well maintained in the operating forces.

to do it, understanding and knowing that it is the right and
creditable thing to do.

A higher tribute to his fellow workers it would be hard for
any business executive to pay. . . . A little later, one finds
Mr. Willard putting the thing more colloquially, saying:

I have heard men in railroad service say in times past,
when questions of wages and working conditions were being
discussed, that they were not personally interested in the success
of their company; that they would just as soon receive their
pay check from a receiver appointed by the court as from a
corporate officer of a railroad; meaning, of course, that even if
a railroad were bankrupt, they would get their wages and be
just as well paid.   I think I can show that that is a very mis-
taken point of view.   There are many men in the employ of
the Baltimore and Ohio Railroad who have been in its service
long enough to have had a personal knowledge of what happens
during periods of depression, as well as during periods of
prosperity.   When business is good and earnings satisfactory,
shops, engines, cars and all facilities are worked to their full
capacity, which of course means a full force of employés.
When business begins to fall off it is first evidenced by the
number of empty cars standing around in yards and on side-
tracks; the number of engines withdrawn from service, which
means fewer train and engine men; roundhouse forces reduced;
back-shop forces curtailed, and, if the business continues dull
for some time, shops may be and are frequently shut down
completely.   But if a period of poor earnings resulting either
from a falling off of business or from inadequate rates should be
prolonged, it will be noticed on most roads, if not all, that in
the effort to still further reduce expenses, forces will be still
further reduced, and then the following things will be noticed:
The engines that are in service while safe to run . . . will not
be in as clean and satisfactory condition as when times are
better.   The shops will not be kept as clean . . . accidents
will occur more frequently; working conditions will become
less attractive, less sanitary, less healthful, less safe. . . . It
is indeed a mistake to feel that money alone represents

everything that is included in the wage. Of course, money is a very essential thing . . . but there comes a time when money is not the most essential part of the wage which one receives. The conditions of employment, the comfort, convenience, health and stability of employment become involved. . . . It is a mistake to think that the employés of a company, particularly of a railroad company, have not a personal interest in the prosperity of that company.

.   .   .   .

There is another very human relationship between the Baltimore and Ohio and its sixty-nine thousand workers that is worthy of comment before the record of the first hundred years is entirely closed. This affects, not so much the active workers, as those who have become, in its service, sick or crippled or even old. Modern industry long since came to recognize its obligation to folk such as these. It found that it could not close its eyes to their many perplexities.

In earlier pages of this history—the year is 1880—one may find John W. Garrett laying the foundations of the Baltimore and Ohio Employés' Relief Association,[1] which, in the course of nearly a half century of very busy and energetic operation, has accomplished a vast deal of good. In 1889, it was reorganized as the Relief Department of the railroad, and its activities divided into three major divisions: relief, savings and pensions.

The first of these has as its chief object the granting of help to employé members in times of sickness or of accident; to their families in the event of death. It is self-supporting, its fund coming from contributions, income from its investments and donations from the company. In the first forty-seven years of its existence, it paid out approximately $38,000,000 in relief benefits.

---

[1] To this work, his son, Robert, then vice-president of the road, gave enthusiastic and whole-hearted personal attention. As long as he lived, the younger Garrett retained his interest in this important phase of the company's work.

It does much more. The railroad company, acting through this function, employs forty-eight medical examiners who examine both members and other employés who have not as yet accepted membership, for sight, hearing, color sense and general physical condition. Back of these men is a reserve corps of surgeons—in number, 696—who may be called upon in case of any emergency. It is part of a railroad's business to be ready for emergencies.

The savings feature of the employé relationship upon Baltimore and Ohio began August 1, 1882. Since that day, nearly $48,000,000 have been deposited with the company by its workers, who have been paid from five to six per cent on their accounts. Upon the other side of the ledger, they have been loaned, chiefly for the purchase or improvement of their homes, an aggregate of over $46,000,000. Over 32,000 Baltimore and Ohio employés have become, for this purpose, borrowers. This speaks volumes for the character of these people. The homes they have erected have come to a total cost of more than $62,000,000. Of themselves, they would form a considerable city.

Last comes the pension feature. Here the railroad company always made the sole contributions. Any employé who has been in the service of the railroad for ten consecutive years and who has reached the age of sixty-five, is entitled to a pension for life, if he is relieved from further active duty. Since its establishment in 1884, more than 4300 employés have been so pensioned, the total amount paid out being well over $7,000,000. Today, an annual sum of more than $850,000 is set aside for this purpose. At the present time, there are 1664 pensioners on the company's rolls.

A final feature of human relationship between the Baltimore and Ohio and its workers comes through the munificence of a former president, the late Oscar G. Murray. Mr. Murray, who died March 4, 1917, bequeathed the greater portion of his considerable fortune to a corporation to be formed and named the Oscar G. Murray Railroad Employés' Benefit Fund.

The income from this fund goes to the assistance of needy widows and orphans of Baltimore and Ohio workers. It is a lasting monument to a much loved executive.

．　　　．　　　．　　　．　　　．　　　．　　　．

So much for the human side of a great American railroad on the threshold of its second century of existence. These facts are but brief and fragmentary. No pen can write fully of the great family feeling within Baltimore and Ohio; of families, which, for four generations, and in many, many ramifications, have been employed by the company; of a vice-president who speaks with pride of his grandfather who drove the first horse car to Ellicotts and one of the earliest locomotives on the Washington Branch. Of a widespread affection and a loyalty which no man may ever hope to measure.

"We shall try to make this railroad a good neighbor," is a favorite phrase of its president. He means it. Means it when he organizes in each of the 158 counties through which the Baltimore and Ohio of today operates its trains, public relations committees, whose duty it is to enhance at all times a friendly feeling between the road and its patrons; who, through frequent meetings, endeavor to feel the pulse of each corner of a far-spread railroad and to sense its wishes as well as its needs, and to translate these into service requirements to be met and cheerfully rendered. Means it when he places in his office a conspicuous sign, "Suggestions always are in order," and leaves that office door open to all callers—employé or patron or chance acquaintance.[1]

Upon the Baltimore and Ohio, the human side comes first—always.

．　　　．　　　．　　　．　　　．　　　．

Yet, the physical side of the development of the road in

---

[1] While this door opens easily to all, it is not to be interpreted that time is to be wasted in the president's office. There is little idling there.

the years that followed the end of government control is not without interest.

Baltimore and Ohio has not yet ceased to expand. In 1917, it purchased the important Coal and Coke Railroad, 175 miles in length, which gave it a direct entrance into the brisk capital city of West Virginia; Charleston, on the Kanawha River. In 1926—at the beginning of the one-hundredth year of its corporate existence—it acquired another road of no little importance: the Cincinnati, Indianapolis and Western, extending due west, 296 miles from Hamilton, Ohio, and bringing another capital city—Indianapolis—into the Baltimore and Ohio fold, as well as affording more direct connections with still another state capital—Springfield, Illinois.

Nor is this to be the end of expansion.

The Transportation Act of 1920 definitely set down national policy in the United States as favoring the consolidations of the railroads—under certain conditions and limitations. By its provisions, the old-time theory of preventing these rather logical combinations, which have been in effect ever since the railroad began its course in America, was completely reversed.

In all the many plans and proposals for these consolidations yet to come, Baltimore and Ohio has preserved both its unity and its honored name. Other roads—and important ones—are destined perhaps to lose their names and identities, to be swallowed up, either into existing companies or into new companies yet to be created. No one has suggested such a fate for Baltimore and Ohio. The name and charter would now seem destined for at least another century of growth and development.

The logical suggestion frequently is made that eventually the Reading Company (the former Philadelphia and Reading) and the Central Railroad of New Jersey, the control of which is held by the Reading, will be combined with the Baltimore and Ohio. The fact that the Baltimore company uses portions of the main lines of each of these roads for its very valuable entrance rights into the port of New York, and already is a

half owner (with the New York Central) of fifty-one per cent
of the Reading's common stock, would tend to give color to
this suggestion.   Nor is the New York–Philadelphia line the
only link of these two affiliated neighboring companies that
is valuable to Baltimore and Ohio.   Ownership or control of
them would give a very valuable direct line, for freight rather
than for passengers, between New York and the West, by way
of Allentown, Reading, Harrisburg and the Cumberland Valley
country to Martinsburg, on the main line of the present Baltimore and Ohio.

Such a new link would save a number of miles between
New York and western points, as well as avoiding the congested
portions of the present Baltimore and Ohio line through
Philadelphia, Baltimore and Washington.   It involves the use
of a number of miles of a branch of the Western Maryland—
between Shippensburg, Pennsylvania, and a point just west
of Martinsburg—and very recently Baltimore and Ohio has
anticipated this very situation by purchasing a substantial
interest in the shares of the Western Maryland.   The line has
much other potential value to the Baltimore company.   It
could be used—and probably will be—to advantage in shortening certain of its routes throughout West Virginia.

In 1927, a final step in a long program of reconstruction,
extending over some fifteen years, was begun when contracts
were let and construction started on the completion of the
double track on the historic Metropolitan Branch between
Washington and Point of Rocks.   Because of the rough
contour of the country, ever since the branch was first completed (in 1867), a short section of the line had been left in
single track.   This was the last bit of single track on the
through passenger line between Washington and Pittsburgh
and Chicago.   The through freight line had been double-
tracked—in some cases, three and four-tracked—ten years
before.

Moreover, the track itself is of the highest type of construction.   The best steel rail, of from 100 to 130 pounds to

THE *Lord Baltimore.*

One of the great mountain-climbing passenger locomotives of the Baltimore and Ohio engine fleet.

From a photograph.

The *President Washington.*

One of the President class, used chiefly in fast passenger service between New York, Philadelphia, Baltimore and Washington.

From a photograph.

the yard, is laid down in main-line construction; while rock-.
ballast foundation has been made the standard for the system.
Signal facilities are of the most modern type; daylight color
signals are (1927) being installed everywhere upon the property; while train control, under the detailed inspection and
authority of the Interstate Commerce Commission, is being
given thorough trial upon representative divisions of heaviest
traffic. And heavy traffic on the Baltimore and Ohio means
heavy traffic. There are few stretches of railroad in the
United States that exceed or even approach the tonnage that
today passes up and down its main stems.

.   .   .   .

With right of way, rolling stock—cars and engines of every
sort—have kept apace.

Baltimore and Ohio has become known throughout the
entire railroad world as a leader in motive power practice.
It has bought and it has built in quick succession, Mikadoes,
Pacifics, Santa Fés—each type a distinct improvement upon
its predecessors. Engines that were considered efficient
and dependable but twenty or thirty years ago, have been
scrapped ruthlessly—when it has been shown that in the swift
competition for best efficiency they no longer were worth their
keep. The growth in strength and power in the locomotive
fleet in the eighteen years of the present administration of the
property is shown not so much in the increase in numbers of
the individual engines—from 1886 in 1910 to 2535 in 1927—
as in the development of the individual locomotive; in the
great aggregate of tractive power of the fleet as a whole; from
58,130,121 pounds to 126,013,265—more than double.

In the summer of 1925, this development of modern motive
power on the Baltimore and Ohio took a dramatic form in the
construction, at the Mount Clare shops of the company, of
one of the largest passenger locomotives ever built, not only
for that road, but for any railroad. This was the huge *Lord
Baltimore*, measuring an even hundred feet from tip to tip,

and capable of hauling, without pusher assistance, twelve heavy Pullmans over the grades of the Alleghenies. The tractive power of this engine is 68,200 pounds.

Very recently, however, twenty new Pacifics of the *President* class have been purchased. These engines, beautifully finished in green and gold, are each named; from the *President Washington* up to and including the *President Arthur*. With their huge driving wheels, eighty inches in diameter, they can, if necessary, make the run of 225 miles between Washington and Jersey City quite easily in four hours and a half.

.   .   .   .

As with the locomotive fleet, the carrying capacity of Baltimore and Ohio is not to be measured in the total number of individual units. The individual car, within the past few years, has doubled and tripled in size. One figures the capacity of a modern freight train, a mile or more in length, not in car numbers, but in tonnage—five thousand tons has become as nothing for one of these giants.

Passenger cars have kept pace with the development of the freight cars. While, in comfort and in beauty, they have gone far ahead of even the longest visioned dreamer of the beginning of the present century. The day coach of today, in every way, is vastly superior to the parlor car of forty or fifty years ago.

Baltimore and Ohio prides itself upon being a "day-coach road." It is part of the inherent democracy of the property. It looks always to the comfort of its day-coach riders. While in the *Capitol Limited* and the *National Limited* it boasts of two of the finest all-Pullman trains in the entire land,[1] it still

---

[1] The *Capitol Limited* operates daily between Baltimore and Washington and Chicago; the *National Limited*, between Washington, Cincinnati and St. Louis. The one train was first put in service May 13, 1923; the other, April 26, 1925. While both offer every modern convenience, including barber shop and bath, secretarial and maid service, their chief pride is in their punctuality. The *Capitol*, operating 823 miles nightly, has in the four years of its operation a record

believes, none the less, in keeping good train service open to the day-coach rider. With this in view, it steadily improves the quality of the vehicle itself. One of its recent moves in this respect has been in furnishing day coaches with individual chair units, not unlike the chairs long used in parlor cars—and all without extra charge to the passenger.

. . . .

It is easy to slip into superlatives in describing a thing which is close to one. It is better by far to let other folk, without prejudice, do the talking. To gain such a perspective, turn to the pages of two publications, often quite opposed in their views: *The Wall Street Journal* and *The Nation*. The occasion which brought forth editorial opinions from these—and many other newspapers—was the Centenary of the chartering of the company, which began to be celebrated at Baltimore by a dinner, on the evening of February 28, 1927. Said *The Wall Street Journal:*

A railroad which has carried on under its original charter for one hundred years, survived three foreign and one civil war and the more insidious destructiveness of the "early days" of transportation development, has a right to celebrate its centenary. Something of the inherent strength of the Baltimore and Ohio, based in coal, steel, cement, glass and grain, is to be inferred from the fact that the property has never been sold at foreclosure. The first rank carriers of which that can be said may be counted upon the fingers. More important, both to those who own and those who use the road, is that it has crowned its first century with its best year, in quality of service rendered and in the margin of its revenues over all its requirements.

Baltimore and Ohio has never been in better condition, nor have its facilities ever been better proportioned to its needs. Its management is aggressive in more ways than one, as recent

of being on time 95 per cent of its runs; the *National*, with a daily operation of 890 miles in each direction, 98 per cent.

shifts in railroad security ownership have demonstrated. Obviously, it is destined to become a greater trunk line system. . . .

A railroad is not always a mere carrier of passengers and goods.   In the Civil War, the Baltimore and Ohio was often a part of the battle front; during the World War, again, its geographical position made it one of the two great highways between the munition factories and the eastern seaboard. . . .

In the real sense, this hundred-year-old Baltimore and Ohio is a young railroad.   Of an investment of roundly $850,000,000, just over $400,000,000, or nearly half, has been created since Daniel Willard became president of the company on January 1, 1910.   In these seventeen years the company's road mileage has increased only from 4435 miles to 5200 miles, but in capacity, in operating method and in the spirit of its personnel it is another railroad.   In this same period the company has experienced a succession of hardships which would have been incredible if any imaginative mind had attempted to depict them in advance.   They are over and done with.   The company has definitely taken its place among the strong railroads; its securities have become investments.

From the opposite wing of American journalism, *The Nation:*

If it was the first and almost the only railroad to build and own a steamship line across the Atlantic; if it was along its line that the first telegraphic message "What hath God wrought" was sent; if it first employed electricity on a standard railroad, these and other facts pale into insignificance compared to its admirable labor standards.   Its relations with its employés are of the best; the railroad has a real pride in its democracy, a real respect for its workers, and a long proved readiness to work with them through their unions. . . .   So the railroad has flourished and has been part of the history of the country. . . .   It came out of the Civil War triumphant and it is today the same Baltimore and Ohio as it was a hundred years ago when railroads were more experimental than radio is today, under the same charter, with the same corporate organization, under its own flag in the business of selling transportation, honestly and squarely.

.   .   .   .

So slips Baltimore and Ohio across the threshold of the second century of its existence. What the second hundred years may hold in store for it, no man may safely predict. What of tragedy, what of accomplishment, what of physical and technical achievement, is masked within the hidden folds of an unseen future. But that Baltimore and Ohio men will continue to work for the future of the road to which their allegiance is so closely bound, as for it they have worked so whole-heartedly in the past, would seem to be a safe conclusion. . . . There is a something in a great railroad organization like a huge army. Something martial, something inspiring. Bands playing. Flags flying. Men in quick and unctuous step. Men trained to obey. Orders are orders. No questions. Heads up. Eyes ahead. Precision always. Discipline and precision. Discipline and precision and team work. Even step, and quick. . . . A modern railroad asks no odds of the finest of modern armies—in heroism, in discipline, in devotion. It demands the best of any man—and almost always it gets it.

So across the threshold and down the long lane of the second century for Baltimore and Ohio. Its own bands are playing; its own gay flags flying. The column moves in good order. In rhythm, in punctuality and precision. Men and still more men—always still more men—the measure of any good railroad. Good men forever making a good railroad. Good men making—always, year in and year out—a good, an efficient, a progressive Baltimore and Ohio.

APPENDIX

THE FAIR OF THE IRON HORSE

The Centenary of a Railroad—The Birthday Dinner at the Lyric
Theater—The Fair of the Iron Horse—Visual History—A
Million and a Quarter Persons Visit Halethorpe and See the
Transport Development of North America.

THAT the one-hundredth birthday of the Baltimore and Ohio
Railroad, which was, to all purposes, coincident with the one-
hundredth birthday of the railroad as a whole in the United States,
should be a matter of national attention, was quite to be expected.
For the first century of the Baltimore road has marked the development of the physical structure of the railroad on this continent.
While one or two other railroad companies had been chartered
before Baltimore and Ohio, it was upon that line that the first
train for the public transport of freight and passengers began to
run (May 24, 1830). In one hundred years, it did its full share
of pioneering in the construction of the railroad and the many,
many things pertaining directly to it. No review of that century of progress could escape the fact that within its pages was
being written almost the entire history of the railroad development
of North America.

The Centenary celebration of the Baltimore and Ohio Railroad
attracted much more than a cursory attention, however. It became a much discussed national event. In the words of an
editorial writer upon the *Baltimore Evening Sun*, it was "one of
the notable public events of the year on the Atlantic seaboard."

The celebration divided itself into two major observances; one
indoors, the other outdoors. The actual centennial birthday of
the company, February 28, 1927, was marked by a large dinner in

Baltimore. It was felt, however, that a dinner would, of itself, not be quite enough. Obviously, at even the largest of these functions, there would not be room for even a tithe of the folk who wished to attend. Therefore it was decided that there also would have to be open-air observance of the occasion. It was equally obvious that February in the North was not an ideal season for outdoor festivities. It was then further decided that the dinner would be the sole function in February; and that later in the Centenary year—preferably in the autumn, when weather conditions in and about Baltimore are at their very best—would be held the open-air festivities.

. . . .

Nearly a thousand men sat down as the company's guests at dinner on the evening of February 28.[1] Accommodations were provided for more than seven hundred of these upon the floor of the Lyric Theater in Baltimore—the largest place available in that city for such a function. An overflow dinner of 250 covers was provided in the ballroom of the nearby Hotel Belvedere. At a later time in the evening, the guests of the two dinners—which were precisely the same in every way—were brought together at the Lyric, where a program of speeches, music and pageant tableaux was given.

It is interesting at this time to notice the difference between a railroad dinner of 1927 and those that were given in the earlier days of Baltimore and Ohio, and which are referred to elsewhere. Elaborate menus, much food and heavy drinking of liquors, as well as endless oratory, good taste today eschews. The simple menu of the dinner on the evening of February 28, of itself, tells the story. Here it is:

[1] In choosing the dinner guests, preference was given to the older officers and employés of the company, and to members of the Maryland Legislature as well as the city officers of Baltimore. The fact that both the Legislature and the City Council had been of such very large help in assisting the struggling railroad to get upon its feet at the outset, was enough reason for this selection. . . . The rest of the dinner list was chiefly made up of citizens of Baltimore, members of the press and the executive officers of other railroads. . . . Not the least important of the guests were the representatives of the actual workers of Baltimore and Ohio —selected through their unions and otherwise—who were present in great force and who gave the dinner a genuine democracy.

Olives   Hearts of Celery   Salted Almonds

Clear Green Turtle Soup   Sunny South Wafers

Chesapeake Bay Diamond Back Terrapin

Maryland Biscuits

Milk-Fed Chicken—Maryland Style

Creamed Hominy   Candied Sweet Potatoes

Dinner Rolls

Hearts of Lettuce, Russian Dressing   Smithfield Ham

Centenary Ices

Fancy Cakes

Cigars   Coffee   Cigarettes

Mints

Contrast this with what was done in the older days. Yet, this is but the beginning. Liquid potables? No more the champagne, the port, the Madeira. Ginger ale and mineral water and plain water and coffee—and no headaches. No more, too, the endless toasts to this thing, or to that, or to the other. Oratory these days is confined. Also it is selected. Thus, at the Baltimore and Ohio dinner, there was only one oration: the fine historical address given by Newton D. Baker, former Secretary of War, but placed upon the program merely as a director of the company.

The dinner had been opened with an invocation delivered by the Most Reverend John Gardner Murray, Presiding Bishop of the Protestant Episcopal Church of America. Daniel Willard, president of the Baltimore and Ohio, acted as presiding officer at the affair. It was his pleasant duty to announce the speakers of the evening; in addition to Mr. Baker, Governor Albert C. Ritchie, of Maryland, and Mayor Howard W. Jackson, of Baltimore. At the last moment, Governor Ritchie was compelled, through a slight illness, to remain at his residence in Annapolis. . . . Mayor Jackson made a few felicitous remarks in behalf of the city of Baltimore.[1] This, together with a few introductory remarks on

---

[1] Archbishop Michael J. Curley, of the Roman Catholic Archdiocese of Baltimore, was invited to deliver the benediction at the close of the exercises, but was prevented by a previous engagement from accepting this invitation.

the part of President Willard and Mr. Baker's address, comprised the speech making for the evening.[1]

There were, however, many other things upon the program: selections by the Baltimore and Ohio Women's Music Club and by the Baltimore and Ohio Glee Club (composed entirely of male voices); and, finally, a series of three episodes upon the great stage of the Lyric, depicting three leading events in the early days of the company. These, connected and given with appropriate music, costumes and stage settings, had spoken passages, written by Miss Margaret Talbott Stevens, of the company's forces.

.   .   .   .

The first of these scenes showed a group of Baltimore business men in the parlor of the home of George Brown, the banker, on a February evening in 1827. Gathered around a long table, which held a single glittering candelabrum, these men discussed their incipient railroad project. At the close of the scene, John V. L. McMahon burst in upon the group with the definite announcement that the Legislature, then sitting at Annapolis, had just granted a charter to the new-born Baltimore and Ohio Rail Road Company— an announcement that was greeted with much applause.

A year had passed before the period of the second scene. The place shifted to the farm of James Carroll at Mount Clare. The citizenry of Baltimore was employed in laying, ceremoniously, the First Stone that marked the actual beginnings of the construction of the new railroad. The event of that Independence Day of 1828 upon the Carroll farm was repeated at the Lyric with careful fidelity to detail. Among the historic personages that walked upon the stage were Charles Carroll of Carrollton, who presently was seen grasping the spade by which he turned the soil for the laying of the Stone; President Thomas of the railroad company, and the

[1] An interesting feature of the Centenary dinner was its souvenirs. These were bronze medals, designed by Hans Schuler of Baltimore. The obverse of the medal shows a modern express train drawn by a large locomotive. The Spirit of Transportation guides the train upon its flight. The inscription on this face reads:

ONE HUNDRED YEARS . . . SAFETY . . . STRENGTH . . . SPEED

The reverse of the medal depicts the *Tom Thumb*. . . . The surrounding inscription reads:

THE BALTIMORE AND OHIO RAILROAD COMPANY 1827–1927

various members of the Masonic lodges who performed the actual laying of the marker.

A third and final scene also was at Mount Clare; on an August afternoon of 1830. In it, the audience saw, not only the first horse car that made the daily trips between Baltimore and Ellicotts Mills, but also Peter Cooper riding upon a close reproduction of the *Tom Thumb*. This brisk scene closed with a dream of the future; Mr. Cooper standing in a spotlight at the front of the stage and viewing through the oncoming years the vision of the great locomotive, the *Philip E. Thomas*, bowling along at tremendous speed.

So ended a dinner marked by restraint and good taste. Many of the out-of-town visitors then crossed the street to the Mount Royal Station, which had been gaily decorated for the Centenary,[1] and boarded special night trains that had been provided for their return to New York.

.   .   .   .

The dinner over, preparations were at once begun for the open-air festivities of the autumn. Even before the celebration in February, the importance of the entire Centenary had been recognized by the Governor of Maryland and the Mayor of Baltimore in the appointment of official committees, composed of leading citizens of the state and of the city. These committees were made up as follows:

The State of Maryland

GEORGE WEEMS WILLIAMS, Chairman

JOHN W. GARRETT	VAN LEAR BLACK
JACOB EPSTEIN	HOLMES D. BAKER
ALEXANDER BROWN	OLIVER H. BRUCE, JR.

The City of Baltimore

WILLIAM F. BROENING, Chairman

GENERAL CHARLES D. GAITHER	HOWARD BRYANT
WILLIAM L. RAWLS	J. CAREY MARTIEN
WILLIAM I. NORRIS	HOWARD BRUCE

---

[1] Flags, smilax and cut flowers filled the interior of Mount Royal; upon its lofty tower a huge American standard was affixed; while just beneath the four clock faces at its top, the familiar electric letters, "B & O," were supplemented by a glowing "1827-1927."

In addition to these official committees, semi-official ones were appointed by the Maryland Bankers Association and the Baltimore Association of Commerce, both of whom at all times showed great interest and gave large coöperation to the Centenary. Their members were:

The Maryland Bankers Association

W. H. GIDEON, Chairman

J. THOMAS C. HOPKINS, JR.	ALBERT D. GRAHAM
WILLIAM O. PIERSON	STEPHENS A. WILLIAMS
TRASKER G. LOWNDES	JOSHUA W. MILES

The Baltimore Association of Commerce

THOMAS E. COTTMAN, Chairman

WALTER B. BROOKS	R. A. McCORMICK
ALBERT D. HUTZLER	WALTER HOPKINS
WILLIAM H. MATTHAI	E. H. BOUTON

A final committee—and a particularly hard-working one—was that of Arrangements, made up of the company's own personnel. This committee was:

DANIEL WILLARD, JR., Chairman

F. X. MILHOLLAND, Personnel	T. C. ROBERTS, Properties
E. W. SCHEER, Transportation	R. M. VAN SANT, Music
OLIVE DENNIS, Costumes	J. J. NUGENT, Vehicles

PAUL FAUSTMAN, Assistant Costumes

The task set out for this last committee was not an easy one—indeed, none of the committees failed to function most actively. But to the Committee of Arrangements was handed the laborious work of taking care of all the details—small as well as large—of the dinner in the spring and of the pageant in the autumn.

．　　　．　　　．　　　．　　　．　　　．　　　．

A pageant came as a development of the original plan to hold—in addition to a historical exhibition—some sort of an outdoor parade of railroad rolling stock of every kind. This original idea, to an extent, was based on a similar parade which had been held, in 1925, in connection with the centenary of the British railways.[1] It was planned at first to move the American parade along the rails of the original Main Stem of the Baltimore and Ohio from Mount Clare to the Relay House, or to Ellicott City.

Gradually, this parade idea was abandoned. It was felt that, not only was the weather risk very great, but that it would hardly be possible to show the parade a single time and bring to it all the folk who would wish to come, without seriously interfering with the operation of the railroad. It was then determined to hold the parade—probably in pageant form—on some piece of property convenient to, but not directly on, the main-line tracks. . . . The city of Baltimore came forward and very generously tendered the use of its parks. This was declined because none of these was exactly suited to such a pageant. After much consideration, it finally was decided to use a plot of land owned by the company at Halethorpe, upon the main line of the Baltimore and Ohio, six miles west of Baltimore.

The Halethorpe plot was located admirably for the purpose. A thousand acres of almost level land—bisected by the railroad, and situated also upon the main highway between Baltimore and Washington (as well as between New York and Florida)—it had every possible advantage of accessibility. While the flat contour of the land—originally, it had been used as a flying field—rendered it ideal for show purposes.

For the movement of the pageant, there was laid down, south of the main line of the railroad, an oval loop of standard railroad track, some 6000 feet in length. While, because some features of this portion of the Centenary celebration depicted highway transport in old days as well as new, a dirt roadway of a somewhat lesser length was placed inside this loop. . . . Facing both, and

---

[1] The British railway centenary was held at Darlington and at Stockton along the line of the original Stockton and Darlington Railway, now a part of the London and North Eastern Railway. It was on this very early line that the historic *Locomotion No. 1* was run, in September, 1825. . . . The chief feature of the British centenary which was held July 2, 1925, was a long parade of rolling stock. In addition, there was, in a nearby car shop, an exhibition of railroad locomotives, cars and other accessories which remained open for a fortnight thereafter.

almost directly alongside the main line of the railroad, was the great grand stand, nearly 1000 feet in length, 24 tiers deep, and seating, with its boxes, 12,048 persons. The canopy which completely covered this stand and which shaded its occupants from the sun, was one of the largest pieces of canvas ever fabricated in America.

The grand stand also faced the Court of Honor, which acted as an effective background for the pageant. This court was flanked upon its other sides by the three principal buildings of the exhibition. Chief of these was the Hall of Transportation, 502 feet in length and 62 feet wide. At the east end of this was the Allied Services Building; and at the west, the Traffic Building.

A uniform style of architecture was adopted for all these structures—a simple adaptation of the so-called Colonial. The fact that they were built of brick and trimmed with wood made them lend themselves easily to this form of treatment. Their roofs, like the roofs of all the other exhibition structures, and the canopy over the grand stand, were striped white and royal blue—the traditional colors of the Baltimore and Ohio. This added to the uniformity of the entire group. . . . The central and dominating Hall of Transportation was crowned by a modest tower, or lantern, of white. In it, hung the oldest bell belonging to the railroad; taken from the belfry of the passenger station at Ellicott City, where it had hung since 1830 and in the long ages had announced the comings and the goings of the trains. At certain times during the Centenary, this bell was again rung.

. . . .

This group of permanent structures at Halethorpe Field was completed by a few others; among these, notably the General Washington Inn—a reproduction of a typical early tavern upon the National Road—which served as an administration and press headquarters; a large coffee house, where more than 400 persons could be served at a sitting and where as many as 9000 meals were served in a single day; a building devoted to the exhibits of the state of Maryland, etc., etc. In addition, there were ample lavatories, hospital facilities and smaller structures devoted to fire service and the like. A huge round booth—which presently became known as the Roundhouse—served as a central souvenir

THIS MEDAL is issued on the one hundredth birthday of the Baltimore & Ohio Railroad Company to commemorate not merely an important milestone in its own history but the rounding out of a century of a definite American railroad achievement.

The Baltimore & Ohio was the first American railroad to operate its line for the public handling of passengers and freight. This was early in 1831. In all the one hundred years of its life it has changed neither its corporate name, its charter nor its fundamental organization.

The obverse of the medal depicts one of the most modern trains of the Baltimore & Ohio—The Capitol Limited or The National Limited—drawn by one of the largest and most modern passenger locomotives built. The spirit of Transportation guides the locomotive in its onward flight.

The reverse shows the Tom Thumb, designed by Alderman Peter Cooper of New York and the first steam locomotive to be built in the United States, even though it was never put into practical service.

Mr. Hans Schuler, director of the Maryland Institute in Baltimore, is the sculptor who designed this medal and it was reproduced direct from its model by the Medallic Art Company of New York City.

THE CENTENARY MEDAL.

Designed by Hans Shuler of Baltimore, this lasting souvenir of a railroad's centennial year was given wide distribution.

From the original.

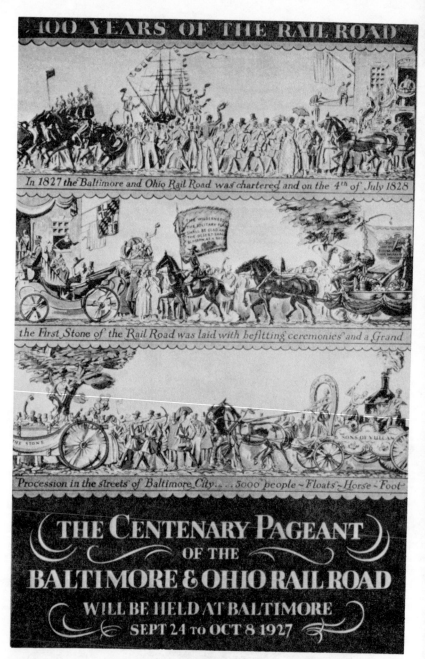

A CENTENARY POSTER.

Designed by Edward A. Wilson, it portrays portions of the parade at the laying of the First Stone, July 4, 1828.

From the original.

stand.[1] Smaller booths dispensed various popular forms of food (sandwiches, "hot dogs" and ice cream), soft drinks and cigars. . . . At the rear of the plot were the dressing-room facilities for the actors in the pageant. These consisted primarily of coaches and sleeping cars for actual dressing rooms, baggage cars for the storage of the six hundred costumes, while a caboose made a most excellent tailor shop. . . . The floats, when not in display, were stored under a huge circus tent. . . . There also were abundant facilities for fueling and watering and otherwise taking care of the locomotives that were in daily showing. This was, in itself, a real function and required the constant attention of a master mechanic (Mr. L. W. Galloway) and a corps of competent assistants.

This, then, the setting for the Centenary Exhibition and Pageant of the Baltimore and Ohio, which speedily became known as the Fair of the Iron Horse. This last name stuck. It caught the popular fancy and was echoed from one end of the land to the other. It served as the basis for quips in the newspapers and upon the stage, and so served to broadcast the centenary still more. Which already had been generously advertised, both in the newspapers and the magazines and by means of posters in the trains and stations of the railroad and elsewhere. The posters, in particular, were of a most artistic type and were widely sought by art museums, art schools and collectors everywhere.

The Fair of the Iron Horse was divided into two basic features: the exhibition and the pageant. Of these, the exhibition might be said to be the foundation; and, of it, the famous Pangborn collection of full-sized models of the early locomotives of the United States and Europe, which was brought together for the Chicago

[1] The Women's Music Club of the Baltimore and Ohio was granted the souvenir concession. These ran a wide gamut, from badges and other small mementoes to electric locomotives, which actually operated under their own power. They all bore, in one way or another, the imprint of the railroad. The young women of the club, in the twenty-three days of the Fair, sold more than $78,000 in souvenirs. In addition to which, they dispensed the official catalogues of the exhibition. Of these, some 55,000 were printed, bound and sold during the progress of the Fair.

World's Fair of 1893, was the beginning. This group of thirty-two models was supplemented by many hundreds of large pictures, showing the development of locomotives, cars, track and appliances, both here and abroad. There were a number of horse-drawn vehicles also in the collection.

The thirty-two locomotive models (including one of the *Old Ironsides*, loaned by the Baldwin Locomotive Works) were ranged down a double track which ran the length of the Hall of Transportation. Room was found upon the south wall for the collection of railroad-development pictures—which was brought up to the moment. Along the north wall were placed a variety of exhibits showing air brake, stoker, injector and signal progress, the development of track appliances and of time service upon the railroad. In preparing these exhibits, active coöperation was given by the Westinghouse Air Brake Company, the General Railway Signal Company, the Union Switch and Signal Company, the Locomotive Stoker Company and other large manufacturers of railroad appliances. Numerous watchmakers and clock makers assisted in the setting up of the time-service exhibit.

Perhaps the most distinctive feature of the Hall of Transportation, however, was the various miniature railroad models that it held. These ran from bridges and cars and engines of many railroads (including even the Egyptian railways) down to various appliances, such as headlights and the like. A single miniature model, 250 feet in length, showed in a most graphic fashion the development of bridges, locomotives and cars upon the Baltimore and Ohio during its ninety-seven years of actual operation. Sharing interest with this, was a model, sixty feet in length, of Harpers Ferry, Virginia, as it stood in the days just preceding the opening of the Civil War.[1] The constant attention given to all of these models justified a prediction that had been made before the Fair that they would attract an interest far greater than that given to flat-surface pictures, of any sort. Seemingly, they made far greater appeal to the average imagination.

. . . .

The Hall of Transportation and the exhibit tracks that sur-

[1] The catalogue of the exhibition, issued by the company at the time of the Centenary, describes these and other features of the exhibit halls and tracks in a very considerable detail.

rounded it, dwelt chiefly upon the actual maintenance and operation of the railroad; both yesterday and today. The series of ten short stretches of track in front of that building, showing the development of this important feature throughout ninety-seven years, also proved to be of absorbing interest to the crowds. As well as the locomotives and various sorts of cars upon the long tracks at its rear.

The Traffic Building, on the other hand, sought, primarily, to show how the railroad seeks and receives its business. Early tickets, waybills and advertisements told something of the story of traffic solicitation. Baggage and baggage handling had its booth. And, again, models came to the fore. There were miniature reproductions, not merely of the Mount Royal passenger station and the central headquarters building in Baltimore, and a bas-relief map of the entire territory traversed by the system, but also showing the actual terminals. The highly modern coal wharves and loading machinery at Curtis Bay were shown in great detail by a working model of the coal-handling plant there; while the center of the Traffic Building was occupied by a large model of the new grain elevator at Locust Point, together with the wharves with which it is closely connected by automatic carriers.

In a similar way, the Allied Services Building gave at least a hint of the various great outside services that always are so closely identified with the operation of the modern railroad. While the dominating feature of this hall was a huge map of Baltimore and Ohio—painted in the ancient manner by George J. Illian,—one saw within it the work of the railway mail, in an exhibit prepared by the United States Post Office Department; of the express, by the American Railway Express; of the telegraph, by the Western Union Telegraph Company; and of the telephone, by the American Telephone and Telegraph Company. In addition to which, there were exhibits, depicting, not merely the modern accounting methods of Baltimore and Ohio, but also its great social and welfare activities, of every sort. . . . The railway mail and the express services also showed their work in actual modern cars on the outside tracks; and so did the Pullman Company,—in an exhibit on wheels which ran from a very old sleeping car of 1859 to one of the most modern of highly modern trains—the *Capitol Limited.*

. . . .

The story of the growth of the railroad, which was told by the exhibit in a quiet and highly detailed fashion, was made even more graphic and picturesque in the pageant, which was held every day, save Sundays, throughout the duration of the Fair. Here was naught of picture nor of model, nor of the iron horse and his convoys standing cold and impotent upon sidings; but here, in all the sharp beauty of actuality, the history of inland transport in America was, in reality, walking down the years. Human beings—more than six hundred of them, each properly attired, with historical correctness—were employed as actors to people the floats, the trains, the horse-drawn vehicles of the highway, even to march afoot down the highroad of progress. With the chief feature of the pageant at all times the long, colorful and elaborate succession of floats and vehicles that showed the many ingenious carriers devised during the past two centuries to transport man and his goods quickly and safely from place to place.[1]

The pageant moved in a single direction around the loop track, from the dressing rooms at the rear of the plot, past the grand stand and the rest of the audience, back to the place whence it came. Placed in a straight line, it would have reached more than four miles. It took an hour and a quarter to pass a given point.[2]

The pageant, which began after the band had marched to its place upon its stand, was headed by the Baltimore and Ohio Glee Club riding on a float, draped with the American flag. This float, like the fourteen others used upon the loop track, was propelled by unseen motors underneath its apron. The drivers of the motor

[1] The pageant also took the form of drama; of a drama, set to music. Miss Margaret Talbott Stevens, who had written the book for the historical episodes at the Lyric in the spring, did a similar service for the pageant in the autumn. Her book was singularly lilting and beautiful. . . . Dr. Sigmund Spaeth arranged a music score, based upon tunes appropriate to the time and the occasion. This was rendered by the Baltimore and Ohio Centenary Band of sixty-five pieces, with Nelson C. Kratz as leader; while Charles Coburn read Miss Stevens' lyric poem. . . . The entire stage direction was under the immediate charge of Mrs. Adele Gutman Nathan, who had supervised the staging of the historical episodes at the Lyric.

[2] The control of this parade was in the hands of Mrs. Nathan, who had her post in a specially built signal tower at the east end of the grand stand. A telephone gave her constant and instant communication with the entrance points, the exits, the dressing rooms and the band stand. In this way, she was at all times in command of the entire situation.

The Fair of the Iron Horse.

A birdseye view of a portion of the grounds at Halethorpe, Maryland, where was given—September 24th to October 15th, 1927—the Centenary Exhibition and Pageant of the Baltimore and Ohio Railroad.

Photograph taken from an aeroplane.

As the Folk in the Grand Stand Saw the Pageant.

They also faced the Court of Honor and the long façade of the Hall of Transportation.

floats also were completely hidden from public view. . . . In front of the grand stand, the float with the Glee Club halted and the men who rode upon it joined with the band and the audience in the singing of *The Star Spangled Banner*. After which, the drama of inland transport went its way.

It began, appropriately enough, with the Indians, who, with their heavily laden pack horses and the primitive travois, passed down the highway. These Indians, members of the Blood and Piegan tribes of the Blackfoot nation, also showed their bull boats and Red River carts of a far later day. They were followed by a float representing Father Marquette, missionary and explorer, accompanied by Joliet and two aides, as well as three Indian servants. . . .

Inland-water transport was depicted, first by an old-fashioned bateau and then by an early canal boat. Both were mounted on floats and peopled with their passengers. The early American highway next showed road wagons and a Conestoga wagon, a variety of stage coaches—four-horse and six-horse—, a gentleman's carriage in which Henry Clay was to be observed riding over the National Road to Washington, and folk riding horseback on their weary travels. . . . The parade in the streets of Baltimore which had preceded the laying of the First Stone, July 4, 1828, was then reproduced, with much faithfulness of detail; including four horse-drawn floats which had been built from the careful descriptions left of their originals.

.   .   .   .

All of this formed the prelude to the coming of the iron horse himself. The earliest experiments with motive power upon the rails of the Baltimore and Ohio—the sailing-car, the treadmill car, the horse car—were, each in turn, depicted; each bore its passengers most bravely. Then the stage was set for the coming of the *Tom Thumb;* and the *Tom Thumb* came, working under its own steam and driven by a Peter Cooper of today. A most faithful reproduction it was, too; built at Mount Clare shops, from the pictures and descriptions of the original. It was necessary similarly to reproduce the *York*. But the *Atlantic* and the *Thomas Jefferson* which followed were the original locomotives, made new only in those parts that had shown the hardest wear. The *Atlantic* hauled two reproductions of the double-decked coaches that Richard

Imlay of Philadelphia built for the Baltimore and Ohio in 1831, and upon these rode the ladies and gentlemen of that early day. They and their early baggage.

The fifth engine in line was another reproduction—of the historic *Lafayette*, which for the Centenary had been renamed the *William Galloway*, after a distinguished early locomotive engineer of Baltimore and Ohio. It hauled two flour cars, each carefully fashioned after those which once had brought thousands of barrels from the mills of Frederick and other Maryland points down to Baltimore City. . . . Thereafter, there were no reproduced engines. But a procession of original locomotives, carefully preserved through all the years and, for the Centenary, made as fit for operation as upon the day in which they were born: the *Memnon*, the *William Mason*, *No. 25* (dazzling in her original green and gold); the *Thatcher Perkins*, *No. 117* (in deep maroon, bright red and gold); the *Ross Winans* (camel), *No. 217*; the *J. C. Davis*, *No. 600*; and the *A. J. Cromwell*, *No. 545*, a consolidation locomotive of 1888 designed and built by A. J. Cromwell, successor to J. C. Davis as chief of motive power of Baltimore and Ohio.[1] A swift passenger puller built in 1896 for Royal Blue Line service, the *1310*, followed, and the *John E. Muhlfeld*, *No. 2400*, designed and built in 1904, and the first Mallet engine to be put in service in the United States. . . . In addition to the *Atlantic* and the *Galloway*, two others of these early engines drew trains; the *Perkins*, which hauled a train of small yellow passenger coaches such as were in almost universal use in the United States in the decade after the Civil War; and the *Ross Winans*, with three hopper coal cars and two small sheet-iron house or box cars—which had been dragged out from obscurity along the system and made seaworthy once again. There was no caboose to the early freight train. The conductor and the brakeman stood atop of one of the little box cars where they might easily survey the landscape and watch the operation of the train.

Interspersed in this section of the pageant were a number of other floats; one showing the Baltimore citizens meeting at the

---

[1] The Cromwell tradition in Baltimore and Ohio is also carried out—in the presence in the company's forces of Oliver C. Cromwell, son of A. J. Cromwell, who is (1927) assistant chief of motive power, and of his son in turn, Howard T. Cromwell.

house of George Brown, another the United States Army officers making the first surveys for the new railroad; still others showing the birth of the telegraph, the arrival of Abraham Lincoln in Washington for his first inauguration, the destruction of Baltimore and Ohio tracks by military forces in the Civil War, and the coming of the electric locomotive in 1895.

A float led the next section of the pageant procession, which was given over to visiting locomotives from railroads of other countries.

Baltimore and Ohio, the oldest of American railroads to operate without change of name or charter, desired to recognize England as the home of the birth of the railroad idea. Therefore, the next float was of Stephenson's *Rocket*—the first thoroughly successful locomotive to be operated anywhere—attended by a feminine figure depicting Britannia. This float was followed by a locomotive sent by the oldest railway in England to operate without change of name or charter—the Great Western Railway, which was incorporated in 1833. To the Fair of the Iron Horse this representative British railway sent perhaps the finest passenger engine yet made by British locomotive builders—the *King George V:* the product of its own shops at Swindon. This fine four-cylindered locomotive —weighing, with its tender, 135 tons—was placed on the steamer *Chicago City* at Cardiff in July and shipped direct to Baltimore, where it was reassembled at Mount Clare and again placed in good working order. . . .[1] At the close of the Fair and after a test run on Baltimore and Ohio between Washington and Philadelphia, in which it gave a very good account of itself, the *King George V* was again taken to Mount Clare, knocked down and prepared for shipment back to England.[2]

[1] The Great Western Railway also sent to the Fair of the Iron Horse, Daniel Gooch's remarkable creation, the *North Star*, built in 1838. Owing to the extremely wide gauge of this engine—seven feet—it was not practical to operate her in the pageant. She was, however, given a place of honor upon the exhibit tracks beside the Hall of Transportation.

[2] As permanent souvenirs of its visit to America, the *King George V* carries upon each side of its cab the bronze medals struck off by Baltimore and Ohio in commemoration of its one-hundredth birthday. Even more conspicuous is the gift from the American railroad that it wears at its pilot—the silver-plated

Two other British locomotives—these, however, from Canada —followed the *King George V*. They were the *Confederation, No. 6100*, of the Canadian National Railways and the *No. 2333* of the Canadian Pacific Railway. Each of these also excited a lively interest.

.   .   .   .   .   .

The foreign visitors past, the pageant returned for a final moment to the beginning days of the American railroad. The locomotive *De Witt Clinton* (1831) of the one-time Mohawk and Hudson Railroad, which with its three coaches had been carefully taken out of its permanent resting place in the Grand Central Station in the city of New York, ran under its own steam and carried a trainload of excited, jabbering, quaintly costumed folk. From its permanent home in the Smithsonian Institution in Washington, came the original *John Bull* (1831) of the Camden and Amboy Railroad, also operating under its own steam and carrying an early coach filled with passengers. The old locomotive *Satilla* (1860) of the Atlantic and Gulf was loaned by Henry Ford, its present owner, and made a gay addition to the show. So did the *William Crooks* (1861), the first locomotive to operate in the Northwest, and which, with its early baggage car and passenger car, was loaned to the Fair by the Great Northern Railway.

.   .   .   .   .   .

To modern days the pageant turned again. Its audience saw one of the new Hudson-type passenger locomotives, designed by the New York Central and placed in service upon that railroad but two months before; a huge passenger engine from the Pennsylvania; a powerful locomotive, with a mighty tender, used by the Western Maryland in hauling its heavily laden coal trains over the stiff grades of the Alleghenies; then the *John B. Jervis*, of the Delaware and Hudson, a highly efficient locomotive, unusual in its appearance, with a water-tube fire box and a boiler capable of carrying a steam pressure of 400 pounds to the square inch. In this engine, the booster was set upon the rear truck of the tender. The *Jervis* marked the complete extinction of the smoke-

---

engine bell, properly inscribed, that speaks the distinctive note of all Baltimore and Ohio engine bells. It is now (1927) the only important locomotive in all Great Britain to carry a bell.

tack upon the American locomotive. That once distinctive eature of the engines of railroads in the United States, which 'eached its veritable apotheosis in the decades of the 'fifties and he 'sixties in the huge, flaring balloon stacks of the old wood ourners, ever since then gradually growing shorter and smaller, is the boiler grew both higher and larger. In the *Jervis*, it had lisappeared from view completely.[1]

.   .   .   .

Modern motive power upon the Baltimore and Ohio Railroad formed the final act of this pageant-drama. For this, there had been chosen a group of representative locomotives, employed both in freight and in passenger services. A ten-wheel passenger engine, the *2024*, used in local trains, with its new green and gold livery, excited general approbation. So did a converted Mikado, the *5005*, a type brought out in 1924, primarily for use upon the swift and heavy passenger trains between Washington and New York. The Mikado itself, *No. 4465*, came into the picture. So did its logical development, the Santa Fé type, *No. 6137*, that immediately followed. But, presently, these were overshadowed; the *Philip E. Thomas* (mountain type), *No. 5501*, came majestically into sight— also wearing the gay new passenger livery of the road. With its tremendous length—100 feet over all—and its trim lines and great show of strength and power, it awakened many cheers from the grand stand. . . . It was followed by a great Mallet type engine (in freight service), the *7151*, hauling a short train made up of representative freight cars, of almost every type in the service of the company. The *7151* is the most modern type of Mallet locomotive—literally two engines in one, although supplied with steam from a single boiler and controlled by a single engineer. In almost every other way, separate. Even to the separate smokestacks, the one placed behind the other.

[1] Baltimore and Ohio also showed a water-tube fire-box locomotive, the *4045*, designed by George H. Emerson, chief of motive power of the company, and finished within a fortnight of the opening of the Centenary exhibition. A novel feature of the boiler was that the tubes could be applied and rolled and the boiler entirely cleaned without requiring a workman to get inside. Because it was desirable to remove some of the boiler plates in order to give a better view of the fire-box construction, this locomotive was not operated in the pageant. It was given a position upon one of the exhibit tracks.

The final locomotive actor upon the giant stage was the *President Washington* (*No. 5300*), attached to the road's most famous train of today, the *Capitol Limited*, which is regularly in service between Baltimore, Washington and Chicago. The replica of the *Capitol Limited* shown in the pageant was, for convenience in handling upon the fairgrounds, made up of but six cars—five Pullmans and a modern colonial dining car, the *Martha Washington*. But each of these was representative of the types operated upon the *Capitol*. In fact, they were actual cars, taken from the spare equipment used daily upon this world-famous train.[1]

In these actual cars also rode actual passengers. And, when the train came to its slow and easy stop in front of the grand stand, these alighted and boarded the modern motor busses that there awaited them. These were actual busses, taken from the Baltimore and Ohio's own fleet at its New York terminals, and used daily in connection with its trains, carrying passengers back and forth between the trainside at Jersey City and various central points both in Manhattan and Brooklyn. . . . A similar bus service is in regular operation between Newark and the railroad station at Elizabeth, New Jersey.

These motor busses represent the very last word in the perfection of railroad auxiliary passenger service. At the Fair of the Iron Horse, one might see for himself the beginning steps in comfort in that service—from the upper decks upon the Imlay double-decked coaches to the early sleeping car, with its clumsy attempts to provide real beds for travelers at night, and so on, down through the years. The skillful correlation of railroad train and motor bus,

---

[1] The *Philip E. Thomas*, as has already been stated, was built at Mount Clare shops in 1926. It is a mountain-type locomotive, with a 4-8-2 wheel arrangement and a tractive power of 68,200 pounds; a weight on its drivers of 275,000 pounds; an engine weight of 400,000 pounds, and a total weight of engine and tender of 653,000 pounds. The diameter of the driving wheels is 74 inches.

The Mallet, *No. 7151*, is a heavier engine, still. Its wheel arrangement is 2-8-8-0 and its tractive power comes to the high figure of 118,800 pounds. The weight of the engine is 491,300 pounds; of engine and tender combined, 702,300 pounds.

The *President Washington* has the high drivers characteristic of a locomotive designed for fast passenger service. Its wheel arrangement is 4-6-2 and the drivers are 80 inches in diameter. Tractive power is set at an even 50,000 pounds. The engine weighs 326,000 pounds; the engine and its tender combined, 540,000 pounds.

MODERN LOCOMOTIVES ON EXHIBITION.

They stood together on the grounds where all might make inspection of them.

From a photograph.

FROM FAR OFF BRITAIN CAME THIS REGAL ENGINE.

The Great Western Railway of England sent this powerful passenger locomotive, the *King George V*, as its delegate to the B...

particularly in terminal service, represents what probably is the most modern of all attempts to improve passenger transport in America. An attempt which now (1927) has proceeded so far that it no longer may be called experimental, but rather a recognized feature of the service of one fairly important railroad of the United States.

. . . . . .

Through long months of orderly preparation, the Fair of the Iron Horse proceeded toward its announced opening day, September 24, 1927. When that hour came finally—a cloudless day of early autumn, neither too hot nor too cold, with the warmth of the sun tempered by a gentle western breeze—the Fair was completed and ready for its visitors. Completed, to the last small detail, the pageant rehearsed to the last fine point of precision and starting on exactly the advertised moment, the Fair of the Iron Horse opened that day to an attendance of 46,000 persons. . . . It had been felt that the average daily attendance might be from 18,000 to 20,000 persons—with possibly twice that number on Saturdays. . . . This proved to be extremely moderate prophecy. The fine weather continued—in the three weeks duration of the Centenary, there were but two rainy days; only one when it was necessary to abandon the pageant. . . . The crowds also continued. They continued to increase. On Saturday, October 1, over 76,000 persons passed through the gateways of Halethorpe Field.

It had been the original intention to close the Centenary on Saturday, October 8, but its popularity was such that the management yielded to public demands and extended the exhibition and pageant for another seven days—to and including Saturday, October 15, when 110,000 persons entered the grounds. The following day, Sunday, the sixteenth, the grounds and exhibits were open to the public; but, as on previous Sundays during the Fair, the pageant did not move. With the close of that day, the total of admissions stood in excess of a million and a quarter. The popular success of the Centenary had exceeded the wildest dreams of the men who promoted it.

As an exposition, the Fair of the Iron Horse defied precedent.

There were no sideshows. The only concessions were the carefully regulated ones that dispensed food and drink and souvenirs to the guests. No one could pay for anything else. The folk who came to the Fair came, literally, as the guests of the Baltimore and Ohio Railroad Company. So there could be no charges for admission or for seats upon the grand stand. These last were given out to all applicants—as long as there were any to be given. Nor was this all. While the Baltimore and Ohio is a railroad, it recognized that many of its guests might prefer to come by automobile. So it laid out at Halethorpe Field a parking space for 3000 motor cars, which later was extended so that, on a given day at a given hour, more than 9000 automobiles were parked there. And, of course no charges to any one.

Nor were the company's guests pestered with advertising. Not at any time were they solicited—directly or indirectly—to use its services. They were not compelled to listen to unbridled oratory. On the opening day, President Willard introduced the Hon. Albert C. Ritchie, Governor of Maryland, who made a brief speech of felicitation. On Baltimore Day—October 8—Mayor William F. Broening, of Baltimore, made a short address. That was all. . . . Many persons of large distinction came to the Fair—Senators, Congressmen, with one exception every member of the Cabinet, the British Ambassador, the Canadian Ambassador, the Argentine Ambassador, many others of the diplomatic corps at Washington, the governors of many states, the mayors of many cities, the presidents and vice-presidents of most of the railroads of the United States and Canada, bankers, scientists, educators—the list runs to great length. . . . But, with all of these, the informal character of the occasion still was rigorously preserved. The Centenary, in its last analysis, was nothing more nor less than a huge birthday party.

So closes this record. . . . The Fair of the Iron Horse ended as it began—in warm sunshine and bright cool air. For a final time, that Saturday afternoon of mid-October, the Centenary Band came briskly marching down the highway, the Indian chieftains rode their horses furiously and then returned to escort the slow-moving travois, Henry Clay rode down the National Pike lifting his hat in fond adieus, the stage-coaches lumbered by, the

First Stone parade of July 4, 1828, once more delighted the multitude, the locomotives—old and new, small and large—for the last time rolled their way around the long loop track. . . . Then the unexpected thing came to pass: The human actors in the pageant marched at its close to the front of the grand stand—as had been their habit at each performance. Only, for the first time, the Indians came too, and the gaily costumed folk from off the floats. With the bands, the seven hundred of them took final position. . . . There was the customary stanza of *America*. . . . Then . . . *Auld Lang Syne*—that eternal song of human memories. Then men laughing . . . women crying—just the least bit—for memory and for the happiness of memory. . . . The inevitable finally had come to pass; the unforgettably happy thing was dying. . . . Men grew a little more sober. . . . Laughter died. . . . A moment of quiet suspense. Then the sharp roll of the drums and again the actor folk marching off—the grand stand clearing itself for the final time.

The Fair of the Iron Horse had slipped into the pages of history.

Humphreys, A. A., "History of the Bridge Across the Ohio at Wheeling," *Report of the Chief of Engineers (U. S. Army)*, 1875, Part 2, pp. 1025 ff.

Laboratory Studies on the Tacoma Narrows Bridge at the University of Washington, July 1941.

Mills, B. D., "Aerodynamic Action on Wires and Bridges," *Engineering News-Record*, Vol. 126 (1941), pp. 163-68.

Moisseiff, L. S., "Growth in Suspension Bridge Knowledge," *Engineering News-Record*, Vol. 123 (Aug. 10, 1939), pp. 46-49.

"Monrose Suspension Bridge," *The Civil Engineer and Architect's Journal*, Vol. 1 (1838), pp. 381, 417. (Bridge in Scotland, built 1829, partially destroyed by a gale on Oct. 11, 1838.)

"Narrows Nightmare," *Time*, Nov. 18, 1940, p. 21.

Pigeaud, F., "Action du Vent sur un Tablier de Pont Suspendu," *Le Génie Civil*, Vol. 87 (1925), pp. 83-85.

Provis, W. A., "Observations on the Effect of the Wind on the Suspension Bridge over the Menai Straits," *Institution of Civil Engineers — Proceedings*, London, Vol. 1 (1841), pp. 74-81.

Rathbone, T. C., and Turner, C. A. P., "Tacoma Narrows Collapse," *Engineering News-Record*, Vol. 125 (Dec. 5, 1940), p. 40.

Raymond, C. W., Bixby, W. H., and Barr, Edward, "The Maximum Practical Length for Suspension Bridges," *Engineering News*, Vol. 32 (1894), pp. 423-25, 444-46, 465-65.

Report of the Board of Investigation, Tacoma Narrows Bridge, to James A. Davis, Acting Director of Highways, Olympia, Wash., 1941.

Robinson, S. W., "The Vibration of Bridges," *Institution of Civil Engineers — Proceedings*, London, Vol. 90 (1886-87), pp. 475-78.

Roebling, J. A., "The Cincinnati Bridge," *Engineering*, London, Vol. 7 (1869), p. 300.

——— *Niagara Suspension Bridge—Report to the Directors of the Niagara Falls International Railway Suspension Bridge Company*, reprinted in *Mechanics' Magazine and Engineers' Journal*, Vol. 2 (1855), pp. 193-95.

——— "Some Remarks on Suspension Bridges, and on the Comparative Merits of Cable and Chain Bridges," *American Railroad Journal*, Vol. 14 (Apr. 1, 1841), pp. 193-96.

Royen, N., "Calculation of Extent to which Cable in Suspension Bridges Takes Up Wind Load," *Der Bauingenieur*, Vol. 10 (1919), pp. 239-43.

Russell, J. S., "On the Vibration of Suspension Bridges and Other Structures; and the Means of Preventing Injury from this Cause," *Journal, Royal Scottish Society of Arts*, Vol. 1 (1839), pp. 305-07. (Describes destruction of span at Brighton, Nov. 30, 1836.)

INDEX

353

TECHNOLOGY AND SOCIETY

An Arno Press Collection

Ardrey, R[obert] L. **American Agricultural Implements.** In two parts. 1894

Arnold, Horace Lucien and Fay Leone Faurote. **Ford Methods and the Ford Shops.** 1915

Baron, Stanley [Wade]. **Brewed in America:** A History of Beer and Ale in the United States. 1962

Bathe, Greville and Dorothy. **Oliver Evans:** A Chronicle of Early American Engineering. 1935

Bendure, Zelma and Gladys Pfeiffer. **America's Fabrics:** Origin and History, Manufacture, Characteristics and Uses. 1946

Bichowsky, F. Russell. **Industrial Research.** 1942

Bigelow, Jacob. **The Useful Arts:** Considered in Connexion with the Applications of Science. 1840. Two volumes in one

Birkmire, William H. **Skeleton Construction in Buildings.** 1894

Boyd, T[homas] A[lvin]. **Professional Amateur:** The Biography of Charles Franklin Kettering. 1957

Bright, Arthur A[aron], Jr. **The Electric-Lamp Industry:** Technological Change and Economic Development from 1800 to 1947. 1949

Bruce, Alfred and Harold Sandbank. **The History of Prefabrication.** 1943

Carr, Charles C[arl]. **Alcoa, An American Enterprise.** 1952

Cooley, Mortimer E. **Scientific Blacksmith.** 1947

Davis, Charles Thomas. **The Manufacture of Paper.** 1886

Deane, Samuel. **The New-England Farmer,** or Georgical Dictionary. 1822

Dyer, Henry. **The Evolution of Industry.** 1895

Epstein, Ralph C. **The Automobile Industry:** Its Economic and Commercial Development. 1928

Ericsson, Henry. **Sixty Years a Builder:** The Autobiography of Henry Ericsson. 1942

Evans, Oliver. **The Young Mill-Wright and Miller's Guide.** 1850

Ewbank, Thomas. **A Descriptive and Historical Account of Hydraulic and Other Machines for Raising Water,** Ancient and Modern. 1842

Field, Henry M. **The Story of the Atlantic Telegraph.** 1893

Fleming, A. P. M. **Industrial Research in the United States of America.** 1917

Van Gelder, Arthur Pine and Hugo Schlatter. **History of the Explosives Industry in America.** 1927

Hall, Courtney Robert. **History of American Industrial Science.** 1954

Hungerford, Edward. **The Story of Public Utilities.** 1928

Hungerford, Edward. **The Story of the Baltimore and Ohio Railroad, 1827-1927.** 1928

Husband, Joseph. **The Story of the Pullman Car.** 1917

Ingels, Margaret. **Willis Haviland Carrier, Father of Air Conditioning.** 1952

Kingsbury, J[ohn] E. **The Telephone and Telephone Exchanges:** Their Invention and Development. 1915

Labatut, Jean and Wheaton J. Lane, eds. **Highways in Our National Life:** A Symposium. 1950

Lathrop, William G[ilbert]. **The Brass Industry in the United States.** 1926

Lesley, Robert W., John B. Lober and George S. Bartlett. **History of the Portland Cement Industry in the United States.** 1924

Marcosson, Isaac F. **Wherever Men Trade:** The Romance of the Cash Register. 1945

Miles, Henry A[dolphus]. **Lowell, As It Was, and As It Is**. 1845

Morison, George S. **The New Epoch:** As Developed by the Manufacture of Power. 1903

Olmsted, Denison. **Memoir of Eli Whitney, Esq.** 1846

Passer, Harold C. **The Electrical Manufacturers, 1875-1900.** 1953

Prescott, George B[artlett]. **Bell's Electric Speaking Telephone.** 1884

Prout, Henry G. **A Life of George Westinghouse.** 1921

Randall, Frank A. **History of the Development of Building Construction in Chicago.** 1949

Riley, John J. **A History of the American Soft Drink Industry:** Bottled Carbonated Beverages, 1807-1957. 1958

Salem, F[rederick] W[illiam]. **Beer, Its History and Its Economic Value as a National Beverage.** 1880

Smith, Edgar F. **Chemistry in America.** 1914

Steinman, D[avid] B[arnard]. **The Builders of the Bridge:** The Story of John Roebling and His Son. 1950

Taylor, F[rank] Sherwood. **A History of Industrial Chemistry.** 1957

Technological Trends and National Policy, Including the Social Implications of New Inventions. Report of the Subcommittee on Technology to the National Resources Committee. 1937

Thompson, John S. **History of Composing Machines.** 1904

Thompson, Robert Luther. **Wiring a Continent:** The History of the Telegraph Industry in the United States, 1832-1866. 1947

Tilley, Nannie May. **The Bright-Tobacco Industry, 1860-1929.** 1948

Tooker, Elva. **Nathan Trotter:** Philadelphia Merchant, 1787-1853. 1955

Turck, J. A. V. **Origin of Modern Calculating Machines.** 1921

Tyler, David Budlong. **Steam Conquers the Atlantic.** 1939

Wheeler, Gervase. **Homes for the People,** In Suburb and Country. 1855

Deane, Samuel. The New-England Farmer; or Georgical Dictionary. 1822.

Dyer, Henry. The Evolution of Industry. 1895.

Epstein, Ralph C. The Automobile Industry: Its Economic and Commercial Development. 1928.

Erickson, Henry. Sixty Years a Builder: The Autobiography of Henry Erickson. 1942.

Evans, Oliver. The Young Mill-Wright and Miller's Guide. 1850.

Ewbank, Thomas. A Descriptive and Historical Account of Hydraulic and Other Machines for Raising Water, Ancient and Modern. 1842.

Field, Henry M. The Story of the Atlantic Telegraph. 1893.

Flinn, A. P. M. Industrial Research in the United States of America. 1917.

Van Gelder, Arthur Pine and Hugo Schlatter. History of the Explosives Industry in America. 1927.

Hall, Courtney Robert. History of American Industrial Science. 1954.

Hungerford, Edward. The Story of Public Utilities. 1928.

Hungerford, Edward. The Story of the Baltimore and Ohio Railroad, 1827-1927. 1928.

Husband, Joseph. The Story of the Pullman Car. 1917.

Ingels, Margaret. Willis Haviland Carrier, Father of Air Conditioning. 1952.

Kingsbury, John E. The Telephone and Telephone Exchanges: Their Invention and Development. 1915.

Labatut, Jean and Wheaton J. Lane, eds. Highways in Our National Life: A Symposium. 1950.

Lathrop, William G[ilbert]. The Brass Industry in the United States. 1926.

Lesley, Robert W., John B. Lober and George S. Bartlett. History of the Portland Cement Industry in the United States. 1924.

Marcosson, Isaac F. Wherever Men Trade: The Romance of the Cash Register. 1945.

Miles, Henry A[dolphus]. Lowell, As It Was, and As It Is. 1845.

Morison, George S. The New Epoch: As Developed by the Manufacture of Power. 1903.

Deane, Samuel. The New-England Farmer, or Georgical Dictionary. 1822

Dyer, Henry. The Evolution of Industry. 1895

Epstein, Ralph C. The Automobile Industry: Its Economic and Commercial Development. 1928

Ericsson, Henry. Sixty Years a Builder: The Autobiography of Henry Ericsson. 1942

Evans, Oliver. The Young Mill-Wright and Miller's Guide. 1850

Ewbank, Thomas. A Descriptive and Historical Account of Hydraulic and Other Machines for Raising Water, Ancient and Modern. 1842

Field, Henry M. The Story of the Atlantic Telegraph. 1893

Fleming, A. P. M. Industrial Research in the United States of America. 1917

Van Gelder, Arthur Pine and Hugo Schlatter. History of the Explosives Industry in America. 1927

Hall, Courtney Robert. History of American Industrial Science. 1954

Hungerford, Edward. The Story of Public Utilities. 1928

Hungerford, Edward. The Story of the Baltimore and Ohio Railroad, 1827-1927. 1928

Husband, Joseph. The Story of the Pullman Car. 1917

Ingels, Margaret. Willis Haviland Carrier, Father of Air Conditioning. 1952

Kingsbury, J[ohn], E. The Telephone and Telephone Exchanges: Their Invention and Development. 1915

Labatut, Jean and Wheaton J. Lane, eds. Highways in Our National Life: A Symposium. 1950

Lathrop, William G[ilbert]. The Brass Industry in the United States. 1926

Lesley, Robert W., John B. Lober and George S. Bartlett. History of the Portland Cement Industry in the United States. 1924

Marcosson, Isaac F. Wherever Men Trade: The Romance of the Cash Register. 1945

Miles, Henry A[dolphus]. Lowell, As It Was, and As It Is. 1845

Morison, George S. The New Epoch: As Developed by the Manufacture of Power. 1903

Olmsted, Denison. Memoir of Eli Whitney, Esq. 1846

Passer, Harold C. The Electrical Manufacturers, 1875-1900. 1953

Prescott, George B[artlett]. Bell's Electric Speaking Telephone. 1884

Prout, Henry G. A Life of George Westinghouse. 1921

Randall, Frank A. History of the Development of Building Construction in Chicago. 1949

Riley, John J. A History of the American Soft Drink Industry: Bottled Carbonated Beverages, 1807-1957. 1958

Salem, F[rederick] W[illiam]. Beer, Its History and Its Economic Value as a National Beverage. 1880

Smith, Edgar F. Chemistry in America. 1914

Steinman, D[avid] B[arnard]. The Builders of the Bridge: The Story of John Roebling and His Son. 1950

Taylor, F[rank] Sherwood. A History of Industrial Chemistry. 1957

Technological Trends and National Policy, Including the Social Implications of New Inventions. Report of the Subcommittee on Technology to the National Resources Committee. 1937

Thompson, John S. History of Composing Machines. 1904

Thompson, Robert Luther. Wiring a Continent: The History of the Telegraph Industry in the United States, 1832-1866. 1947

Tilley, Nannie May. The Bright-Tobacco Industry, 1860-1929. 1948

Tooker, Elva. Nathan Trotter: Philadelphia Merchant, 1787-1853. 1955

Turck, J. A. V. Origin of Modern Calculating Machines. 1921

Tyler, David Budlong. Steam Conquers the Atlantic. 1939

Wheeler, Gervase. Homes for the People, In Suburb and Country. 1855

Olmsted, Denison. Memoir of Eli Whitney, Esq., 1846

Passer, Harold C. The Electrical Manufacturers, 1875-1900, 1953

Prescott, George B[artlett]. Bell's Electric Speaking Telephone, 1884

Prout, Henry G. A Life of George Westinghouse, 1921

Randall, Frank A. History of the Development of Building Construction in Chicago, 1949

Riley, John J. A History of the American Soft Drink Industry: Bottled Carbonated Beverages, 1807-1957, 1958

Salem, F[rederick] W[illiam]. Beer, its History and Its Economic Value as a National Beverage, 1880

Smith, Edgar F. Chemistry in America, 1914

Steinman, D[avid] B[arnard]. The Builders of the Bridge: The Story of John Roebling and His Son, 1950

Taylor, F[rank] Sherwood. A History of Industrial Chemistry, 1957

Technological Trends and National Policy, Including the Social Implications of New Inventions. Report of the Subcommittee on Technology to the National Resources Committee, 1937

Thompson, John S. History of Composing Machines, 1904

Thompson, Robert Luther. Wiring a Continent: The History of the Telegraph Industry in the United States, 1832-1866, 1947

Tilley, Nannie May. The Bright-Tobacco Industry, 1860-1929, 1948

Tooker, Elva. Nathan Trotter: Philadelphia Merchant, 1787-1853, 1955

Turck, J. A. V. Origin of Modern Calculating Machines, 1921

Tyler, David Budlong. Steam Conquers the Atlantic, 1939

Wheeler, Gervase. Homes for the People, In Suburb and Country, 1855